Organizations and Popular Culture

Throughout its history, popular mass-mediated culture has turned its attention to representing and interrogating organizational life. As early as Charlie Chaplin's cinematic classic *Modern Times* and as recently as the primetime television hit *The Simpsons*, we see cultural products that engage reflexively in coming to terms with the meaning of work, technology and workplace relations. It is only since the late 1990s, however, that those who research management and organizations have come to collectively dwell on the relationship between organizations and popular culture – a relationship where cultural meanings of work are articulated in popular culture, and where popular culture challenges taken-for-granted knowledge about the structure and practice of work. Key to this development has been the journal *Culture and Organization* – a journal that has been centre stage in creating new vistas through which the 'cultural studies of organization' can be explored.

This book brings together the journal's best contributions which specifically address how popular culture represents, informs and potentially transforms organizational practice. Featuring contributors from the UK, USA, Europe and Australia, this exciting anthology provides a comprehensive review of research in organization and popular culture.

Carl Rhodes is Professor of Organization Studies at Swansea University, UK. His research interests focus on ethics and politics in organizations, organizations in popular culture, and theory and method in organization studies. He is currently senior editor of the journal *Organization Studies* and associate editor of the journal *Organization*. Previous publications include *Bits of Organization* (2009, with Alison Pullen), *Critical Representations of Work and Organizations in Popular Culture* (2008, with Robert Westwood) and *Humour, Work and Organization* (2007, with Robert Westwood), and many journal articles.

Simon Lilley is Professor of Information and Organization, and Head of the School of Management at the University of Leicester, UK. He is editor of the journal *Culture and Organization*. His research interests focus on the relationships between (human) agency, technology and performance. Previous publications include *Management and Organization: A Critical Text, 2nd Edition* (2009, with Stephen Linstead and Liz Fulop), and numerous journal articles.

The essays edited by Carl Rhodes and Simon Lilley on Organization and Popular Culture collect some of the best articles published in the journal *Culture and Organization*. Ranging from studies of how popular culture represents business and organizational institutions to how corporations make use of popular culture, these studies demonstrate that scholars within the field of management and organization studies provide interesting perspectives on key aspects of contemporary culture and society.

Professor Douglas Kellner, UCLA, USA

A virtuoso conceptualization of today's managerial and production regimes, *Organizations and Popular Culture* is a magnificent book because of its contemporary relevance: it helps us to appreciate postmodern information, representation, and their transformative powers through literature and media, gender, music, pleasure, performativity, and, especially, good humour. *Organizations and Popular Culture* thus serves as a splendid introduction to the importance of the connections between the business of culture and culture of business.

Professor John Armitage, Northumbria University, UK

Organizations and Popular Culture

Information, Representation and Transformation

Edited by
Carl Rhodes and Simon Lilley

Routledge
Taylor & Francis Group

LONDON AND NEW YORK

First published 2012
by Routledge
2 Park Square, Milton Park, Abingdon, Oxon, OX14 4RN

Simultaneously published in the USA and Canada
by Routledge
711 Third Avenue, New York, NY 10017

Routledge is an imprint of the Taylor & Francis Group, an informa business

British Library Cataloguing in Publication Data
A catalogue record for this book is available from the British Library

ISBN13: 978-0-415-69239-7 (hbk)
ISBN13: 978-0-415-69238-0 (pbk)

Typeset in Times New Roman
by Saxon Graphics Ltd, Derby

Publisher's Note
The publisher would like to make readers aware that the chapters in this book may be referred to as articles as they are identical to the articles published in the journal. The publisher accepts responsibility for any inconsistencies that may have arisen in the course of preparing this volume for print.

MIX
Paper from
responsible sources
FSC
www.fsc.org   FSC® C004839

Printed and bound in Great Britain by
CPI Antony Rowe, Chippenham, Wiltshire

Contents

CONTENTS

Permissions

Chapter 2
Studies in Cultures, Organizations and Societies (former title), Vol. 5, No. 1, 1999, 13–41

Chapter 3
Culture and Organization, Vol. 15, No. 1, March 2009, 21–38

Chapter 4
Culture and Organization, Vol. 15, No. 2, June 2009, 203–220

Chapter 5
Culture and Organization, Vol. 11, No. 1, March 2005, 17–31

Chapter 6
Culture and Organization, Vol. 15, No. 1, March 2009, 89–108

Chapter 7
Culture and Organization, Vol. 9, No. 2, June 2003, 121–137

Chapter 8
Culture and Organization, Vol. 8, No. 4, December 2002, 293–306

Chapter 9
Culture and Organization, Vol. 11, No. 3, September 2005, 195–208

Chapter 10
Culture and Organization, Vol. 15, No. 2, June 2009, 221–235

Chapter 11
Culture and Organization, Vol. 11, No. 3, September 2005, 153–166

Chapter 12
Culture and Organization, Vol. 16, No. 1, March 2010, 37–54

Chapter 13
Culture and Organization, Vol. 15, No. 2, June 2009, 151–165

List of contributors

David Boje, Professor of Management and Bill Daniels Ethics Fellow, New Mexico State University, USA.

Yue Cai, Assistant Professor of Management, University of Central Missouri, USA.

Miguel Pina e Cunha, Professor, Nova School of Business and Economics, Lisbon, Portugal.

Barbara Czarniawska Professor of Management Studies, Gothenburg Research Institute, School of Business, Economics and Law, University of Gothenburg, Sweden.

João Vieira da Cunha, Assistant Professor, Nova School of Business and Economics, Lisbon, Portugal.

Michaela Driver, Professor of Business Administration, Department of Business, Accounting and Economics, Western State College of Colorado, USA.

Richard Godfrey, Lecturer in Strategy, School of Management, University of Leicester, UK.

Nuno Guimarães-Costa, Visiting Assistant Professor, Nova School of Business and Economics, Lisbon, Portugal.

Ruud Kaulingfreks, Philosopher of Art lecturing in organisational philosophy at the University of Humanistics Utrecht, The Netherlands, and the University of Leicester School of Management, UK.

Kate Kenny, Lecturer in Political Science and Sociology, National University of Ireland, Galway, Ireland and Research Fellow at Judge Business School, University of Cambridge.

Hugo Letiche, Research Professor, University of Humanistics Utrecht, The Netherlands.

Geoff Lightfoot, Senior Lecturer in Entrepreneurship and Accounting, School of Management, University of Leicester, UK.

Simon Lilley, Professor of Information and Organization, School of Management, University of Leicester, UK.

Paula McDonald, Associate Professor of Management, Queensland University of Technology Business School, Australia.

Anna-Maria Murtola, member of the editorial collective of the journal *ephemera*.

Martin Parker, Professor of Organisation Studies, Warwick Business School, University of Warwick, UK.

Alf Rehn, Professor of Management and Organization, Åbo Akademi University, Finland.

Carl Rhodes, Professor of Organization Studies, School of Business and Economics, Swansea University, UK.

Annette Risberg, Associate Professor, Department of Intercultural Communication and Management, Copenhagen Business School, Denmark.

David Sköld, Senior Lecturer in Industrial Engineering and Management, Ångströmlaboratoriet, Uppsala University, Sweden.

Janne Tienari, Professor of Organizations and Management, Aalto University School of Economics, Finland.

Eero Vaara, Professor of Management and Organization, Hanken School of Economics, Finland.

Introduction: Studying Organizations Through Popular Culture

Carl Rhodes and Simon Lilley

The iconic 1936 film *Modern Times* sees Charlie Chaplin's character the Little Tramp working on a factory assembly line. As the conveyor belt of the line whizzes in front of him he repeatedly screws nuts on to passing unidentifiable pieces of machinery. Spanner in hand, the drudgery and monotony of the work are portrayed starkly and coldly. But this is of course a comedy and Chaplin uses the industrialized and mechanized workplace to great humorous effect, most especially by showing how his character, supposedly also expected to enact his role in a machine like way, simply cannot perform these mechanical duties effectively. With slapstick conviction and satire driven pathos the man reduced to machine is trapped in a world of rationalized production technology that he must either yield to or be rejected by. And even when he seeks some solace from a lonely cigarette in the bathroom, in anticipation of modern surveillance technology, the factory boss's face appears projected on the wall telling him to get back to work. Rationalized, mechanized and bureaucratized, the world of Chaplin's factory requires, indeed demands, compliance and efficiency; neither of which the Little Tramp can offer. The machinery can't really offer it either; especially in the form of an automatic feeding machine designed to enable the workers to eat at their work stations. This automation just sets the stage for a (food) fight between machine and worker. Scientific management never had it so good! Chaplin's character is not the machine he is meant to be and the unbearable repetitiveness of the task coupled with his technical ineptitude finally drive him insane. Rampaging through the factory and being twisted out of shape by the machines, he finally loses his mind; the ultimate escape from the unrelenting infliction of rationality and the worship of efficiency.

Chaplin's politically driven parody of modern factory work was a huge hit in its day and remains a cinema classic. It marks also the beginning of Chaplin's use of cinema comedy for the purpose of social commentary, an approach culminating in 1942 with his spoof on Adolf Hitler in *The Great Dictator*. With *Modern Times* clearly there was (and still is) an audience that finds Chaplin's shenanigans hugely entertaining. What is also interesting is the way that the film mirrored, and potentially even informed, social concern over the dehumanizing and alienating effects of industrial production technologies. There is a certain cultural circularity at play here where the filmic representation draws on both cultural critique and popular sentiment while at the same time informing and even transforming them through their artistic rendition. In this case, as Lohof (2004) explains, the circumstances that Chaplin attacked with such pathos and satire were so 'compelling and ubiquitous [...that...] the subordination of the skilled artisan to the sophisticated mechanism, and the replacement of the unique item by the uniform product – became major leitmotifs in the history of the industrial revolution' (p. 519). Chaplin's film also serves as a vivid and emotionally sensitive illustration of some important sociological ideas and concerns that were circulating at the time. As Curtis (2009) suggests, for example, *Modern Times* 'can be seen to visually illustrate what Weber noted – once Capitalism really took hold and the original Protestant ethic and spirit of Capitalism was lost (n.p)'. Void of any even secularized religious calling that might inform a work ethic suited to enduring factory labour, the Little Tramp's life becomes unbearably meaningless – a meaninglessness that leads him to insanity. We can note too that Chaplin's film was released more than 20 years before Weber's work was translated and published in English. Further, as a 'classic critique of the machine age' we have a film that in some ways foreshadows Braverman's (1974) *Labour and Monopoly Capital* in its illustration and critique of factory life and the compliant, de-skilled and alienated workers that it demands and tries to produce (Tolich, 1992: 244).

Modern Times is a complex cultural product. The rapid developments in technology spawned in and after the industrial revolution made a whole new era of cultural production and transmission possible. No longer restricted to live performance, the advent of cinema, radio and the phonograph meant that cultural products could be produced for a mass audience each of whom could consume exactly the same performance at different times and in different places. In one sense the technological and industrial developments that afforded Chaplin the ability to make movies were the very same things that created the mass-production systems whose effects he was criticizing. Moreover the capitalist system within which such production is located is the same system that sells cinema for profit and that made Chaplin one of the most successful movie stars in history. It is clear from the outset that culture does not follow a single line of rationality. In this case what we have is a mass mediatised popular culture that uses capitalist industrial technologies in order to provide and widely disseminate a critique of capitalist industrialized technologies. For many the unforgiving irony of this is too much to bear, and dominant theoretical positions have long rested on the general blandness of popular culture, its inferiority to more lofty cultural pursuits, and even its capacity for social control and the reproduction of capitalist practice and ideology; the latter position most notoriously promoted by Theodor Adorno and Max Horkheimer in their book *Dialectic of Enlightenment* (1947). For them popular culture presents a distorted perspective on the realities of capitalist cultural economic relations; a culture not only produced by the capitalist system, but also reinforcing of its ideology. Most especially this reinforcement is achieved, so the story goes, because it placates emancipatory impulses through the satisfaction of false needs and by distracting its consumers from the true grasp of socioeconomic realities.

The 'culture industry' as Adorno and Horkheimer dubbed it, was a mechanism of 'mass deception' that made cultural dopes of a people robbed of authentic cultural experience. With another irony, however, it would seem that Chaplin was suggesting a similar tendency as it relates to the production process; after all the workers in his factory are similarly reduced to mindless automatons drudging their time through the work day, else they are driven mad by non-conformism and the desire for individual expression. The issues we have been discussing are of central relevance to the themes this book, themes that revolve around the relationship between organizations and popular culture and the cultural contradictions embodied therein. We attest here that this is no straightforward relationship, nor one that befits simple generalizations no matter how critically well intended. What we do know, however, is that popular culture is an organized phenomenon orchestrated and enabled by technology and business. We also know that work and organizations, in their many guises, are regular and widespread subject matter for popular culture. Throughout its history popular mass-mediated culture has turned its attention to representing and interrogating organizational life whilst simultaneously nurturing itself from it. This can be traced back as early as Charlie Chaplin's silent movies and as recently as the primetime television mega hit *The Simpsons*. From Chaplin's factory to the Springfield Nuclear Power Plant we see a reflexive engagement with coming to terms with the meaning of work, technology and workplace relations.

Since the 1990s there has been a groundswell of interest from researchers in management and organizations seeking to collectively dwell on the relationship between organizations and popular culture; a relationship where the cultural meanings of work are represented in popular culture and where popular culture comes to inform the meaning and practice of work itself. There had been, of course, some important earlier studies of the industrial and commercial arrangement that went into the production of popular culture (e.g. DiMaggio, 1977; Lawrence and Phillips, 2002) as well as considerations of how business activity is represented in literary novels (DeMott, 1989; Czarniawska-Joerges and de Monthoux, 1994). Even as early as 1956 Whyte had considered how popular fiction could be used to read changes in popular belief – in his case how it related to the rise and fall of the protestant ethic. It has also been argued that Weber, whose work is central to the founding of organizations studies, 'was rather less a classical management theorist and rather more a student of culture, practising what today we would call "cultural studies"' (Clegg, 2005: 528). In a sense we can thus suggest that theoretical attention that has been placed on fictional works in organizational studies is more of a return to culture than a fresh departure; one that can be traced back at least to Marx's use of classical mythology and then contemporary literature to examine the emergence of the factory system (Lilley and McKinlay, 2009). Despite such provenance, however, until recently what was largely left out in contemporary study of management and organizations was a consideration of the meaning and value of the films, songs, books, magazines and television programs made possible by industrial production and technology. This started to change in the 1990s as work began to appear in organization and management journals that edged towards consideration of popular culture in that way. Early examples included Ingersoll and Adams' (1992) study of the dominance of technical rationality in children's books and its implications for management, Corbett's (1995) investigation into what science fiction films might tell us about organization and technology, Foreman and Thatchenkery's (1996) consideration of the narrative structure of films about organizations, as well as Grice and Humphreys (1997) use of the *Star Wars* films as a motif and structure through which to interrogate the development of critical management studies.

A text that bolstered this emerging trend was the edited collection published by John Hassard and Ruth Holliday entitled *Organization-Representation: Work and Organization in Popular Culture* (1998). In that book the editors brought together a number of papers that collectively focused on the ways that work and organizations are *represented* in popular culture as well as the ways that these representations can in turn influence knowledge and practice. The work done by that book significantly shaped the off shoot of the discipline of Organization Studies that subsequently became focussed on the analysis of media representations of organizations. The book illustrated that the ways that work and organizations were represented in the popular media offered more striking, powerful, and dynamic insights than those representations that are found in academic work. The issue wasn't necessarily about whether popular culture's depictions of work where better or worse, or more or less accurate than those common to theory, but rather that they were different; and, moreover, it was this difference that offered a valuable source of knowledge.

Core to this difference, Hassard and Holliday argued, was that rather than privileging a view of organizations as rational, unemotional and disembodied, popular culture showed organizational life as an everyday activity that was embodied, personal and affectual. Subsequent to the publication of Hassard and Holliday's collection studies have been published that have explored themes as diverse as gender performativity at work in television comedy (Tyler and Cohen 2008); counter cultures to organization and their embedding in mundane cultural artefacts (Parker, 2006); carnivalesque organization critique in television animation (Rhodes, 2000); gender and embodiment in Hollywood cinema (Höpfl, 2003); work based utopianism in rock music (Rhodes, 2004); the production of collective memory in war films (Godfrey and Lilley, 2009); managerial machismo in popular films (Panayiotou, 2010) and critical management in science fiction (Parker, 1998). This points to but a handful of examples yet illustrates the variety of directions that the study of organizations and popular culture has taken. Also suggestive of the importance of these developments are the number of books and special issues of journals dedicated to the subject. This includes Parker, Higgins, Lightfoot and Smith's (1999) *Amazing Tales,* Smith, Higgins, Parker and Lightfoot's (2001) *Science Fiction and Organization,* Rhodes and Westwood's (2008) *Critical Representations of Work and Organization in Popular Culture,* Bell's (2008) *Reading Management and Organization in Film,* Rhodes and Parker's (2008) *Images of Organizations in Popular Culture* and Parker's (2011) *Alternative Business: Outlaws, Crime and Culture.* 'Popular Culture' even features as an entry in *The International Encyclopedia of Organization Studies* (Rhodes, 2008).

As Philips had already argued in 1995, mainstream cinema, as a core form of popular culture, contains the narrative resources to study important but often overlooked organizational phenomena. Phillips pointed especially to issues such as racism, sexism, frustration at work and the human effects of layoffs. What Phillips also argued was that popular culture enabled researchers to appreciate and study cultural knowledge that was difficult to access through standard social scientific research methods and data sources. Supporting this, Czarniawska and Rhodes (2006) have argued that the value of popular culture to the study of organizations lies in the way it serves as a propaedeutic for management and organizational practice as well as furnishing a means through which such practice can be understood. What they highlight are the ways that the repertoires of 'emplotment' used in popular culture serve to distribute a set of dominant means through which people can interpret, understand and inform their working lives. They suggest that the abstract models and theories proffered by management theorists are much less powerful in actually informing or even transforming practice; detective stories or adventure movies seem to have done the job much better. As they speculate, white male baby boomer managers would appear to have been more influenced in their practice by John Wayne than Peter Drucker. While popular culture might provide modes of emplotment that inform practice, Czarniawska and Rhodes also argue that such culture additionally serves to draw attention to and undermine the taken-for-grantedness of such plots so as to offer the potential for critical and transformational readings of conventional management knowledge. Indeed this issue of the ways that the mass media can offer a 'critique in culture' rather than a 'critique of culture' (Rhodes, 2004) has become a dominant theme especially as it relates to the whether and how culture reinforces or resists organizational authority structures. A cornerstone of the study of organizations and popular culture that has been established is the relatively ambivalent relationship between the two. This does not suggest a lack of conclusiveness; more a willingness to engage with particular instantiations of culture at the expense of the cold comfort of generalization. Culture is no monolith and the expectation of a uni-directional and all encompassing explanation of the relationship between the different elements within it is, at best, naive and, at worst, politically and intellectually irresponsible. Popular culture can thus be approached in terms of how it contains within in a counter-culture to dominant organizational culture in some instances (Parker, 2006) as well as how it works to reproduce dominant and oppressive cultural norms in others (Coltrane and Adams, 1997).

Studies of popular culture are commonly understood as being outside of the 'mainstream' of research interests in management and organizations. Perhaps so, but it is also the case that organization studies more generally has long been understood as "a contested discursive terrain, within which there has always been (and continues to be) a variety of voices engaged in a political process of claims for recognition, acceptance and dominance" (Westwood and Clegg, 2003; 2). Moreover, the institutionalized heterodoxy that this infers has made for "an enormous expansion of organization theory [...] simply by virtue of researchers turning to issues that were typically not discussed in the past" (Jones and Munro, 2005: 5). In such a context it is because of rather than despite contestation that studies of organizations and popular culture have, since the 1990s, become an established niche within organizations studies; the examples cited earlier attest to this. At least in part this is a legacy of the influence of 'postmodernism' as it came to mark various debates within and approaches to organization studies in the 1990s. In one sense this provided increased legitimacy for researchers to investigate hitherto non-conventional subjects in non-conventional ways. Further the focus on textuality and representation that characterised post-structural theory and came to be associated with postmodernism defined the terms through which popular culture could be investigated; a move, as Jeffcut (1994) would have it, from 'interpretation to representation'. This move is related also to the attention that narrative has attracted in organization studies as a legacy of the influence of postmodernism (Calas and Smircich, 1999). In one vein this has resulted in the analysis of the 'real' stories told about organizations and by people in organizations. But in another it has extended to considering the intellectual value of those 'fictional' stories that are also told about organizations, both literary and popular. What was thus recognized, either explicitly or implicitly, was the value of narratives embedded in 'popular culture as exemplars of knowledge about organizations and management [...and...] a realization that there are others outside of academic research who are much more practiced and skilled [than those within] at telling stories about work and organizations' (Rhodes and Pullen, 2009: 594). Such developments can also not be divorced from the massive popularity of the notion of 'organizational culture' in both the theory and practice of organizations. If anything what studies of popular culture have done is to broaden research interests outside of the culture than occurs within office and factory walls to that which exists in the realm of leisure and entertainment as well (Rhodes and Parker, 2008).

Key to the developments discussed above has been the journal *Culture and Organization*, a publication that has been centre stage in creating new vistas through which the 'cultural studies of organization' (Parker, 2006) can be explored. This book brings together the journal's best contributions that have specifically addressed how popular culture represents, informs and potentially transforms organizational practice. Featuring contributors from Great Britain, the United States, Europe and Australia the book provides a state of the art review of research in organization and popular culture.

In editing the book we reviewed the journal's full contents since its foundation in 1995; originally entitled *Studies in Cultures Organizations and Societies* (SCOS) in shared acronym with the annual *Standing Conference on Organizational Symbolism* with which it is associated, the journal changed its name to *Culture and Organization* in 2002. Our selection of which papers to include in the book was guided by the themes outlined above. Essentially we wanted to incorporate those papers that showcased the different ways that popular culture had been investigated and deployed in relation to the study of work, organizations and management. Indeed, in having done this we found that this theme had been present in the journal almost since its inception, although relevant contributions had grown in frequency in recent years, again suggesting a trend of the increasing establishment of such studies as a mainstay of the discipline more generally.

The papers begin in chapter two with a piece by Barbara Czarniawska entitled 'Management she wrote: organization studies and detective stories'. In this chapter Czarniawska turns her attention to the popular literary genre of the detective story, arguing that the detective and the social scientist have much in common despite the misplaced but dominant common sense that the two endeavours are quite different. Positioning itself against the 'scientization' of the social sciences the chapter suggests that detective stories, rather than 'just' being entertainment or pulp, provide social scientists with a model through which they can transgress the limitations of their own disciplinary strictures by experimenting with localized stories based on the experience of inquiry. While Czarniawska focuses on the methodological lessons that can be learned from popular culture, in chapter 3, '"We just make the pictures…?" How work is portrayed in children's feature length films', Paula McDonald treats popular culture as a set of texts to be studied in order to consider how they might inform the worldviews of those who consume them. Suggestive of the importance of 'audience response' as a key part of how popular culture is studied, the chapter explores how adult work is portrayed in some 42 contemporary children's films that were under widespread circulation. The chapter assesses how such films might change the way children anticipated their own futures and the ways that the films might serve to limit the possibilities of those expectations; especially as it relates to the gendered division of labour and unequal power relations at work. Continuing with the cinema, Richard Godfrey's 'Military, masculinity and mediated representations: (con)fusing the real and the reel', turns its attention to films about the military but again with a focus on gender. For Godfrey the military, as it is depicted in popular culture, wields an important influence on the experience and understanding of masculinity. As with McDonald, Godfrey regards popular culture in general, and the cinema in particular, as being a valuable source of knowledge about our understanding and expectations of real organizations. This knowledge, as the chapter evinces, offers a nuanced and complex appreciation of the experience of organizational life both within the military and beyond.

Chapter 4, '"I love the dough": Rap lyrics as a minor economic literature', continues with the theme of examining the meaning of economic activity's representation in popular culture but turns away from the cinema towards popular music. Alf Rehn and David Sköld attend to rap music, especially its reference to 'bling-bling': the demonstration of wealth and success through the wearing of oversized jewellery. Contesting the idea that capitalism is a totally colonizing set of economic relations, the chapter shows how with rap music, and the vernacular it deploys, we have a form of re-appropriation that uses dominant economic narratives for the purpose of subversion and provocation. Chapter 5 focuses on a quite different form of music. In Nuno Guimarães-Costa, Miguel Pina e. Cunha, and João Vieira da Cunha's 'Poetry in motion: protest songwriting as strategic resource (Portugal, circa 1974)', the spotlight is on how music can be used instrumentally as a resource for socio-political influence. Focussing on Portuguese history before, during and after the 1974 revolution, the chapter demonstrates the power of popular culture in terms of protest songs to help people make sense of a changing social and political world. Popular culture is considered here as engaging in an iterative process whereby it both shapes and is shaped by the context in which it occurs. Analysing this in terms of the relationship between power and discourse suggests that protest singers and critically oriented scholars have much in common, albeit with the former being more popular and influential.

While the chapters outlined so far have focussed on creative and fictional examples of popular culture, in Chapter 6 we have a consideration of the relations between popular news media and organizations. In 'Making sense of a transnational merger: Media texts and the (re)construction of power relations', Annette Risberg, Janne Tienari, and Eero Vaara consider the cultural dimensions associated with the media coverage of the merger between a Swedish and a Finnish organization. Applying critical discourse analysis to these texts, the chapter explores power relations in as related to national identity, demonstrating how the media can both reflect and reinforce cross-cultural structures of domination; reportage is rendered here as a cultural phenomenon. By this account the popular media serves the function of furthering oppressive cultural relations as reflective more generally of post-colonial forms of domination. While Risberg, Tienari and Vaara examined the representations of real organizations in the realist genre of the news media, in Chapter 7, 'Coffee and the business of pleasure: The case of Harbucks vs. Mr. Tweek', Carl Rhodes is interested in how real organizations are represented in fiction, specifically the animated television cartoon *Southpark*. This involves a detailed analysis of one episode of this program which features a parody of the global coffee shop chain *Starbucks*. This chapter shows how popular culture may provide both a critique of contemporary business practice and also a critique of popular criticisms of it. *Southpark*, it is argued, provides an exemplary case of how popular culture contains within it sophisticated (and funny!) appreciations of the vicissitudes and contradictions of the social meaning and evaluation of exploitative business practices.

The theme of humour continues in Chapter 8, David Boje, Michaela Driver and Yue Cai's 'Fiction and humor in transforming McDonald's narrative strategies'. In this case what is investigated is the way that corporations, and McDonald's in particular, deliberately produce corporate fiction and humour. Through an examination of the character of Ronald McDonald and the cartoon series in which he stars, the authors explore how popular culture can be used instrumentally for strategic business transformation. What this enables, they argue, is that organizations, for better or for worse, can engage in a form of dialogical imagination that exceeds more rational understandings of business strategy and also potentially exceeds the possibility of strategy being under the rational control of organizations. There is more humour in Chapter 9, Kate Kenny's '"The performative surprise": parody, documentary and critique'. In this instance the question asked is the extent to which parody harbours real critical potential. The example of popular culture interrogated is the television documentary *Yes Men*, taken as parody of the World Trade Organization. Responding affirmatively Kenny illustrates how, in this case, parody does offer what she refers to, following Judith Butler, as a 'performative surprise': a case where norms and expectations are disrupted or subverted. What this demonstrates more generally is how popular cultural parodies are able to highlight the contingency of commonly accepted institutional and institutionalized identities so as to render them more explicit and hence open to critique and re-imagining.

Continuing with the possibilities for critique that can be found in popular culture, in Chapter 10, Martin Parker's 'Organizational gothic', we have a review of the tradition of gothic representations of organizations. Beginning with Marx's association of capitalism with the vampiric and extending through to contemporary film, Parker shows how the gothic tradition offers a mode of cultural critique through representation of organizations as sites of darkness. While rich in historical antecedents, Parker shows how that it is in post 1970s cinema that organizational gothic takes full hold of our collective imagination as an expression of contestation to, and struggle with, neo-liberal managerialism. In keeping with the contemporary meaning of historically established cultural symbolism, in Chapter 11, 'Commodification of utopia: The lotus eaters revisited', Anna-Maria Murtola uses the story of the lotus eaters from Homer's *Odyssey* to explore the cultural commodification of utopia. At stake are not specific cultural or media texts, but the more general cultural phenomena of the shopping mall. The myth of the lotus eaters is invoked as a means of understanding a particular cultural tendency for a seemingly narcotically induced apathy to capitalist realities that masks a deeper seated melancholia. This is achieved, Murtola argues, through the commercial appropriation of utopia as exemplified by the shopping mall, a utopia both culturally attractive yet in need of resistance. The final chapter in the book comes in the form of Ruud Kaulingfreks, Geoff Lightfoot and Hugo Letiche's 'The man in the black hat'. Again we are dealing with the power of cultural symbolism; in this case in the form of the cowboy as portrayed in Western films and fiction. The chapter argues that the cultural imagery of the cowboy continues to shape the ways we think about the relationship between individuals and organizations; but not in a straightforward way. At issue is the perpetuation of the myth of freedom and its association with individuality and solitude that is deeply sedimented in capitalist culture. It is within such culture that the cowboy-hero is filled out by representations of the figure of the entrepreneur. This entrepreneurial figure, the chapter argues, is equally 'fake' as the cowboy on account of a mythical freedom being encased in the confining realities of organization and commercial culture.

It is our hope that the collection of papers housed in this book illustrates the depth and richness with which the relation between organizations and popular culture has been treated within the formal study of management and organizations. These papers show how popular culture has been invoked to develop innovative methodological, theoretical, empirical and political contributions. While the specific approaches vary, as do the evaluation of the positive, negative or ambivalent prospects for popular culture, what is common is an engagement with the particular; that is with specific instances and examples of popular and media discourse. Eschewing more generalized pronouncements on the meaning of culture, these studies exemplify a sustained collective engagement the meaning and practice of organizing that draws inspiration and meaning from everyday cultural texts and practices. It is also our hope that the book serves as an inspiration for further enhancing the line of research that it represents. The ubiquity and importance of popular culture cannot be denied and the possibilities for further studies of its relationship with work, management and organizations is still fecund as an area of study. If it is true, as Bruce Springsteen once sang, that '[w]e learned more from a three minute record than we ever learned in school' then it remains incumbent on those of us still in (business) school to listen to those three minute records (as well as the television programs, magazines, movies and other cultural texts) and treat them as central to the meaning of what goes on in and around work organizations.

References

Adorno, T. and Horkheimer, M. (1947/1972) *Dialectic of Enlightenment,* New York: Herder and Herder.

Bell, E. (2008) *Reading Management and Organization in Film*, Basingstoke: Palgrave.

Calas, M.B. and Smircich, L. (1999) Past Postmodenrism? Reflections and Tentative Directions, *Academy of Management Review*, 24, no. 4: 649-671.

Clegg, S.R. (2005) Puritans, Visionaries and Survivors, *Organization Studies*, 26, no. 4: 527-545.

Coltrane, S. and Adams, M. (1997) Work-Family Imagery and Gender Stereotypes: Television and the Reproduction of Difference, *Journal of Vocational Behaviour*, 50: 323-347.

Corbett, M. (1995) Celluloid Projections: Images of Technology and Organizational Futures in Contemporary Science Fiction Film, *Organization*, 2, nos. 3-4: 467-488.

Curtis, H. (2009) Themes Within the Movies of Charlie Chaplin, *Helium: Movie Analysis*, 17 May 2009 (available at http://www.helium.com/items/1451627-charlie-chaplins-modern-times, visited 1 June 2011).

Czarniawska, B. and Rhodes, C. (2006) Strong Plots: The Relationship Between Popular Culture and Management Theory and Practice, in P. Gagliardi and B. Czarniawska (Eds.), Management Education and Humanities. pp. 195-218. Edward Elgar: London.

Czarniawska-Joerges, B. and Guillet de Monthoux, P. (1994) *Good novels, better management: reading organizational realities*, Chur: Harwood Academic Publishers.

DeMott, B. (1989) Reading Fiction to the Bottom Line, *Harvard Business Review*, 67, no. 3: 128-134.

DiMaggio, P. (1977) Market Structure, the Creative Process, and Popular Culture: Toward an Organizational Reinterpretation of Mass-Culture Theory, *Journal of Popular Culture*, 11, no. 2: 436-45.

Foreman, J. and Thatchenkery, T.J. (1996) Filmic Representations For Organizational Analysis: The Characterization Of A Transplant Organization In The Film *Rising Sun, Journal of Organizational Change Management*, 9, no. 3: 44-61.

Godfrey, R. and Lilley, S. (2009) Visual consumption, collective memory and the representation of war, *Consumption Markets, and Culture,* 12, no. 4: 275-300.

Grice, S. and Humphries, M. (1997) Critical Management Studies in Postmodernity: Oxymorons in Outer Space, *Journal of Organizational Change Management*, 10, no. 5: 412-415.

Hassard, J. And Holliday, R. (1998) *Organization-Representation: Work and Organization in Popular Culture*, London: Sage.

Höpfl, H. (2003) Becoming a (Virile) Member: Women and the Military Body, *Body and Society*, 9, no. 4: 13-30.

Ingersoll, V.H and Adams, G.B. (1992) The Child is 'Father' to the Manager: Images of Organizations in U.S. Children's Literature, *Organization Studies*, 13, no. 4: 497-519.

Jeffcut, P. (1994) From Interpretation to Representation: Postmodernism, Ethnography and Organizational Symbolism, *Organization Studies*, 15, no. 2: 241-274.

Jones, C. And Munro, R. (2005) Organization Theory, 1985-2005, in C. Jones and R. Munro (eds.) *Contemporary Organization Theory*, pp. 1-15. Oxford: Blackwell.

Lawrence, T.B. and Phillips, N. (2002) Understanding Cultural Industries, *Journal of Management Inquiry*, 11, no. 4: 430-441.

Lilley, S. And McKinlay, A. (2009) Matters of fact/matters of fiction: imagining and implementing institutional change, *Culture and Organization*, 15, no. 2: 129-133.

Lohof, B.A. (2004) Hamburger Stand: Industrialization and the American Fast-food Phenomenon, *Journal of American Culture*, 2, no. 3: 519-513.

Panayiotou, A. (2010) 'Macho' managers and organizational heroes: competing masculinities in popular films, *Organization*, 14, no. 7: 659-683.

Parker, M. (1998) Judgement Day: Cyborganization, Humanism and Postmodern Ethics, *Organization*, 5, no. 4: 503-518.

Parker, M. (2006) The Counter Culture of Organisation: Towards a Cultural Studies of Representations of Work, *Consumption, Markets and Culture,* 9, no. 1: 1-15.

Parker, M. (2011) *Alternative Business: Outlaws, Crime and Culture*, London: Routledge.

Parker, M., Higgins, M., Lightfoot, G. and Smith, W. (eds.) (1999) Amazing Tales: Organization Studies as Science Fiction, Special Issue of *Organization*, 6, no. 4: 579-590.

Rhodes, C. (2000) The Simpsons, popular culture, and the organizational carnival, *Journal of Management Inquiry*, 10, no. 4: 374-383.

Rhodes, C. (2004) Utopia in Popular Management Writing and the Music of Bruce Springsteen: Do You Believe in the Promised Land? *Consumption Markets & Culture*, 7, no. 1: 1-20.

Rhodes, C. (2008) Popular Culture, in S.R. Clegg and J.R. Bailey, J.R. (eds.) *The International Encyclopedia of Organization Studies 4 Vols.*, pp. 1257-1260. Thousand Oaks: Sage.

Rhodes, C. and Parker, M. (eds.) (2008) Images of Organizing in Popular Culture, Special Issues of *Organization*, 15, no. 5: 627-637.

Rhodes, C. and Pullen, A. (2009) 'Narrative and Stories in Organizational Research: An Exploration of Gendered Politics in Research Methodology', in D. Buchanan and A. Bryman (eds.) *The Sage Handbook of Organizational Research Methods*, pp. 583-601. London: Sage.

Rhodes, C. and Westwood, R. (2008) *Critical Representations of Work and Organization in Popular Culture*, London; Routledge.

Smith, W., Higgins, M., Parker, M. and Lightfoot, G. (2001) *Science Fiction and Organization*, London: Routledge.

Tolich, M. (1992) Bringing Sociological Concepts Into Focus in the Classroom with *Modern Times, Roger and Me* and *Annie Hall*, *Teaching Sociology*, 20, no. 4: 344-347.

Tyler, M. and Cohen, L. (2008) Management in/as Comic Relief: Queer Theory and Gender Performativity in The Office, *Gender, Work and Organization*, 15, no. 2: 113-132.

Westwood, R. and Clegg, S.R. (2003) The Discourse of Organization Studies: Dissensus, Politics and Paradigms, in R. Westwood and S.R. Clegg (eds.) *Debating Organization: Point-Counterpoint in Organization Studies,* pp. 1-42. Oxford: Blackwell.

Whyte, W.H. (1956) *The Organization Man*, New York: Simon and Schuster.

Management She Wrote: Organization Studies and Detective Stories

Barbara Czarniawska

It has been postulated that social sciences in general and organization theory in particular can profit from parallels and analogies with fiction literature. As the main form of expression in social sciences, like in literature, is a written product, inspired imitation can visibly improve the literary forms of organization theory, without diminishing its specificity. This essay argues that one genre in fiction literature is especially suitable for such comparisons. This is the genre of the detective story, where the detective, much like the researcher, must untangle the social tissue to arrive at an explanation.

Social Science and Literature

Together and Apart

The idea that scientific and non-scientific writing might have much in common is neither especially remarkable nor particularly new. The very fact that so much effort has been invested into differentiating art from science since Plato's Republic would suggest a proximity that was disquieting – at least to some audiences who demanded a clearer demarcation between the two. At the same time, there were always voices like that of Giambattista Vico, intent on abolishing this difference. Anyone keen on periodization as a sense-making device would be able to discern periods when one or the other school of thought was in ascendance.

One such period worth mentioning is the early eighteenth century, when modern natural sciences began to assume their present shape. In Schaffer's rendition of those "Augustan realities" (1993), scientists such as Isaac Newton and Jeremy Bentham did tremendous "cultural work", gaining legitimacy for their science through commited political writing and public spectacles, of which the most spectacular example is the autopsy of Bentham's body performed, at his request, in the presence of his friends at his house. This part of history is relatively well known; what attracts less attention is the meta-activity of erasing the traces of artistry and politics from their work, the accomplishment of having established a genre of scientific realism as "a philosophical position that distracts attention from this cultural work of representatives of nature, and points it toward the adequacy of nature's representations … the 'amnesia' of realism, in which the work that establishes representations is forgotten" (Schaffer, 1993, p. 279).

The realistic style has earned a legitimate place in two genres: in scientific realism and in the realist novel. Some more work was thus needed to establish the difference between the two, and especially between the realist novel and the social sciences which both emerged at about the same time in the nineteenth century. This time around, the legitimizing efforts were directed not only at establishing each of them as genres in their own right, but also at distinguishing between what initially looked very much alike (Czarniawska-Joerges, 1994). One of the victims of this legitimating process was Emile Zola, who, failing to see the way things were going, became an ardent admirer of Auguste Comte and his positive science of sociology, and considered his own work the embodiment of the new scientific ideal. As a result, he was judged unscientific by the scientists and non-literary by the literati.

The matter of difference/no difference was not settled, though. The years 1950-1970, exploiting the scientific contributions to World War Two, brought another wave of "scientization" to the social sciences (Lepenies, 1989). The late 1970s, however, witnessed what is often called a "linguistic turn" in the social sciences which was soon accompanied by a "literary turn". Examples abound: rhetorical analysis in economics (McCloskey, 1985) and in most of the social sciences and humanities (Nelson *et al.,* 1987), the reconstruction of the burnt bridges between sociology and literary theory (R.H. Brown, 1977; Bruss, 1982; Bakhtin, 1928/1988; Agger, 1989; Lepenies, 1989), the knitting of close ties between anthropology and literary theory (Geertz, 1973, 1988; Marcus and Fischer, 1986) and the on-going debate about the importance of narrative knowledge (Lyotard, 1976; MacIntyre, 1981; Fisher, 1984, 1989; Bruner, 1986, 1990; Polkinghome, 1987).

There are many routes accessible for establishing the validity of treating scientific writing as a literary genre. I will choose a short one, composed of only two steps: summarizing the current debate which conceptualizes science as a conversation rather than an accumulating representation of reality, and considering in more detail the possible knowledge status of my own discipline – organization studies – in such a redefined realm of science.

One possible place to begin is the refutation - by the new pragmatist philosophy - of the metaphor of science as "the mirror of the mind", where the mind itself was supposed to be a receptor of the "true world (Rorty, 1980).

The ground for this kind of refutation had been prepared by the many variations of constructivism - from Schützian phenomenology, carried on by Berger and Luckrnann (1966) and Burkard (1968) to Goodman's (1978) "irrealist" claim that we are all world-makers. The realist ontology turned into a belief; and a very practical one. Levine (1993) recalls a routine conversation with a "true" scientist who invariably asks him at parties whether a deconstructionist (or a constructionist, for that matter) would die falling off a high tower. To which Levine supposedly (and routinely) responds that he would not know before seeing the event, but expects any deconstructionist of his acquaintance to steer safely away from the edges of high towers. It is practical to believe in the world of causes 'over there'; it works most of the time. This does not equal saying that there are ways of describing this world which represent it 'as is': "We need to make a distinction between the claim that the world is out there and the claim that truth is out there" (Rorty, 1989, p. 4). As a consequence, the sophisticated notion of episteme (knowledge) becomes equalized with doxa (opinion), held traditionally in disdain by science (Rorty, 1991). All people have opinions on all kinds of matters (indeed, the 'self' can be seen as a constantly reweaving web of beliefs) and test them in action; as a result, what works matters usually more that what is 'true' (besides, for whom is it true? for how long?). It is – sometimes – the object of those opinions and – always – the conventional (for given time and space) ways of expressing it which form differences between "science" and "everyday knowledge" or "science" and "literature".

Science, in this view, is a conversation of the humankind, and its logic of inquiry is rhetorical (Oakeshott, 1959; McCloskey, 1986). Much of this conversation takes place in written form, thus making it legitimate to apply various kinds of literary analysis to it; for instance, genre analysis.

Is Organization Theory a Genre?

A genre is usually conceived as a system of action which has become institutionalized and is recognizable by repetition; its meaning stems from its place within symbolic systems making up literature and culture, acquiring specificity by difference from other genres (Bruss, 1976, p. 5). Does organization theory qualify?

Organization science began as a "practical" science. When, around the turn of the century, its forefathers (plus Mary Parker Follet) began forming the subject, they did so, with the promise of solving any problems companies and administrative organizations might possibly have. At the same time, however, this kind of knowledge was becoming a strictly academic subject, with PhDs and professors, refereed journals and international conferences. Organization science was thus following the footsteps of other practical sciences, such as law, medicine and engineering.

More recently, however, other self descriptions have come to light. In a provocative article, Astley and Zarnmuto (1989) claimed that organization theory is nothing but a language-game in its own right. If one were to understand this statement broadly, as a refutation of correspondence theory, in which all use of language is a language-game, the conceptualization is convincing but does not yield much heuristic value. If, as the authors seem to suggest, one should take it more strictly, as a languagegame played for the fun (sic) of it amongst a group of people closeted in academia, it loses much of its appeal and becomes a rather claustrophobic concept.

More appealing is thus a suggestion by Sandelands (1989), who proposes treating theory production as a kind of practice. The product of theoretical thinking is metaphor (see Morgan, 1986), which, not necessarily directly connected to practice, can give practice inspiration and evoke interesting associations, just like art does. Consequently, disciplines like business administration, management science, etc. are academic disciplines eager to remain in close contact with practice, not with the purpose of dictating the order of things, but of reflecting and provoking via basic research and theory. Thus, the art of writing (and of speaking; the persuasive skills in general) become extremely important, and their critical development a crucial task in its own right.

It is this understanding of organization science - as a practice, that is a system of action which has become institutionalized and recognizable – which makes the notion of organization theory analogous to that of a literary genre. After all, all that organization researchers do is read (listen) and write (speak). So in that sense Astley and Zammuto were right: organization researchers are involved in a linguistic practice. But there is more to it than "just talking": it is important to point out that texts are actions (strictly speaking, material traces of such, but they both result from action and provoke a further action), and actions are texts, in the sense that they must be legible to qualify as actions at all, and not, let us say, movements or behaviors. "Action" and "text" are good metaphors of each other, but even more than that (Ricoeur, 1981, pp. 197-221). Actions, especially institutionalized actions, produce texts; texts not only "fix" other actions – their production and interpretation assumes actions.[1]

Actions, in order to be legible, must relate to some context accessible to those who attempt to make sense of them, and such a relation can be seen as a constraint. Just what such constraints and the ways of dealing with them are is well rendered in a description of a literary genre:

---

[1]It should be clear by now, that in this notion of action no agency is implicated: actions are events to which intentions have been ascribed.

All reading (or writing) involves us in choice: we choose to pursue a style or a subject matter, to struggle with or against a design. We also choose, as passive as it all may seem, to take part in an interaction, and it is here that generic labels have their use. The genre does not tell us the style or the construction of a text as much as how we should expect to "take" that style or mode of construction - what force it should have for us. And this force is derived from a kind of action that text is taken to be (Bruss, 1976, p. 4).

The term "choice" should not mislead the reader into assuming a rational choice: what Bruss calls "a passive choice" can be also understood as following the "logic of appropriateness", as March and Olsen (1989) call the usual logic of action which aims not at the choice of an optimal alternative but at an action which will be recognized and accepted by an audience residing within the same institutional setup:[2]

In that sense – evoking expectations by using a label organization theory is undoubtedly a genre; perhaps, in fact, more a genre than a discipline. A useful reflection could then focus on what are the constraints and possibilities of this genre, how does it develop historically, and what are its actual and potential connections to other genres.

The Advantages of Genre Analysis

Genre analysis is often used as a classificatory device (for the most famous example, see Northrop Frye, 1957/1990). Although a system of categories as such is relatively easy to construct and has a strong heuristic power, its application to concrete works is more problematic. After all, a genre is but a space within which one can position various works, and it would be their vicinity or distance to other works that would establish their genre. Genre analysis in literature places most works between genres; disagreement thus remains as to where the genre-borders should run and whether it makes sense to draw them at all (Lejeune, 1989). The best known attempt at genre analysis within organization theory, Burrell and Morgan's classification of the main paradigms (1979) revealed its heuristic power in provoking massive protests and re-classifications. One can thus envisage an alternative of creating an interpretative space which will be able to contain and relate to each of many other approaches without ascribing strict positions to them. McCloskey suggested, for instance, that literary criticism can offer economics a model for self understanding:

"Literary criticism does not merely pass judgements of good or bad; in its more recent forms the question seems hardly to arise. Chiefly is *concerned with making readers see how poets and novelists accomplish their results*" (1986, p. xix, italics added).

Such reflection, or self reflection, makes a genre more distinct and more elaborated. The analysis of a genre is one of its main constitutive forces. Social scientists busy themselves constructing the institutions they describe. Describing what they do, organization researchers can increase the legitimacy of their own genre.

Not everybody is of that opinion. There are voices saying that problematizing what one does is not a good way to institutionalize it, that attracting attention to the process, inevitably exposing its messiness and lack of a *priori* criteria is the last thing a discipline in need of legitimation wants (Pfeffer, 1983). This might be true in the case of nascent disciplines, which are vulnerable to any form of doubt, but different phases of the life cycle require different legitimation tactics. The most established disciplines, such as philosophy, mathematics or theoretical physics, like nothing more than a public soul-searching in order to renew and re-legitimate themselves. This is helped by the fact that the very attempt

---

[2]On difference between the logic of action and the logic of decision, see Brunsson, 1985.

to define a genre, as Lejeune (1989) pointed out, is paradoxical: it can only be done by exploring its grey zones and borderline cases. Genres blur as soon as you look at them at close range.

Neither paradoxicality nor the presence of conflict need to debilitate a field; on the contrary, they enhance its controlling power. Institutions emerge and renew themselves "by generating just the right kind of tension or even conflict, creative rather than destructive" (MacIntyre, 1981/1990, p. 171). Delineating borders facilitates transgressions, stabilizing gives a basis for experimentation, routinizing unleashes creativity. As language renews itself via paradox (Lyotard, 1979), so social practices renew themselves via tensions and contradictions.

Genres Compared

One of the obvious ways to perform a genre analysis is by contrasting an analyzed genre with other genres. I have suggested elsewhere (Czarniawska-Joerges, 1994) that novels can become models for organization theory – not for imitation, but for inspiration. They are versions of the world, and insofar as these are relevant and valid, it is not by virtue of correspondence with 'the world', but by virtue of containing proper ("entrenched") categories and of being acceptable (Goodman, 1984). Such versions of worlds gain acceptability, not in spite of, but because of their aesthetic features. It is the power of creative insight and not documentary precision that makes novels both a potential competitor of and a dialogue partner for organization theory.

But the analogy between the novel and organization theory is not well-balanced: the novel is a very broad genre, best compared to all social sciences. Organization theory is at best a sub-genre in the social sciences, and therefore could be fruitfully compared to a sub-genre of the novel. Many such comparisons are possible. I have chosen one to concentrate on: the subgenre of the detective story.

One striking and specific analogy between detective stories and organization studies is a preference for a realist style dictated by an interest in social life. They are both built around problem-solving in a social context. The narratives are constructed in a similar way: there is something amiss, it is neither clear nor obvious what it is (there are many false clues), this "something" must be explained (the problem must be diagnosed) and – although this is optional in both detective story and in organization studies – the way of solving the problem ought to be prescribed. When this last condition is upheld, there is often another striking similarity between the main characters - the detective and the consultant. Otherwise, in case the authorship is hidden, as it were, the invisible character of the researcher tells the story, including the solution, without being part of it.

Another analogy concerns the narrative structure, shared by classical detective novels and organization studies. The plot of a detective novel consists of two stories: one is the story of criminal action, which is hidden, and which is revealed through the second story, that of investigation, or acquiring knowledge, which is mystifying to the reader, who does not understand the actions of the detective until the first story is uncovered, and sometimes not even afterwards (Hühn, 1987). The story of investigation seems, in a study of an organization, open to the inspection of the reader, as it is clearly demarcated in a chapter or a section entitled "Method"; however, its highly ritualistic structure is only a different mystifying procedure. Instead of running to and fro with a magnifying glass, the researcher "applies a technique", and in both cases the reader is left to believe that "there is a method in this madness". In the case of the detective story, the actual action is revealed and its underlying pattern is hidden; in the case of an organization study the pattern is presented as such, but the reader never knows how it was actually applied in situ. Both genres often use a variation including a third story to explicate the second: a naive observer, like Dr. Watson in Sherlock Holmes, who can indulge in stating the obvious since he has a professional status to save him from a suspicion of lack of intelligence, or a researcher who tells the story of investigation made by a true hero usually a Leader. The researcher becomes thus a Dr. Watson who is protected by the scientific method, and who can safely be in awe of Sherlock Holmes – the practitioner.[3]

Even the readers who became convinced of the correctness of the above analogy, might be put off by the thought of making it. The detective novel is not precisely on the Pantheon of fiction writing. Why compare organization studies to a genre which is by many considered trash, not worthy of a serious reader, on a part with science fiction and only just keeping ahead of cheap romance? There are two famous arguments in the defense of the detective story, one formulated by Raymond Chandler from the point of view of the writer, and another formulated by Umberto Eco from the point of view of the reader.

Chandler begins with the somewhat unfortunate statement by Dorothy Sayers (unfortunate for her, as all of Chandler's argument is built up at her expense), according to which the detective story "does not, and by hypothesis never can, attain the loftiest level of literary achievement" (after Chandler, 1950, p. 191). According to Chandler, there are no criteria of absolute loftiness:

"It is always a matter of who writes the stuff, and what he has in him (this apparently includes Ms. Sayers) to write it with. .. there are no dull subjects, only dull minds".

In Chandler's opinion, the greatness of literature is decided by its realism, in the sense of sociological portrayals of the everyday life of everyday man (sic) in the everyday world. And this is where I see the additional point of convergence between the detective story and organization studies: in both, an exceptional event (murder, loss of profits, decline, fraud) is an interruption which – for a short moment – reveals the well-ingrained structure of the everyday world, which is forgotten and institutionally sealed from inspection in everyday proceedings.

Eco's (1979) argument is somewhat more ambiguous. He claims that most of popular fiction earns its appeal thanks to its iterative scheme, thanks to a relaxing redundancy it provides to the cultivated readers, who find in it the well-earned repose from the inquisitive search to which their life is dedicated. Thus even detective stories, which are read supposedly to satisfy the need for surprise and the unexpected, are actually valued for their comforting repetitiveness.

Eco's reasoning can be easily paraphrased for the present purpose. Like popular fiction, social science studies are recognizable, what is more, defined, by their repetitive structure. Indeed, there is more structural deviance in detective stories than in doctoral dissertations. Whether this iteration offers comfort and relaxation is another matter (although I would claim that it does). But, just as with detective stories, the redundancy can be all that there is, or else the iterative scheme and the familiar characters can serve as a stabilizing frame through which to reach novel insights into the complexity of social life, due to the lack of distraction usually produced by structural innovations. In what follows I wish to speak of examples of just such work.

---

[3]Keith Hoskin (1996) has another interesting conjecture on this matter. He claims that the prototype of the detective is an academic teacher, with the ultimate right to examine. This model originated in Edgar Allan Poe's repeated failure in academic examinations, which he revenged by inventing a new character – and a new genre.

Two Ways of Writing Murder – and Organization

In principle, both detective stories and social science studies are supposed to build on analytical logic and employ deduction or induction. In practice, formal logic is a rare guest in both. Although Hercule Poirot is supposedly a master of deduction in contrast with Jane Marple's genius of induction, only a very indulgent reader could actually support this claim. Similarly, Glaser and Strauss (1964) following many other critics of the received theory of knowledge, such as Winch (1955) and Feyerabend (1957/1988), showed convincingly that although social sciences attempt to use deduction and induction in their approaches, they owe their insights mostly to abduction. It is thus easier to find writings which prescribe the way to proceed deductively or inductively than actual studies which apply analytical logic, especially among those which use field material (Czarniawska, 1997).

It is abduction, also called the "logic of discovery", which dominates both genres. Another way of proceeding, which should perhaps not be called "logic" at all but is sometimes denoted as "logic of inquiry", is often connected to a "postmodern attitude" which denies formal logic any superior value, appreciates the power of speech, and heeds chance, random events and paradoxes – with bitterness or in a celebratory mood. While the notion of abduction originates in the works of Peirce, his pragmatism and semiotic analysis, the other approach can be fruitfully related to new pragmatism and deconstruction.

Abduction in Fiction

Abduction in a detective story is attributed above all to Sherlock Holmes, who collects observations of which he produces a conjecture, a hypothesis, and then experiments, which sometimes lead to refutation of certain elements or the whole hypothesis, and finally presents the solution to the equally stupefied criminal, Dr. Watson and, sometimes, a police inspector or other witnesses.

It has been suggested that Holmes in fact never verifies his hypotheses, thus failing to follow strict logic and opening himself to a number of parodies which emphasize just this defect (Truzzi, 1983). It is an interesting suggestion which can be seen as correct or incorrect depending on what is assumed to be Holmes' "method". If, as suggested by most, it is abduction, there is no need for Holmes to verify his hypotheses – at the point when no refutations occur (and they usually do in the course of detecting), the conclusion can be presented.

Besides, as pointed out by Bonfantini and Proni (1983), Holmes uses abduction not to revolutionize general laws, as Peirce suggested, but to arrive at narrow-range theories, theories of a particular case, fitting in well the received view of the universe. Holmes does "normal science".

It is pertinent to notice that, like any researcher, Holmes himself does not claim to use abduction, but strictly deduction: "… when this original intellectual deduction is confirmed point by point by quite a number of independent incidents, then the subjective becomes objective and we can say confidently that we have reached our goal".[4] Like in most studies, the talk of "method" is usually loosely coupled to an actual reporting on the procedure, step-by-step. When Holmes pontificates about his "method", Watson is invariably impressed and inscribes it word for word. When Holmes describes what he

---

[4]"The Adventure of the Sussex Vampire", *The Penguin Complete Sherlock Holmes*, 1981, p. 1042.

does, the effect is invariably disillusionment on the part of his public, creating situations like the one in "The Red-Headed League":

Mr. Jabez Wilson laughed heavily. "Well, I never!"
"I begin to think, Watson," said Holmes, "that I made a mistake in explaining.
'Omne ignotum pro magnifco', you know, and my poor little reputation, such as it is, will suffer shipwreck if I am so candid."[5]

Sebeok and Umiker-Sebeok (1983) registered the many ways in which Holmes intentionally mystifies Watson, and made a useful analogy with the medical profession, usually taken as the source of inspiration for the character of Holmes, where a touch of magic in diagnosing supposedly helps recovery. The alleged "elementary, my dear Watson", albeit nonexistent in Doyle's texts, summarizes the usual techniques utilized by the experts to put down the lay-people. Holmes also shares with the modern scientist the habit of admitting that, although strict deduction is his model, frequent deviations occur: "One forms provisional theories and waits for time or fuller knowledge to explode them. A bad habit, Mr. Ferguson, but human nature is weak. I fear that your old friend here has given an exaggerated view of my scientific methods".[6] In other words, a classic case of an aspiring positivist who dabbles in deductive reasoning but depends on abduction for the main result. Where he deviates from the research model is, as I said before, in actual step-by-step reporting of his deeds and thoughts.

One could make a conjecture that the reason why Holmes now and then reveals his procedure, although it is invariably ridiculed by his public and requires an intensification of mystification attempts, is that Doyle needs to show it to the reader. There is no such need when presenting a doctoral dissertation, although such stories often give color to informal seminars and talks with friends. Attempts to legitimize them by introducing them into the main discourse of the dissertation, although recently more frequent, bristle with difficulties (see Ashmore, 1989).

The procedure and the method reflect not only the habits of the scientific community then and now, but also a certain way of seeing the world, a certain cosmology, which Holmes and social scientists share, to a degree. In many analyses of Holmesian detection a parallel is made between the detective and the physician, and through it a generalization is reached concerning the "useful sciences" (such as law, medicine, although management sciences can be easily included in this group). This is what Ginzburg calls "an attitude oriented toward an analysis of individual cases, reconstruable only through traces, symptoms, indices" (1983, p. 109, trans. BC). Sherlock Holmes is interested in society, but society is accessible to him through the minute and multiple inscriptions it makes on individuals, together with biology. The dedication in reading those signs makes him, in the eyes of the critic, an admirable semiotician. As far as organization studies are concerned, here is where the qualifier I used before – "to a degree" – most strongly applies. Many organization studies share with the Holmesian approach the belief that individuals are the only accessible study object, as organizations can be apprehended only by studies of individuals, but not necessarily the understanding and the devotion of a semiotician. The obvious is a red rag to Holmes' eyes, but it is – more often then not – taken for obvious in organization studies.

---

[5] *The Penguin Complete Sherlock Holmes,* 1981 p. 177.

[6] "The Adventure of the Sussex Vampire", *The Penguin Complete Sherlock Holmes,* 1981, p. 1038-39.

... and in Organization Studies

Alvin Gouldner's *Patterns of Industrial Bureaucracy* begins, as it should, with a description of a disturbance in the existing social order by a demise: pre-modern, "organic solidarity", which previously ruled Gypsum Plant, is killed. Modern, industrial bureaucracy is introduced in its place. The issues to detect are several: is this a crime, a misdemeanor, or just a death from old age? And who, among the suspects, is the real perpetrator: the new plant manager, the new social order, or the Zeitgeist? The detective, called in by the head office, as it seems, is a team of undergraduate students and their tutor, most of them ex-GIs Gust like in Holmes' stories, most of Watson's chums are ex-rnilitary).[7] The reader is informed that the study has been guided by a deductively derived (from Weber's theory of bureaucracy) hypothesis, but the detectives emphasize the openness of their methods, so that no relevant information could escape them (which, as in Holmes' case, will cost them many an apology.. .)

In the process of detection, many interesting details of local and universal folklore are detected and created: the miners' tales, familiarizing the danger in their jobs, but also "a Rebecca myth", Daphne du Maurier's metaphor which the researchers pick up to throw light on their findings.

From many tales, observations and reflections, emerges a picture of two distinct groups: "the miners", representing and maintaining the old, organic solidarity, and "the surface", which is already much more bureaucratic when the central events begin. The informal solidarity of the miners is produced both by the spatial arrangement of their jobs, and the constant threat they experience. This, in a sense, justifies their resistance to bureaucracy. On the other hand, they are perceived by the management as unreliable (high level of absenteeism, due partly to their drinking and gambling habits), and thus in need of bureaucracy. Here, the readers have an opportunity to see how abduction works in practice:

Did this perception of undependability of the miners' work attendance arouse bureaucratic efforts, which our hypothesis as presently formulated would imply, and if not, why not? An illuminating example was the case of the "no-absenteeism" rule. Supervisors in the mine did, at first, attempt to enforce this rule. Very shortly thereafter, however, they bowed to strong informal opposition and declared that this rule just could not be enforced in the mine.... . This suggests the following modification in our original hypothesis: Even if supervisors see subordinates as failing in the performance of their role. obligations, the adoption of bureaucratic solutions will depend, in part, upon an estimate of whether they will work. The mine supervisors had to ask themselves, would the introduction of bureaucratic discipline into the mines, and an emphasis on strict conformity to work regulations, *succeed here?*

There were important features of the mining situation which made supervisors decide that question in the negative... . Management's conception of the miners encouraged them to accept the status quo in the mine, forestalling efforts at bureaucratization, however desirable these might seem (Gouldner, 1954, pp. 142-143).

Lest it be thought that I am forcing the analogy of the detective pursuit on an unwilling author, here is Gouldner's introduction to the last part of the book:

In seeking to account for the development of bureaucracy we have, so far conformed to the time honored canons of the working detective; that is, we sought to demonstrate first, the "motives," and then the "opportunity." In considering the first, it has been suggested that the "motives" comprise an effort to solve the problem of worker

---

[7]For the record, although one woman joined the team at a later stage, it was an all-male operation, including the bonding between the miners and the researchers. And so are Sherlock Holmes stories: women have quite a defined role there, and never that of a detective or his assistant.

"apathy"; in examining the "opportunity," attention has been given to the recalcitrance of the human material, and to the question of whether the "victim" is cussedly resistant or quietly acquiescent.

By analogy, we are not so much interested in the "crime" as in the career of the criminal, and this, of course, is shaped by more than his motives or opportunities. It depends also on what happens in the course of such a career. Whether the criminal escapes or is caught is no petty detail: whether he satisfies his motives or frustrates them influences the development of his career (Gouldner, 1954, pp. 157-158).

"The criminal" is bureaucratic patterns, of course. And now to another piece of analogy, the chapter of method. True to form, the "Appendix" mixes the description of the actual procedure with apologies for its constant deviation from the "scientific method":

The purpose of this appendix is not to show how our procedures conformed to the canons of scientific method, but to describe in some detail what we actually did and how we did it. This does not mean that we were insensitive to methodological requirements. As the contrast between mine and surface may indicate, we tried to orient ourselves to the logic of controlled experiment - at least as much as our recalcitrant research predicament would permit. Our case study, however, is obviously not a venture in validation. Instead, it is primarily exploratory and comprises an effort to develop new concepts and hypotheses which will lend themselves to validation by experimental methods (Gouldner, 1954, p. 247).

One wonders whether they really believed that a "validation by experimental methods" was possible. At any rate, the conclusions, as usual in detective stories, involve a redefinition of the problem and, as usual, the research team knew that from the very beginning (see footnote on p. 145). With deference to tradition, I will abstain from revealing the conclusions in detail: suffice it to say that they had considerable influence on the ways of seeing bureaucracy in the years to come. Not so the study pattern, though: Gouldner's efforts, like Dalton's later, were much lauded and little imitated. But my choice of this study had little to do with its being typical. It is not that most or even many organization studies resemble Sherlock Holmes' stories. The point is that an organization study might resemble the Sherlock Holmes' story. The final reason why my choice fell on Gouldner is namely that it reads like a detective story, it engages and fascinates the reader. The appropriate language games are in place, ensuring the pleasure of an iterative scheme, but there is also suspense. Old-fashioned suspense, I admit. Nowadays there are other ways of writing detective stories, and doing organization studies.

Postmodern(ist) Options in Detective Fiction ...

The genre of the detective stories seemed to become stale and rigid in the 1920s and the 1930s, when the attempts of genre analysis led to establishing canonical rules, used to discipline the new adepts by the established figures such as S.S. Van Dine or Ronald Knox (Hiihn, 1987). Chandler spoke with spite of "a few badly scared champions of the formal or the classic mystery who think no story is a detective story which does not pose a formal and exact problem and arrange the clues around it with neat labels on them" (1950, p. 197). But, as it can be said that impressionism was produced by the French Academy (which by consistent rejection of paintings not conforming to the rules provoked the opening of the Independent Salon), so one can claim that the rigidification of the rules of the genre made the transgressions easier. Thus the emergence of the "hardboiled" novel, whose foremost representative, Dashiell Harnmett, is now celebrated as one of the first postmodern writers. Before engaging in unpacking this claim, a brief look at the meaning of this ambiguous adjective might be useful.

The adjectives "postmodern" and "postmodernist" are among the most used in contemporary social science and humanities writing. Sometimes they stand contrasted to "modern" and "modernist", sometimes not; sometimes they are used synonymously, sometimes not. I have no ambition to sort out the semantic confusion once and for all, but I wish to propose a temporary order for the purposes of this text. I shall use the word "postmodern" to denote a special kind of attitude, a sensibility which has its roots in one or another kind of disenchantment with what Lyotard calls "The Modern Project" (1979). It comes in two versions: a despairing and a celebratory one. The former concentrates on a feeling of disorientation, meaninglessness and fragmentation (Wilson, 1991). The latter is an attitude of skepticism towards the solutions of modernism ("more control, better control") combined with the realization that actions aimed at wringing order out of disorder seem to be necessary, albeit they are at best only temporarily successful. In other words, it is an attitude of an observer who sees the paradoxicality of life and yet, as an actor, bravely engages in daily efforts to *deparadoxify* (Luhmann, 1991) with not too many expectations of predictable results and lasting effects, and the acceptance of the inevitability of unexpected consequences.

The term "postmodernist" will be used below in the narrow meaning of a literary form of aesthetic sensibility, developed as a follow-up and on the basis of, modernism as a trend (Fokkema, 1983). There are many points of connection between the two. To begin with, one can claim that postmodern sensibility produced postmodernism. But the two do not coincide completely: postmodern sensibility can find expression in surrealism, magic realism, modernism (see, for example, a plea for "modernist anthropology", Marcus, 1992), and, in its celebrating version, in many such forms at once (of which the best example is provided by the works of Paul Auster).

There exists an interesting attempt to read the detective novel as a quasi-postmodernist genre, namely, as an exercise in deconstruction (Hiihn, 1987). As mentioned before, classical detective fiction contains at least two stories: that of a crime and that of an investigation. If one takes a detective as reader, as Hiihn does, the criminal is an author who then tries to write another story – composed of false clues – to cover up the original one, which is inscribed in various material traces of the crime. The detective has to deconstruct the false story – being especially aware of all kind of institutionalized reasoning. The criminal is usually a master of enthymeme: leaving cues which should be completed in a certain – misleading – whole while hiding the premises.

The process of deconstruction is hampered on at least two sides. There are namely other authors, guilty not of a crime in question, but of something else which they wish to conceal, and they either corroborate the criminal's story or write other false stories which must be deconstructed as well. On the other side there is a competitive reader – the police – which is inept in deconstruction and attempts to close the text before its possibilities have been explored.

The detective differs from a deconstructivist mostly in one respect: refusing to admit the infinity of possible deconstruction and insisting on reconstruction of the "only true story", thus heeding the demands of a conventional analysis. Even at that point, notes Hiihn, the realist stance is somewhat weak: rather than presenting "the evidence" the detective presents yet another narrative, betraying the ultimate faith in the constituting power of the narrative.

There was, however, one author of detective stories whose anti-classic attitude became in time read as a forerunner of a postmodern attitude and a postmodernist kind of writing: Dashiell Hammett. The postmodern attitude is the way in which his characters conceive of the social life in which they participate. The most cited example (Marcus, 1974; Parker,

1988) is the case of Flitcraft, a tale which Spade tells Birgit O'Shaughnessy in *The Maltese Falcon* in order to explain his way of seeing the world.[8]

The tale could have been used by Zygmunt Bauman (1992) to illustrate his concept of a postmodern identity: it is a story of a man who, prompted by a chance event, understood that the way he lived – ordered, rational and moral – did not correspond with the nature of existence which is "opaque, irresponsible and arbitrary" (Marcus, 1974, p. xvii). Flitcraft abandons his previous existence, wanders aimlessly around the world, and then establishes a new life, taking on the name of Charles Pierce (which, says Marcus, can hardly be a randomly chosen name), and then recreates his life as it was before. Here, says Marcus,

we come upon the unfathomable and most mysteriously irrational part of it all – how despite everything we have learned and everything we know, men will persist in behaving and trying to behave sanely, rationally, sensibly and responsibly. And we will continue to persist even when we know that there is no logical or metaphysical, no discoverable or demonstrable reason for doing so (Marcus, 1974, p. xviii).

Whereas at this point Marcus himself seems to be on the verge of a metaphysical insight about the "irreversible and inscrutable human nature", one can point out, in accordance with the argument in this essay, that what Flitcraft/Pierce discovers is the futility of the correspondence theory of truth, and the convenience of living according to a story which has an institutional legitimacy in a given time and place. A person living randomly in a world constructed by people who value rationalism may find it rewarding – if, like Hammett did (according to Marcus), he or she finds complexity, ambiguity and paradoxicality pleasurable. Otherwise such a person might find it more practical to adjust to the dominant story of the time, as Flitcraft did, The insight may, after all, not concern the nature of anything – world or people – but the status of knowledge and its uses. And from this perspective, although the main structure of Hammett's stories runs along the genre lines as sketched above, his detectives are consistent deconstructionists, to the bitter end.

Hammett's detective encounters at the outset a "reality" as accounted for by the others, which, however, soon shows the traces of the fabrication process that went into its production: inconsistencies, lack of coherence. multiple voices selling different versions and adjusting them all the time. The detective sets out to deconstruct those fictions and arrive, true to the ethos of the genre, at the "true" story. But this final story happens to be just the last story of the text, no more true or plausible than the magnitude of versions spun all through the text. This final version seems to fit the detective and his present conditions best, is most feasible, or simply is good enough: the pragmatic attitude is clear. A postmodern antihero applies postmodernist skills in his reading/writing activity of the detective. Behind a fiction there is always another fiction – it is turtles all the way down.

Postmodernist before his time, Hammett presented a problem to his readers, and even to his pupils. His most ardent follower, Raymond Chandler, could not accept the final ambiguity of Hammett's texts and the denial of the role of the "harbinger of Truth":

But all this (and Hammett too) is for me not quite enough…. In everything that can be called art there is a quality of redemption. It may be pure tragedy, if it is high tragedy, and it may be pity and irony, and it may be the raucous laughter of the strong man. But down these mean streets a man must go who is not himself mean, who is neither tarnished nor afraid. The detective in this kind of story must be such a man. He is the hero, he is everything…. The story is this man's adventure in search of a hidden truth and it would be no adventure if it did not happen to a man fit for adventure. … If there were enough like him, I think the world would be a very safe place to live in, and yet not too dull to be worth living in (pp. 197-199).

---

[8]This story was not included in John Huston's movie.

This is the cry of a romantic against the seeming acceptance of the wrongs of the world by a postmodern hero, a nostalgia for a Superman. Chandler himself did not create such a hero because his penchant for parody prevented him from this: even in *The Big Sleep* his hero is somewhat alike Archie Goodwin. But recently another pupil of Hammett's created such a person, although she happens to be a woman: this is V.I. Warshawski,

Sara Paretsky's creature, Warshawski defies easy classification: an ardent deconstructivist, a skillful saboteur of the chauvinist language, she nevertheless presents a basically modern attitude: the world is run and distorted by the rich, and the truth lives on the side of the underdogs. But she does not restore order in the world by finding "the truth" of a case; the world remains as is, which puts V.I. into a bad mood then directed at her friends and people dear to her.

V.I.'s stories make explicit and premeditated the variation of the genre initiated by Hammett's stories in a way unparalleled in all other Hammett's followers. The detective's reading of the crime story changes the story, and changes the detective herself (Hiihn, 1987). Being on the side of the underdogs and therefore morally right, she nevertheless implicates herself in the story, becoming at least implicitly guilty and sometimes explicitly criminal in her own actions. As Hiihn put it, speaking of Hammett's heroes, "[t]he influence this has on his self image together with the insight into the inextricably complex ramifications of the crimes tends to produce frustration and disillusionment in him, which finally leave him in a paralyzed state of profound weariness and melancholy" (1987, p. 461). V.I., however, having invested in a postmodern capacity for self reflection, knows very well what is ailing her, and therefore takes a bath, awhisky, soaks her battered body and conscience, and starts anew.

Melancholy and disillusionment are, as we said at the outset, not the only possible consequence of a postmodern attitude. Carl Hiaasen is as much socially sensitive as Sara Paretsky, and each of his books is a small sociological treatise on some kind of societal wrong. His characters, men and women alike, do not bother to fret about the hopelessness of society and its disorders – they take them for a fact. Keen not so much on restoring justice, which they do not see as an original state of affairs at any rate, they do not differentiate between crime and non-crime, between what is legitimate or illegitimate, but employ any means, the more outrageous the better, in order to fight against what they consider an ultimate outrage. Nor are they lonely heroes – there is always a small "interpretive community" who reads the wrongs of the world in the same way and who is equally disenchanted with the legitimate means of protest. The best example is a character who is present in many stories, the ex-governor of Florida who was completely powerless in his post, but as Skink, living on the edge of society, he is able, with help of other people who think alike, to prevent much crime and injustice – by perpetuating more crime. The reader is forever on a roller coaster – first laughs then glimpses the massacre caused by these peculiar do-gooders, but then continues to laugh again.

Hiaasen's textual strategies may prove too advanced for organization studies, although the use of irony and absurdity could be much increased. But it is still V.I. Warshawski who may serve as a realistic model for an organization researcher, who, after all, usually would like to see the world somewhat better, but cannot avoid noticing that all the changes for the better are at best limited.

When siding with the rulers, the diligent student of organizations cannot but notice that there are victims on the opposite side; while siding with the underdogs, such a student notices, like Burawoy (1989) and Kunda (1992) did, that power also has its complications. They all share a general solicitude for the Other, an understanding of entrapment and liberation possibilities provided by the language, and a skepticism toward the Modern

Project which would fix all the wrongs of the world once and for all in the march of Progress.

... and in Texts on Organizations

The two examples I chose, Richard Pascale's "The Real Story Behind Honda's Success" (1984) and Marta Calh and Linda Smircich's "Voicing Seduction to Silence Leadership" (1991) share quite a few similarities but also reveal instructive differences, due partly to the time lapse between them (many mores changed during the seven intervening years).

Pascale begins with Webster's definition of "strategy", only to move from it to a more pragmatic view which emphasizes varying uses of the word relative to the cultural context. While the concept acquired quite a special meaning in the Anglo-Saxon world of management, this use, more, the notion as such, is alien in the Japanese context. Consequently, the application of the notion on events and developments taking place in a non-Anglo-Saxon world becomes a peculiar operation, which is the focus of Pascale's article.

In the Boston Consulting Group's rendition of Honda's entry into the U.S. market, the company's success is explainable in terms of their strategy. "Honda is portrayed as a firm dedicated to being the low price producer, utilizing its dominant market position in Japan to force entry into the U.S. market, expanding that market by redefining a leisure class ... segment, and exploiting its comparative advantage via aggressive pricing and advertising" (Pascale, 1981, p. 51).

Pascale confronts this story with one produced by himself in a group interview with the six Japanese executives responsible for the events which took place in 1959. "The story that unfolded, ... highlights miscalculation, serendipity, and organizational learning - counterpoints to the streamlined "strategy" version related earlier" (p. 5 1).

It does indeed: here follows a funny story of blunders, chance happenings and sheer persistence. Enough to say that while the (then) young executives were trying to sell larger bikes, their future hit – the 50cc – became known to the public only because they used them as cheap means of transportation when destitute in Los Angeles.

The use to which Pascale puts the two contrasting stories oscillates between "the old" and "the new" style of organization studies. On the one hand he says that both stories are valuable, on the other he proceeds to choose the second as "most appropriate in the environmental context of the eighties" (p. 57) on the basis of another streamlined story, this time produced by himself. On the on hand, he criticizes the traditional theory for its simplifications and reductionism, for its ignorance of "the givens of organizations" which are "ambiguity, uncertainty, imperfection, and paradox" (p. 65). On the other, he mainly proposes to extend the list of the determining factors from one item (strategy) to six, (the "excellence" list of 6 Ss), which should take care of everything, ambiguity and paradox included. Finally, the sub-title itself – the "real" story" suggests a powerful commitment to the idea that there is one story which is "truer" than all the others – or, perhaps, that six stories are truer than one.

These oscillations are absent from Calás & Smircich's work, Here, the "text detectives" make their perhaps first appearance in organization studies. "Reality" is a moot point in this exercise: interesting readings of well-known texts are the point. Unlike Pascale, who represented "the truth", the two authors have a "standpoint", which is a feminist one.

As in Pascale's text, a dictionary makes an appearance early in the text, but in a role which has become paradigmatic since. The lexical quotes neither attempt to establish "the accurate meaning of the word" nor, as in Pascale's text, to contrast the dry simplification of a dictionary with living usage (which builds a parallel to the contrast between the "Honda strategy" and "Honda real" stories). They serve as a brief review of the history of uses ("genealogy"), sedimented in etymology, "witnesses", as it were. Calás and Smircich then re-read four classical texts on leadership in terms of ... seduction.

Is the "seduction" reading of the texts "truer" than the "leadership" one? Certainly not, especially as this criterion does not carry much relevance in the present context. "Truer" to what? Author's intentions? Yes and no, as Mintzberg's agitated answer indicates (1991, p. 502): he refuses "leadership as seduction", but admits "writing as seduction", making the detectives into perpetrators, another typical turn of fate for a post-modern detective. As the literary theory taught us a while ago, however, if the readers were constrained by authors' intentions, the whole civilization would not get very far. Luckily for both the authors and the readers, the writers write more than they know.

Is, then, "seduction" a complementary perspective which, together with "leadership", will tell us all about organizations? Again, although Pascale and Calás & Smircich make a seemingly identical point about the value of multiplicity of perspectives/meanings, the consequences are not the same. For Pascale, six is better than one, but six happen to exhaust the interpretive possibilities (a lucky number?). For Calás Smircich the readings are endless; in fact, they continue with three "utopias" which are in a sense "further" readings beyond the edge of what is (organization literature). There is an interesting spatial parallel in Pascale's and Calás & Smircich's percourses. He stops at Peters and Waterman, who provide the answer to all his troubles. They put Peters and Waterman just before the edge (sitting' safely on the mainland, as it were), and then cross the edge, leaving Peters and Waterman behind.

The readings are endless only in principle; in practice, as pointed out many a time, and most convincingly as regards the social sciences by Ashmore (1989), the fear of "endless semiosis" or "aporia" is greatly exaggerated. The institutional frame of time and space limits the repertoire pretty much, and such social mechanisms as fashion and imitation introduce further limitations (for example, they seem to have chosen the "untrue" Honda's story instead of Pascale's). The organization theory detectives do not claim that two stories are twice as good as one; it is just that they cannot ignore noticing many stories always floating around, which makes suspense greater rather than less. Too great, as some readers claim.

How do these two organizational texts compare to the detective stories mentioned above? Hiaasen's heroes and heroines, upon discovering a version of a story which contradicts the official one, commit outrages; Pascale runs for help to "normal science" (police?), choosing to fit his discovery to the legitimate frame, rather than trying to break the frame. Calás and Smircich commit an outrage, just like V.I. Warshawski would. Like she, they are engaged in a relentless battle against gender discrimination crimes committed in language. The difference between Warshawski and Calás & Smircich is that she is also an ethnographer, documenting a new angle of contemporary life in all her adventures. In this sense, she is closer to such organizational detectives as Gideon Kunda (1992) and Robin Leidner (1993). After all, a genre is a space, not a point. How does it look, however, when the time dimension is added? A large shift occurred between Pascale and Calás & Smircich articles. What can we expect of the future? After all, genre analysis is dynamic: it registers the emergence of genres, their transformations and possible death.

Who, If Not the Butler?

Genres in Change

It has been claimed, in fact, that the postmodern detective story is a harbinger of its own demise. Although the detective

is frequently still able to read the truth in the text, he can no longer extract it, as it were, and employ it to remedy injustice and disorder in society. In short, he cannot publish the story anymore ... the truth is useless and ineffectual, because society is not interested in finding the hidden meaning, nor is there a general consensus about the necessity of detection at all. ... The detective reading venture is thus no longer supported or even legitimized by an interpretive community. The story has lost its social function and potential power (Hiihn, 1987, pp. 461-462).

Hiihn's reading, so close to Chandler's lament above, collapses the fate of the detective into the fate of the detective story. Is this justified? It is certainly correct, as Thompson (1993) pointed out, that while the modern detective traded knowledge for power, the postmodern detective earns only confusion in this transaction. But why should the powerlessness of the detective equal the powerlessness of the genre? The market success of Faretsky and Hiaasen, to name only two, tells quite a different story. In fact, Hiaasen's heroes and heroines do remedy justice and disorder in society in their peculiar, hard-boiled way. One could rather speak of a revival and a renewal within the genre: Hammett, a marginal phenomenon in the popular heyday of Doyle and Christie, is situated by his followers in the mainstream, in the center. What is more, the "high-culture" fiction seems to be approaching this popular genre rather than distancing itself from it.

With its origins attributed to Borges, a sub-genre of "metaphysical detective story" is emerging (Rowen, 1991). Contemporary works such as Paul Auster's *City of Glass,* Patrick Suskind's *Petjiume,* Haruki Murakami's *Hard-boiled World* and Jeanne Winterston's *Passion* are all detective stories – in a fashion. They all retain the iterative scheme as a reflexive allusion or a pastiche, and remake the simple mystery, to be straightened out by a clever detective, into the mystery of individual life and social order. At the end, the mystery deepens, if anything, and yet the readers feel richer and wiser, or perhaps just comforted by company.

Rowen, who analyzed Auster's *City of Glass,* points out that Auster's character, Quinn, seeks in the detective story "a refuge from the metaphysical chaos that he finds around him" (1991, p. 226).[9] What he finds are other people engaged in a similar quest, to the point of self annihilation.

The paradoxical lesson is that looking for final order is nothing but the final madness.

Is it not the lesson which is quite easily transferred to the world of organizations where it has been pointed out that the uncurbed quest for control threatens with annihilation not only of those who seek but also the whole world? Might it not be so that the two genres are changing in the same way? That swift and simple remedies are out of fashion, in detective stories and in organization studies?

---

[9] It should be pointed out that her reading differs dramatically from that given Auster by the doyen of British crime stories, Julian Symons, who labels *The City of Glass* a "clever, sterile book" (1992, p. 267), reading in it a contempt rather than a celebration of the detective story tradition. In terms of frequency, however, Rowen's reading is more common.

Not only an Analogy

Much to my delight, there now exist experiments in "scientifiction" which are hybrids of two genres, which indicate that this must be the case. Two I wish to mention are Latour's *Aramis, or the Love of Technology* (1996) and Goodall's *Casing a Promised Land* (1994). In Aramis, the Master and his Pupil, modeled, to my eye, most closely on William of Baskerville and Adso in Eco's *In the Name of the Rose,* are given a task to solve the mystery of death of beautiful Aramis, or Agencement en Rames Automatises de Modules Independents dans les Stations (arrangement in automated trains of independent modules in stations). The Master is a sociologist of science and technology, the Pupil an engineer who takes courses in social sciences at h o l e des Mines, and Aramis is a piece of transportation machinery, whose cars couple and decouple automatically, following the programming of the passengers. Born in the late 1960s, Aramis promised to be the kind of technology that serves humans and saves the environment, and yet in November 1987 it was nothing but a piece of dead machinery in a technology museum.

Who killed Aramis? Engineers? Politicians? Economists? Secret allies? Fate? Hypotheses multiply and the plot thickens, as the young engineer learns that "adding variables" does nothing for understanding complex events.

Goodall's book reminds one more of Dennis Potter's *Singing Detective* by its autobiographical character. Six stories portray six detective adventure of an organizational communication specialist who, by default and by design, enters various organizational settings, looking for clues and reading them. The mystery revealed by degrees is an identity of an organization researcher, spiraling around in the familiar and strange world of US corporations. Is he in or is he out?

There are many interesting similarities and differences in these two books. They are both placed in technology-intensive settings, and yet while Latour subjectivizes things and machines, Goodall does a careful purification work, sifting the human project (symbolization) from the maverick objects. Only once he seemed to be on the verge of being seduced by technology: inside the space-shuttle simulator. But then, once again outside, he (and his colleagues, university professors) was ashamed of brushing shoulders with things so closely as to forget what they symbolize.

According to the authors' self descriptions, *Aramis* is a realist work while *Autobiography* is surrealist. Short of those labels, the reader might easily think that it is the other way around. This teaches the contemporary reader a lesson or two: one is, never believe the author's self classifications and look for yourself; the other is that there are a great variety of realisms.

A better clue to their differences is to be found in their model detectives. I compared Latour's Master and Pupil to Baskerville and Adso not only because of the obvious analogy, but also because Baskerville and Adso are themselves repositories of many models of detection. The Master mentions Holmes and Colombo, and incorporates this unlikely mixture of self assurance and humbleness. Goodall dedicates his work to Raymond Chandler, and indeed there is a similar romanticism and a strong trace of the humanist project in his play with words and events. The Master is truly post-modern in his project of embracing the machines with sincere affection, no matter how non-human they are.

What the two works have in common, and what is of utmost relevance for me, is that they are not "fiction written by social scientists". There were many attempts of that kind which ended either with success, thus redefining the scientist as a novelist, or else with failure, which seemed further to prove that the two do not mix. Latour and Goodall do not dabble in fiction: they propose, seriously, and to my mind very successfully, to hybridize the two genres into a new one.

The Future as a Mystery

The "time-honored" analogy between the detective and the scientist, pointed out by many authors before me (Nicolson, 1946; Porter, 1981; Hiihn, 1987), was supposed to reside in the two characters' common ability to reveal the true meaning, to re-affirm the rule of reason, and to re-impose order on chaos. Hiihn suggests that it was actually science that first suffered from the tremors of self doubt, from the coup d'etat of relativity, and that the scientists turned to detective stories as the last place where order can be kept in spite of all threats. That might no longer be true, and yet there are still many things to be found in detective stories. After all, as Lyotard pointed out, the demise of metanarratives – of Progress and Emancipation makes a lot of room for the little narrative, which "remains the quintessential form of imaginative invention, mostparticularly in science" (Lyotard, 1979, p. 61). The postmodern detective story provides an encouraging example showing the variety of experimentation with such "little narratives" that can be achieved once the rules of the genre are well understood and used – not as a means to control and discipline, but as a spring-board for transgression.

References

Agger, Ben (1989) *The Decline of Discourse: Reading, Writing and Resistance in Postmodern Capitalism.* Basingstoke: The Falmer Press.

Ashmore, Malcolm (1989) *The Reflexive Thesis: Wrighting Sociology of Scientjk Knowledge.* Chicago: The University Chicago Press.

Astley, Graham W. and Zammuto, Raymond F. (1992) Organization science, managers, and language games. *Organization Science,* 3(4): 443-460.

Bakhtin, Michail M./Medvedev, P.N. (f192811985). *The Formal Method in Literary Scholarship. A Critical Introduction to Sociological Poetics.* Cambridge, MA: Harvard University Press.

Bauman, Zygmunt (1992) *Intimations of Postmodernity.* London: Routledge.

Berger, Peter and Luckrnann, Thomas (1966) *The Social Construction of Reality.* New York: Doubleday.

Bonfantini, Massimo A. and Proni, Giampaolo (1983) To guess or not to guess? in: Eco, Umberto and Sebeok, Thomas A. (1983) *Il segno dei tre: Holmes, Dupin, Peirce.* Milano: Bompianti, 139-155.

Brown, Richard H. (1977) *A Poetic for Sociology: Toward a Logic of Discovery for the Human Sciences.* New York: Cambridge University Press.

Bruner, Jerome (1986) *Actual Minds, Possible Worlds.* Cambridge, MA: Harvard University Press.

Bruner, Jerome (1990) *Acts of Meaning.* Cambridge, MA: Harvard University Press.

Brunsson, Nils, (1985) *The Irrational Organization.* London: Wiley.

Bruss, Elisabeth W. (1976) *Autobiographical Acts. The Changing Situation of a Literary Genre.* Baltimore: John Hopkins University Press.

Bruss, Elisabeth W. (1982) *Beautiful Theories.* Baltimore: John Hopkins University Press.

Brunsson, Nils, (1985) *The Irrational Organization.* London: Wiley.

Burawoy, Michael (1979) *Manufacturing Consent.* Chicago: University of Chicago Press.

Burrell, Gibson and Morgan, Gareth (1979) *Sociological Paradigms and Organizational Analysis.* Aldershot, UK: Gower.

Calas, Marta and Smircich, Linda (1991) Voicing seduction to silence leadership. *Organization Studies,* 12(4): 567-601.

Chandler, Raymond (1950) The simple art of murder. In: *Pearls are a Nuisance.* London: Penguin, 181-199.

Czarniawska-Joerges, Barbara (1994) Realism in the novel, social sciences and organization theory. In: Czarniawska-Joerges, Barbara and Guillet de Monthoux Pierre (eds.) *Good Novels, Better Management.* Reading, UK: Harwood Academic Publishers, 304-325.

Czarniawska, Barbara (1997) The four times told tale: Combining narrative and scientific knowledge in organization studies. *Organization,* 4(1) 5 1-74.

Eco, Umberto (1979) *The Role of the Readel: Explorations in the Semiotics of Texts.* London: Hutchinson.

Eco, Umberto and Sebeok, Thomas A. (1983) *Il segno del tre: Holmes, Dupin, Peirce.* Milano: Bompianti.

Feyerabend, Paul (1988) *Against Method.* London: Verso.

Fisher, Walter R. (1984) Narration as a human communication paradigm: The case of public moral argument. *Communication Monographs,* 51: 1-22.

Fisher, Walter R. (1987) *Human Communication as Narration: Toward a Philosophy of Reason, Value, and Action.* Columbia, South Carolina: The University of South Carolina Press.

Fokkema, Douwe W. (1984) *Literary History, Modernism and Postmodernism.* Amsterdam: John Benjamins.

Frye, Northrop (195711990) *The Anatomy of Criticism.* London: Penguin.

Geertz, Clifford (1988) *Works and Lives: The Anthropologist as Author.* Stanford: Stanford University Press.

Ginzburg, Carlo (1983) Spie. Radici di un paradigma indiziario. In: Eco, Umberto and Sebeok, Thomas A. (1983) *Il segno dei tre: Holmes, Dupin, Peirce.* Milano: Bompianti, 95-136.

Glaser, Barney and Strauss, Anselm (1967) *The Discovery Of Grounded Theory.* Chicago: Aldine.

Goodall, H.L. Jr. (1994) *Casing a Promised Land The Autobiography of an Organizational Detective as Cultural Ethnographer.* Carbondale: Southern Illinois University Press.

Goodman, Nelson (1978) *Ways of Worldmaking.* Indianapolis: Hackett.

Goodman, Nelson (1984) *Mind and Other Matters.* Cambridge, MA: Harvard University.

Gouldner, Alvin (1954) *Patterns of Industrial Bureaucracy.* Glencoe, IL: Free Press.

Holzner, Burkhard (1966) *Reality Construction in Society.* Cambridge, MA: Schenkman.

Hoskin, Keith (1996) A seminar at London School of Economics, March 5.

Hdhn, Peter (1987) The detective as reader: Narrativity and reading concepts in detective fiction. *Modern Fiction Studies,* 33(3): 451-466.

Kunda, Gideon (1992) *Engineering Culture: Control and Commitment in a High-tech Organization.* Philadelphia: Temple University Press.

Latour, Bruno (1996) *Aramis or the Love of Technology.* Cambridge, MA: Harvard University Press.

Lejeune, Philippe (1989) *On Autobiography.* Minneapolis: University of Minnesota Press.

Lepenies, Wolf (1988) *Between Literature and Science: The Rise of Sociology.* Cambridge, UK: Cambridge University Press.

Levine, George (1993) Looking for the real: Epistemology in science and culture. In: Levine, George (ed.) *Realism and Representation· Essays on the Problem of Realism in Relation to Science, Literature, and Culture.* Madison, Wisconsin: The University of Wisconsin Press, 3-26.

Luhmann, Niklas (1991) Sthenographie und Euryalistik. In: Gumbrecht, Hans Ulrich and Pfeiffer, Karl-Ludwig (eds.) *Paradoxzen, Dissonanzen, Zusammenbruche. Situationen ofSener Epistemologie.* Frankfurt: Suhrkamp, 58-82.

MacIntyre, Alasdair (19811 1990) *After Virtue.* London: Duckworth Press.

March, James G. and Olsen, Johan (1989) *Rediscovering Institutions. The Organizational Basis of Politics.* New York: The Free Press.

Marcus, George E. (1992) Past, present and emergent identities: requirements for ethnographies of late twentieth-century modernity worldwide. In: Lash, S. and Friedman, J. (eds.) *Modernity & Identity.* Oxford, UK: Blackwell, 309-330.

Marcus, George and Fischer, Michael M. (1986) *Anthropology as Cultural Critique: An Experimental Moment in the Human Sciences.* Chicago: The University of Chicago Press.

Marcus, Steven (1974) Introduction to Hammett, Dashiell: The Continental Op. New York: Vintage Books, vii-xxix.

McCloskey, D.N. (1986) *The Rhetoric of Economics.* Wisconsin, MD: The University of Wisconsin Press.

Mintzberg, Henry (1991) A letter to Marta Calas and Linda Smircich. *Organization Studies,* 12(4): 602.

Morgan, Gareth (1986) *Images of Organization.* London: Sage.

Most, Glenn, and Stowe, William (eds.) (1983) *The Poetics of Murder: Detective Fiction and Literary Theory.* San Diego: Harcourt.

Nicolson, Marjorie (1946) The professor and the detective. In: Haycraft, Howard (ed.) The art of the mystery story. New York: Simon, 110-127.

Oakeshott, Michael (19591 1991) The voice of poetry in the conversation of mankind. In Oakeshott, Michael, *Rationalism in Politics and Other Essays.* Indianapolis, IN: LibertyPress, 488-541.

Parker, Robert B. (1988) Introduction to Hammett, Dashiell: *Woman in the Dark.* New York: Vintage Books, ix-xiv.

Pascale, (1984) Perspectives on strategy: The real story behind Honda's success. *California Management Review,* XXVI(3): 47-72.

Pfeffer, Jeffrey (1993) Barriers to the advance of organizational science: Paradigm development as a dependent variable. *Academy of Management Review,* 18(4): 599-620.

Polkinghome, Donald (1987) *Narrative Knowing and the Human Sciences.* Albany, NY: State University of New York Press.

Porter, Dennis (198 1) *The Pursuit of Crime: Art and Ideology in Detective Fiction.* New Haven: Yale University Press.

Ricoeur, Paul (1981) *Hermeneutics and the Human Sciences.* Cambridge: Cambridge University Press.

Rorty, Richard (1989) *Contingency, Irony and Solidarity.* New York: Cambridge University Press.

Rorty, Richard (1991) Inquiry as recontextualization: An anti-dualist account of interpretation. In: *Objectivity, Relativism and Truth. Philosophical Papers.* Vol. 1. New York: Cambridge University Press, 93-110.

Rowen, Norma (1991) The detective in search of the lost tongue of Adam:
Paul Auster's 'City of Glass'. *Critique,* XXXII(4): 224-234.

Sandelands, L.E. (1990) What is so practical about theory? Lewin revisited. *Journal for the Theory of Social Behaviour,* 20(3):235-262.

Schaffer, Simon (1993) Augustan realities: Nature's representatives and their cultural resources in the early eighteenth century. In: Levine, George (ed.) *Realism and Representation. Essays on the Problem of Realism in Relation to Science, Literature, and Culture.* Madison, Wisconsin: The University of Wisconsin Press, 279-318.

Sebeok, Thomas A. and Umiker-Sebeok, Jean (1983) "Voi conoscete il mio metodo": Un confront0 fra Charles S. Peirce e Sherlock Holmes. In: Eco, Umberto and Sebeok, Thomas A. (1983) *11 segno dei tre: Holmes, Dupin, Peirce.* Milano: Bompianti, 27-64.

Symons, Julian (1992) *Bloody Murder.* London: Macmillan.

Thompson, Jon (1993) *Fiction, Crime and Empire. Clues to Modernity and Postmodernity.* Urbana: University of Illinois Press.

Todorov, Tzvetan (1972) *The Poetics of Prose.* Oxford: Blackwell.

Truzzi, Marcello (1983) Sherlock Homes: Psicologo sociale applicato. In: Eco, Umberto and Sebeok, Thomas (1983) *11 segno dei tre: Holmes, Dupin, Peirce.* Milano: Bompianti, 65-94.

Winch, Peter (1958) *The Idea of a Social Science.* London: Routledge and Kegan Paul.

'We just make the pictures...?' How work is portrayed in children's feature length films

Paula McDonald

This article explores how adult paid work is portrayed in 'family' feature length films. The study extends previous critical media literature which has overwhelmingly focused on depictions of gender and violence, exploring the visual content of films that is relevant to adult employment. Forty-two G/PG films were analyzed for relevant themes. Consistent with the exploratory nature of the research, themes emerged inductively from the films' content. Results reveal six major themes: males are more visible in adult work roles than women; the division of labour remains gendered; work and home are not mutually exclusive domains; organizational authority and power is wielded in punitive ways; there are avenues to better employment prospects; and status/money is paramount. The findings of the study reflect a range of subject matters related to occupational characteristics and work-related communication and interactions which are typically viewed by children in contemporary society.

Introduction

'We just make the pictures, and let the professors tell us what they mean' (Bell, Haas and Sells 1995). This well-known statement of Walt Disney suggests that movie-making is a naïve and innocuous activity, yet it is well established that the socialization of children and adolescents is strongly influenced by various forms of media. Films, magazines, television dramas, cartoons, video games, music videos and advertising have all been scrutinized with respect to the way they influence young people. In the main, these studies have focused on either gender analyses or the impact of media violence on its audience. While a few studies have explored the nature of specific occupations in some media forms, little previous work has addressed broader work-related themes which are exhibited to youth. Yet the role of paid worker is one of the most important transitions from childhood/adolescence to adulthood. Moreover, a growing body of empirical work suggests that these choices are influenced by social and cultural media such as parents' occupational roles and attitudes, geographic contexts, peers and education (e.g., Furnham and Stacey 1991; Gouvias and Vitsilakis-Soroniatis 2005). This study explores the way in which adult paid work is portrayed in feature length films. While it makes no empirical, 'conditioning' claims, there is an implicit speculative argument that texts (books, films and so on) have the capacity to inform the worldviews of those who experience them (Grey 1998), or at least reflect and reinforce the cultural prevalence of such views. Hence, the findings reflect a range of employment-related subject matters which are typically viewed, and are potentially internalized, by children in contemporary society, including the integration of paid and unpaid work, the nature of interactions between employees and employers and how structural factors influence workplace experiences.

Enculturation through media

Recent studies concur that youth spend a great deal of time consuming entertainment media. Children under age six watch an average of two hours of television each day, while eight to 17 year olds are spending an increasing amount of time using 'new media' like computers, the internet and video games, without cutting back on 'old media' such as television and music (Kaiser Family Foundation 2005; Rideout et al. 2003). Increasing consumption, as well as greater accessibility of children's films as a consequence of developments in video, DVD and the internet, suggests the influence of this form of media may have become more pervasive (Huczynski and Buchanan 2004). Indeed, it is argued that the motion picture industry is the most influential media entity shaping consciousness today, with the worldwide industry generating a record US$26.7 billion at the box office in 2007 (Pritham 2003; Motion Picture Association of America 2008). Increasing efforts by movie production companies to systematically market and promote products to youth is also a significant change in the broader youth media culture. Wasko (2008), for example, details the intensive contribution to the commercialization of youth culture by the Disney Company, in the United States and worldwide. Strategies designed to dominate the youth market include the distribution of animated and live-action films and home videos; merchandising – to all ages including babies and toddlers; theatrical productions of successful animated films; children's publishing; online, interactive software, television and websites; major theme parks; and television programming (Wasko 2008). Thus, the broader, commercial media environment is increasingly targeting younger audiences in more strategic ways.

Concerns about the effects of movies and other media on children have been voiced and studied for over 100 years. Butsch (2001) tracks these historical social discourses, which were predominantly based on class, beginning with the silent movie era following the turn of the twentieth century when reformers identified movie content as the root of children's misbehaviour. Other research on the effects of television and radio on children continued through the 30s, 40s and 50s. Findings often reported that subordinate groups were more susceptible to suggestion and more influenced by media messages (Butsch 2001), reflecting dominant cultural views and middle class concerns about the 'polluting' effect of working-class practices (Cohen 1972). More recently, analyses of the changing media environment and the appropriation of cultural meanings and practices have more carefully considered the importance of the temporal, spatial and social dimensions of children's lives, as well as questions of meaning, voice and the values underpinning the regulation of children's leisure (Livingstone 2002).

Academic media and cultural research concerned with the content of children's media has explored a range of diverse topics such as representations of mental illness, cultural/racial analysis, body image, and death and grief (e.g., Beveridge 1996; Cox et al. 2005; Miller and Rode 1995; Minnebo and Acker 2004; Sedney

2002; Tiggemann 2005). The bulk of studies, however, have focused on two constructs of interest; gender and violence. Gender roles have been explored in a number of different media contexts including advertising, television, film, print media, children's literature and video games. Researchers almost unanimously conclude that the media retell a familiar and enduring tale about power relations in a gender hierarchy (Beres 1999; Dundes 2001; Grey 1998; Massoni 2004).

While gendered themes in feature films have not received the same level of recent scrutiny as television and commercials (see for example Johnson and Young 2002; Kim and Lowry 2005; Stevens, Aubrey and Harrison 2004), a few studies discuss their relevance to wider social and political concerns. For example, McLeer (2002) examined two popular films from the 1960s, viz. *Mary Poppins* and *The Sound of Music*. Both films, McLeer (2002) argues, reconceptualize the relationship of the patriarch to the traditional and ideal domestic household in response to mid-1960s cultural anxieties over social and ideological upheavals such as feminism, masculinity and the role of fathers. Furthermore, Hannon (1997) explored gender and age depictions in seven Disney films produced in the previous decade and found that males appeared in major roles more than twice as often as females. In this study, major male characters were also older than major female characters, and all major females were romantically involved. Depictions in Disney films were also examined by Tanner et al. (2003), who found that couple relationships are created by love at first sight, are easily maintained, and are often characterized by gender-based power differentials (Tanner et al. 2003).

The other major area of interest in critical media studies has been the way that media violence influences youth. Studies strongly suggest three important trends in the findings (see Anderson et al. 2003 for a review). First, modern media contains an extensive presence of violence (Dietz 1998). Second, many children and youth spend a large amount of time consuming violent media (Wilson et al. 1998). Third, media violence increases the likelihood of aggressive and violent behaviour (Anderson et al. 2003). Experimental studies and cross-sectional surveys suggest that exposure to violent media has an immediate causal effect on physical and verbal aggression, in addition to aggressive thoughts, emotions or tolerance for aggression (e.g., Bushman and Huesmann 2001; Geen 2001). Longitudinal surveys also reveal that frequent exposure to media violence in childhood (six to 11 year olds) results in high-level aggressive behaviour in early adulthood (Huesmann et al. 2003).

Studies on gendered and violent themes in contemporary media are predominantly derived from the psychological literature and are characterized by theories and questions about how children consciously and unconsciously learn from observed sources such as media characters. Cahill (1994) argues, for example, that children use precedents such as television and movie characters in support of their definitions of social constructions and that they rarely challenge the authority of these examples. Such theoretical perspectives include priming and observational learning theory, which argue that (a) the media operates as an active, ubiquitous and influential agent in the process of socialization and construction of identity, and (b) images and messages are internalized by their audiences and reproduced in society (e.g., Currie 1999; Kellner 1995). Priming, where an encounter with some event or stimulus activates related concepts and ideas in a person's memory (Bargh and Pietromonaco 1982; Fiske and Taylor 1984) has also been applied in studies that examine how occupations are portrayed in the media (e.g., Massoni 2004) and also as a means to explain the way gender schemata are activated and reinforced (Nathanson et al. 2002). Observational learning theory (Bandura 1977) suggests that children learn specific behaviours but also more generalized, complex social scripts or sets of 'rules' for how to interpret, understand and deal with a variety of situations (Anderson 2003).

Importantly, dominant psychological perspectives on the influence of media on children have not been unquestioned. Some sociological literature, for example, has attempted to broaden the research agenda on childhood and media, encompassing diverse, interdisciplinary approaches that situate children as active in the construction of their own lives, of those around them and of the society in which they live (Livingstone 2002). These so-called *child-centred* perspectives reject the attribution of social and cultural changes to features (including the content) of the technology itself (an approach referred to as *media-centred*), but rather consider the meaning, context and contingencies in practices of media use. In essence, these diverse approaches reflect fundamental epistemological questions and differences – those around the nature and scope of knowledge itself. The child-centred and media-centred approaches, in addition to other perspectives such as commercial ones which support a rights-based recognition of consumerism as a defining element of youthful leisure (Beck and Beck-Gernsheim 2002) also illustrate broader debates over the cultural values that society should promulgate to its children (Drotner and Livingstone 2008).

Representations of organizations and employment

During childhood and adolescence, young people progressively develop notions of adult employment and expectations for their own involvement in paid work. Research that explores how young people learn about work tends to focus on educational and occupational aspirations (Gouvias and Vitsilakis-Soroniatis 2005), job value acquisition (Daehlen 2005) and education and training that emphasizes preparation for tertiary education or post-school occupations (Malley et al. 2001). However, school education tends not to focus on more macro issues related to employment, such as rights and responsibilities in the labour market or the way in which gender impacts on employment. Further, while civic education and participation in the political realm are the focus of curriculum attention (e.g., Hahn 1998), the same cannot be said of industrial education. And this is despite the fact that teenagers typically start work three to five years before they can vote.

The portrayal of occupations in various media sources has been addressed in a few previous studies. For example, Massoni (2004) explored occupations embedded in *Seventeen Magazine* and found that the labour market was presented as heavily skewed toward professional occupations, particularly in the entertainment industry. Whilst the roles depicted were consistent with teens' occupational aspirations, they neglected entire occupational categories, such as blue collar and high-skilled jobs. Other studies that have identified different occupations in prime-time televisions' programs found that more prestigious, glamorous and exciting occupations, such as doctors, police and lawyers, were over-represented and less prestigious jobs such as blue collar and clerical-type jobs were under-represented (Signorielli 2004; Signorielli and Kahlenberg 2001). Research has also found that children's media consistently portrays women, compared with men, as either not working, particularly if they are married, or in occupations that cannot be categorized (Signorielli 2004; Signorielli and Bacue 1999). Even in media where women's work roles are featured prominently, distinctive gender patterns are portrayed.

Other work has looked beyond the visibility of occupations specifically towards more nuanced analyses of organizations and organizational life. Whilst most recent work in this area has focused on representations in adult-targeted forms of media, Grey (1998) demonstrated, through an analysis of children's novels, how subtle messages about organizations, such as the operation of rule-based organizations and how skilled work invests one with moral worth, are woven into stories. In analyses of humorous representations of work found in popular culture, Rhodes and Pullen (2007) explored work-based masculinity through a parody of the male body in *The Simpsons* and Linstead (2007) examined organizational bystanding as a condition for moral harassment in *Seinfeld* (both programs are arguably targeted at, and watched by children as well as adults).

These studies, whether they have explored specific occupational content or broader organizational discourses, have contributed to the sketch of contemporary understanding of employment-related themes communicated to children. However, such studies are relatively few and there remains a paucity of knowledge of notions of employment that extend beyond occupations to individuals' rights and responsibilities at work, the nature of employment relationships such as negotiation, power and authority, and structural elements such as legal protections, the role of unions and remuneration issues. The way these issues have been depicted in the media, and film more specifically, as well as the nexus between work and the media in a broader sense, has been largely neglected in scholarly work.

This study addresses these issues by exploring adult employment roles and relationships in children/family genre feature films. Films are a globalized medium designed to be consumed on a worldwide scale rather than for specific national audiences (Bell 2008). Like narratives in other media, films also contain embedded explanations for events and offer frames of reference for the interpretation of actions (Huczynski and Buchanan 2004). Foreman and Thatchenkery (1996) further argue that film equates with organizational research to the extent that both genres generate outputs that carry knowledge, focus on the complexity of experience, pose questions about the social and organizational world, test ideas, and generalize findings. Such fictional representations can therefore be seen as a point of access into the 'realities' of organizational life (Grey 1998). Hence, films are useful for examining not only the occupations characters are engaged in, but how the structural and relational elements of work are arranged and negotiated.

Methods

Sample

Forty-two post-1990 feature length films were explored. Given that recent media studies have found more equal representations of men and women in professional occupations (Signorielli and Kahlenberg 2001), later movies were thought to illustrate a 'best-case scenario' of depictions of gender, social diversity and political correctness. Films were included in the sample if they (a) received a G/PG rating (children/family genre); (b) had widespread circulation in Australia; and (c) included at least one adult (either 'real' or computer animated) engaged in paid work in an identifiable occupation. These criteria excluded television programs, films where adults work roles were either absent or minimal (e.g., *Polar Express*), films released before 1990 (e.g., *Mary Poppins)* and traditionally animated films (e.g., *Snow White*) because the characters were insufficiently life-like to portray 'real' adult roles. Computer animated movies

Table 1.   Sample of feature length children's / family films by year of release (N = 42).

Title	Date	Title	Date	Title	Date
101 Dalmatians	1996	*Dr Doolittle*	2001	*Lemony Snickets*	2003
Agent Cody Banks	2003	*Ella Enchanted*	2004	*Like Mike*	2004
Addams Family Values	1993	*Fantastic 4*	2005	*Matilda*	1996
Annie	1999	*Flubber*	1997	*Millions*	2004
Baby's Day Out	1994	*Free Willy*	1993	*Mrs Doubtfire*	1993
Cat in the Hat	2003	*Garfield the Movie*	2004	*Nanny McPhee*	2005
Cats and Dogs	2001	*Grinch, The*	2000	*Peter Pan*	2003
Catch that Kid	2004	*Herbie Fully Loaded*	2004	*Phantom*	1996
Charlie & Choc. Factory	2005	*Holes*	2003	*Princess Diaries*	2001
Cheaper by the Dozen 1	2002	*Home Alone*	2002	*Racing Stripes*	2005
Cheaper by the Dozen 2	2003	*Ice Princess*	1996	*Santa Claus, The*	1994
Christmas w the Kranks	2004	*Incredibles, The*	1993	*Sky High*	2005
Cool Runnings	1993	*Inspector Gadget*	1999	*Snow Dogs*	2002
Daddy Daycare	2003	*Jumanji*	1995	*Stewart Little*	1999

where animals were central to the storyline (e.g., *Finding Nemo*) were also excluded. Where originals and sequels to family films were available (e.g., *Home Alone*), only the original film was reviewed, with the exception of *Cheaper by the Dozen 1* and *II*, since work roles were central to these films' content. Table 1 lists the study sample.

Procedure and analysis

The exploratory nature of the research questions required an inductive approach which involved identifying themes directly from the data. First, the types of occupations portrayed in each film were listed, including the gender of each worker. Where multiple individuals of the same gender in the same occupation were portrayed (such as four male police officers arriving at a scene), these were counted as one. This strategy was designed to elicit the number of 'appearances' in the films of different occupations and the gender of individuals engaged in them. Given the tendency of several jobs undertaken predominantly by men to appear in groups, counting occasions of appearance allowed for a conservative, though arguably more realistic estimate of the visibility of jobs by gender, compared to counting individuals. Second, themes were identified by exploring the films' content for recurring patterns of employment-related behaviours or interactions. In order to maximize validity of themes, disconfirming evidence was actively sought and relevant quotes were transcribed.

Results

Occupations: types, seniority and visibility

Many different occupations were portrayed in the films, from roles commonly depicted in television and adult films, such as police officers, lawyers and nurses, to more unusual roles such as dog catchers and make-up artists. The breadth of occupations was also wide, spanning high-status, professional roles to manual and trade-related occupations, to low-status, low-paid, routine jobs such as wait staff, factory workers and maids. The most commonly featured occupations were journalists (14), police officers (14), waiters (11), business owners/employers (11), business executives/ managers (9), school teachers (9), security guards (9), and receptionists (8).

Depictions of men's work roles were far more visible than those of women. Indeed, appearances of male occupations outnumbered women's occupations more than two to one (205 compared to 93). Occupations predominantly undertaken by men (e.g., police officers on 14 occasions and athletes on 4 occasions) also often appeared in groups of individuals, whereas this was not the case for women. Where women appeared in work roles, they usually appeared on their own or in rare circumstances (such as maids), as groups of two maximum. Male work roles were also allocated far greater screen time in most movies, which contributed to the overall greater visibility of male roles.

Although some occupations were gender balanced (e.g., school teachers, waiters, journalists), most were not. Depictions of male work roles heavily outstripped females by more than three to one in sport/recreation (e.g., coaches, managers, sports judges), transport/travel (bus drivers, couriers), and law and order (e.g., police officers, detectives, judges; security guards). Not a single female was portrayed in a manual/trades occupation. Depictions of men were also heavily weighted in occupations representing power, wealth and prestige. Chief executive officers of companies were all men (4 men, 0 women) and business executives/managers and business owners/employers were predominantly men (9:1 and 10:1 respectively). The only category of occupations where women were disproportionately featured was in the traditionally female area of administration. The majority of receptionists, personal assistants and clerks were women (11 women, 3 men). Where categories of work roles were more gender balanced, such as health, men were over-represented in the professional, highly-trained occupations (doctors/dentists), while women were portrayed as para-professionals (nurses).

In some films, women were portrayed as highly-trained professionals (e.g., 1 veterinarian, 1 general practitioner, 1 pharmacist, 1 judge, 1 social worker, 1 security design expert), but these were more atypical than a strong trend. There were also 2 cases where women were portrayed in traditionally male jobs, but their femininity was highly visible, which masked the status typically associated with these roles. These examples included one of the major characters, who in the movies *Agent Cody Banks* and *The Fantastic 4*, played a CIA agent and scientist, respectively. These characters were tall, attractive and wore tight, revealing clothing throughout the movie.

The gendered division of labour

Couples with children were depicted in 21 of the 42 films explored in this study. In 13 (62%) of these films (viz. *Cheaper by the Dozen 2, The Santa Claus, Stuart Little, Dr Doolittle, The Incredibles, Baby's Day Out, Peter Pan, Matilda, Charlie and the Chocolate Factory, Holes, Christmas with the Kranks, Free Willy, Jumanji*), the mother did not engage in paid work, but instead took care of the children and completed domestic work. In *Charlie and the Chocolate Factory*, for example, Charlie's father worked in a toothpaste factory, while his mother stayed at home to cook, clean and care for her four elderly, infirm parents and parents-in-law. In *Stuart Little*, Stuart's mother kisses her suit-clad husband goodbye at the door each morning and takes the children to school before returning home to complete a range of domestic tasks. In six films, both parents worked outside the home. Their paid work

Table 2. Occupations portrayed in films and number of males and females in each role.

Occupational Title		M	F	Occupational Title		M	F
Hospitality	Chef	4	0	Transport/travel	Flight attendant	0	3
	Waiter	5	6		Bus driver	5	0
	Caterer	1	1		Truck driver	1	0
	Bar tender	3	0		Flight booking off.	1	1
	Maitre 'D	1	0		Courier	3	0
Sport/recreation	Sports coach	4	2		Pilot	1	0
	Sports commentator	3	0		Taxi driver	1	0
	Pro. sportsperson	4	0	Science/technic.	Technician	3	0
	Team manager	3	0		Video designer	1	0
	Umpire	1	0		Scientist	3	2
	Cheer leaders	0	1		Security design expert	0	1
	Race caller	1	2		Biologist	1	0
	Sports judge	3	1		Inventor	1	0
	Horse trainer	1	0	Business	CEO	4	0
	Jockey	1	0		Business exec./manager	9	1
	Book maker	1	0		Business owner	10	1
Entertainment	Make-up artist	1	0		Accountant	1	0
	Musician	2	1	Law and order	Police officers	14	0
	Actor	2	1		Police detectives	4	0
	Casino worker	1	0		CIA agents	1	1
Health/medical	Pharmacist	0	1		Judge	4	1
	GP	4	1		Lawyer	2	0
	Nurse	0	5		Customs officer	1	0
	Vet	0	1		Security guard	7	2
	Obstetrician	1	0		Social worker	3	1
	Dentist	2	0		Court stenographer	1	0
	Psychiatrist	2	0	Retail	Store employee	2	3
Administration	PA	1	3	Trades/manual	Mechanic	3	0
	Receptionist	0	8		Farmer	1	0
	Clerk	2	0		Gardener	2	0
Personal service	Group home coord.	1	1		Butcher	1	0
	Group home staff	1	1		Welder	1	0
	Maid	0	6		Fire officers	3	0
	Butler	3	0		Wharf worker	1	0
	Chauffeur	2	0		Groundsperson	2	0
	Camp director	1	1		Storeman	1	0
	Nanny/childcare	0	4		Construction worker	2	0
	Milk deliverer	1	0		Removalist	1	0
	Hotel doorman	1	0		Fishing boat operator	1	0
	Real estate agent	3	2		Soldier	1	0
	Postman	1	0	Sundry	Dog catcher	1	0
	Cleaner	1	1		Factory worker	2	2
	Librarian	0	1		Sailor	1	0

Table 2. (*Continued*).

	Occupational Title	M	F		Occupational Title	M	F
	Driving instructor	1	0		Priest	1	0
Education	School teacher	5	4		Animal trainer	0	1
	School principal	2	3	Journalism/Med	Newsreader	3	1
	College academic	3	2		Journalist (field)	7	7
Fashion/design	Fashion designer	0	1		Media producer	2	0
	Interior designer	0	1		Author	0	1
	Architect	1	0		Camera technician	3	0
				Public officials	Mayor	0	2

Note: Where multiple individuals of the same gender were portrayed in the same occupation, these were counted as one appearance.

was of relatively equal status in *Cats and Dogs, Catch that Kid, Daddy Daycare* and *Sky High*, while the mother's job was of higher status in *Mrs Doubtfire*. Only *Cheaper by the Dozen 1* depicted a full-time working father and part-time working mother. In the remaining two films depicting couples with children (*The Addams Family, Home Alone*), neither parent was shown in paid work.

In households where there was a single parent (4 single fathers, 2 single mothers), these parents were in full-time, paid work. In *101 Dalmatians,* where a couple with no children was portrayed, Anita, a fashion designer, remarked to her employer about her future plans for leaving work when she had children: 'If I left here it wouldn't be for another job…. If I met someone, if working here didn't fit in with our plans…'. Her employer, Cruella De Vil, a fashion house owner, replied: 'More good women have been lost to marriage than to war, famine, disease and disaster. You have talent darling, don't squander it'. This statement was (perhaps) intentionally ironic because while it directly challenged the traditional roles of women as wives and mothers seen in many of the films, it was delivered by the ambitious, unlikeable, evil character, Cruella, reducing the potential for a convincing alternative position of women as talented and career-oriented.

Work-life integration

Around one-third of the movies sampled depicted some kind of conflict between work and home. In three movies (*Mrs Doubtfire, Cat in the Hat, Catch that Kid*), a working mother was interrupted at least once at work in order to deal with a crisis at home. In six films (*Mrs Doubtfire, 101 Dalmatians, The Incredibles, Flubber, Daddy Daycare, Nanny McPhee*), one of the central characters was shown working at home, either predominantly or partially. In *Flubber*, for example, Phillip Brainard, a college professor, has a full laboratory in his basement and is shown working long hours to the exclusion of all else. Indeed, he misses his own wedding three times because he is distracted with his inventions. Four additional movies (*Cats and Dogs, Dr Doolittle, Catch that Kid, Mrs Doubtfire*) portrayed long working hours interfering with home life, especially in relation to childcare or family leisure time. *Cheaper by the Dozen 1* was the only film that depicted the family in the workplace. Tom Baker, a football coach, is shown directing a game with a set of infant twins on his front, while his wife, Kate Baker, is shown writing as a journalist with three children around her desk. The moral of this movie, however, is that these arrangements are far from ideal, a long way from the expectations of employers and that significant career trade-offs must be made when a family comes along.

Nevertheless, the content of most films suggested that the characters engaged in paid work derived significant satisfaction from it. Employment was relatively central to many characters lives, above and beyond its function as a means to earn money or derive status or expertise. This was evidenced in voluntarily spending long hours at work (e.g., *The Santa Claus*, *Flubber*), the forming of meaningful relationships at work (e.g., *Mrs Doubtfire*, *Cheaper by the Dozen*) and the sense of contribution to others or the broader community (e.g., *Dr Doolittle*, *Free Willy*). This is despite the fact that work interfered from time to time with family responsibilities and other pursuits. Similarly, satisfaction also appeared to be derived from the unpaid, home-based work performed by many women (particularly mothers) in the films (e.g., *Stuart Little*). Indeed, the role of paid employment in many films was painted as realistically complex and ambivalent – simultaneously meaningful and engaging, yet frustrating with respect to high workloads and unrealistic employer expectations.

Perhaps the most obviously illustrated example of employer expectations of unhampered commitment to the workplace was portrayed in *Charlie and the Chocolate Factory*. Willy Wonka employed Oompa Loompas to run his factory, individuals who were numerous and perfect clones of one another. They were obedient, loyal and unencumbered by families or other outside work responsibilities or interests. They lived at the chocolate factory and did not need to leave for any reason. The loyalty and service of the Oompa Loompas is couched in terms of being a fair exchange for their rescue from the 'terrible Loompa-land' and protection from the outside world. Nevertheless, when Willy Wonka offers his chocolate factory to Charlie, he has the same expectations of commitment and unhampered loyalty: 'You can't run a chocolate factory with a family hanging over you like an old dead goose. You have to go solo and run free and follow your dreams'. While the film ends on a more positive note, with Charlie's entire family moving to the chocolate factory, the themes described provided an illuminating depiction of the tensions that exist in integrating paid work and other 'life' commitments.

The boss as a bully

Sixteen films depicted a senior work colleague, most commonly the CEO of the company or president of a financial institution that was providing money to a business enterprise, chastising a more junior employee or associate. These episodes portrayed derogatory language, shouting, threats and serious conflict. A demonstration of authority that should not be challenged was highly visible in these interactions, as were signs and symbols representing the status, wealth and power of the person in charge. The issue of money, particularly the extent to which the employee was contributing to the financial success of the company, was also clearly evident in these conflicts. However, the extent to which the interaction was punitive varied neither by gender, nor by the seniority of the employee being chastised.

An example that effectively illustrates these altercations was *The Incredibles*, where the boss calls Bob (Mr Incredible) into his office and dresses him down for approving too many insurance claims and losing money for the shareholders. In *Mrs Doubtfire*, Daniel, a voice-over actor, has a conflict with his boss over the issue of showing a cartoon character smoking. The production manager responds as follows: 'Daniel, listen to me. This session is costing the studio thousands of dollars. If you want a pay cheque you stick to the script. If you want to play Gandhi, then do it on somebody else's time… If you leave, then you're not coming back in. I'm not taking any crap from you pal'. In *Racing Stripes*, Mrs D, a race-horse owner and chairman of the board, responds to one of her trainers when he tells her he is certain he has a winning horse: 'Well, he'd better be Mr Cooper. Give me less than a victory and you'll be back shovelling manure'. In *Catch that Kid*, Mrs Phillips, a security design expert, is called in by the CEO of the bank in order to explain her time-line for completing the security system. He states that: 'The primary shareholder will be here for the opening of the bank next Friday night… That party will take place Mrs Phillips, with or without your consent… Don't tell me how to run my bank. You work for me remember'.

In four movies (*Cat in the Hat, Charlie and the Chocolate Factory, The Phantom, Daddy Daycare*), an employee was summarily dismissed by their employer, sometimes for minor offences (e.g., *Cat in the Hat)* or for operational reasons (e.g., *Charlie and the Chocolate Factory)*. None of these cases showed any avenue of redress for the employee such as being able to negotiate their job back or the involvement of a union, legal representative or other advocate in order to seek reinstatement or compensation. Rather, dismissals were portrayed as events that had to be passively accepted by employees. The only option open to them was to seek another job.

Avenues to better employment prospects

Six movies (*Mrs Doubtfire, Dr Doolittle, The Incredibles, Peter Pan, Charlie and the Chocolate Factory, Nanny McPhee*) depicted a solution to low-paying, repetitive jobs. These solutions included demonstrating talent, hard work, acquiring technical skill or developing better relationships with employers. In *Peter Pan*, Mr Darling was a bank clerk for a large financial institution in a corral beside many other identical-looking men in suits. His sister suggested that his lowly status (and subsequently that of his daughter) could be improved by means of a strengthened personal relationship with senior employees at the bank: 'The daughter of a clerk cannot hope to marry as well as that of a manager. You must attend more parties, make more small talk with your superiors at the bank'.

An alternative solution to poorly paid, repetitive jobs was suggested through the acquisition of technical skills in *Charlie and the Chocolate Factory*. Early in the movie, Mr Bucket worked at a toothpaste factory putting lids on the toothpaste tubes – 'the hours were long and the pay was terrible'. He was retrenched when the factory installed an automated machine that completed the same job more efficiently. However, later in the story, when chocolate sales increased with a concurrent rise in cavities and toothpaste sales, he was re-employed as a technician who fixed the machine that had replaced him. Yet another solution to repetitive, poorly paying jobs was suggested in *Mrs Doubtfire* when Daniel worked his way up from a lowly storeman: 'Well you take all these cans, you box 'em, you ship 'em, then you box those cans over there, ship them, then more of them will come in, you box those, you ship those. Any questions?' to the host of a children's television program, by demonstrating acting and impersonation talent to his boss.

Discussion

This study extends existing literature on the social construction of childhood through an examination of how organizations and paid work are represented in children's/

family feature length films. Some implications of these findings are discussed with respect to career expectations, the reproduction of gendered stereotypes and the avenues through which enculturation may occur. In the sense that studies of film pose questions about the social and organizational world and focus on the complexity of experience (Foreman and Thatchenkery 1996), the findings also contribute to broader organizational research agendas. In a similar way to previous research addressing organizational life in popular culture, the films examined were not neutral, but offered certain positions such as the reinforcement of gender stereotypes and the normalization of existing organizational power structures (Hassard and Holliday 1998). As such, the study was an opportunity to explore the films' points of view in relation to our own experiences and values (Huczynski and Buchanan 2004).

Occupational characteristics and roles

The visibility and status of male work roles, the volume of unpaid, domestic work performed by women, in addition to the conflict between work and family, paint a bleak picture of any recent shifts in the portrayal of gender roles in the media. Furthermore, there were no apparent differences in gendered themes across the 15-year production span of the movies sampled, or between stories that were historically-based compared to those in the present day. Thus, while the age of a film often has little bearing on its thesis (Huczynski and Buchanan 2004), the nature and degree of prestige attached to occupations in which characters are cast provide distinct messages about who works and who does not and illustrates the value and importance of various work roles (Signorielli 2004).

An argument could be made that this is simply 'art imitating life', that is, women do indeed perform the majority of domestic duties and occupy inferior positions in the labour market. Overall, however, the movies portrayed situations more conservatively than even labour force statistics would suggest. For example, women make up around 50% of medical graduates (Australian Medical Workforce Advisory Committee 2004), yet they were outnumbered in these films seven to one. Female police officers constitute one-fifth of the police force (Goward 2002), yet not a single female police officer was depicted. In addition, nearly two-thirds of mothers in two-parent families in these films did not engage in any paid work. Movies with very large viewing audiences have huge potential to promote a fair and equitable society by providing alternatives to traditional themes that can be internalized and reproduced by their audiences. As Hassard and Holliday (1998) argue, films are not neutral in their representations but offer positions, reinforce stereotypes and normalize existing power structures and inequalities. Pritham (2003) captures this idea poignantly. He cites a catch phrase from the 2002 movie *Spider-Man*: 'With great power comes great responsibility' and suggests that the advice is not only for fledgling superheroes but is also appropriate for the all-powerful motion picture industry.

It was encouraging that the range of different occupations portrayed in family movies was very large, potentially broadening exposure to occupational choice for younger audiences. This finding is in contrast with previous studies of television occupational portrayals which have found that police officers, lawyers and doctors dominate the screen (e.g., Signorielli and Kahlenberg 2001). Notwithstanding the gendered themes discussed previously, occupations covered a wide spectrum of industries, including sport and recreation, hospitality, education, health, journalism and manual trades and a diverse range of occupations within these industries. This exposes children to paid work possibilities beyond those of their parents and other immediate social contacts.

Films showing progression of a major character from a low paid, repetitive or dissatisfying job which had a corrosive effect on identity and family, to one that is better paid and more fulfilling, was another positive theme arising from the analysis. Rather than a 'rags to riches' scenario, this progression, and the various avenues through which it could be achieved, tended to be realistically portrayed. Indeed, despite a range of employment 'problems' such as difficulties achieving work-life integration and conflict with authoritarian figures, work itself was clearly a source of significant meaning and intrinsic satisfaction for many of the films' characters.

Power and authority

The nature of hierarchical employment relationships portrayed in the films was clearly problematic. Power and wealth were strongly associated with owning large corporations, especially financial institutions, and this power was often wielded in castigatory and even violent ways. The large differential in authority between the top of the organizational hierarchy and those further down the food chain was not dependent on qualifications or position. That is, even trained professionals or highly competent business executives were chastised by their employers in many of the films examined for the study. Several films also depicted employees being dismissed summarily without any apparent access to compensation or legal redress. Furthermore, the films were completely silent with regard to the role of unions or other collective bargaining mechanisms that assist workers whose employment relationships break down.

Negotiation was depicted as a process that was almost completely one-sided, with the employer holding all the power in the employment relationship and employees being completely at the whim of their fickle and profit-driven bosses. Indeed, the value of stock and other financial outcomes was the principal concern and focus of the interaction in most of these conflicts. Of course, the conflict depicted in the films is to some extent a function of plot development – a way of complicating the heroes' path, inserting obstacles in their progression and demonizing those (managers, employers) who have authority over the 'good guy'. Such plots make for an engaging storyline, reflecting a template that has been designed for mass-market films in the process of training contemporary screenwriters to embed and formalize certain 'rules' of plot construction and characterization (Bordwell 2006). However, there was clearly an imbalance between the consistent conflict-driven themes and enormous power differentials between employees and employers on the one hand, and depictions of negotiated solutions or possible structural avenues of redress on the other. As a powerful agent of socialization, it would seem important for plots to reflect a range of solutions or avenues of negotiation that, while still allowing for an exciting storyline, reflect some of the effective institutions and open, productive employment relationships that many adults enjoy.

Avenues of enculturation

Although the findings of this research paint a rather negative picture of the way in which adult employment is portrayed to children, some caveats are worthy of mention. Previous research on the effects of media violence on children's aggression suggests a number of moderating factors that may influence the relationship between media consumption and adopting or internalizing the themes portrayed. Several of these factors may also apply to the influence of paid work portrayed by the media. For example, observational learning theory suggests that children who identify strongly with a character or perceive a scene as realistic are especially likely to be influenced by the portrayal and to imitate the character or acquire a variety of beliefs, attitudes and schemas (Anderson et al. 2003). Thus, characters which are very different to real-life adults with whom children interact are likely to be less influential than those more closely aligned to their own experiences. For example, the school principal in *Matilda*, who is a nasty bully who terrorizes her pupils and uses physical punishment, may be less influential than the employer-subordinate interactions portrayed in *Mrs Doubtfire*, which are more believable. Indeed, by excluding animated and most computer animated films, the content in the sample films was very realistic. They portrayed, in many cases, 'real life' families, that is, interactions and themes to which many children could not only relate, but would have experienced personally.

As with other moderator effects, it is important to note that because there is increased risk when perceptions of realism and identification are high, does not mean that there are no deleterious effects when levels of realism are low (Anderson et al. 2003). For example, numerous studies have found significant effects of media violence on aggression even when the media violence is clearly fictional and unrealistic (Anderson et al. 2003). Although we may not be able to directly extrapolate the findings of studies of the influence of media violence to conclusions about the way in which children are influenced by portrayals of work roles, the underlying mechanisms of internalizing schemas are convincing enough to warrant further attention in a range of media themes beyond depictions of violence.

Content characteristics such as the age, gender and race of the actors, in addition to the consequences of the characters' choices and behaviour, may also impact on the way in which children integrate these roles and relationships into their own cognitive schemas. Aspects of the social environment including culture, socio-economic status and the influence of parents may also moderate the relationship between what is portrayed in the media and children's understanding of the world. Parents who critique the movies their children consume, for example, are likely to influence the extent to which children are able to discern media content. Singer and Singer (1986a, 1986b) proposed that, when parents take an active approach toward television viewing by their children, including commenting regularly and critically about realism, justification and other factors that could influence learning, children are less likely to be negatively influenced by media content. Nathanson (1999) provides some support for this view. She found that children whose parents discuss the inappropriateness of television violence with them or restrict access to violent television report lower aggressive tendencies than children whose parents do not.

The study of popular children's culture inevitably raises difficult questions about the authority of the critic and about the distance between the cultural critic and the ordinary consumer (Buckingham 1997). Concerns about negative media influences have been voiced since motion pictures were first screened when middle- and upper-class reformers worried about the lower classes absorbing dangerous ideas from such movies (Butsch 2001). In retrospect, these concerns seem at best patronizing, and at worst, an active attempt by those with power to restrict pluralism and maintain control. Drotner (1992) also points out that as each new medium (cinema, comics, radio, television, VCR, the Internet) is introduced, we come to accept, through a kind of historical amnesia, the medium that preceded it, moving from censorship and direct social control, to tacit paternalism and the advocacy of moral education. Thus, it is important not to over-state any potentially negative influences that contemporary films may have on youth. It is also crucial in any media analysis to identify positive influences as well as negative ones. However, given that film is rarely neutral, but presents a point of view that shapes understanding of social and organizational life (Huczynski and Buchanan 2004), the traditional themes identified in this study suggest there may be a role for movie producers and script writers to challenge dominant discourses around employment which persist in feature films. Jauss (1982) refers to these discourses or paradigms as 'horizons of expectation' which are created in the social consciousness through exposure to previous texts. This perspective acknowledges that authors of texts are subject to the same neo-conservative ideas as viewers and as such, they may be blind to the stereotypical themes which they perpetuate. Importantly, film makers are also subject to commercial imperatives, being required to exaggerate, sensationalize and glamorize characters and events (Buchanan and Huczynski 2004), which may limit their ability to alter traditional themes.

Conclusions

When Walt Disney made the statement, 'We just make the pictures, and let the professors tell us what they mean', he underestimated or ignored the wide-reaching influence of the motion picture industry and failed to acknowledge the role it could play in changing children's expectations for the future. While some positive messages were highlighted in this study, the strongly gendered portrayal of occupational roles and the consistently negative interactions between employers and employees suggest there may be opportunity for movie producers and script writers to offer alternatives to the gendered and largely disempowering employment themes which are typical of children's films today. While no claims to direct influences on youth can be made on the basis of this study, popular film offers dramatic, intense and dynamic representations of organizations (Hassard and Holliday 1998) and organizational life that have the potential to be internalized.

Ultimately of course, children create their own, child-centred cultural practices and meanings, uses and impacts of media, just as media cultures in turn, contribute to shaping the experience of childhood and youth (Marsh 2005; Livingstone 2002). In this sense, future research should acknowledge the importance of various contexts in the way media messages about work and organizations are used, while at the same time recognizing the salience and potential influence of narratives that illustrate the 'heart of organizational life' (Bell 2008; Hassard and Holliday 1998, 1). Important issues of context include the simultaneous adoption and use of multiple information and communication technologies that provide multifaceted and sometimes competing cultural messages in children's homes, schools and communities. Other contextual factors which may impact how messages about work and organizations are internalized (or rejected) include social, cultural, economic, or family arrangements. Despite this complexity, we should not throw 'the baby out with the bathwater', but rather recognize that media themes, in and of themselves, are fundamentally important in shaping youth's expectations and consciousness on various issues. Studies have repeatedly and consistently demonstrated a range of negative, causal effects of children's exposure to highly gendered, violent or stereotyped media themes and it is evident that children, for better or worse, are spending much greater periods of time engaging with various media forms and in a more commercialized way. The findings of this study have illustrated one significant, though little examined group of messages communicated to children and youth – those relating to adult paid work in feature films. Children, of course, are by no means passive recipients of film messages. However, the motion picture industry should be urged to consider the scope for innovation within the rigid structure of creativity in producing a saleable film (Bordwell 2006), especially given the existence of significant social and labour market problems in industrialized countries, such as growing gaps between rich and poor, ageing populations, skill and labour market shortages and the associated need for more women to be able to combine employment and child-rearing. Such innovation ultimately attends to the fragile nexus between 'art and life'.

References

Anderson, C.A. 2003. Violent video games: Myths, facts and unanswered questions. *Psychological Science Agenda: Science Briefs* 16, no 5: Oct.

Anderson, C., L. Berkowitz, E. Donnerstein, L. Huesmann, J. Johnson, D. Linz, N. Malamuth, and E. Wartella. 2003. The influence of media violence on youth. *Psychological Science in the Public Interest* 4, no. 3: 81–110.

Australian Medical Workforce Advisory Committee. 2004. Annual Report 2003–04, AMWAC Report 2004.5, Sydney.

Bandura, A. 1977. *Social learning theory.* New York: General Learning Press.

Bargh, J., and P. Pietromonaco. 1982. Automatic information processing and social perception: The influence of trait information presented outside of conscious awareness on impression formation. *Journal of Personality and Social Psychology* 43: 437–79.

Beck, U., and E. Beck-Gernsheim. 2002. *Individualization.* London: Sage.

Bell, E. 2008. *Reading management and organization in film.* Basingstoke: Palgrave Macmillan.

Bell, E., L. Haas, and L. Sells. 1995. Introduction: Walt's in the movies. In *From mouse to mermaid: The politics of film, gender and culture,* ed. E. Bell, L. Haas, and L. Sells, 1–20. Bloomington: Indiana University Press.

Beres, L. 1999. Beauty and the Beast: The romanticization of abuse in popular culture. *European Journal of Cultural Studies* 2: 191–207.

Beveridge, A. 1996. Images of madness in the films of Walt Disney. *Psychiatric Bulletin,* 20: 618–20.

Bordwell, D. 2006. *The way Hollywood tells it.* Berkley, CA: University of California.

Buchanan, D., and A. Huczynski. 2004. Images of influence. 12 angry men and thirteen days. *Journal of Management Inquiry* 13, no. 4: 312–23.

Buckingham, D. 1997. Dissin' Disney: Critical perspectives on children's media culture. *Media, Culture and Society* 19: 285–93.

Bushman, B., and L. Huesmann. 2001. Effects of televised violence on aggression. In *Handbook of children and the media,* ed. D. Singer, and J. Singer, 223–54. Thousand Oaks, CA: Sage.

Butsch, R. 2001. A history of research on movies, radio and television. *Journal of Popular Film and Television* 29, no. 3: 112–20.

Cahill, S. 1994. And a child shall lead us? Children, gender and perspectives by incongruity. In *Symbolic interaction: An introduction to social psychology,* ed. N.J. Herman and L.T. Reynolds. Dix Hills, New York: General Hall.

Cohen, S. 1972. *Folk devils and moral panics: The creation of the mods and rockers.* Oxford: Basil Blackwell.

Cox, M., E. Garrett, and J. Graham. 2005. Death in Disney films: Implications for children's understanding of death. *Omega* 50, no. 4: 267–81.

Currie, D. 1999. *Girl talk: Adolescent magazines and their readers.* Toronto, Canada: University of Toronto Press.

Daehlen, M. 2005. Changes in job values during education. *Journal of Education and Work* 18, no. 4: 385–400.

Dietz, T. 1998. An examination of violence and gender role portrayals in video games: Implications for gender socialization and aggressive behaviour. *Sex Roles* 38, nos. 5–6: 425–42.

Drotner, K. 1998. Modernity and media panics. In *Media cultures: Reappraising transnational media,* ed. M. Skovmand and K. Schroeder. London: Routledge.

Drotner, K., and S. Livingstone, eds. 2008. *The international handbook of children, media and culture.* London: Sage.

Dundes, L. 2001. Disney's modern heroine Pocahontas: Revealing age-old gender stereotypes and role discontinuity under a facade of liberation. *Social Science Journal* 38: 353–65.

Fiske, S., and S. Taylor. 1984. *Social cognition.* Reading, MA: Addison-Wesley.

Foreman, J., and R. Thatchenkery. 1996. Filmic representations for organizational analysis: The chartertization of a transplant organization in the film *Rising Sun. Journal of Organizational Change Management* 9, no. 3: 44–61.

Furnham, A., and B. Stacey. 1991. *Young people's understanding of society.* London and New York: Routledge.

Geen, R. 2001. *Human aggression* (2nd ed.). Philadelphia: Open University Press.

Gouvias, D., and C. Vitsilakis-Soroniatis. 2005. Student employment and parental influences on educational and occupational aspirations of Greek adolescents. *Journal of Education and Work* 18, no. 4: 421–49.

Goward, P. 2002. Both sides of the thin blue line. Speech delivered at the Women and Policing Globally Conference, Canberra, Australia, 20 October.

Grey, C. 1998. Child's play: Representations of organization in children's literature. In *Organization/representation: Work and organizations in popular culture,* ed. J. Hassard and R. Holliday. Sage, London.

Hahn, C. 1998. *Becoming political.* Albany, USA: SUNY Press.

Hannon, C. 1997. Aging with Disney: Depiction of gender and age in seven Disney animated fairy tales. Dissertation Abstract 58–02, 331.

Hassard, J., and R. Holliday, eds. 1998. *Organizational representation: Work and organization in popular culture.* Thousand Oaks, CA: Sage.

Huczynski, A., and D. Buchanan. 2004. Theory from fiction: A narrative process perspective on the pedagogical use of feature film. *Journal of Management Education* 28, no. 6: 707–26.

Huesmann, L., J. Moise-Titus, C. Podolski, and L. Eron. 2003. Longitudinal relations between children's exposure to TV violence and their aggressive and violent behaviour in young adulthood: 1977–1992. *Developmental Psychology* 39: 201–21.

Jauss, H.R. 1982. Literary history as a challenge to literary theory. In *Towards an aesthetics of reception,* 3–45. Minneapolis: University of Minnesota Press.

Johnson, F., and K. Young. 2002. Gendered voices in children's television advertising. *Critical Studies in Media Communication* 19, no. 4: 461–80.

Kaiser Family Foundation 2005. *Generation M: Media in the lives of 8–18 year olds.* http://www.kff.org/entmedia/entmedia030905pkg.cfm. Accessed online 12 may 2008.

Kellner, D. 1995. *Media culture: Cultural studies, identity and politics between the modern and the postmodern.* London: Routledge.

Kim, K., and D. Lowry. 2005. Television commercials as a lagging social indicator: Gender role stereotypes in Korean television advertising. *Sex Roles* 53, nos. 11–12: 901–10.

Linstead, S. 2007. The comedy of ethics: The New York four, the duty of care and organizational bystanding. In *Humour, work and organization,* ed. R. Westwood and C. Rhodes. Abingdon: Routledge.

Livingstone, S. 2002. *Young people and new media. Childhood and the changing media environment.* London: Sage.

Malley, J., P. Ainley, and L. Robinson. 2001. *Witnessing evolution: A report on the growth of workplace learning in Australian schools to 1999.* Sydney, Australia: Enterprise and Career Education Foundation.

Marsh, J., ed. 2005. *Popular culture, new media and digital literacy in early childhood.* London: RoutledgeFalmer.

Massoni, K. 2004. Modeling work: Occupational messages in *Seventeen* magazine. *Gender and Society* 18, no. 1: 47–59.

McLeer, A. 2002. Practical perfection? The nanny negotiates gender, class, and family contradictions in 1960s popular culture. *NWSA Journal* 14, no. 2: 80–101.

Miller, S., and G. Rode. 1995. The movie you see, the movie you don't: How Disney do's that old time derision. In *From mouse to mermaid: The politics of film, gender and culture,* ed. E. Bell, L. Haas, and L. Sells. 86–103. Bloomington: Indiana University Press.

Minnebo, J., and A. Acker. 2004. Does television influence adolescents' perceptions of and attitudes toward people with mental illness? *Journal of Community Psychology* 32, no. 3: 257–65.

Motion Picture Association of America 2008. Research and statistics. Available at http://www.mpaa.org/researchStatistics.asp. Accessed online 25 August 2008.

Nathanson, A. 1999. Identifying and explaining the relationship between parental mediation and children's aggression. *Communication Research* 26, no. 2: 124–43.

Nathanson, A., B. Wilson, J. McGee, and M. Sebastian. 2002. Counteracting the effects of female stereotypes on television via active mediation. *Journal of Communication* 52, no. 4: 922–37.

Pritham, Y. 2003. Medicine, myths, and the movies Hollywood's misleading depictions affect physicians, patients alike. *Postgraduate Medicine* 113, no. 6: 9–13.

Rhodes, C., and A. Pullen. 2007. Representing the d'other: The grotesque body and masculinity at work in *The Simpsons*. In *Humour, work and organization,* ed. R. Westwood and C. Rhodes. Abingdon: Routledge.

Rideout, V., E. Vandewater, and E. Wartella. 2003. *Zero to six: Electronic media in the lives of infants, toddlers, and preschoolers.* Menlo Park, CA: Kaiser Family Foundation.

Sedney, M. 2002. Maintaining connections in children's grief narratives in popular film. *American Journal of Orthopsychiatry* 72, no. 2: 279–300.

Signorielli, N. 2004. Aging on television: Messages relating to gender, race and occupation in prime time. *Journal of Broadcasting and Electronic Media* 48, no. 2: 279–301.

Signorielli, N., and A. Bacue. 1999. Recognition and respect: A content analysis of prime-time television characters across three decades. *Sex Roles* 40, nos. 7–8: 527–44.

Signorielli, N., and S. Kahlenberg. 2001. Television's world of work in the nineties. *Journal of Broadcasting and Electronic Media* 45, no. 1: 4–22.

Singer, J., and D. Singer. 1986a. Family experiences and television viewing as predictors of children's imagination, restlessness, and aggression. *Journal of Social Issues* 42, no. 3: 107–24.

Singer, J., and D. Singer. 1986b. Television-viewing and family communication style as predictors of children's emotional behaviour. *Journal of Children in Contemporary Society* 17: 75–91.

Stevens Aubrey, J., and K. Harrison. 2004. The gender-role content of children's favorite television programs and its links to their gender-related perceptions. *Media Psychology* 6: 111–46.

Tanner, L.R., S.A. Haddock, T.S. Zimmerman, and L.K. Lund. 2003. Images of couples and families in Disney feature-length animated films. *American Journal of Family Therapy,* 31, 355–74.

Tiggemann, M. 2005. Television and adolescent body image: The role of program content and viewing motivation. *Journal of Social and Clinical Psychology* 24, no. 3: 361–81.

Wasko, J. 2008. The commodification of youth culture. In *The international handbook of children, media and culture,* ed. K. Drotner and S. Livingstone, 460–74. London: Sage.

Wilson, B., D. Kinkel, D. Linz, J. Potter, E. Donnerstein, S. Smith, E. Blumenthal, and M. Berry. 1998. Violence in television programming overall: University of California, Santa Barbara study. In *National television violence study,* vol. 1, ed. M. Seawall, 3–204. Thousand Oaks. CA: Sage Publications.

Military, masculinity and mediated representations: (con)fusing the real and the reel

Richard Godfrey

In this paper I argue that it is time to rethink the military within Management and Organization Theory. The starting point for this discussion is a juxtaposition of the (lack of) study of the military within Management and Organization Theory compared with the recent (and sustained) interest in depicting war, the military and the military subject within popular culture. I argue that the military is a gendered and gendering organization that has wider discursive effects on the lived experience of masculinity. Having laid down these conceptual claims, I then argue for the value of film, and popular culture more broadly, as an important source of 'knowledge' about organizational life. To elaborate this claim, I conduct a close reading of four films that represent post-Cold War conflicts and identify three recurring themes that tell particular 'truths' of the experiences of the contemporary military organizational subject. I conclude that there is something meaningful and relevant in the contemporary popular culture of war that can help address the limitations of the exploration of the military within Management and Organization Theory.

Introduction

'Military' and 'organization' have a long and shared history. For example, some of the earliest forms of organized groups were hunting bands that fought for and over precious resources. Furthermore, the earliest permanent, large-scale organizations were military forces, such as the armies of ancient Greece, Rome and China. As Davies (2003, 156) has noted: 'More than 2000 years before Ford and General Motors, these armies practised division of labour, routines, span of command and planning.' The language of management and organization is also regularly and overtly militaristic. We hear competitors referred to as the *enemy* who occupy *positions* on the *battlefields* (marketplace). These competitor/enemies are then regularly *engaged* by our own (labour) *forces* and *fought* with in the marketplace/battlefield, often with the goal of *beating*, *destroying*, and *out-manoeuvring* them.

However, within the theory of management and organization, the military is seldom afforded a position of importance or relevance. There is a significant under-theorising of the military within the discipline, and where it is considered it is frequently used as an example of how not to do things.

This lack of serious study is indexed through the rarity with which discussions of the military appear in the major management and organization journals. Elsewhere, a stream at the 5th *Critical Management Studies* conference in 2005 on the military and militarism (a rarity in itself) not only failed to attract many papers, but of those which were presented, a significant number merely employed the military in a loose meta-phorical sense in order to speak of other issues, (see, for example, John Armitage's paper on 'Militarised education factories'). A lack of interest was also confirmed through the fact that the stream failed to attract any notable audience beyond those presenting.

Conversely, within popular culture in recent years, we find that there has been something of a renewed interest in representing war, the military and the military subject. Across a broad spectrum of textual forms, from the wealth of commemorative and documentary television programmes that occupy many spots on the digital networks, to the new genre of video games that seek to represent specific conflicts, to the abundance of (auto)biographies of experiences of war, to (what might be conceived of as) a new genre of the war film in Hollywood film-making, it seems the military occupies a position of significant and sustained attention within the culture industries.

Whilst much of this textual outpouring takes as its reference point World War Two, there are also a small but significant number of texts that seek to represent post-Cold War conflicts and military actions. This is especially so in the non-fiction biographies of serving soldiers and war commentators. Within this subgenre there are also a small number of film texts, notably: *Three Kings* (1999); *Behind Enemy Lines* (2001); *Black Hawk Down* (2001); and *Jarhead* (2005). (A short synopsis of each film can be found in Appendix 1.)

In this paper, I offer a reading of these films in order to consider some of the ways in which they might help inform not only a particular conceptualisation of the experiences of the contemporary military subject, but also how they might be used to help expand our limited understanding of the military within Management and Organization Theory.

In relating this discussion back to the call for this issue of *Culture and Organization*, it strikes me that here is a situation in which the 'fiction' of the military can help inform the 'fact'. In other words, there is something meaningful and relevant in the contemporary popular culture of war that can, I would argue, address the limitations of the exploration of the military within Management and Organization Theory. This has particular relevance when we consider that for most of us our relationship to the military is a mediated one. Few of us have direct experience of the military organization, nor open access to it. As such, our attitudes and feelings towards it are, potentially, heavily influenced by the ways in which it attends to us through our television sets and cinema screens.

The paper is laid out as follows. First, I draw a number of connections between military, masculinity and organization (theory). I make an argument for the military as a gendered and gendering organization, and that through numerous discursive practices the masculine gendered structure of the military has been pervasive on a wider, societal level. Second, and having outlined the importance, as I see it, of this relationship, I then move on to make an argument for the value of popular culture as a source of inquiry into organizational life. Once this is done, I undertake an analysis of four films that represent post-Cold War conflicts, with particular emphasis on the representation of the military subject – the soldier. I conclude that, in this case, the study of 'fictional' texts has something meaningful to add to discussions of the military within Management and Organization Theory.

Military, masculinity and organization (theory)

Where the military is considered in Management and Organization Theory, something of an orthodox position has emerged which, it seems to me, essentially downplays the role, value and importance of the military as an organization worthy of academic study. Whilst this in itself is cause for concern, when one reads the military through the lens of gender its value and relevance to Management and Organization Theory becomes even more readily apparent, as does the relative lack of discussion in this area (for exceptions, see Barrett 2001 and Höpfl 2003).

As Alvesson and Billing (1992) argue, most occupations, in most organizational sectors, have some kind of gendered imagery associated with them. That is to say, we associate certain jobs and certain organizations with either masculine or feminine imagery. In this regard, the military can be seen as an example of a masculine-gendered organization. Indeed, Morgan (1994) suggests that the military is a *key* site for the study of masculine performance. Hirschfeld (cited in Schneider 1997) goes even further to argue that: 'Of all occupations that are allotted to one or the other sex, none has been considered so much a male privilege as that of the soldier' (186–87).

By extension, it can be surmised that the relationship between notions of masculinity and notions of militarism have been so closely connected that in many societies, throughout history, war fighting becomes a form of male rite of passage; 'to be a real man is to be ready to fight' (Cockburn 2001, 20).

This is a crucial point worth elaborating. Primarily, what is being argued here is that the military, and the act of making war, have become significant factors in wider conceptions of what it means to be a man (subject) and how Man (discourse) has been constructed. The testing, or measuring, of manhood, in militaristic terms, has had far reaching consequences both in terms of theorising masculinity but also in the everyday lives of men. As Hopton's (1999, 72) survey of the literature suggests:

> Many writers who have analysed the psychology and sociology of masculinity have commented on the close links between masculinity, male power and militarism (e.g. Weeks 1981; Morgan 1987; Theweleit 1987; Enloe 1988; 1989; Rogers 1988; Smith 1993). For example, explorations of the psychology of masculinity show that in Western cultures military traditions have a profound influence in shaping men's ideas about masculinity (e.g. Harris 1995). Similarly, Myriam Miedzian has commented upon the close relationship between militarism and what she terms the 'masculine mystique', which is characterised by toughness, domination, competition and aggression. (Miedzian 1992)

There is an imagery, a mythology, around military forms of masculine performance that has pervaded many societies and cultures. Historically, part of the explanation for this connection may well rest with the fact that significant numbers of men had, at some time or another, served in military organizations, whether in times of war or peace. Not only would a form of socialisation take place whilst serving in the military but it is also conceivable that, given the disciplinary nature of this socialisation process, these men would then carry the marks of their military service with them when they returned to civilian life (see Godfrey 2008 for a reading of this socialisation process).

Beyond this, the pervasiveness of the military regarding wider conceptions of masculinity can also be located in the 'pleasure culture' of war that emerged during the nineteenth century (see Paris 2002) and which persists to this day (some of its most recent manifestations might include paint-balling, adventure weekends, survival holidays, as well as the popular cultural texts identified earlier).

Through this range of practices, structures and experiences, then, war, the military and the warrior-ideal have come, in a great many instances, to occupy a position of elevated status within many societies, to the point that they become imbued with notions of national identity:

> The warrior becomes the emblem of a nation's identity. We call on the warrior to exemplify the qualities necessary to prosecute war – courage, loyalty, and self-sacrifice... The soldier is often whom we want to become, although secretly many of us, including most soldiers, know that we can never match the ideal held out before us. (Hedges 2002, 11)

This last point is significant. What is being conceived of here, it seems to me, is an idealised, even fictional, version of masculine performance, one that few can ever achieve but which, importantly, has discursive effects on the lives of men. I call this ideal-type: 'military-masculinity'.

This particular ideal of masculinity is marked by many of the 'common' traits of masculinity. However, so interwoven has the imagery become that it is difficult to separate out the masculine from the militaristic and vice versa. For example, if we take a definition of the 'prevailing Western masculinity' from an introductory textbook on Management and Organization Theory (Brewis and Linstead et al. 2004, 78–79), we find that it revolves around being:

> rational, objective, sure of oneself, logical, decisive, unemotional, tough and competitive. This masculinity centres on control. It means being explicit and assertive, saying what you think and speaking your mind plainly; being outer-focused, possibly aggressive; valuing work, sports and organized activities; being action-oriented, liking to get things done, a doer; being analytical or calculating about situations, rather than intuitive, relying on hunches or gut feelings; being dualistic, or tending to see things as black or white, either/or; preferring quantitative solutions which involve numbers to qualitative solutions which involve opinion; linear thinking rather than lateral thinking; being rationalist, valuing reason more than emotion or playfulness; being reductionist, liking to reduce things to their simplest terms and principles, rather than relishing subtle differences; being materialist, with a constant eye on resources, costs and benefits; being constantly aware of one's position in a hierarchy, engaging in one-upmanship with colleagues, striving to maintain the upper hand and protect oneself from challenges; and isolating oneself from others and rejecting dependence on them.

These characteristics, to me, have clear militaristic undertones and they capture a particular conceptualisation of what it means 'to be a man'; one that has, importantly, been elevated, celebrated and commemorated in the Anglo-West over much of the nineteenth and twentieth centuries.

However, more recently it seems that this particular imagery has come under increasing scrutiny and even attack; its traits increasingly seen as negative, harmful and destructive, rather than noble, valiant and worthy of aspiration. This particular critique has appeared at a time when, according to some, the pervasiveness and popularity of the military as a whole has begun to wane (see Shaw 1991; Morgan 1994; Connell 1995; Hopton 1999).

The Vietnam War (and its subsequent mediated representation) was, I would argue, fundamental to this shifting attitude. It called into question the virtuous warrior image that had existed in the popular consciousness since before World War Two. Images sent back from Vietnam of atrocities perpetrated by US troops further reinforced this feeling. The hostile treatment many veterans of the war reported on returning home testifies to the changing attitudes towards war, the military and the military subject. Today, civilian perspectives towards the military are increasingly those of disinterest, ambivalence and, certainly in the context of ongoing military operations in Iraq and Afghanistan, outspoken disagreement and challenge.

Furthermore, in an era also increasingly defined by consumerism and post-industrialisation, more 'acceptable' practices of masculine performance have emerged as cultural ideals; masculinities more given to the conditions of global capitalism. These developments and the resultant 'unbalancing' of wider gender relations has lead a number of authors to suggest that we are currently living through a 'crisis of masculinity' (see Brod and Kauffman 1994; Connell 1995; Connell and Wood 2005; Kimmel and Messner 1995; MacInnes 2001; Whitehead and Barrett 2001; Beynon 2002; Whitehead 2002).

Under such conditions, and with far fewer of us now having experienced military service, the key question guiding this paper might be: Given its steady loss of status in our cultural construction and practices of masculinity, why is it that since the late 1990s there has been a sudden resurgence of interest in imaging/imagining the military and the warrior ideal across a broad range of popular cultural forms? What are the normative messages they seek to convey about war, the military and the military subject? How might analysis of these representations help inform our understanding of the military organization? It is with regard to film texts representing post-Cold War conflicts that this paper seeks to offer some answers to these questions.

Before doing this, however, it is first necessary to say a little more about the mediated representation of the military (and masculinity) and why it might be useful to read the latter through the former. It is to this I now turn.

Military and masculinity as mediated representation

Representations of war are, arguably, inextricably tied up with representations of masculinity. The military and the image of the warrior-soldier have served throughout human history as signifiers of masculinity. Furthermore, the war film itself has become something of a 'masculine genre par excellence' (Horrocks 1995: 4).

Part of the explanation, I think, for the appeal of the war film (to adapt Horrocks's argument) is that it has 'been constantly elaborated over time, until it has achieved the complexity and richness of more ancient mythologies. It provides a set of symbols which are instantly recognisable" (60). Dirks usefully summarises the recurring narrative motifs that tend to characterise this genre:

> Typical elements in the action-oriented war plots include POW camp experiences and escapes, submarine warfare, espionage, personal heroism, 'war is hell' brutalities, air dogfights, tough trench/infantry experiences, or male-bonding buddy adventures during wartime. Themes explored in war films include combat, survivor and escape stories,

tales of gallant sacrifice and struggle, studies of the futility and inhumanity of battle, the effects of war on society, and intelligent and profound explorations of the moral and human issues.

The final theme that Dirks notes, that war films through their narrative structures regularly explore contemporary issues of relevance, is particularly pertinent in the context of this paper. Indeed, I would go so far as to argue that the images offered in contemporary (post-1998) war films constitute a new 'genre' of the war film; one that is marked by a redefinition of war, the military and the military subject in order, once again, to reflect contemporary concerns, political debates and socio-cultural movements.

Of course, one may ask why study film at all: what value can it serve in the discipline of Management and Organization Theory? In attempting to address this question, the first point to make is that films should not just be seen as banal forms of entertainment, nor even (only) works of art, but that they can be more productively considered as 'texts', that is: 'coherent, delimited, comprehensive structures of meaning' (Kolker 2000, 10). By extension, and in following Brewis (1998, 85), as texts these films constitute 'pieces of knowledge': in this instance, pieces of knowledge about war, the military and the military subject. When conceived of as pieces of knowledge they are, to my mind, legitimate sources of data.

Indeed, such a view is becoming increasingly widespread to the point where it is now quite common to see issues of management and organization explored through the full spectrum of popular cultural forms, such as novels (Knights and Willmott 1999), science fiction (Parker et al. 1999), TV cartoons (Rhodes 2001), plays (Feldman 2003), and popular music (Clegg and Hardy 1996). It is perhaps worth reciting here some of the arguments made by such authors in terms of thinking through the productive value of popular culture as a field of inquiry.

Using 'fictional' data

A commonly cited benefit of using popular cultural texts is in their ability to dig beneath the surface of what is so frequently represented about organizational life in the more 'academic' literature. Hassard and Holliday (1998) suggest that:

> popular culture offers more dramatic, more intense and more dynamic representations of organization than management texts. Consequently, where organization studies texts present rationality, organization and monolithic power relations, popular culture plays out sex, violence, emotion, power struggle, the personal consequences of success and failure, and disorganization upon its stage. (1)

To this list of themes, Phillips adds the 'fear, humour, lust, envy, and ambition that drives so much of organizational behaviour' (1995, 629).

Phillips also makes the obvious, but often overlooked point that we are all organizational members. We belong to a range of institutions and organized bodies. Equally, we all, to varying degrees, engage with popular culture. We go to the cinema, watch TV, read trashy novels and flick through magazines. As such, Phillips argues, the choice of popular cultural texts read in any specific organizational context can become, in itself, an important topic of inquiry: Why these texts? How do they relate to the organization and to its subjects? How are they utilised within the context of the organization? These are important questions that can offer 'further insight into the symbolic infrastructure of the phenomena of organization' (Phillips 1995, 639).

Another reason for studying popular culture (and one of particular relevance to this paper) is the way in which it enables exploration of organizations and events that we may not have access to through more traditional methods:

> fictional sources provide insight into the organization of Soviet prison camps, the work organization of the 1940s, or the organization of a jazz band in the early 1900s. Fictional sources such as these provide a window on a set of organizational events and experiences and present particular aspects of the phenomena of organization in a distilled form that could never, in all probability, be observed by an ethnographer. (Phillips 1995, 639)

This is not to suggest that more 'academic' texts do not address such issues, but as Parker (2002) observes: 'Simply put, an average popular film or book reaches more people than an academic "best seller"' (144).

Finally, perhaps the most important use of fictional texts is their capacity for storytelling and the narrative techniques they employ. To quote from Phillips again:

> in telling a story [narrative fiction] creates a space for the representation of the life-world within which individuals find themselves. This space provides room for the reader to enter into the life-world constructed by the text. It also allows for a more complex representation of organizations; or, to put it another way, it allows researchers to develop more complex hypotheses of organizational functioning. Many different viewpoints can be included in the text, each represented by a character. No final sense of closure needs to be created and none is implied by the presence of the omnipotent author of traditional research reports. Much more room remains for doubt, uncertainty, contradiction, and paradox, aspects of organization that necessarily disappear under 'rigorous' analysis. (1995, 628–29)

This, for me, underscores the value of this type of approach, for it rests, not on its ability to unearth some final solution, a panacea that is able to 'correct' a 'problem': instead, it considers a particular set of organizational issues situated in a particular time and space. It looks to disclose the complexities and contradictions it finds therein, and seeks to identify the normative representations being conveyed whilst also conceiving of points of resistance and challenge. Frequently, it does nothing more than provide a language for that which is often already implicitly or intuitively known. But in doing so, it regularly draws attention to themes and concerns that are so often without representation in much of the literature on management and organization. This, for me, is its value, and in this it is valuable enough to be a legitimate methodological approach to the study of management and organization.

Having made this claim, I now move on to the substantive analysis of the films texts in order to consider some of the themes that emerge, in terms of how they seek to represent the military organization and the military subject. Specifically, I highlight three key themes that emerge in these films. First, the films suggest an increasing sense of separation and isolation of the military subject from civilian life. Second, they point to the confusion, uncertainty, frustration and boredom inherent in contemporary experiences of war. Third, against the critical representation of the military subject found in much of the (previously dominant) Vietnam film genre, these films portray the soldier in an ultimately positive light – reaffirming, it seems to me, the mythic status of military-masculinity.

Imaging/imagining the contemporary military subject

Separation and isolation

A dominant and recurring theme with these films is a sense of separation, and a feeling of isolation, of the military from the civilian. This is a significant theme when read against recent representations of World War Two in films such as *Saving Private Ryan* (1998)*, Pearl Harbor* (2001) *and U-571* (2001). In the construction of the warrior image of World War Two, there was a clear (albeit perhaps in substantial proportion post hoc, given the subsequent rewriting of underlying Allied intent as related to a battle against genocide) moral imperative behind the soldier's cause. Motivation to fight largely revolved around family, unit and country (see Godfrey and Lilley [forthcoming] for a discussion of war, the military and the military subject in recent filmic depictions of World War Two).

However, in the representation of post-Cold War conflicts, allegiance now seems to stop at unit. Chris Hedges (a war correspondent) discusses this point. Recalling a conversation in the field, he states:

> 'Just remember,' a Marine Corps lieutenant colonel told me as he strapped his pistol belt under his arm before we crossed into Kuwait, 'that none of these boys is fighting for home, for the flag, for all that crap the politicians feed the public. They are fighting for each other, just for each other.' (2002, 38)

This dialogue is almost literally recreated in *Black Hawk Down*. At the end of the film, when the surviving US Army Rangers have made it to the safety of the UN camp, Delta Force Sergeant 'Hoot' Hooten, as he prepares to go back into the city to recover more (American) bodies, says to Eversmann: '*When I go home people ask me: "Hey Hoot, why do you do it, man?" … I won't say a goddam word… They won't understand why we do it… They won't understand it's about the men next to you. And that's it. That's all it is.*' Of course, this is not to suggest that in previous wars comradeship and unit did not always come first. Rather, what is being suggested is that in these films this particular level of attention has taken on added significance.

This sense of separation and isolation and the subsequent rationalisation of loyalty have particular consequences. One that emerges repeatedly through these films is the military ethos (at least for the American military) that no man is left behind. The political significance of this attitude is keenly felt when one reads these films against Vietnam (as war, image and discourse), where American soldiers were regularly left behind or abandoned (see, for example, *Apocalypse Now* [1979], *Rambo First Blood Part 2* [1985], *Missing in Action 2* [1985] and *Platoon* [1986]). Furthermore, in positioning the military subject through notions of loyalty and comradeship, one cannot help but read this as, amongst other things, a critique of the individualism and consumptive greed of contemporary society: or at least that is what Ridley Scott suggests in his DVD commentary on the film!

As if to signify its central importance, 'leave no one behind' became the tag line to the release of *Black Hawk Down,* and was a central theme within the film's narrative. The most explicit display of this conviction comes in the actions of Gordon and Shughart, two Delta Force snipers who feature in the film. In a scene in which a second Black Hawk helicopter is shot down, the two snipers make repeated requests to go in and secure the crash site alone. The following dialogue takes place:

General Garrison:	*This is Garrison. I want to make sure that you understand what you're asking, so say it out loud.*
Gordon:	*We're asking to go in and set up a perimeter until ground support arrives.*
General Garrison:	*You realize that I cannot tell you when that might be, it could take a while.*
Shughart:	*Roger that.*
General Garrison:	*And you still want to go in there?*
Gordon:	*Yes sir.*

Shughart and Gordon secure Durant's crash site and hold off a Somali mob for a period of time before both they lose their lives and Durant is taken hostage. It was Gordon's body that was later pictured by the world's media being dragged around the streets of Mogadishu.

It is not just in *Black Hawk Down* that 'leave no man behind' is a key narrative structure. In *Three Kings* it functions through the quest to rescue Troy, who is captured by Iraqi forces, and in *Behind Enemy Lines* it is witnessed in the commitment to rescuing Burnett (an action Admiral Reigart knows will cost him his job). 'Leave no man behind' is a paradoxical creed – admirable but costly. Until the first Black Hawk helicopter gets shot down, only one (US) fatality has been incurred. However, in the desire to retrieve the bodies of the downed helicopter pilot, seventeen more American soldiers will die, as will hundreds of Somalis.

Emanating from this sense of isolation and detachment, and through the conditions of contemporary war, what comes across as the primary experience of these soldiers in relation to their role, their purpose, their identity as warriors, is a sense of confusion, uncertainty, frustration and even boredom. To this theme I now turn.

'Experiencing' war

The contemporary politics of war is a central trope in the narrative structures of the films under consideration. In each, there is a key scene early on in which the film's main protagonist questions their current role, attempting to come to terms with the new purpose for which they fight. In *Three Kings*, during the celebrations that mark the end of the first Gulf War, Gates says, '*I don't even know what we did here. Just tell me what we did here?*' Gates, a Special Forces officer two weeks from retirement, is a seasoned and experienced soldier, but he is an artefact of the Cold War, and struggles to understand and accept this new type of conflict. In *Black Hawk Down*, Eversmann, an idealistic young Army Ranger, believes that they are in Somalia to '*make a difference*', but by the end of the film he will come to question the very possibility of this notion. In *Jarhead*, it is displayed through Swofford's general lack of interest or commitment. He notes early on how he only entered the military out of some (misplaced) sense of family tradition, both his father and uncle being Vietnam veterans. In *Behind Enemy Lines*, Burnett, a young Navy pilot, offers his resignation because he is tired of being '*a cop walking a beat nobody cares about*', of '*watching, not fighting*'. He is bitter that he will never have the opportunity to '*punch a Nazi in Normandy*'. By the end of the film, however, Burnett, having seen his co-pilot executed, been forced to hide himself amongst rotting corpses in a mass burial grave, spent three days being hunted by a Serbian assassin, and having seen the destruction and brutality of war up close, asks for his letter of resignation back. It seems Burnett approves of this version of war, and certainly does not want to disconnect from it!

The contemporary politics of war also reveal their 'iron cage of bureaucracy'. In the opening scenes of *Black Hawk* Down, we see US military gunships looking on as Somali militia assault and kill unarmed civilians at a Red Cross food station. Eversmann says: '*Chief, we got unarmed civilians getting shot here.*' The reply comes in: '*I got it Matt. I don't think we can touch this.*' The pilot radios in to base to request permission to engage the militia. An anonymous voice informs him: '*UN's jurisdiction, 64. We cannot intervene.*' The soldiers, surrounded by military technology and weaponry, look on, helplessly constrained by policy. This scene in *Black Hawk Down* also serves another function. It helps position the blame for inaction in Somalia at the feet of the United Nations. Whereas in the Vietnam films of the 1980s, it was often the US Government that frequently received blame for the failures and limitations of the war, today Hollywood looks to the international defence community as the signifier of bureaucracy and inaction.

This discourse of blame recurs in the other films, most notably in *Behind Enemy Lines* in relation to Admiral Reigart's frequent attempts to rescue 'his boy', Burnett. The situation is made more immediate by virtue of the fact that a Serbian military force, having already executed his co-pilot, is hunting Burnett. However, Admiral Piquet, commander of NATO forces, continually restrains Reigart in his rescue attempts. Piquet is fearful that any intervention by the US will unbalance a delicate peace accord on which a current ceasefire rests. As such, the UN is prepared to sacrifice a single (American) life even if the US, it appears, is not. Much of the film's narrative turns around this question, and at times it seems as though there is no suitable resolution. For example, in one altercation between the two admirals following Reigart's decision to leak the story of his downed pilot to the media, a tactic employed to garner public support for his non-sanctioned rescue mission, Piquet confronts him: '*Do you know how much damage this may cause to the peace process?*' Reigart replies: '*All I know is, the American people want their pilot back.*' '*Exactly,*' Piquet retorts, '*Americans. All you care about is your own damn pilots! What happens when the fighting starts again? Will America recommit its forces to stop a major war?... You might have helped save your man today. And I emphasize "might". But you have risked the lives of thousands tomorrow.*'

At first this appears to be a criticism of American self-interest. However, by this point in the film we, the audience, know that the evil other in the film is using the ceasefire to plan future attacks, and that they are trying to kill the American pilot because he has witnessed mass burial sites; sites that would later come to the public's attention as the conflict subsided and the immensity of the genocide in Yugoslavia became more apparent.

The film (released in 2001) plays on our prior knowledge of the genocide to further the plot. It adds justification to Reigart's mission to rescue his pilot, the only one who has the 'proof' necessary to expose this war crime. It also constructs Piquet, and all that he signifies, as an obstacle to this revelation. By incorporating the genocide into the narrative, the film implicitly seeks to lay the blame for the failures of the war squarely at the feet of the international community. So, in *Behind Enemy Lines*, what starts out as a potentially powerful critique of American military practice becomes a justification for it.

As well as a sense of confusion and frustration, the films also reveal, on the part of the soldiers, a sense of detachment not only from the rest of society but also from any sense of purpose. The opening scene of *Three Kings* plays beautifully on these ideas. It begins when the war ends with the sound of footsteps. The camera pans around to a close-up of Troy: he has spotted an Iraqi soldier in the distance. He shouts out to another US soldier:

Troy: *Are we shooting?*
Reply: *What?*
Troy: *Are we shooting people or what?*
Reply: *Are we shooting?*
Troy: *That's what I'm asking.*
Reply: *What's the answer?*
Troy: *I don't know the answer! That's what I'm trying to find out!*

[Meanwhile, the Iraqi soldier stands on top of his bunker, waving at Troy. The camera pans around to the anonymous US voices engaged in banal conversation. Some are arguing over chewing gum: '*I already gave you a piece.*' '*No you didn't.*' Another has something in his eye, '*I can see a grain of sand in there. I just can't get it out.*' All the time Troy is locked in a potentially lethal stand-off.]

Troy: *I think this guy has a weapon! ... Yeah he does!*

[The Iraqi soldier now has a gun in one hand and a white flag in the other, which he is waving at Troy. Troy shoots him, the Iraqi falls. Troy runs up to check. When he arrives, a young Iraqi man dying from his wound looks up at him. The other US soldiers finally take notice and run up to join Troy.]

Conrad: *Congratulations, my man, you shot yourself a raghead! Dag. Didn't think I'd get to see anyone shot in this war.*

Another soldier poses with the corpse and calls out: *Take my picture.*

Although tragic-comical to watch, the scene is loaded with the kind of confusion, ambiguity and lack of interest that these films seek to portray as symptomatic of the current experience of military personnel. As Fuchs notes in his review of the film:

[T]he movie [shows] U.S. soldiers who are bored and confused. They're used to wait-ing, for orders, action, something to do. Now the waiting seems to be over: the war has been 'won' by smart bombs and video-game-like technology. With their 'mission' deemed accomplished, the soldiers might wonder what the hell they're doing here. (1999)

This trope of boredom and confusion structures much of the narrative of *Jarhead* also. In one scene, whilst supposedly in the middle of a war, Swofford offers some advice on how to manage the situation:

Swofford: *Suggested techniques for the Marine in the avoidance of boredom and loneliness; masturbation, rereading of letters from unfaithful wives and girlfriends; cleaning your rifle; further masturbation; rewiring Walkman; arguing about religion and meaning of life; discussing in detail every woman the Marine has ever fucked; debating differences, such as Cuban versus Mexican; Harleys versus Hondas; left- versus right-handed masturbation; further cleaning of rifle; studying of Filipino mail-order bride catalogue, further masturbation; planning of Marine's first meal on return home; imagining what the Marine's girlfriend and her man Jody are doing in the hay, or in the alley, or in a hotel room.*

This sense of boredom and uncertainty can be read against the foil of Vietnam. Anthony Swofford (on whose biography the film *Jarhead* is based) notes in his DVD commentary that for those military personnel who served in the first Gulf War, the Vietnam film genre was one of the primary means through which they 'understood' war: *'our base knowledge of war was through these films'*. To the soldiers watching them, the Vietnam films were an insight into what they (believed they) could expect when they themselves went to war. These films also functioned as a form of exhilaration to help combat the fear associated with such a prospect. *'To them, they are not anti-war films: all anti-war films are pro-war to Marines.'* (Mendes, *Jarhead* DVD commentary)

In *Jarhead*, Vietnam representations serve as a recurring motif and, importantly, as these soldiers' experiences of war become more and more discordant with Vietnam representations, so their relationship toward these texts become increasingly less positive. For example, on the eve of going to the Gulf the Marines watch *Apocalypse Now*, and we join them during one of the most iconic scenes of that film; the massacre of a Vietnamese village by American gunships. Swofford and his fellow Marines cheer, pre-empt dialogue and actions, sing along to the *Ride of the Valkyries* soundtrack, boo the Vietnamese and cheer the Americans. The destruction of the Vietnamese village is met with chants of: *'Come on, start running, motherfucker'*, *'Shoot the motherfucker'*, *'Die!'*

As *Jarhead* progresses however, the love affair with Vietnam becomes more tainted. The Marines realise that their war, their experiences, do not live up to their expectations, to the rhetoric and the images they have been fed: all they kill is time. In one scene, a Marine is sent what he believes is a copy of *Deer Hunter* by his wife, only for it to have been erased and copied over with a home movie of her having sex with a neighbour: *'Who's fucking around now, Brian?'* she asks. In another scene, whilst Swofford and his platoon patrol the empty desert, US helicopters fly by with *'Break on Through'* by the Doors blaring out. No longer do the Marines sing along. Instead Swofford calls out: *'That's Vietnam music. Can't we get our own fucking music!?'*

Boredom and confusion are also key tropes in *Black Hawk Down*. Army Ranger Grimmes complains: *'I made coffee during Desert Storm, I made coffee through Panama.'* In *Behind Enemy Lines*, Burnett is resigning due to his frustration at his role as a Navy pilot in the context of the war in Yugoslavia. In *Three Kings*, our protagonists go in search of stolen Kuwaiti gold as a way of trying to at least salvage something of value from their (non)experience of a (non)war.

It is also in these moments of boredom and confusion (or perhaps because of them) that the more negative representations of the military subject emerge. The portrayal of the American soldier in the Vietnam film genre has opened up space for thinking about, and depicting, American soldiers committing negative acts. In *Jarhead*, Fowler is caught mutilating a dead Iraqi soldier. In *Three Kings*, our American heroes are ultimately nothing more than would-be thieves.

However, despite this confusion and uncertainty, despite the frustration and boredom, despite the (isolated and occasional) negative representation, ultimately these films still reproduce a dominant discourse of the war film genre; that of the quality of the average US fighting man (*sic*). Indeed, even if these films are read as anti-war, critical of US foreign policy or international politics, they are certainly not anti-soldier. Against the shadow of Vietnam, these films are careful to construct the heroism, courage and moral integrity of the individual soldier on the ground.

Celebrating a (mythical) military subject

More in line with recent representations of the World War Two military subject, the films discussed here offer, in the final analysis, a positive portrayal of the average soldier. Within these films this is most frequently constructed through the relationship between a young, inexperienced, naive soldier and the seasoned, experienced veteran. The latter is regularly presented as a mentor figure that helps induct the younger soldier (and the audience) into the 'realities' of war and the military: In *Behind Enemy Lines* this occurs in the relationship between Burnett and Admiral Reigart; in *Jarhead* between Swofford and Sergeant Sykes; in *Three Kings* it occurs in the relationship between Troy and Gates. Despite Gates's despondency about the war and his role in it, he is still a skilled and experienced soldier, and with that he carries a certain moral responsibility. Hence his decision to intercede on the part of Iraqi civilians against the oppression of Saddam's military, knowing full well the consequences (not only the immediate danger but also in terms of his career and for retaining the gold). The self-serving interest that motivates the heist is replaced by a moral imperative to safely deliver Iraqi refugees across the Iranian border.

Perhaps the most explicit version of this relationship occurs in *Black Hawk Down*, in the relationship between Eversmann, the idealistic young Ranger, and Hoot, the experienced Delta Force operator. The two share a number of scenes that reveal some of the tensions played out in the changing role and purpose of the contemporary military. Eversmann, when asked why they are in Somalia, says: '*Look, these people, they have no jobs, no food, no education, no future. I just figure that, I mean, we have two things that we can do. We can help or we can sit back and watch the country destroy itself on CNN. Right?*'

He is there not to fight – he has never seen 'action' before – but 'to make a difference'. Eversmann is serious, self-conscious, doubting, inexperienced. Hoot, on the other hand, has seen it all; he is calm, confident, pragmatic. When Eversmann says to him: '*You don't think we should be here?*' he replies: '*You know what I think? It doesn't matter what I think. Once the first bullet goes past your head, politics and all that shit just goes right out of the window.*' Eversmann replies: '*I just want to do it right today.*' To which Hoot says: '*Just watch your corner. Get all your men back here alive.*'

The character of Hoot in *Black Hawk Down* is an interesting one. He is the archetypal warrior; tough, fearless, quiet, a loner. He encapsulates the ideal of military-masculinity most forcibly. Hoot fights not for country, flag or the future, but 'for the man next to you'. He shuns authority and sees himself as detached from, not fighting for, his country or the military machine. He stands out in the film as the exemplar of this stark form of a mythical militarised masculinity. When chaos and confusion rain down, he is the figure of calm and understated experience. When the first bullets fly and the first Ranger is killed, it is he who immediately takes control. When the vehicle convoy he is travelling in comes under heavy fire, he puts himself in danger to return fire. Later, when his vehicle column cannot find the crash site of a downed Black Hawk, he decides to go it alone on foot, through the streets of Mogadishu. When the mission is done and the other men savour the safety of the UN base, he prepares to go back out alone. He tells Eversmann that: '*we still got men out there*' and, when Eversmann makes a move to go with him, tells him to forget it: he works better alone.

In some respects, the inclusion of Hoot can be read as a way of redressing the critical representation of the military subject found so often in the Vietnam film. This is made more apparent when one learns that Hoot is the only *fictional* character in the film (all of the other American characters are 'real' people). There was no Hoot in Somali: he is, as Ridley Scott (the film's director) notes, an amalgam of assorted Delta Force characters rolled into one super-soldier.

The decision to include a character such as a Hoot in a film that strives, for the most part, to recount a specific event as it actually occurred, is an important one. It highlights the need (our need) to perpetuate such myths, to provide those with an eye on the military with figures still worthy of aspiration. Hedges (2002, 86) captures the argument well:

> [E]ven in the new age of warfare we cling to the outdated notion of the single hero able to carry out daring feats of courage on the battlefield. Such heroism is about as relevant as mounting a bayonet or cavalry charges. But peddling the myth of heroism is essential, maybe even more so now, to entice soldiers into war. Men in modern warfare are in service to technology. Many combat veterans never actually see the people they are firing at nor those firing at them, and this is true even in low-intensity insurgencies.

In drawing this discussion to a close, I have suggested that these films present a particular conception of the military subject. Against the shadow of Vietnam and the contemporary celebratory commemoration of World War Two, they reflect the complexity and contradiction inherent in experiences of war. They tell of characters not with the determination and moral clarity so apparent in representations of World War Two, but of individuals bored, confused, frustrated. But at the same time they are also depicted, for the most part, as decent, upstanding, moral men.

Conclusion

From a starting point that sought to locate the relationship between masculinity, militarism and organization, I proceeded by arguing that the notion of military-masculinity has had far-reaching discursive effects on the lives of men. Specifically, I made an argument for the importance of notions of militarism to discourses of masculinity, and for military-masculinity to be seen as a particular idealised conception of masculine performance, albeit one currently under increased scrutiny and resistance.

Having laid out this particular theoretical concern, my attention moved on to question why it is that we have seen a return to representations of war, the military and the military subject in popular culture and, importantly, what messages they seek to convey. In order to explore this question, I undertook an analysis of a series of war films released during the period 1999–2005. Given that these films depict wars that occurred after Vietnam, they do not have available the comfort of a retrospective account of a pre-Vietnam era (one afforded the recent World War Two genre). As such, these films make a number of moves in their representation that seek, not to rewrite Vietnam (as war, image and discourse) but to renegotiate its legacy. Within this act of 'renegotiation', these films share with the recent re-imagining of World War Two numerous points of similarity in their depiction of the military subject. Perhaps most importantly, by and large they still paint a very positive, celebratory picture of the military subject, and in doing so they also extol certain values of military-masculinity as a productive, beneficial means of organizing masculinity. Within contemporary performances of military-masculinity, we still see the importance of loyalty, duty, collective identity and the elevation of the group over the individual. These films present a picture of the importance of the military and, most explicitly, of the military subject. As Horrocks (1995) puts it:

It matters that we repeatedly reaffirm the important values of humanity that escapes from the cracks of doom in battle. While the savage fighting seems the antithesis of civilisation, the nobility of intent within that framework is crucial to society's ongoing belief and trust in the virtues elevated by these stories. (4)

In relating this discussion back to the wider literature on Management and Organization Theory, the claims that I can make here are, at best, modest. By conceiving of films as textual pieces of knowledge, I believe they are a relevant source of material for exploring the worlds of work and organization. By offering a particular reading of a particular set of themes within a particular set of films, my goal has been merely to open up a small space from which to rethink the military within Management and Organization Theory. Even within the parameters of this short and very narrowly defined study, I find that there is something significant about the experiences and activities of these organizational members (at least through their mediated representation) that refuses to fall neatly into the (often simplistic) ways in which they are regularly represented within the management and organizational literature.

In conclusion, through a reading of these films, I simply do not recognise the picture of the military that predominates in Management and Organization Theory. These popular cultural texts have something meaningful to say about the military at the current time and, I would argue, can and should serve as an important source in developing a more nuanced account of this organization within the literature.

Acknowledgements

The author would like to thank Simon Lilley, Gavin Jack, Jo Brewis, Pauline Maclaren, Alan McKinley and the anonymous reviewers for their comments upon earlier versions of this material. Inadequacies that remain are, of course, all my own.

References

Armitage, J. 2005. Faith and militarised discourses. Paper presented at the 4th Critical Management Studies Conference, 4–6 July 2005, Cambridge University.

Alvesson, M. and Y.D. Billing. 1992. Gender and organization: Towards a differentiated understanding. *Organization Studies* 13, no. 12: 73–102.

Barrett, F. 2001. The organizational construction of hegemonic masculinity: The case of the US Navy. In *The masculinities reader,* ed. S. Whitehead and F. Barrett, 77–99. Cambridge: Polity.

Behind Enemy Lines. Directed by John Moore, Twentieth Century Fox, 2001.

Beynon, J. 2002. *Masculinities and culture.* Buckingham: Open University Press.

Black Hawk Down. Directed by Ridley Scott, Revolution Studies, 2001.

Brewis, J. 1998. What is wrong with this picture? Sex and gender relations in disclosure. In *Organization/representation: Work and organizations in popular culture,* ed. J. Hassard and R. Holiday, 83–99. London: Sage.

Brewis, J. and S. Linstead. 2004. Gender and management. In *Management and organization: A critical text,* ed. S. Linstead, L. Fulop and S. Lilley, 56–92. Hampshire: Palgrave Macmillan.

Brod, H. and M. Kaufman, eds. 1994. *Theorizing masculinities.* Thousand Oaks, CA: Sage.

Clegg, S. and C. Hardy. 1996. Representations. In *Handbook of organizational studies,* ed. S. Clegg, C. Hardy and W. Nord, 676–708. London: Sage.

Cockburn, C. 2001. The gendered dynamics of armed conflict and political violence. In *Victims, perpetrators or actors? Gender, armed conflict and political violence,* ed. C. Moser and F. Clark, 13–29. London: Zed Books.

Connell, R. 1995. *Masculinities.* Cambridge: Polity Press.

Connell, R. and J. Wood. 2005. Globalization and business masculinity. *Men and Masculinities* 7, no. 4: 347–64.

Davies, P. 2003. Military strategy. In *Strategic management: A multi-perspective approach,* ed. M. Jenkins and V. Ambrosini, 153–74. Hampshire: Palgrave.

Dirks, T. The greatest films. http://www.filmsite.org/warfilms4.html (accessed 27 November 2007).

Feldman, S. 2003. Weak spots in business ethics: A psycho-analytic study of competition and memory in Death of a Salesman. *Journal of Business Ethics,* 44: 391–404.

Fuchs, C. 1999. *Three Kings* review. http://www.popmatters.com (accessed 15 July 2005).

Godfrey, R. 2008. *Military, masculinity and mediated representations.* Doctoral thesis, Keele University.

Godfrey, R. and S. Lilley. Forthcoming. Oh what a lovely war: Filmic re-imagining and the new regime of memory of World War Two. *Consumption, Markets and Culture.*

Hassard, J. and R. Holliday, eds. 1998. *Organization/representation: Work and organizations in popular culture.* London: Sage.

Hedges, C. 2002. *War is a force that gives us meaning.* Oxford: Public Affairs.

Höpfl, H. 2003. Becoming a (virile) member: Women and the military body. *Body & Society* 9, no. 4: 13–30.

Hopton, J. 1999. Militarism, masculinism and managerialism in the British public sector. *Journal of Gender Studies* 8, no. 1: 71–82.

Horrocks, R. 1995. *Male myths and icons: Masculinity in popular culture.* Hampshire: Macmillan.

Jarhead. Directed by Sam Mendes, Universal Pictures, 2005.

Kimmel, M. and M. Messner. 1995. *Men's lives.* Boston: Allyn and Bacon.

Knights, D. and H. Willmott. 1999. *Management lives: Power and identity in work organizations.* London: Sage.

Kolker, R. 2000. The film text and film form. In *Film studies: Critical approaches,* ed. J. Hill and P. Church Gibson, 9–27. Oxford: Oxford University Press.

MacInnes, J. 2001. The crisis of masculinity and the politics of identity. In *The masculinities reader,* ed. S. Whitehead and F. Barrett, 311–29. Cambridge: Polity Press.

Morgan, D. 1994. Theater of war: Combat, the military, and masculinities. In *Theorizing masculinities,* ed. H. Brod and M. Kaufman, 165–82. London: Sage.

Paris, M. 2002. *Warrior nation: Images of war in British popular culture, 1850–2000.* London: Reaktion Books.

Parker, M. 2002. *Against management: Organization in the age of managerialism.* Cambridge: Polity Press.

Parker, M., M. Higgins, G. Lightfoot and W. Smith. 1999. Amazing tales: Organization studies as science fiction. *Organization* 6, no. 4: 579–90.

Phillips, N. 1995. Telling organizational tales: On the role of narrative fiction in the study of organizations. *Organization Studies* 16, no. 4: 625–49.

Rhodes, C. 2001. D'oh: The Simpsons, popular culture and the organizational carnival. *Journal of Management Inquiry* 10, no. 4: 374–83.

Schneider, J. 1997. The pleasure of the uniform. *Germanic Review* 72, no. 3: 183–201.

Shaw, M. 1991. *Post-military society: Militarism, demilitarization and war at the end of the twentieth century.* Cambridge: Polity Press.

Three Kings. Directed by David O. Russell, Warner Bros. Pictures, 1999.

Whitehead, S. 2002. *Men and masculinities.* Cambridge: Polity Press.

Whitehead, S. and F. Barrett. 2001. The sociology of masculinity. In *The masculinities reader,* ed. S. Whitehead and F. Barrett, 1–26. Cambridge: Polity Press.

Appendix 1
Three Kings (1999)

Set in the aftermath of the first Gulf War, *Three Kings* tells the story of a group of confused and bored US soldiers who come across a secret map detailing the location of Kuwaiti gold stolen by Saddam Hussein during the war. The soldiers, all part-time reservists, are joined by experienced Special Forces officer, Major Archie Gates, and proceed into the desert to retrieve the gold for themselves.

The film depicts their experiences in the desert as they follow the clues that will finally lead them to the gold. Along the way they witness the oppressive treatment experienced by the civilian population at the hands of Saddam's Republican Guard. Eventually having seized the gold, the point comes that Gates decides he can no longer stand back and watch, and so intercedes on the part of the civilians against these forces. What follows is a series of gun battles between the American soldiers, who are joined by Iraqi rebels, and the Iraqi military. In the process, Troy is captured and subsequently rescued and Conrad is killed.

Following these battles, the American soldiers finally agree to transport the rebels across the Iraqi border to the safety of Iran in return for supplies and help with carrying the gold, which they also agree to share with the rebels. All the while, hot on their trail, is Adriana Cruz, a reporter in search of the stolen gold story, and Colonel Horn, wanting to know where his men have disappeared to.

Just as the rebels are about to cross the border, Colonel Horn finally catches up with the group and prevents them from carrying out this 'illegal' action. A standoff ensues which is ultimately resolved, partly through Cruz's presence with a film crew, when Gates agrees to give up the gold in return for the safety of the rebels. Horn agrees.

Behind Enemy Lines (2001)

Behind Enemy Lines is set during the war in Yugoslavia in the mid-1990s. The story begins with Burnett's decision to resign from his role as a navy pilot because he is bored and finds no fulfilment in the military in which he serves. Following an altercation with his ship commander, Admiral Reigart, he is assigned a reconnaissance mission of the kind he has done many times before.

When Burnett and his co-pilot, Stackhouse, stray off course in order to explore some non-sanctioned military units, his jet is targeted by anti-aircraft missiles and, following a protracted chase, is eventually shot down. Both pilots eject but Stackhouse is injured. Burnett decides to leave the wounded Stackhouse in order to reach higher ground to send out a distress beacon. As he does so, the Serbian forces that shot them down find Stackhouse and proceed to execute him. Alerted by Burnett's involuntary screams, the Serbs then pursue Burnett through the Serbian countryside for a number of days, aware, as they are, that he has seen their illegal build-up of military forces during an agreed ceasefire. Meanwhile, Admiral Reigart makes repeated attempts to rescue Burnett, but is continually restricted in his actions by NATO commander Admiral Piquet, who does not want to upset the current, supposed, peace accord.

What follows is a series of events in which Burnett, pursued by a ruthless Serb tracker, travels on foot to a series of grid references in order for safe evacuation only to be told, once there, that it is no longer viable and to move on to another position. Along his way, Burnett has several encounters with his pursuers and also with local rebels, until finally he realises what he has seen and decides to return to the site of his crashed fighter plane in order to recover the digital camera that contains proof of the military build-up. By now, Reigart has decided to ignore his orders and lead a personal rescue mission. The film culminates with a fire-fight at the crash site where Burnett finds the camera, battles and kills the Serb tracker, and is rescued by Reigart just before the might of the Serbian army descends.

Black Hawk Down (2001)

Black Hawk Down is based on the true story of America's intervention in Somalia in 1993. Following years of civil war and the murder of two UN peacekeepers, American Army Rangers and Delta Force operatives are sent to Mogadishu to support UN actions. The film centres on an American military operation to capture two senior Somali militia officers who work for the most dangerous of the Somali warlords, Aided.

This is to be a fast snatch-and-grab operation, and so the soldiers will use Black Hawk and 'Little Bird' helicopters to make the pick-up and then extract via armoured 'Humvee' road vehicles. The grab mission is a success, but before the US forces can extract one Army Ranger falls from his Black Hawk helicopter and another Black Hawk is shot down. Based on the US military creed to 'leave no man behind', the extraction vehicles are then sent to retrieve (dead or alive) those shot down. What ensues is a battle lasting a day and a night in which the US forces try, often in vain, to reach their increasing number of downed helicopters and injured men whilst facing intensive resistance from Somali militia deploying basic but effective guerrilla fighting tactics.

The film follows the experiences of the US soldiers, now spread out across the city, during these hours until, at the end of the film, they finally 'escape' to the safety of the UN base the following morning.

Jarhead (2005)

In short, *Jarhead* recounts a portion of Anthony Swofford's autobiography of his time spent in military service. Specifically, it shows Swofford's experiences of basic training in the Marine Corps, his training to become a Scout Sniper and then his involvement in the first Gulf War. Focusing on Swofford's platoon of highly trained Scout snipers, under the direction of Sgt. Sykes, the film follows them through the military build-up in the Gulf and the endless 'exercises' they endure, through to their move up to the front line, and finally to the war's end, just a few days later, with none of the snipers ever having been able to fire their weapons.

The film depicts these (non)events from a soldier's point of view. It shows boredom, uncertainty, anxiety, fear, humour, excitement and fraternity, all in equal measure. In recounting the (non)experiences of this group of soldiers in this (non)war, the film shows a different side to war and the military, a certain reality that is seldom captured in film.

'I Love The Dough': Rap Lyrics as a Minor Economic Literature

ALF REHN and DAVID SKÖLD

Whereas literary and cinematic representations of economy and management have been analyzed for some time (see e.g. Czarniawska and Guillet de Monthoux, 1994; Hassard and Holliday, 1998), precious little interest has been directed to similar aspects in popular music. Consequently, this paper analyzes economy as it is portrayed and disseminated in rap music. By discussing how conspicuous consumption and economic discourses are used in rap lyrics to convey the image of success and possibility, the paper attempts a reading of contemporary capitalism in a particular cultural setting through the notion of a minor literature as theorized by Deleuze and Guattari. The multidimensionality and ironical approach held to the 'bling-bling' thus problematizes simplified analyzes of economic language as colonizing (cf. Gibson-Graham, 1996) and instead opens up to a reading of economy as openness.

'I just signed my contract worth $100 million on Friday. I ain't worried about saving. I'm ballin' outta control'.

Baby, CEO of Cash Money Records,
interviewed in *The Source* #158 (2002)

INTRODUCTION

In contemporary society, the grand narrative of economy and the market seems to hold fast, regardless of what Lyotard (1979) claimed. In an age where these notions have become both iconic and anthropomorphic, there is clearly a need for reflection regarding the ways in which we narrate the economic, and specifically in the less obvious ways in which this might be done. As has been shown by various writers on social theory, the notion of economy as merely one thing is highly suspect (cf. Bataille, 1967/1991; Baudrillard, 1996; Benedict, 1934; Derrida, 1992; Mauss, 1924/1990, among others), and in order to comprehend the complex interrelationships between culture and economy (cf. Callon, 1998; du Gay and Pryke, 2002) we need more subtle and more complex readings of economic phenomena. The feminist scholars J.K. Gibson-Graham—two co-authors writing under a penname—have argued that the common view of an economic order (read: capitalism) as totalizing is insufficient, and that the image of e.g. capitalism as a force capable of perfectly colonizing every sphere it enters is insufficiently analytic. In *The End of Capitalism (as we knew it)* (Gibson-Graham, 1996) they argue that our readings of economy often stumble due to our tendency to polarize the issue, where capitalism is seen as a binary issue, either not there or there as total colonization. They instead exhort us to analyze the ways in which economic 'hybrids' are created, cultural mixtures of capitalism and resistance where the straw-man of 'bourgeois capitalism' is placed in a cultural context and subsequently mutates. This text aims at analyzing one such hybrid.

In order to do so, this paper will discuss a specific economic language, and do so in an empirical fashion. More specifically, this paper deals with how narratives regarding economy and organization materialize within popular music. Whereas literary and cinematic representations of economy and management have been analyzed for some time (see e.g. Czarniawska and Guillet de Monthoux, 1994; Hassard and Holliday, 1998), precious little interest has been directed to similar aspects in popular music. This is interesting particularly as the argument for analyzing e.g. literary works usually has been that it gives us a perspective as to how notions of management and economy are translated into more popular depictions, and that one through this can learn something about such popularization. At the same time, popular music is far more 'popular' than either the novels of e.g. Martin Amis or the movies of e.g. Terry Gilliam, arguably making it a far more potent 'mirror of production'. Consequently, we will analyze specific narratives in popular culture, ones that praise capitalism, that revel in the market economy, and that exhibit an almost rapturous attitude towards material goods. We will focus on the bling-bling.

> I be that nigga with the ice on me /
> If it cost less than twenty it don't look right on me /
> […]Diamonds worn by everybody that's in my click /
> Man I got the price of a mansion, 'round my neck and wrist
> (B.G., 'Bling-Bling')

The term 'bling-bling' refers to the gleam that is projected into the eyes of the observer when rays of light reflect and refract from jewelry and gold. As a term it arises in rap vernacular, and has now entered the language of popular culture more generally. More specifically, it refers to a particular fashion of ostentatious displays of wealth, one where oversize jewelry is the norm (cf. Codere, 1950). As the seminal and eponymous rap-anthem quoted above shows, it has to do with proving your place in the world through specific displays—such as boasting that the chains one wears around one's neck and wrists are worth as much as a major piece of real estate. What is interesting about it in the perspective of this article is less the fashion statement it represents, and more how it shows us a narration of life under capitalism that is almost comically affirmative. In bling-bling one can find a way to *perform capitalism*, and it is this trope of re-appropriation that we wish to explore here. Whereas most writing on the use of literature to understand organization(s) has tended to be in a critical vein, and thus focus on more pessimistic texts, this article is interested in the ways in which narratives of the economic can be used in a provocative manner, as a micro-politics unto itself. We will here use some ideas from Deleuze and Guattari (1986, 1987) to read the 'capitalist language' in (some) rap music as political. This is done specifically to create a counterpoint to the idea that the colonization of language that capitalism is capable of could not be counteracted. The bling-bling, to us, thus represents a hybrid language, one where the accouterments of capitalism are used in a subversive fashion.

THE ART OF STORYTELLING & ROLLIN' WITH RUSH

> Back in the day a nigga used to be asked out /
> Now a nigga holding several money-market accounts
> (Busta Rhymes, 'Dangerous')

Rap music is a form of rhymed storytelling accompanied by highly rhythmic, electronically based music [which] began in the mid-1970s in the South Bronx in New York City as a part of hip hop, an African-American and Afro-Caribbean youth culture composed of graffiti, breakdancing, and rap music. (Rose, 1994: 2)

Rap has always dealt with storytelling, and one could well say that rap *is* storytelling. Often these stories have featured the hardships and the struggles involved in coping with everyday life in 'the 'hood': with, and against, drugs, violence, poverty, an oppressive establishment, of man-woman relationships and the like. And often these stories have told of aspirations and desires of moving 'up' and perhaps 'out', socially and spatially—another classic theme in African-American cultural expressions, e.g. as articulated by Bobby Womack in *Across the 110th Street* (1972). Since rap music's first major break in 1979, with Sugar Hill Gang's hit *Rappers Delight*, which brought about an interest in the music by the mainstream music industry (for more extensive accounts of the evolution of hip-hop culture and its antecedents, and of hip-hop culture growing into an industry, see e.g. Boyd, 1997; Foreman, 2002; George, 1998; Potter, 1995; Rose, 1994), and which made hip-hop a plausible way of escaping the harsh conditions of the 'hood—Cornel West (1989, 2001) argues that the entertainment industry, especially throughout the late 20th century, has been an option of hope for 'upward' mobility for African-Americans (sports has of course been another such option)—the storytelling has often focused on money, on how one is going to get some of that 'precious green'. In the title cut to their classic debut album *Paid in Full*, released in 1986, Eric B. and Rakim fantasize about how their talent for rhyming and scratching (DJing/putting together beats) along with their contacts at the record company, will bring them pots of gold. Kool G Rap and DJ Polo further emphasize a Lutheran work ethic as a necessary foundation for succeeding (economically) in the hip-hop classic *Road to the Riches* (1989). Furthermore, songs about money—or cheese, cheddar, chips, dough, cream, cake, scrilla, green, loot, paper, dead presidents, or Benjamins to name but a few of the terms in circulation—and different aspects thereof more explicitly, have come by in great numbers. Some examples are Outsidaz' *Money Money Money* (2001), Bone Thugs-n-Harmony's *Money Money* (2002), and Ol' Dirty Bastard's *Got Your Money* (2000)—in which he lisps and slurs, perhaps partly due to his gold and jewelry capped teeth. And we could go on, and on, and on, for quite some time.

[Eric B]: Yo Rakim, what's up?
[Rakim]: Yo, I'm doing the knowledge, E., I'm trying to get paid in full.
[E]: Well, check this out, since Nobry Walters is our agency, right?
[R]: True.
[E]: Kara Lewis is our agent.
[R]: Word up.
[E]: Zakia/4th & Broadway is our record company.
[R]: Indeed.
[E]: Okay, so who we rollin' with?
[R]: We rollin' with Rush.
(Eric B. and Rakim, *Paid in Full*)

Erick Sermon and Parrish Smith, of the legendary group EPMD (acronym for Erick and Parrish Making Dollars) further accentuated the business aspect of getting into the music industry in the late eighties, making the notion of business a gimmick imbuing almost all their work. They released their first record *Strictly Business* in 1988 and followed it up with *Unfinished Business* (1989), *Business As Usual* (1990), *Business Never Personal* (1992), *Back In Business* (1997) and *Out Of Business* (1999). Moreover a number of rap classics read like manuals for the entrepreneurial youngster: The Notorious B.I.G. told of *The Ten Crack Commandments* which outline best practice in the drug trade (1997), whereas E-40 released the album *Blueprint of a Self-Made Millionaire* (1999).

What is notable, especially in the excerpt from the Eric B. and Rakim lyrics, is that rap artists in a conscious way use the cachet of being good business men and having business contacts as a way to enhance their art. Referring to their agent, their business manager and their record company not as something to be revered (i.e. they are not forced to advertise their label), but as something that in a way belongs to them, as a part of their network, and as something they can be proud of 'having', implies a strategy of self-actualization through business. While referring to an agent or ones management team would seem wildly out of place in the context of a pop song [there are some counter-examples, though; for instance, Lynyrd Skynyrd recorded the track *Working for MCA* and AC/DC stated *Ain't No Fun (Waiting Round To Be A Millionaire)*], it is part of the legacy of rap music. Making music is not only a cultural strategy, it is a form of metaphorical survival—making it in the world.

ALL ABOUT THE BENJAMINS

Rap lyricists have probably never been more inclined to talk business than they were a couple of years into the 20th century. Reading hip-hop magazines like *The Source* in 2003/2004, you will learn more about rap artists' financial strategy and career plans, than about their music. In connection with the release of *The Black Album* in 2003, the celebrated rapper Shawn 'Jay-Z' Carter was featured as a super-entrepreneur in *TIME Magazine*. At that time Jay-Z declared that *The Black Album* was his farewell to the rap game. Instead, he said he wanted to be able to fully concentrate on the business empire surrounding Roc-A-Fella Records that he, Damon Dash and Kareem 'Biggs' Burke had built off of record sales (Tyrangiel, 2003). In November 2004, these efforts resulted in Jay-Z being appointed the position as president of Universal's Island Def label—part-owner of Roc-A-Fella Records.

> Willies wanna rub shoulders, ya money too young /
> See me when it gets older, ya bank account grow up /
> Mine is one zero zero zero o'ed up…
> (Jay-Z, 'Money Ain't a Thang')

Speaking of Jay-Z, it ought to be pointed out that he has not only been a rapper talking and bragging about his business endeavors in his lyrics. He has also been a full-fledged bling-bling rapper, which he demonstrates, for instance, in his 1998 lyric quoted above—a flawless example of what bling-bling might sound like. A year before Sean John Combs—performing under the name Puff Daddy (today using P. Diddy)—had declared that 'It's All About the Benjamins!' in the song with the same name. And The Notorious B.I.G. sings an ode to luxurious consumption habits in *I Love the Dough*, released posthumously (only about two weeks after his death) in 1997.

> We hit makers with acres /
> Roll shakers in Vegas, you can't break us /
> Lost chips on Lakers, gassed off Shaq /
> Country house, tennis courts on horseback /
> Ridin', decidin', cracked crab or lobster? /
> Who say mobsters don't prosper?
> (The Notorious B.I.G. (feat. Jay-Z & Angela Winbush), 'I Love the Dough')

It could easily be argued, and it has been argued, that the bling-bling attitude—here represented by Jay-Z, Jermaine Dupri, The Notorious B.I.G. and P. Diddy—in the latter part of the 1990s and in the beginning of the new century had come to be *the* dominating attitude in rap music, and in hip-hop culture. In forums designated to intellectualize hip-hop culture, such as the Internet site *urbanthinktank.org*, one can even find references to the bling-bling as an '-ism', a movement: 'bling-bling-ism'—a 'supercilious rampage of material worship and indulgence' (Tyson, 2001). We have no interest in proving that that is the case, we simply state that bling-bling exists.

Having said this, it might be worth pointing out that bling-bling rappers do frequently voice an attitude quite contrary to that of the homage to 'makin' it', namely an attitude bearing witness of the very harsh life one has experienced/experiences in the 'hood, and of telling things how they really are—an attitude of 'keeping it real' and of telling 'the naked truth' [unlike an establishment which often is seen as shutting its eyes for the social problems found in the 'hood, and which marginalizes, oppresses and enslaves the African-American population (see George, 1998, and the film *Letter to the President*)].

These two strategies in rap as a cultural mode of self-expression, the need to 'keep it real' and the portrayal of possibilities could be viewed as a dialectics of sorts. Whereas the first, as a textual strategy, might be seen as a form of ghetto realism, the second is closer in style to the fairy tale. Such stories, as Vladimir Propp (1968) so famously pointed out, tend to consist of a fairly simple structure: a young protagonist is given a task and solves this in a way that brings him fortune and glory (and a girl, as a bonus). As the 'realist' tales represented in rap music tend to describe a fairly dark world, one where poverty, random violence and socio-pathic behavior is rife, it follows the narrative logic that this is then juxtaposed with tales about abundance and a kind of *Scharlaffenland*. When 'keeping it real' one may talk about food stamps, government cheese, dealing drugs and going hungry, but this is countered with tales where one chooses between 'cracked crab or lobster', drinks 'Cris(tal)' (a brand of champagne) and drives a customized Mercedes-Benz. In other words, the task at hand for a young hero is—as we have seen—to go from one state to the other, to escape poverty. And as soon as this has been accomplished, to portray this escape by economic ostentation, through capitalist imagery.

This specific rhetoric regarding the market economy and organized capitalism that prevails in rap lyricism is important for two reasons. One, it presents us with a case of narrative knowledge regarding economy/organization that offers us an alternative to 'high literature'. Unashamedly part of popular culture, rap lyricism still is a specific brand of literary representation, and might show us other ways of understanding how economy can be told as a narrative. Whereas the use of literature to teach/understand organization and economy has usually focused on 'great books', the 'sticking to the rawness' and 'keeping it real'-ethos of rap does not allow for finery, and may give us an empirical counterpoint. Two, it presents us with a case where economic language is used in a positive, affirming way (regardless what one thinks of the veracity of such tales) by a subculture that is usually seen as repressed and downtrodden by the very capitalism it celebrates. This paradox, the marginalized celebrating that which marginalizes, may give us a case to specifically analyze the functioning of economy as language. Instead of observing how economy enters into narrations, we can in these cases see how economy is *performed* through narration, i.e. how one in a specific cultural setting can *do* economy.

BATTLING IT OUT, AND UP

Even though the struggles and the strategies for getting money often have been central to expression in hip-hop, another form of expression has always been present: the battle. The role of the rapper has often been to keep the party hyped by yelling out call-and-response party chants such as: 'All the ugly people be quiet!' Other times however, the role of the MC has been to battle other MCs. Battles such as those starring Eminem as Bunny Rabbit in *8 Mile*, have been one of the main characteristics of hip-hop culture from the very beginning. Entire sound system crews have battled each other out by sheer volume, DJs have battled each other out behind the turntables, dancers have battled each other out 'on the floor', and graffiti artists have been battling it out by painting subway trains in ever more difficult locations, with ever more refined motives. And MCs have battled each other out on stage as well as on records. Hip-hop, claims Rose (1994: 36), 'remains a never-ending battle for status, prestige, and group adoration, always in formation, always contested, and never fully achieved'.

This never-ending battle has often been manifested in MCs 'dissing'—disrespecting, dismissing or disparaging—other MCs or entire hip-hop crews. Sometimes it has occurred live on stage and sometimes recorded—on dedicated 'diss tracks' or as short passages appearing on any regular track. Whatever the forum, oftentimes the disses have lead to more withstanding disagreements or feuds, *beefs*. Concentrating on the abundance of feuds within hip-hop culture, the movies *Beef* and *Beef II* line up (and possibly exaggerate) such disagreements by the dozen. Disregarding the possible magnification these disputes undergo in the process of becoming entertainment, what is notable for our purposes is an idea brought forth in the film *Beef II*, namely that beefs and disses—from the time when the UFTO song *Roxanne Roxanne* was released and answered up by Roxanne Shante with *Roxanne's Revenge* in 1985, both of which climbed the charts that same year—have been recognized and later on exploited as strategic ways of enticing listeners and boosting record sales in hip-hop culture (For accounts of the emergence of a hip-hop industry, including the dissemination of hip-hop media, see Foreman, 2002: 106–45, 213–51). Drawing a lot of (media) attention to particular artists and songs, the film suggests that the battle and the disses became means deployed strategically to reinforce record sales and increase profits.

Should this observation be valid (which seems reasonable, although we believe it would be a gross exaggeration to state that *all,* or even a majority of the disagreements between rap artists are strategic business moves), what follows in the wake of the battle in general, and the disses in particular, is an enhanced music genre fueled by internal controversies—by and large also entailing a more potent culture industry. The disputes are doing hip-hop media and films—such as *Beef* and its sequel—a big favor (if not creating the very conditions for their existence altogether), providing them with good stories to tell, to boost and to feed off of. Hence, the battle emerges as a mechanism inherent in hip-hop culture, possessing a force driving it both artistically and business-wise.

However, in a culture where such a mechanism is present and where 'art' and 'business/ economy' are so inextricably linked together, the boundaries between these two spheres become blurred. In the case of the narratives, some strategically shaped (perhaps into down-right attacks on other rappers' economic status, as we shall soon see) so as to enhance sales and profits, they are turned into business endeavors, which may in turn well be the topic of yet another narrative, turned into business. Over and over again; the two being heavily inter-twined, making it a futile project to attempt to distinguish the art of storytelling from the business endeavor. As an analytical tool, and as a meaningful means for making different aspects of a phenomenon distinct from one another, the two spheres of art and economy/ business collapse into one another, becoming one and the same.

SHOWING OFF THE KITSCH AND THE GLAM—STILL BATTLING

The battle is not always manifested in explicit disses. Returning to the bling-bling, we can see that the use of supercilious consumption in part exists for bragging purposes – the battle has become one of posing. Assuming that most rap artists come from modest means, or at least exist in a culture where economic hardship is seen as characteristic for lived experience ('keeping it real'), having achieved financial success is not necessarily something one would keep quiet about. Rap lyrics keep a very high profile in relation to this. Where economic success in a middle-class culture would be signaled in a fairly modest way, in the rap culture the signaling of poverty and affluence seems to be performed *in extremis*. If we take the eponymous track *Bling-Bling*, it is recorded by a larger group known as the Cash Money Millionaires (the track is officially credited to B.G. featuring Big Tymers and Hot Boyz), a group formed in the 'Dirty South', i.e. a part of the US that still lags behind the rest of the country when it comes to economic development, and where abject poverty among the black population is widespread.

> Hit the club and light the bitch up /
> Cash Money motto is to drink til' we throw up /
> Nigga point the hoe out, guaranteed I can fuck /
> Woady 'cause I'm tattooed and barred up /
> Medallion iced up, Rolex bezelled up /
> And my pinky ring is platinum plus /
> Earrings be trillion cut /
> And my grill be slugged up /
> My heart filled with anger, 'cause nigga I don't give a fuck /
> Stack my cheese up /
> Cause one day I'm a give this street life up
> (Baby rhyming on 'Bling-Bling')
>
> A lil' nigga seventeen, playin' with six figures /
> Got so much ice you can skate on it, nigga
> (Lil' Turk rhyming on the same track)

This sheer mass of jewelry is obviously a matter of great pride. In Lil' Turks hyperbole, the 'ice'/diamonds are portrayed less like adornments and more like a rhetorical weapon—a skating rink made out of one of the most expensive materials in known existence. A medallion with diamonds, a Rolex covered in more of the same, lavish earrings, stacks of cash and gold all over your teeth [your smile is your 'grill', and a player will get this 'slugged up', i.e. fitted with caps in precious metals—according to the hip-hop magazine *The Source* #158 (November 2002), Baby's current dental embellishments are made out of platinum, since gold teeth were becoming too common] seem to represent a uniform of sorts. The track further contains references to private jets, customized cars and a helicopter with a candy-color paintjob and leather interior. Brand names are not massively present, as could be the case in the lyrics of the now deceased Notorious B.I.G., but several allusions to a particular type of 'rims' (i.e. custom rims for car tires) are made. A somewhat more 'demure' version of the same ethos can be found in the lyrics of Lil' Kim ('Big Momma Thing'):

> I got lands in the Switzerland /
> Even got some sands in the Marylands /
> Bahamas in the spring /
> Baby, it's a big momma thing

And further, in a display of brand-awareness, The Notorious B.I.G. ('Hypnotize') can be found outlining his own shopping preferences:

> I put ho's in NY onto DKNY /
> Miami, D.C. prefer Versace /
> All Philly ho's, dough and Moschino /
> Every cutie wit' a booty bought a Coogi

The list could be made endless: Ludacris professes to 'smelling like Burberry cologne', Snoop Dogg to owning '50 dollar socks, a hundred thousand-dollar-shoes', Tupac referred to himself as a 'self-made millionaire', and Jay-Z boasts that his new house is so opulent that 'you'd have to film *MTV Cribs* (a show that showcases the lifestyles of the newly rich and famous) for a week'. Foxy spits: 'Who could talk about that money better than me? / Who could stay so hood femininely?' Eminem has even used direct sales-figures to diss enemies – such as when he on a track compared the sales of Everlast's latest album (claiming this to be a paltry 40,000 copies in its first week) with himself 'making records break'. And so on.

Without leaving the notion of the battle (but rather using it as a bridge onto, and a tool for the next stage of the analysis), we now wish to claim that one way to understand the lyricism of rap music (keeping in mind that this is just one 'genre' of rap music) is to analyze it as an economic literature, with bling-bling serving as an economic language. In other words, rap lyrics can be seen as a way to convey narratives of economy within a sub-culture, so that economic success takes on a political dimension. 'Making it' is in such a perspective proof that the hardships presented by ghetto life can be overcome, and further (which is a more provocative statement), that one can develop a notion of success that isn't tethered by the aesthetic notions of the white plutocracy and through this a culturally specific 'economy'. One can, for instance, note the importance put on having and advertising a self-owned record label/company or a clothing label. To take but a few examples, Jay-Z owns (among other things) Rocawear, Diddy owns Bad Boy Records and Sean John Clothing, Master P the No Limit-group of companies, and Snoop Dogg assorted businesses. All of them frequently name-check these in their lyrics, something portrayed in both music and magazines as 'ghetto entrepreneurialism'. Still, our point is not to claim that such an economic movement exists, nor that rap lyrics and bling-bling:ism would be a solution to the real economic problems in urban areas. Rather, it is to show how a particular kind of narrative representation can be understood in context.

> Snoop Dogg is a ghetto Martha Stewart. His ultimate commodity is a way of life. Everything he sells and endorses (the Blunt Wrap tobacco tubes for smoking Buddha, the K-Nine clothing for the pimps, playas, and ho's, the 'Freak Line' phone sex service, the rap music, the films, and so on) designates, validates, and delineates a specific mode of urban existence. He makes it easier to be ghetto, in the way Martha Stewart makes it easier to be bourgeois. (Mudede, 2001)

THE BATTLE AND THE DELEUZIAN COMBAT...

> The combat-between is the process through which a force enriches itself by seizing hold of other forces and joining itself to them in a new ensemble: a becoming. (Deleuze, 1995: 132)

What the inherent battle in hip-hop culture (manifested in the bling-bling) reveals is not, however, an apparent battle against, say, the establishment. Nor is it a battle directed against the politics pursued by the establishment or against oppressive attitudes in society—although rap music has been prone to partake in such battles. Instead it is a battle carried out within hip-hop culture, between MCs or hip-hop crews. To borrow a concept and an expression from Gilles Deleuze (1995), it is a combat 'between its own parts', rather than an external combat against something exterior. Instead of trying 'to repel or destroy a force' repressing, subjugating or marginalizing African-American culture, the bling-bling seems—partly self-reflexively it seems, and through the battle that is carried out between Itself—'to take hold of a force, and make it [its] own'.

> And no doubt the combat appears as a combat against judgment, against its authorities and its personae. (Deleuze, 1995)

With regards to language the battle-between has (among other things) been fought with words, but it has not been a battle against an Other economic language (with a plethora of vernaculars, rules, norms and terminology)—one which one might acquire by attending a typical business school or reading e.g. the *Wall Street Journal*. In a sense, it has been minding its own business. But, whereas the disses and the old school on-stage-battling display a 'combat-between' with rappers attempting to subjugate one-another in every thinkable way, the bling-bling is, as we have seen, to a large extent a battle fought by out-posing one another; one of showing off and 'looking past', rather than one of wiping out and 'looking down' at one's contestant. And doing so by using economic terminology. So, while this first type of lyrical battle might well have reinforced hip-hop's position and status as a music genre and as a culture industry, the internal battle that makes out the bling-bling positions hip-hop as an economic language, and as a combatant Itself, with a force of its own that is also exerted externally, working on an Other body of economic languages—hence becoming a combat against, in every sense political.

...FOUGHT WITH A LACK OF TALENT...

Sticking to the assumption that most bling-bling rappers do come from modest means, or at least exist in a culture where economic hardship is seen as characteristic for lived experience, we might further develop the idea of speaking about the economic as something which cannot be resisted. For many rappers this seems to be the case: lying at the heart of the every-day struggle, the economic has become a topic impossible not to speak about. At the same time has the culture in which the rappers exist by tradition been excluded from many a discourse regarding major economic issues and issues, and is hardly one where e.g. reading *The Wall Street Journal* is common or where attending business school is an option even to a small minority.

The cultural capital of 'sophisticated' ways in which to brag and discuss economic matters is thus less likely to be accumulated in the setting from which rap emerges. To deploy a dominant mode – i.e. mainstream, white, establishment ways – of speaking about the economic is not a plausible option, but rather an impossibility – which opens for innovation. To borrow yet another expression from Deleuze and Guattari, we might say that talent to speak about the economic is lacking in hip-hop culture. One has to take what lies at hand, for instance gangster manners, in a gangster slang, picked up on the street.

> Eh-yo, the bottom line is I'm a crook with a deal /
> If my record don't sell I'ma rob and steal...
> [...]
> I'll snatch Kim and tell Puff, 'You wanna see her again?' /
> Get your ass down to the nearest ATM...
> (50 Cent, 'How To Rob')

Appreciating that bragging about economic achievements is an ubiquitous activity in Western culture, and that this mechanism might well be a major driving force in capitalism, 50 Cent demonstrates how bragging in rap music turns explicit. 'Fiddy' brags of his ability to steal, threatens 'industry niggas', and does so as the head of G-Unit Records. In a sense, the bling-bling rapper speaks about the economic, but without the 'proper' knowledge of how to do so. Hence, in a way bling-bling rap has stolen an element central to capitalism, but instead of following conventions of how to treat it, expresses it without temperance and breaks every possible rule of how to speak of such things, 'stealing the baby from its crib' (cf. Deleuze and Guattari, 1986).

What is proposed here is that the forms of expression we've outlined in rap lyricism show similarities to the idea of a 'minor literature'. Deleuze and Guattari famously draw upon the works of Franz Kafka to explain what they mean by such a literature: Kafka, who was a Czech Jew, lived in Prague but wrote in German. His German was a Prague German, with a withered vocabulary and an incorrect syntax, and it was influenced by Yiddish. This made his German a rare mutation, and it 'allowed him the possibility of invention' (Deleuze and Guattari, 1986: 20). As all minor authors, according to Deleuze and Guattari, he was a 'foreigner to [his] own tongue'.

> Kafka does not opt for a reterritorialization through the Czech language. Nor toward a hypercultural usage of German with all sorts of oneiric or symbolic or mythic flights (even Hebrew-ifying ones), as was the case with

the Prague School. Nor toward an oral, popular Yiddish. Instead, using the path that Yiddish opens up to him, he takes it in such a way as to convert it into a unique and solitary form of writing. [...] He will make the German language take flight on a line of escape. (Deleuze and Guattari, 1986: 25–6)

The Prague German in which Kafka wrote his novels had, according to Deleuze and Guattari, the power to deterritorialize the 'high' German. In a similar manner the bling-bling talks with one (or several) Black English(es), developed and nurtured on the streets, which makes use of a particular vocabulary, ignores grammatical rules and conventions (as specified by a Master language). The influences are numerous and the creativity seems to be flourishing—but probably moving beyond the limits of what is accepted in the realms of business. As rappers go from being exploited entertainers, coming from social groupings that usually don't occupy a space in the economic discourse, to owning their own companies and showing it off, this street language enters into 'larger' and more 'serious' economic realms. And similar to Kafka's deterritorialized Prague German it deterritorializes the ways in which business is being spoken and thought of.

That it is written in a major language, but from the margin, the position of a minority, is the first outlining characteristic Deleuze and Guattari attributes a minor literature. It thus changes the rules of the major language, changing it from within and is 'affected with a high coefficient of deterritorialization' (Deleuze and Guattari, 1986: 16). By changing the major language according to its own positions, it moves the borders of that language, changing the way in which it occupies a specific ideological/political (economic?) territory.

...AND WHICH CAN'T BE WON

Let us yet again return to the notion of the battle: as Rose (1994) points out, it cannot be won. There is no border to transgress, and which determines who the winner is. There is no judge proclaiming a winner. But since hip-hop culture is not one unified culture, there are many voices and opinions within it. Who wins and who loses is subject to an ongoing debate, but never quite settled. Media, award juries and fans—all hunger to take part in the debate, but all also hunger for new debates. The never-ending battle is perhaps best understood not as a consequence of someone's desire to win or seize power, but a desire for something else—perhaps escaping the oppression experienced by people in the 'hood altogether—and might best be described a 'continuum of desire' imbuing the entire culture (cf. Deleuze and Guattari, 1986). A desire of both 'makin' it' and of staying behind, 'keeping it real'; a desire for the 'hood and the people living there to obtain redress. But also a desire to sell another record, to top another sales list with yet another song, to win another award, and to engage in another battle, to diss another rapper for his or her fake-ness or inauthenticity.

Thus, we find ourselves not in front of a structural correspondence between two sorts of forms, forms of contents and forms of expression, but rather in front of an expression machine capable of disorganizing its own forms, and of disorganizing its forms of content in order to liberate pure contents that mix with expressions in a single intense matter. A major, or established, literature follows a vector that goes from content to expression. Since content is presented in a given form of the content, one must find, discover, or see the form of expression that goes with it. That which conceptualizes well expresses itself. But a minor, or revolutionary, literature begins by expressing itself and doesn't conceptualize until afterward... (Deleuze and Guattari, 1986: 28)

Picking up on the remark made earlier on the collapse of art and business as two distinct spheres meaningful to deploy when analyzing the bling-bling, yet another collapse becomes evident when dealing with this phenomenon. As has been demonstrated above talk of the economic often make up the (form of) content of the rap lyrics. Accompanied by beats, melodies and other musical arrangements, this content is of course packeted and sold as music (recorded or performed live), making up one of bling-bling's form of expression. Due to the nature of the content—i.e. its often provocative attitude towards other rappers—the music and its content, and what is going on around it (e.g. beefs involving economic issues), is constantly cast around, magnified and speculated upon in hip hop media (making out other forms of expression dealing with bling-bling content), with lyrics being subjected to interpretations, and rappers, fans and experts being interviewed and cross-examined. New songs are written to answer back, to what by now might be a highly distorted version of the controversy. What in one instance was a form of expression, makes out the content in the next, although perhaps this time appearing as a heated argument conducted in an unpolished language between two rappers with the benefit of pushing magazines sales.

Take for instance the beef involving the rappers Eminem (who is one of few white rappers in the industry) and 50 Cent on one side, and the rapper Benzino and the hip-hop magazine *The Source* (proclaiming to have a journalistic mission) on the other: the latter side accusing Eminem of stealing sales from black rappers has led 50 Cent (who is a protégé of Eminem) to exclaim: 'Fuck *The Source*, I'm on the cover of Rolling Stone', in the song *The Realest Killaz*. Dragging in even more parts of the cultural expressions and their contents in the feud might well enhance the profits as noted earlier, but it also creates a new situation, with new conditions—where the borders between content and expression are dissolved, turning bling-bling into what Deleuze and Guattari would call an 'expression machine' which connects wildly in any direction, and which 'begins by expressing itself and doesn't conceptualize until afterward' (Deleuze and Guattari, 1986: 28)—which uses its connections as levers to work on its surroundings, exerting forces on e.g. the industry, using the masses as leverage, and on attitudes prevailing in the 'hood. Bragging and retaliating, becoming political in the process.

> I dumb down for my audience and double my dollars /
> They criticize me for it, yet they all yell 'Holla' /
> If skills sold – truth be told /
> I'd probably be lyrically Talib Kweli /
> Truthfully I wanna rhyme like Common Sense /
> But I did five mill' /
> I ain't been rhymin' like Common since.
> (Jay-Z, 'Moment of Clarity')

As Jay-Z implies in the quote above, the topics dealt with in his lyrics are not really those that he is most concerned with, but those which have proven saleable. Presumably the white middle class consumers are not as interested in rappers going on about social inconveniences and political matters that really concern those living in impoverished urban areas. For Jay-Z the bling-bling has thus become an instrument for doing something else: a way of redrawing the industry map, of moving borders and upsetting governing orders within the music industry. A means with deterritorializing powers which has enabled him as a rapper and former crack-dealer from the streets of Brooklyn to succeed in entering the industry, upsetting it from the inside.

COLLECTIVELY ACTING WITHIN A CRAMPED SPACE

According to the second characteristic Deleuze and Guattari ascribe to the minor, it is, at its very core, political. With the minor the individual becomes the social, and also thoroughly political: 'its cramped space forces each individual intrigue to connect immediately to politics. The individual concern thus becomes all the more necessary, indispensable, magnified, because a whole other story is vibrating in it' (Deleuze and Guattari, 1986: 17). Over the years rap music has been prone to speak explicitly about political matters and to engage in issues concerning societal inequalities, disenfranchisement and racism, passing/carrying on a tradition of black activism. Now, what seems to be a common reaction to the bling-bling attitude, is regarding it as a threatening counter-movement to that hip-hop music which displays a political awareness; as a sign of black politics declining in America; and as a threat to African-American culture (see Harris, 2002; Kelley, 2004; Tyson, 2001). Or, brushing it off—as the rap legend KRS One does in an interview in the film *Letter to the President*—as sheer buffoonery. Without explicitly speaking about politics, the bling-bling irritates and upsets, or is waved aside as something trivial.

Herein lies a clue to a power we posit the bling-bling to possess, namely that it ties directly to politics. Without getting caught in the criticized notion that 'all rap is conjoined with spaces of urban poverty' (cf. Foreman, 2002), the bling-bling attitude exists in a social context—the 'hood—where it is inevitable not to stand out, should you show off some of that wealth. Jermaine Dupri will not go unnoticed driving down Nostrand Avenue 'In the Ferrari or Jaguar, switchin' four lanes, with the top down, screaming out: Money ain't a thang'. Even dwelling in the 'hood once you've 'made it'—or returning there to visit old friends—seems to be a complicated matter (see the documentary *Black Picket Fence*). But so does moving to more fashionable areas, for the 'hood stays with you. 'Now we buy homes in unfamiliar places / Tito smiles every time he see our faces', exclaims The Notorious B.I.G., supposedly referring to the servant of his new neighbors in the fashionable Hamptons. Assumedly the money is too new, the language too crude and the manners too explicit. Even taken outside its geographical boundaries, the 'hood, as a mentality, seems to be acting within a cramped space. Again bling-ing offends, frightens, and evokes nervous laughter from the vicinity. In doing so, it is highly political.

Also in relation to the music industry—to a great extent governed by 'white capital' both with regards to the major customers consuming hip-hop music, and to industrial tycoons to a high degree controlling the American music industry—a rapper's ability to navigate the industry seems limited. Recall, for instance the point just made with regards to Jay-Z's *Moment of Clarity*. There seems to be limits to what he, being a black man from the projects, can express in his lyrics—if he wants to keep up his sales figures. The way in which he, and other bling-bling rappers who run their own record labels, seem to handle this issue—partly by exploiting the Industry and the Market on its own terms, and possibly causing a redistribution and accumulation of mainly white capital into (at least partly) African-American domains—emerges, however, as a possible inroad to the industry.

In our view the bling-bling thus becomes an economic language and a political movement which works on the industry, by attaching ever more independent record labels to it (e.g., Lil' Kim's Queen Bee Records, Missy Elliott's Gold Mine, Mos Def and Talib Kweli's Good Tree Records), run by a minority which by tradition has been excluded from the decision-making realms of trade and industry. And even if it would be naïve to believe that the (still) predominantly white music industry doesn't also prosper from these businesses and the sales figures, it seems to us as if the bling-bling contributes to opening up the industry for outside elements, which might well go about their business in dissimilar styles, with dissimilar values, and with a dissimilar language than we are used to be seeing—moving the borders for 'how' and 'by whom' business can be conducted.

This political nature of a minor literature is further inseparable from its collective value. Deleuze and Guattari (1986: 17) explain this inextricability:

> [B]ecause talent isn't abundant in a minor literature, there are no possibilities for an individuated enunciation that would belong to this or that 'master' and that could be separated from a collective enunciation. Indeed, scarcity of talent is in fact beneficial and allows the conception of something other than a literature of masters; what each author says individually already constitutes a common action, and what he or she says or does is necessarily political, even if others aren't in agreement. The political domain has contaminated every statement (énoncé). But above all else, because collective or national consciousness is 'often inactive in external

life and always in the process of break-down,' literature finds itself positively charged with the role and function of the collective, and even revolutionary, enunciation.

The excerpt above of course ties back to the notion of talent to speak and act the economic being something which is lacking in hip-hop culture. Supposedly bling-bling rappers do neither have 'proper' training in speaking about the economic, or come from a culture one would necessarily associate with business life, but rather stem from a culture which by tradition has been excluded from that which Marx would label 'the superstructure' of professional life. By this, we don't mean to imply that a knowledge of how to deal with business is an entirely alien issue in hip-hop culture—as Jay-Z points out in *Rap Game/Crack Game*, even dealing in drugs might not be all that different than navigating the music industry and selling records—but merely suggest that the languages deployed in the two trades, at least on a street level of the former, are different.

In a later section of *Kafka: Toward a Minor Literature*, Deleuze and Guattari (1986: 83) pose the question: 'in what sense is the statement always collective even when it seems to be emitted by a solitary singularity like that of the artist?'. The explanation presented is that the statement 'doesn't refer back to an enunciating subject who would be its cause, no more than to a subject of the statement who would be its effect' (*ibid.*: 84). Instead, when an artist produces a statement 'it occurs necessarily as a function of a national, political, and social community' (*ibid.*: 84).

So Jay-Z speaks of the economic in the voice of a street hustler, and he speaks out of Marcy, as a function of his background in the projects. 50 Cent gives voice to 'Brooklyn' thieves. In an interview in the film *Letter To the President,* he claims to be showing off his neck-chain simply to convey the message 'I am better than you!', a desire immanent in a part of society which has a history of being marginalized and oppressed. Taking what vernaculars, values and expressions that lie at hand, the bling-bling thus turns into an airing of collective desires of 'makin' it'.

CONCLUDING REMARKS

Economy, which is often read as synonymous with capitalism, is of course a language. It has its own vernacular, its own particular grammar. What this text has attempted is to highlight a specific way in which this language has been used, in practice, within a specific cultural setting. Our claim is not that we, being white outsiders, would have any greater insight into the thinking and the lived experience of urban black communities, as this claim would be dubious in any number of ways. What we have tried to do is to show how specific economic behaviors, here exemplified by 'bragging', can be understood as cultural and further as performances of the economic language—performing capitalism.

Further, what we have attempted to show is that the discussion regarding organization/ economy and literature can be extended out into the popular culture and into song lyrics. As a scholar in organization theory is still far more likely to go on about the organizational implications of the at times terminally dull *À la recherche du temps perdu* than the very real economies of the at times fabulous *Anna Nicole Show*, one could make a case for the claim that the interest in literature within organization studies is mainly about scholars amassing cultural capital than analytical potential. This text can thus be seen as an extension to this, as two academics writing about the often crass, coarse and crude 'literature' they actually enjoy rather than the good literature their mothers were pushing. Of course, this invites the question whether we aren't just being wiggas (wannabe/white niggas), amassing our own cultural capital by proving that we are far more hip, cool and with it than those who would still try to dredge something out of Maurice Blanchot's poor, mangled corpse. These are difficult and important questions. We will, though, not make an effort to sort them out here. We will, however, claim that there exists a bias towards 'high literature' within the subfield of organization/literature, and that this needs to be addressed.

This text should thus be seen as an outline of a project. By using Deleuze and Guattari's concept of 'minor literature' we have not wished to show that bling-bling is a way out, a real political alternative, merely that one can read bling-bling in such a manner and that one can situate the ways in which the economic language is used. Nor do we claim that bling-bling should be viewed as a major form of bragging in a specific culture, just that it is an example of a more widespread way to talk the economic. What we do claim, however, is that rap lyrics can be seen as presenting an alternative way to address economic issues, and that this can be analyzed. Bling-bling, to us, is a hybrid. It has obviously bought into the larger capitalist project of amassing wealth, measuring all things in money, conspicuous consumption. Nevertheless, it has done so whilst retaining specific cultural markers, and part of its attitude can be seen as defiance against another form of capitalism, the racialized white capitalism that still works to keep ethnic minorities in a subjugated position. Word.

References

Bataille, Georges (1967/1991) *The accursed share,* New York: Zone Books.

Baudrillard, Jean (1996) *The system of objects,* London: Verso.

Benedict, Ruth (1934) *Patterns of culture,* Boston: Houghton Mifflin.

Boyd, Todd (1997) *Am I black enough for you? Popular culture from the 'hood and beyond,* Indianapolis, IN: Indiana University Press.

Callon, Michel (Ed.) (1998) *The laws of the markets,* Oxford: Blackwell.

Codere, Helen (1950) *Fighting with property,* New York: American Ethnological Society.

Czarniawska, Barbara and Guillet de Monthoux, Pierre (Eds) (1994) *Good novels, better management*: Reading Organizational Realities, Chur: Harwood Academic Publishers.

Deleuze, Gilles (1995) *Essays clinical and critical,* Minneapolis: University of Minnesota Press.

Deleuze, Gilles and Guattari, Felix (1986) *Kafka: toward a minor literature,* Minneapolis: University of Minnesota Press.

Deleuze, Gilles and Guattari, Felix (1987) *A thousand plateaus: capitalism and schizophrenia,* Minneapolis: University of Minnesota Press.

Derrida, Jacques (1992) *Given time, Vol. 1: counterfeit money,* Chicago, IL: University of Chicago Press.

Foreman, Murray (2002) *The 'hood comes first—race, space and place in rap and hip-hop,* Connecticut: Wesleyan University Press.

du Gay, Paul and Pryke, Michael (Eds) (2002) *Cultural economy,* London: Sage.

George, Nelson (1998) *Hip-hop america,* New York: Viking Penguin.

Gibson-Graham, J.K. (1996) *The end of capitalism (as we knew it): a feminist critique of* Political Economy, Cambridge, MA: Blackwell Publishers.

Hassard, John and Holliday, Ruth (1998) *Organization-representation: work and organizations in popular culture,* London: Sage.

Harris, Janelle (2002) Last call: the need for revolution in contemporary Hip Hop. Available at http://www.urbanthinktank.org/lastcall.cfm.

Kelley, Norman (2004) Black power(less): the decline of black politics in America. Available at http://www.urbanthinktank.org/blackpowerless.cfm.

Lyotard, Jean-François (1979) *La condition postmoderne: rapport sur le savoir,* Paris: Minuit.

Mauss, Marcel (1924/1990) *The gift: the form and reason for exchange in* archaic *community,* New York: W.W. Norton.

Mudede, Charles (2001) Ghetto capitalism: Snoop Dogg's 'tentacular Zaibatsu'. Available at http://thestranger.com/2001-11-01/film2.html.

Potter, Russel A. (1995) *Spectacular vernaculars: hip-hop and the politics of postmodernism,* New York: State University of New York Press.

Propp, Vladimir (1968) *Morphology of the folk tale,* Austin, TY: University of Texas Press.

Rose, Tricia (1994) *Black noise: rap music and black culture in contemporary America,* Hanover, NH: Wesleyan University Press.

Simmons, Russell, with Nelson George (2002) *Life and def: sex, drugs, money, + God,* New York: Three Rivers Press.

The Source #158 (2002) November.

Tyson, Christopher (2001) Exploring the generation gap; and its implications on African *American* consciousness, online publication? Available at http://www.urbanthinktank.org/generationgap.cfm

Tyrangiel, Josh (2003) In his next lifetime, *TIME Magazine,* December.

West, Cornel (1989) *The American evasion of philosophy: a genealogy of pragmatism*, Madison: University of Wisconsin Press.

West, Cornel (2001) *Race matters* (Second Vintage Books Edition), Boston, MA: Beacon Press.

Poetry in motion: protest songwriting as strategic resource (Portugal, circa 1974)

Nuno Guimarães-Costa, Miguel Pina e Cunha and João Vieira da Cunha

In this article, we use protest songs written in Portugal in the periods surrounding the Carnations Revolution to suggest that artists have the capacity to use their artistic discourses as strategic resources, attempting to shape socio-political reality. We identify three periods in the Portuguese revolution wherein this instrumental use of art becomes patent. We further suggest that organisational managers should take into account the subjective artistic reality, especially in periods when it can affect the organisational context.

Research on the representations of organisations in popular culture tend to draw, with some notable exceptions (e.g., Chan and Clegg's 2007 paper on the Chinese long march), from popular culture in periods of relative stability in which the role of organisations in society is not at stake. Popular culture has been used to discuss the impact of organisations on topics as diverse as opposition to dominant groups (Pelzer and Pelzer 1996) and urban lifestyles (Ritzer 2002). The use of popular arts in the study of organisations is also common and includes theatre (Meisiek 2004), music (Bastien and Hostager 1988) and literature (Puffer 1991).

In this article, we seek to uncover new meanings, understandings, and utilisations of the organisation, which result from the artistic interpretation of this supposedly well-known social phenomenon. As such, we study the representation of organisations in popular culture, namely in protest songs written at a particular moment of recent Portuguese history, the one immediately preceding, covering and just following a change in 1974 from a Right-Wing dictatorship to a full-fledged democracy.

The discourse of protest songs

We chose protest songs as the cultural artefact under scrutiny because songs, and protest songs, are a particularly resilient and powerful medium during regimes that engage in censorship. Indeed, their diffusion does not require formal publication and they can be performed in open or in clandestine settings since they enjoy a licence similar to poetry. More at hand than poetry itself, protest songs help ordinary people to cope with their everyday challenges and make sense of the social world around them. In the case of our setting, protest songs could be considered a form of poetry in motion for reasons that will be discussed later.

Hence, we interpret protest songs written during the movement of social change taking place in Portugal in the years before, during and after the 1974 *coup d'etat* as an artistic rendition of Portuguese capitalists and their organisations. We draw on the (dis)similarities surfaced by the various representations of capitalists and organisations in protest songs to explore the creative figuration of both, as well as the pattern of evolution of these cultural products *vis-à-vis* the political surrounding events. We link the discourses produced by protest singers/songwriters with the particular historical and social context where they were produced. Our case, specifically, is also interesting because it covers a process of change that follows the three stages considered by Lewin (1951) and focuses particularly on attempts at institutional change by a particular group. This case, then, presents some subtleties that may be pertinent to the study of role of discursive strategies in the institutional process. Firstly, the revolutionary process considered here is an attempt at non-isomorphic change, a part of the institutional process that is not fully explained by institutional theory (Munir and Phillips 2005). Secondly, it particularly centres on the attempts at unfreezing, and studies how different forms of eliciting radical change are used in succession as the social context changes. Thirdly, it uses an understudied form of text (the protest song), produced by a peripheral societal stakeholder (the artistic community), that may be more relevant than is usually considered in organisation theory, namely due to the channels of diffusion at its disposal and to its reputation of independence, amongst other possible reasons. In other words, the texts produced by protest singers are widely available, their consumption is very easy when compared with other discourses, and their artistic value may be taken as a genuine attempt to improve society. Fourthly, by opening our discussion to this stakeholder, we contribute to the analysis of the relationship between discursive activity produced in one institutional field and societal discourses surrounding the field, a topic that, as noted by Hardy and Phillips (1999), promises to add explanatory value to our knowledge of the constitution of institutional fields.

We therefore uncover a utilisation of discourses, 'sets of texts ... which bring an object into being' (Hardy, Palmer and Phillips 2000, 1231), as strategic resources that shape and are shaped by the social context where they happen to be created (Clegg, Courpasson and Phillips 2006) and that actively contribute to the social construction of reality. As noted by Hardy and colleagues (2000), subjects who have the right to produce texts and to engage in discursive practice, such as songwriters and musicians, may be in an especially good position to shape the way others represent the social world around them. In this sense, discourse may be viewed as strategic resource: by virtue of their position, these artists may see themselves as having a louder voice than more common voices (Potter and Wetherell 1987). Therefore, songwriters, as producers of discourse, can engage in discursive practices that extend beyond their immediate field, that of the arts. They interpret capitalists and their organisations through their creative lenses to give shape to an artistic, thus immaterial, entity that is to be utilised as a political weapon in the social space.

We organised the paper as follows. Firstly, with the purpose of framing the rest of the article, we briefly describe the political context in which the artistic movement discussed here evolved. We describe, in other words, the context of our text. Secondly, we explain the method followed, including the steps to select songwriters and songs.

Thirdly, we show the resulting findings of the exhaustive reading, re-reading, analysis, and grouping of songs. We divide the findings into three periods and explain the reasons why we choose to do so. Then, we explore the differences between those periods. In the discussion section of the article, we draw on our findings to suggest that songwriters used protest songs as discursive strategic resources during the movement of social change taking place in Portugal during the 1960s and 1970s. Finally, we establish connections between our case and other contexts.

Our interest in this topic resulted from a number of factors. First, the importance of these songs for the country where we all live, Portugal, is still highly visible three decades after the 1974 *coup d'etat*. Second, we believe that organisations, as a central part of society, are reflected in many different ways in other parts of society. The intentional criticism to which organisations and their owners are submitted in these songs, possibly deserves some attention. In a sense, protest singers/songwriters are the popular equivalents of authors in the critical tradition. Their potential for changing social representations may, however, be much more significant given their wider visibility, in contrast with most academics' low profile. Third, we consider that discourses about organisations circulating amongst peripheral stakeholders, may be more than mere curiosity. Recent research on peripheral vision suggests that severe threats incubate at the periphery. Their consideration, then, may be more than intellectual pleasure. Radical, transformational discourses, often start at some periphery before moving to the centre. All these reasons justify the academic interest of our study, which considers the political interplay between text and context in Portugal's instability *circa* 1974. The role of the discursive context has been considered central in discourse studies. If, as pointed out by Hardy and Phillips (2004, 303), 'no statement occurs incidentally', then the articulation between discourse and context is crucial. The exceptionality of the 1974 *coup d'etat* provides a unique context to study the strategic use of discourse. To explore the text/context interplay, we start with a brief introduction of the socio-political scene where all this occurred. The interested reader may further pursue the topic in the volume edited by Pinto (2004).

The artistic context: Portugal in transition

Isolated from the outside world, with an increasingly disquieted intellectual elite, impoverished by colonial wars that began in 1961 and consumed 50 percent of public spending per year (Barreto 2004; Teixeira 2004), Portugal was set to experience a regime change on April 25, 1974. The transition was an unusually peaceful military coup – popularly known as The Carnations Revolution, because revolutionary troops garnished their weapons with carnations to celebrate victory. Tanks stopped at traffic lights and not one bullet was fired. A chronology of events that contextualise our discussion is in Appendix 1.

The excitement of the liberation from the previous dictatorship was short-lived and replaced by the more riotous PREC (*Período revolucionário em curso*, or revolutionary period in progress). The pacifism that marked the day the regime changed was replaced by mass demonstrations across the country, attempted counter-coups, and *ad-hoc* arrests. A civil war between Far-Left radicals and Centre-Left democrats (the Right fled to exile or kept silent in fear of further harassment) seemed imminent during the period that became known as the *Verão Quente de 75* (Hot Summer of 75), which lasted up to the middle of autumn. On 25 November, Centre-Left moderates took over the country, putting an end to radicalism and laying the foundation for a democratic regime in Portugal.

The political instability continued until 1979 but the trend to fully-fledged democracy seemed unstoppable. Both communists and the Extreme-Left were democratically removed from power. Their hope of implementing a communist regime was definitively thwarted in 1979, when a moderate Right-Wing coalition won the parliamentary elections with more than half of the popular votes.

The events were accompanied by diverse cultural manifestations – painting, literature, poetry, and music – created by Portuguese artists and intellectuals. In the following section, we describe the method we followed to single out specific cases within the larger cultural vessel of one of the most visible cultural manifestations mentioned above: protest songs.

Materials

Bearing in mind the purpose of uncovering novel perspectives of the organisation, we followed the tenets of qualitative content analysis whilst exploring protest songs. This method seeks and interprets meaningful patterns from emergent relationships between concepts intentionally ingrained in texts and expressions (Krippendorff 2004). It entails reading and re-reading songs, in search not only of common words, but also of common intentions and meanings beyond the words.

The first step in the research process concerned the definition of the starting point. Both songs and songwriters had to be central to the context of the Portuguese revolution. Therefore, we looked for a sample of songs selected by one or more members of the community of protest songwriters. We chose a compilation of 40 Portuguese protest songs put together by José Niza, a prominent musician of that genre, on the 25th anniversary of the coup that overthrew the dictatorial regime. This compilation was organised in a set of two CDs, the first including the 20 most relevant songs before the revolution, and the second the 20 most relevant songs written *after* the revolution.

The second step entailed enlarging the sample of songs. For that, we collected the lyrics created by each of the authors included in the set. In doing so, we were able to establish the beginning of the relevant period in 1963 – no song was written by the selected authors *before* that date. We selected all lyrics written until 1979, the year that marked the end of the revolutionary process as perceived by most observers.

The third step consisted of selecting the songs that were relevant to our research. To be included, songs had to allude either directly or indirectly to concepts such as organisations, capitalists, or workers. We made use of the allowance given to researchers of ascribing meanings to the texts under scrutiny (Krippendorff 2004, 21), in the sense that we recurred to our own judgement, based on experience, shared knowledge, and cultural heritage, to identify the metaphorical meaning of some of the messages included in the surveyed songs. As such, words like 'lords', 'masters', 'power', and 'boss' indicated to us that a song should be included in our sample. Likewise, we included songs that referred to metaphors such as 'vampires', 'beasts of darkness', 'clowns', or 'beasts of capital'.

After selecting the songs, we read each lyric, taking note of its inspirational motif, language, and subject. Throughout the process, we repeated reading whenever a comparison with another song emerged, or when we could fine-tune our interpretation of meaning. The thorough analysis of contents of the utilised words and their meanings and of the overall intent of each song allowed us to conclude that there were major differences between songs according to different chronological periods. Since songs within each period shared a set of characteristics that distinguished them from songs pertaining to any other period, chronology emerged as the natural grouping criterion, thus determining three different groups. The first, marked by resistance, includes songs written between 1963 and 1973. The second, euphoric and revengeful, spans 1974 to 1975. The final group, disillusioned and sad, includes the songs composed between 1976 and 1979. Both passages between groups were marked by historical and disruptive moments, which explain why there is a clear demarcation in terms of content between each group of songs. A list of authors and songs can be found in Appendix 2.

In the next section, we describe the identified chronological periods in terms of historical events and corresponding songs' characteristics. We give examples of songs that illustrate each of the periods, which, when put together, allow for a clear picture of the evolution of events over the entire 17-years period. One of the notable things about this change is its sharpness and lack of overlap: the change in style is so marked that it is possible to separate songs from this and the previous period in function of the lyrics: the poetic, oblique style of the first period, is suddenly replaced by an explosion of directness in the second period and by a bitter resentment in search of the *lost opportunity* in the third period. These periods are discussed next.

The patterns

Resistance (1963–1973)

The Portuguese dictatorial regime lasted for 48 years, but whereas it was largely accepted until the end of World Word II, it was increasingly challenged until it was overthrown in a military coup. The waning popularity of the regime was due to two major circumstances. One was the concentration of wealth and economic power in a handful of families that supported the regime. The other was the war in Portugal's African colonies, which were seeking independence from the colonial power. During this period, composers wrote songs to expose the lack of freedom, social inequality and damages created by prolonged conflict in the African colonies, the lack of freedom and the economic fragility of the country (see Anderson 1962 (a, b, c) for an overtly critical view, in line with the view of the songwriters we consider here).

Given the ever-present threat of the political police (PIDE) and the existence of censorship, writers had to be imaginative in order to reach their public. They could not write about social problems directly, but had to resort to allegories and other forms of metaphor, as exemplified in the following verse retrieved from the 1963 song 'Vampiros' (Vampires) by José Afonso:

In the grey sky, under the silent planet
Flapping their wings through the quiet night
They come in flocks with velvet feet
To suck the fresh blood from the herd

Vampires represent the powerful and the wealthy. Afonso denounces the unlimited 'hunger' held by these social vampires, 'they eat everything, leaving nothing behind'. Censorship was thus avoided because the song explicitly refers to vampires. However, the metaphor of the vampire is frequently featured in the protest against capitalism and the managerial society. It was used long ago by Karl Marx (1867/1976, 342), and is one of the better-known images of a gothic representation of the capitalistic firm (see also Godfrey, Jack and Jones 2004; Parker 2005).

The protest songs of this initial period referred mainly to power relations, poverty and submission. The divide between *them* and *us* – a recurrent theme throughout the three periods analysed – is, however discreetly, already present in the beginning. *Them* relates to those with power and wealth, those that keep *us* under their thumb, those that inflict *us* with pain and sorrow, those that feed on *our* poverty. In the 'Trova do Vento que Passa' (Ballad for the Blowing Wind), Manuel Alegre, a poet who became a prominent member of the Socialist Party, wrote:

I saw the green branches bloom
Straight and turned to the sky.
And those that enjoy having masters
I've always seen with bending shoulders.

Given their simultaneous role of signals and agents of change, songs became more explicit as the 1960s unfolded. The pressure of a continuing war compounded by the absence of reformation intentions by the government led authors to a more direct discourse, albeit the use of metaphors. Songwriters evoke the courage of a single worker of the land as a symbol of all the oppressed labour forces; or they use a house-maid's resolute refusal to obey her master's orders as an image of revolt. Explicit references to poverty and social inequality were included; lyrics exposed oppression and opulence and denounced those who collaborated with the regime as well as their masters. Later songs in this period discard the use of implied references, becoming blunter, as in this excerpt from 'Que Força É Essa?' ('What is that strength?'), written in 1971 by José Mário Branco:

I saw you toiling the whole day
Building cities for others
Carrying stones, wasting
Much strength for too little money
I saw you toiling the whole day
Much strength for too little money
[...]
Don't say you never felt
A strength mounting through your fingers
And a rage growing in your teeth

In this song, there is an open divide between *them* and *us*. The author is talking to a 'friend', asking him what kind of strength keeps him away from himself, working against his own interests and favouring his master. *Them* is oppressive, does not deserve the efforts that '*us*' actually do for *them*, in a process that keeps the status quo instead of challenging it.

Tellingly, in the beginning of the 1970s, songs include many references to the need for change and revolution. Lyrics are used as threatening messages to those that are seen as oppressors, such as in this excerpt from 'Embora os meus olhos sejam' (However my eyes may be), by Francisco Fanhais:

You, that away from your empire
Are promising a new world
Be silent since the people may
Want a new world for real

As the revolution approached, poets and songwriters target capitalists in more direct although still poetic ways. They are depicted as conmen taking advantage of the work of others; as false moralists seeking common pleasures; as traitors to their own species. Capitalists, wealthy and influential individuals, all become the targets of anti-regime anger: if oppression is to be attacked, then songwriters will tell a story about a wealthy individual who mistreats his employees; if the need for revolution is to be extolled, then a song such as 'Casa Comigo, Marta' (Marry Me, Marta), released in 1971 by José Mário Branco, appears:

Her name was Marta
He was Sr. Dr. Gaspar[1]
She was poor and young
He was rich and powerful
(...)
Marry me, Marta
I lend and bail and I intermediate investments
(...)
I will force you to marry me
(...)
I will never marry you,
Your can only take me if you put me in a coffin

This had been a period of resistance and hope where poets and songwriters were both interpreters of a recurrent reality and early voices for change. This growing need for change, and sense of urgency shape the messages throughout this period: from allegoric and metaphoric subtlety conditioned by censorship in the early 1960s to progressively overt threat, albeit somehow metaphoric, in the years immediately preceding the revolution. The military coup that ended the dictatorship would radically alter the social and political structure of the country and, with it, the artistic interpretation of politics and society. An abrupt change also took place in the shape of protest songs.

Revolution (1974–75)

On 24 April 1974, at 22:55 precisely, 'E Depois do Adeus'[2] by Paulo de Carvalho was broadcast. This was a signal for the military to start the revolution. Some hours later, another song advised the military leaders that the coup was going as planned. This song was José Afonso's 'Grândola Vila Morena',[3] which became the veritable hymn of the Carnations Revolution.

The demise of the dictatorial regime brought about profound social and organisational change. If on 25 April people were unsure about the political direction the country was taking, shortly thereafter it became clear that the revolution had been against not only the political regime, but also against the hitherto economic powers. Political sensibility by that time rushed to single out the main Portuguese business families as the 'ancient regime''s prime collaborators and supporters. Rapidly, private property and private ownership were the new foes, and a sense of public prosecution pervaded parts of the population. Anyone accused of being 'wealthy' risked imprisonment or, at least, public harassment. In companies, self-management by blue-collar workers took the place of professional managers, who were forced either to abandon their companies or to heel to the new self-appointed workers' committees. In reaction to an attempted right-wing counter-coup on 11 March 1975, the Government started a radical process of nationalisation. Within a few days, every bank and insurance company, the telecom-

munications company, public transports, utilities and other medium-to-large companies became state-controlled, capitalists and top managers were arrested (a few even
assassinated by undisciplined elements of radical far-left movements) and a frantic rush
to communism seemed to seize many members of the government. A developed discussion of this period can be found in Gomes and Castanheira (2006).

The end of censorship, the sudden blast of freedom and the notion that everything
was now allowed, broadened the variety of songwriters and songs, giving birth to
simpler contents and messages. Sergio Godinho's 'O Grande Capital' (The Big
Capital), written in 1974, is an example of the reinvention of the genre:

> That's it: the Big Capital
> The one with that special little taste
> Taste as lemon
> Taste as ginger
> Taste as oppression
> On a salver
> Taste of oppression
> On a salver

This song is a play on words based on the advertising campaign of a popular coffee
brand. It is appealing to a general audience because of its simple, linear verses. In fact,
this tendency pervades most of the lyrics written at this time. Authors who used
allegorical figures such as vampires before the coup, began to use words such as
'monkeys' and 'big monkeys' to describe the more powerful social classes. Metaphors
are thus either put aside or made more explicit, simpler, and thus more understandable
by the average person.

Praise for the revolution and the end of oppression are the most common themes
found in protest songs written in this period. But these themes occasionally
succumbed to a cathartic attack on those who held the power during the dictatorship.
In such cases, themes changed to threats against capitalists and their firms, denouncing social cleavage and imminent social change. Mirroring the surrounding events,
songwriters started to speak aggressively of businesspeople, as in the song 'O Patrão
e Nós' (The Boss and Us), by Fausto:

> Look at that man (…)
> The suitcase full of money
> Which he carries by hand (…)
> He lives in a mansion (…)
> (…)
> But get hold of him because he is a thief
> He is useless and a son of a bitch
> But now look at us
> Wearing rags (…)
> We live in a hut
> Working all year round
> (…)
>
> But this will come to an end
> Smacking the Boss!

The subtlety that marked the previous period has been almost eradicated, and
abstraction largely replaced by expressions such as 'ass' or 'son of a bitch' when
referring to capitalists and other business people. While owners were vilified, workers

were praised. Workers were seen as the only ones capable of managing wealth and productive resources: 'give the wine barrels to the people/only they can keep them', claims one song; 'the people are the ones who command/the people are the ones who work', can be found in another. This discourse stresses and deepens the divide between *them* and *us*, reproducing it in the cultural arena, if nowhere else.

Yet, a new disruptive event in the convulsive period of the PREC, the 25 November that removed left-wing radicals from power, reshaped protest songs for the second time.

Revolt (1976–79)

The end of Left-Wing radicalism put Portugal on the path to full-fledged democracy. This, however, was far from a straight course, both economically and politically. There was a succession of coalition and minority governments, which would rarely outlast their first year, making long-term policy-making next to impossible. The worldwide economic instability caused by the three oil crises, worsened by a State-controlled economy, drove most economic indicators into a dramatic low. The International Monetary Fund intervened, imposing stringent economic policies that led to social unrest and further instability. The Portuguese Communist Party (PCP) and other Far-Left movements were politically active in their attempts to reverse events and put Portugal back on the track toward Soviet communism, promoting strikes and other forms of protest against much needed reforms. In 1976, the Communist Party organised the first edition of the *Festa do Avante,* a music festival profoundly and purposefully ideological, to try to capitalise on social unrest to rule the country.

Despite all the efforts, the Communist Party failed. By the end of 1979, Parliament leaned toward Centre-Right and the Presidency was supported by all moderate political forces, in a move against the radicalisation of the Left. Songwriters were quick to react to these political changes. Protest songs entwined two themes: denouncing social injustice and inciting workers to struggle for their rights, such as in José Afonso's 1976 song 'Os Índios da Meia Praia' (The Indians from Meia-Praia):

> You work all year round (…)
> They suck you down to your bones
> They suck you up to your head
> I wish we could have
> The courage of Agostinho
> To feed our nerve
> To break the bourgeoisie's neck

Power, working conditions, the need for change, social differences and poverty were subjects inherited from the previous periods. In fact, in its first stages – between 1976 and 1977 – a lingering hope for communism gave place to anger and threats against those perceived as opposing it, as in the following passage from the 1976 song 'Foi a Trabalhar' (While I Was Working):

> The one that uses me does not deserve me
> He, who abuses my strength and competence,
> Even my impatience to feed my children,
> Deserves only my loathing.
> (…)

If still today I remain acquiescent
The one that dominates me has his days numbered
My fight is not fought alone
There are several in the same pace
Arm to arm we can be counted as many

These threats often sank into disillusionment. Songwriters resorted to irony, meta-phors and allegory to voice the increasing realisation that communism was making little if any progress and that the structure of power and wealth remained unchanged: José Barata Moura's 1977 song, 'Vamos Brincar à Caridadezinha (Let's Play a Little Charity) illustrates this sentiment:

Let us play a little charity
(...)
In this world of institutions
Even hearts are catalogued
They pay with boots and rations
They steal a lot but they give presents
And their chests will be adorned
With commendations

Sérgio Godinho, in his song 'Venho Aqui Falar' (I Come Here to Speak) written in 1978, voices the disillusionment stemming from a stalled revolution, urging the people not to give up. In a series of analogies, Sérgio Godinho describes a waning revolution, with worrying signs of a complete halt. In fact, as later events showed, the people he is referring to no longer appear to be interested in this type of radicalisation:

Today, I come here to speak
About something that is worrying me
(...)
How can socialist people
Give up socialism

(...)
They are freeing PIDES[4]
 and bombers
Probably to imprison workers
It is like freeing snakes into the street
And put freedom in a cage

(...)

Maybe tomorrow I am no longer here
(...)
I am not the only one to think
That we have to be united
As grapes in a vineyard

The most emblematic song of this period is possibly FMI[5] (the Portuguese acronym for the International Monetary Fund), a twenty-four minute long monologue by José Mário Branco. In this historical song, all the early joy and final sorrow felt by the revo-lutionary poets, all the incomprehension about the reasons why communism was never implemented, is described in such a dramatic manner that it goes from open laughter to complete silence to discreet tears. In 'FMI' – politicians, capitalists, businessmen, companies, big corporations, international institutions – every symbol of current democracy is put at stake. All the efforts made to implement communism, all the hope and joy lived in the revolutionary years, are emotionally described. 'FMI' was written in a single shot, late on a winter night in 1979, soon after José Mário Branco's expulsion from the Portuguese Communist Party because of his radical ideas.

The differences in content and meaning that we found in our sample of protest songs written across the three periods identified, the distinct way they interact with the events, either denouncing or shaping them, and the varying intentionality with which songs are publicised allows us to suggest that protest songs are discursive resources that may be used strategically. We take the next section to detail our suggestion.

Discussion

After analysing the content of the protest songs written between 1963 and 1979 concerning the view poets and songwriters had on capitalists and their organisations, we interpreted the discourses of protest singers according to the framework offered by Hardy, Palmer and Phillips (2000). These authors suggest that the understanding of discourse as strategic resource involves the interplay between the circuit of activities of the individuals who are trying to use discourse strategically (the individual creation of discursive resources), the circuit of performativity, which refers to the engagement of other actors (how the text penetrates the context), and the circuit of connectivity, which refers to the intersection of the two previous circuits of action and engagement (how the new resources and the context interact to produce a result).

Resistance

In this phase, poets and songwriters carefully selected each word and verse in order to avoid censorship and get people's attention. Metaphors and allegorical speech had to be subtle enough to attain both objectives. While protest songs might not have been recognised as such by the public, they were not overlooked by poets, songwriters, intellectuals and opponents to the regime. The bonds created between several artists were signs of this. Different individuals gave a complementary coverage of the ongoing events, creating an increasingly dense texture of protest. Diversity of themes in protest songs was a means to trigger hope for change in such fields as politics, organisations, economy and the society as a whole. Once the artistic movement was audible enough, it was believed, its results would probably become apparent. Indeed, the bluntness detected in the final years of the *resistance period* can be rooted in a belief that revolution was nigh and protest songs could contribute to shape the events.

The artistic movement was crucial at this stage. In giving their voice to the voiceless, songwriters played a strategic role through composition and performance. In pointing to capitalists and politicians alike as those to be held responsible for suffering and oppression, they became the judges. Some of them, in their role as artists in exile, divested from everything, even from the right to live in their own country, became equals in soul to those who saw capitalists and politicians as the perpetrators of their misery. As interpreters of the surrounding reality, they created, then fixed and eventually communicated their reading of the existing boundaries between right and wrong to their audience: the people. Thus, the authors of protest-songs were not mere spectators, but indeed actors in the events that led to the Carnations Revolution.

Revolution

During the *revolutionary period*, the end of censorship, the sense of fresh democracy and above all, freedom, led to a discursive explosion in the explicitness of protest songs. All things that were kept silent could be shouted in the open, every feeling could be expressed, thus explaining the use of harsh words and threatening and vengeful lyrics, as we have found in many of the songs in this period. Since business owners were seen as the major beneficiaries of the former political situation, they naturally became the easy targets of all the rage suddenly unleashed.

The overall tone of protest songs in this period results from the emergence of several social forces. Curiously, this natural radicalism can explain songs' metaphorical simplicity. In fact, by depriving their poems of literary adornments, poets and songwriters were implicitly claiming the supremacy and justness of their beliefs as well as aiming to keep the population mobilised (Duarte 2007). For the same reason, the directness and metaphorical parsimony add incisiveness and facilitate action from the listeners' side.

Poets and songwriters became *de facto* telling interpreters and actors of the contemporary reality when they openly denounced practices, people and political events as wrong and incited their listeners to action. By doing so, they were transforming their artistic interpretation of the organisational reality and its agents into material attitudes and behaviours toward that same reality. Thus, the artistic discourse was utilised as a strategic resource to shape, define, and interfere with some stakeholders' perspective of organisations. Never before, or ever since, has reality been so close to being a sentimental interpretation of art.

Revolt

After 25 November 1975, the public disappearance of many of the most enthusiastic yet less creative songwriters and singers was a clear signal that the initial euphoria was fading away. Given that events were heading in the opposite direction wished by poets and songwriters, they changed their circuit of activity, recovering the 'song as a weapon' stance that had been somehow lost during the revolutionary period. The absence of censorship explains why lyrics became more explicit in denouncement and incitement. The renewed use of metaphors is explained by the sorrow felt by them for what was seen as something of a return to pre-revolutionary times; only metaphors could reinforce irony to clearly stress the extent to which things were going out of hand. The same disenchantment with the course of events may be witnessed in the literature of the time, as noted by Santos (2004). The choice of words and the nature of discourses thus evolves according to the dynamics of the social network of power relations, as discussed by Foucault (1977). Subtlety and metaphor, crudeness and directness, are used according to the circumstances. This was the artists' last attempt to influence events, and through their discourses, to shape the non-artistic organisational reality. Different times call for different words and different positions of textual subjects in the power circuit (Clegg 1989). The right words at one time may be the wrong words at another, hence the dynamic shift in the three circuits considered by Hardy et al. (2000).

In the case of Portugal after 1975, *momentum* had been lost. In fact, society was changing and the artistic movement was not able to accompany that change; instead, poets and songwriters stuck to ideals that only a few believed in and cared to listen to.

Art was, in this case, confined to the limits of its agents' interpretation of reality: for the first time since 1963, protest songs were useful for contemplation and sensible fruition, but no longer for keeping the engine of social change working.

Final comment

We were interested in exploring the contents of organisations and capitalists in Portuguese protest songs between 1963 and 1979. We suggested, in line with authors such as Hardy, Palmer and Phillips (2000), that songs may be interpreted as strategic resources ignited to produce strategic outcomes (Oswick, Keenoy and Grant 2000), texts that shape and are shaped by the context, which we found to be sharing similar characteristics within three distinct periods: before, during and after the revolutionary process.

Art and society evolve in tandem, mirroring each other (Foster and Blau 1989). Like the oeuvre s/he creates, the artist is both influenced by and influencer of the surrounding reality. In this sense, art cannot be dissociated from the surrounding events, and the artist is a powerful mediator between the two realities. In fact, an effective mechanism is available to artists in their generic relationship with non-artistic reality:[6] a three stages process that entails (a) a cognitive analysis of non-artistic reality, followed by (b) dematerialisation in the non-artistic and subsequent materialisation in the artistic reality, and (c) eventual instrumental re-materialisation into the non-artistic reality.

We contributed to the literature on culture and organisation along several dimensions. We suggested that the analysis of discourse might provide refreshing views of the evolution of institutional fields (Munir and Phillips 2005). In our case, we considered how strategic discourses with an explicit ideological content might be created with the strategic purpose of influencing social reality. Therefore, our case offers a clear interplay of the three-dimensional nature of discourses (Munir and Phillips 2005, 1667): texts and discourses are considered in their social and historical contexts. Folk songs, in particular, can be engaging and emotional artefacts in a political struggle that includes voices at the very periphery of organisations and the business system. The form of these texts/resources, as we discussed, is flexible and accommodates to the socio-political environment. In fact, it co-evolves with the environment.

Recent research suggests that scrutinising the periphery may provide valuable information on how distant stakeholders view reality, which in turn may be a source of relevant, actionable knowledge (Day and Schoemaker 2004). We specifically showed how agents adapt their discourse to changes in social reality, and that there is a clear change in the use of this strategic resource in times of social upheaval. This suggests that Shrivastava's (1986) claim that the *rapprochement* between managerial interests and societal stakeholders may include dialogue with the artistic community. As we concluded, this community was critical to the diffusion, to the general public, of concepts that were instrumental to the creation of a certain representation of capitalists (e.g., the gothic metaphors) and of the necessary actions to resist them (e.g., fraternity). The circulating images of organisations may thus be influenced by messages travelling from the periphery.

Our paper may also be viewed as an exercise of contrast with the abundant production on varieties of corporate and other organisational discourses. In this case, we considered the role of critical, non-organisational voices that seek to reshape the system of power existing in a specific context. We therefore contribute to an explanation of how certain actors try to influence, through textual production and diffusion, a given system of power relationships (Hardy and Phillips 2004). We also suggested that the emotionality associated with music might make these texts particularly compelling for their audiences. Their diffusion via radio means, additionally, that they may reach a very wide public. The fact that some of these songs were actually used to put the revolution in motion, gives them a particular meaning: they were symbols that participants appropriated not because of their meaning but as hidden tokens for coordination, or as we suggested in the title, poetry in motion – literally.

We have explored, in summary, the complex relationship between power and discourse. Our analysis illustrates the two sets of influences conceptualised by Hardy and Phillips (2004, 312): the way in which discourse produces the objects that shape power relationships, and the way the nature of power relationships in a given space influences the production and reproduction of texts. The case also illustrates the 'two sidedness' of the social (Palmer and Dunford 1996, 23): the agency of individuals and the constraints imposed upon them by the social context. We studied this dynamic in a context of macro-transformational change. As noted by Hardy and Phillips (2004), the discursive perspective may provide an interesting alternative to mainstream work on power and politics in organisational contexts. We suggested that the consideration of less mainstream discourses, such as protest songs, might add to the texture of this debate.

Postscriptum

After 1979, the most respected songwriters of the resistance period continued their artistic careers beyond the timeframe covered in our analysis, as active and respected musicians. José Afonso, who died in 1987, is an icon of the revolution. Adriano Correia de Oliveira, who passed away in 1982, is still remembered as a central name in popular music at the time. Sérgio Godinho and José Mário Branco are active and respected musicians as we write. Branco is still at the margins and his music maintains clear similarities with the protest song. He labelled his 2007 shows 'Mudar de Vida' (A Change of Life), and during a concert in the city of Oporto he screamed 'Wake up, you men who sleep!' (Pacheco 2007). Godinho is one of the most popular and respected musicians in Portugal. He cooperates regularly with new pop-rock and hip-hop bands. Manuel Alegre is an important politician, poet and novelist who ran in second place for President in the 2005 Presidential Elections. A recent two CD compilation of themes associated with 25 April, 'E Depois do Adeus', is easily attainable.

Acknowledgments

The authors would like to thank the reviewers for their help on an earlier version of this article.

We are grateful to one of the anonymous reviewers for a comment that led us to revisit the songs. Following our method, we rechecked the songs written by the authors that appear in the selected collection to seek points of continuity and overlap. We confirmed that in terms of both content and form they are nonexistent. Nevertheless, one can detect an artistic continuity in the creative style of some of the songwriters, detectable in the music and way of singing. In fact, the author cannot dissociate her/himself totally from her/his creation. For instances, the artistic style of Sérgio Godinho or José Afonso was clearly the same during the period under analysis, as it continued to be the same after 1979 (still today, Godinho has a distinctive way of singing that leads to the immediate identification of his songs). The lyrics, however, can be chronologically organised with recourse to the descriptors obliqueness, directness, and bitterness.

Notes

1. *Senhor Doutor*, literally 'Doctor Sir', a deferential treatment of someone perceived as having special status and education.
2. Which can be translated as 'After Saying Farewell'. It can be found at http://www.youtube.com/watch?v=89LBNSX_vig
3. Which can be translated as 'Grândola, Sunbathed Village'. It can be found at http://www.youtube.com/watch?v=PBK7bd3UYow
4. Former secret police agents.
5. It can be found at http://www.youtube.com/watch?v=ZUJts90HIHc (Part 1/2) and http://www.youtube.com/watch?v=wj7LKI8rIUoandfeature=related (Part 2/2).
6. The discussion about the nature of reality and the real is beyond the scope of this paper. We use the term 'artistic reality' when referring to the creative oeuvre of the artist, as opposed to 'non-artistic reality', which stands for all the rest. Much as Magritte's pipe belonging to the realm of artistic as opposed to the original pipe, that served as a model and belongs to the realm of the real.

References

Anderson, P. 1962a. Portugal and the end of ultra-colonialism (part 1). *New Left Review* May–June: 83–102.

Anderson, P. 1962b. Portugal and the end of ultra-colonialism (part 2). *New Left Review* July–August: 88–123.

Anderson, P. 1962c. Portugal and the end of ultra-colonialism (part 3). *New Left Review* Winter: 85–114.

Barreto, A. 2004. Mudança social em Portugal: 1960–2000. In *Portugal contemporâneo,* ed. A.C. Pinto, 137–162. Lisboa: Dom Quixote.

Bastien, D.T., and T.J. Hostager. 1988. Jazz as a process of organisational innovation. *Communication Research* 15: 582–602.

Chan, A., and S.R. Clegg. 2007. *Total institutions as instruments of Chinese cultural genocide and their peculiar echoes in management and organisation theory.* Paper presented at the 23rd EGOS colloquium, Vienna.

Clegg, S.R. 1989. *Frameworks of power.* London: Sage.

Clegg, S.R., D. Courpasson, and N. Philips. 2006. *Power and organisations.* London: Sage.

Day, G.S., and P. Schoemaker. 2004. Peripheral vision: Sensing and acting on weak signals. *Long Range Planning* 37: 117–21.

Duarte, L. 2007. A canção como arma. *Público/P2,* May 5, 22.

Foster, A., and J. Blau, eds. 1989. *Art and society: Readings in the sociology of the arts.* Albany: State University of New York Press.

Foucault, M. 1977. *Discipline and punish.* London: Allen and Lane.

Godfrey, R., G. Jack, and C. Jones. 2004. Sucking, bleeding, breaking: On the dialectics of vampirism, capital, and time. *Culture and Organisation* 10: 25–36.

Gomes, A., and J.P. Castanheira. 2006. *Os dias loucos do PREC.* Lisboa: Expresso/Público.

Hardy, C., and N. Phillips. 1999. No joking matter: Discursive struggle in the Canadian refugee system. *Organisation Studies* 20: 1–24.

Hardy, C., and N. Phillips. 2004. Discourse and power. In *The Sage handbook of organisational discourse,* ed. D. Grant, C. Hardy. C. Oswick, and L. Putnam, 299–316. London: Sage.

Hardy, C., I. Palmer, and N. Phillips. 2000. Discourse as a strategic resource. *Human Relations* 53: 1227–48.

Krippendorff, K. 2004. *Content analysis: An introduction to its methodology.* (2nd ed.). London: Sage.

Lewin, K. 1951. *Field theory in social science. Selected theoretical papers.* London: Tavistock.

Marx, K. 1867/1976. *Das kapital.* Hamburg: O. Meissner.

Meisiek, S. 2004. Which catharsis do they mean? Aristotle, Moreno, Boal and organisational theatre. *Organisation Studies* 25: 797–816.

Munir, K., and N. Phillips. 2005. The birth of the 'Kodak moment': Institutional entrepreneurship and the adoption of new technologies. *Organisation Studies* 26: 1665–87.

Oswick, C., T.W. Keenoy, and D. Grant. 2000. Discourse, organisations and organising: Concepts, objects and subjects. *Human Relations* 53: 1115–23.

Pacheco, N. 2007. Ele veio de longe, de muito longe, e agora quer que mudemos de vida. *Público/P2,* May 2, 13.

Palmer, I., and R. Dunford. 1996. Reframing and organisational action: The unexplored link. *Journal of Organisational Change Management* 9:12–25.

Parker, M. 2005. Organisational gothic. *Culture and Organisation* 11: 153–66.

Pelzer, P., and M. Pelzer. 1996. *The Gothic experience: Gothic music as an example for role and function of contemporary culture.* Paper presented at the 14th international SCOS Conference, Los Angeles.

Pinto, A.C., ed. 2004. *Portugal contemporâneo.* Lisboa: Dom Quixote.

Potter, J., and M. Wetherell. 1987. *Discourse and social psychology: Beyond attitudes and behavior.* London: Sage.

Puffer, S.M. 1991. *Managerial insights from literature.* Boston, MA: PWS Kent.

Ritzer, G. 2002. *The McDonaldization of society* (2nd ed.). Thousand Oaks, CA: Pine Forge Press.

Santos, J.C. 2004. A literatura portuguesa contemporânea. In *Portugal contemporâneo,* ed. A.C. Pinto, 217–49. Lisboa: Dom Quixote.

Shrivastava, P. 1986. Is strategic management ideological? *Strategic Management Journal* 12: 363–77.

Teixeira, N.S. 2004. Entre a África e a Europa: A política externa portuguesa 1890–2000. In *Portugal contemporâneo,* ed. A.C. Pinto, 87–116. Lisboa: Dom Quixote.

Appendix 1. A chronology of events.

Period		Major events
1961–1973	1961:	• Colonial War starts in Angola
	1962:	• Students unrest and strikes in several Portuguese universities, such as Lisbon and Coimbra. Several clashes with police forces
		• Guinea-Bissau starts guerrilla activities against the Portuguese presence
	1963:	• Mozambique enters the Colonial War against Portugal
		• Protests during Labour Day lead to violence and one person killed
	1965:	• Opposition's former Presidential candidate Humberto Delgado is assassinated in Spain by the Portuguese secret police
		• Several terrorist attacks perpetrated by organised radical movements
	1967:	• Major robbery at the Bank of Portugal. The money was stolen to fund the creation of a radical opposition movement, LUAR
		• Several communist leaders are arrested
	1968:	• Oliveira Salazar, ruler for the previous 35 years, falls from a chair and is replaced in power by Marcelo Caetano, a 'pro-regime' politician associated with reformist ideas
	1969:	• Students unrest at Universidade de Coimbra
	1970:	• A bomb explodes in a military ship, as a result of a terrorist attack performed by the ARA, the Communist party military wing
	1972:	• The Chapel of Rato is invaded by police to put a stop to reformist gatherings of opposition Catholics
	1973:	• Sabotage attacks in both Continental Portugal and the colonies by the Revolutionary Brigades
		• Congress for the Democratic Opposition takes place in Aveiro, a coastal town 250km north of Lisbon; this meeting ends in clashes between protesters and police
		• General elections boycotted by the major opposition movements
		• First signs of military unrest that eventually led to the 25 April military coup
1974–1975	1974:	• Carnations Revolution (25 April)
		• All the political detainees are granted amnesty.
		• The political exiles – e.g., the future President Mário Soares and the Communist leader Álvaro Cunhal - return to Portugal
		• Abandoned houses and palaces are occupied by the people, after their owners have fled the country (May)
		• Moderates publicly show their discontent concerning the radical path the revolution appears to be taking, leading to a growing clash between moderates and radicals and the fear of a civil war (September)
		• The government asks workers to 'offer' a day of work to the Nation; there is a massive response from workers (October)
	1975:	• Portuguese government begins the process of decolonisation (January)
		• Occupation of land in rural areas begins (February)
		• An attempted coup by right wing radicals fails, leading to the radicalisation of both political and economic reforms – The Hot Summer of '75 begins (March)

Appendix 1. *(Continued).*

Period	Major events
	• An encompassing nationalisations programme is launched: banks, insurance companies, utilities, transports become publicly owned. At the same time, several arrests are ordered: moderate politicians, large company-owners and eventually anyone who could be regarded as a wealthy person were targeted as a potential anti-revolutionary and, thus, imprisoned (March) • Free general elections to form a Constitutional Assembly (April) • Growing tensions between radicals and democrats increase the prospects of a civil war and result in political unrest. Some governments last less than a month (July) • Political radicalisation of the government. All moderates are expelled (August) • A moderate government is appointed with the aim of cooling some radical abuses (September) • Increasing violence between moderates and radicals. Clashes between employers and employees in several economic sectors. (starting in September, major events in October) • Government goes on strike (November) • In fear of a radical coup by military extremists, the armed-forces moderate wing launches a counter-coup, putting an end to the Hot Summer of '75 and to its radicalism (25 November) • Government resumes its functions, ending its strike
1976–1979 1976:	• Terrorist bombings of several left-wing sites, such as political parties and other organisations associated with the left (January) • Several popular rallies seek the release of those imprisoned after the 25 November coup (February) • A new democratic Constitution is approved (April) • General elections for the Legislative Assembly. The moderates (including moderate socialists and right-wing conservatives) win 75% of the votes (April) • Presidential elections. Ramalho Eanes, who had led the 25 November counter-coup and is supported by the socialist party and all the right-wing parties, is elected with 61.5% of the vote (June)
1977:	• Due to a deep economic depression, characterised by an inflation rate of 30% and unemployment up to 20%, IMF was forced to intervene directly in the definition of economic reforms.
1978:	• President Ramalho Eanes removes the government led by Mário Soares. A new government is appointed, based on the current parliament (July) • Another government appointed by the President, based on the same parliament (October)
1979:	• New extraordinary general elections that give an absolute majority to a centre-right coalition led by Francisco Sá Carneiro. This government endures until October 1980, when new regular general elections take place (these last elections are won by the same coalition with an absolute majority – its leader dies soon after in a suspicious plane crash. Until today, it is undecided if that was an accident or an assassination, yet official discussions about it lingers).

Appendix 2. The list of songs.

Song	Poet / Songwriter	Year
First Period: Resistance		
Vampiros	José Afonso	1963
Trova Do Vento Que Passa	Adriano Correia de Oliveira	1964
Coro dos caídos	José Afonso	1964
Poema do fecho éclair	Carlos Mendes	1967
Por aquele caminho	José Afonso	1967
Vai, Maria, vai	José Afonso	1969
Qualquer dia	José Afonso	1969
Os Eunucos	José Afonso	1970
Protesto	Francisco Fanhais	1970
Que força é essa	Sérgio Godinho	1971
O charlatão	José Mário Branco / Sérgio Godinho	1971
Cantiga do fogo e da guerra	José Mário Branco / Sérgio Godinho	1971
Casa comigo Marta	José Mário Branco / Sérgio Godinho	1971
Cantiga para pedir dois tostões	José Mário Branco / Sérgio Godinho	1971
Coro da Primavera	José Afonso	1971
Cantiga da velha mãe e dos seus dois filhos	Sérgio Godinho	1971
Que bom que é	Sérgio Godinho	1971
O Cantigueiro	Samuel	1972
Calçada de Carriche	Carlos Mendes	1972
Tourada	Fernando Tordo	1973
Porque	Adriano Correia de Oliveira / Padre Fanhais	1973
Gastão era perfeito	José Afonso	1973
Venham Mais Cinco	José Afonso	1973
Embora os meus olhos sejam	Francisco Fanhais	1973
Second Period: Revolution		
Viva o poder popular	José Afonso	1974
Foi na Cidade do Sado	José Afonso	1974
Só ouve o brado da terra	José Afonso	1974
O grande capital	Sérgio Godinho	1974
Antes Que Seja Tarde	Paulo de Carvalho	1974
Só De Punho Erguido	José Jorge Letria	1974
O Povo Unido Jamais Será Vencido	Luis Cilia	1974
Somos Livres	Ermelinda Duarte	1974
O Patrão E Nós	Fausto	1974
O Que Faz Falta	José Afonso	1974
Tejo Que Levas As Águas	Adriano Correia de Oliveira	1975
Desta Vez É Que É De Vez	Sérgio Godinho	1975
Ó patrão dê-me um cigarro	Vitorino	1975
O Facho	Paulo de Carvalho	1975

Appendix 2. *(Continued).*

Song	Poet / Songwriter	Year
Third Period: Revolt		
Os Fantoches de Kissinger	José Afonso	1976
Os Índios da Meia Praia	José Afonso	1976
Chula da Póvoa	José Afonso	1976
Como se faz um Canalha	José Afonso	1976
Foi a trabalhar	Sérgio Godinho	1976
Sul, Norte, Campo, Cidade	Sérgio Godinho	1976
Um tractor	Sérgio Godinho	1976
O Fado Das "Caixas"	Paulo de Carvalho	1976
Vamos Brincar À Caridadezinha	José Barata Moura	1977
O galo é o dono dos ovos	Sérgio Godinho	1978
O homem fantasma	Sérgio Godinho	1978
Lá isso é	Sérgio Godinho	1978
Ali está a rio	José Afonso	1978
Tinha uma Sala Mal Iluminada	José Afonso	1978
Arcebispíada	José Afonso	1978
Barracas Ocupação	José Afonso	1978
Eu, o Povo	José Afonso/ Fausto	1978
Venho Aqui Falar	Sérgio Godinho	1978
Rainha	José Afonso	1979
FMI	José Mário Branco	1979

Making Sense of a Transnational Merger: Media Texts and the (Re)construction of Power Relations

ANNETTE RISBERG, JANNE TIENARI and EERO VAARA

In this study of symbolic power relations in a transnational merger, we suggest that the popular media can provide a significant arena for (re)constructing national identities and power in this kind of dramatic industrial restructuring, and are an under-utilized source of empirical data in research studies. Focusing on the press coverage of a recent Swedish-Finnish merger, we specify and illustrate a particular feature of discursive (re)construction of asymmetric power relations; superior (Swedish) and inferior (Finnish) national identities, which, we argue, are embedded in the history of colonization and domination between the two nations. The findings of the present study lead us to suggest that a lens taken from post-colonial theory is particularly useful in understanding the wider symbolic power implications of international industrial restructuring.

INTRODUCTION

Mergers and acquisitions are of perennial interest in organization and management studies. In addition to the traditionally dominant strategic perspective (Haspeslagh and Jemison, 1991), these dramatic organizational and industrial restructurings have been studied from human resource and cultural perspectives (Buono and Bowditch, 1989; Nahavandi and Malekzadeh, 1988). Further, as mergers and acquisitions across national borders have become increasingly popular, cross-cultural studies have also looked at transnational mergers from the perspective of national culture (Calori *et al.*, 1994; Very *et al.*, 1998; Lubatkin *et al.*, 1998; Olie, 1994; Søderberg and Holden, 2002). However, much of the culture-oriented literature in this field has been based on an essentialist conception of culture and has focused on cultural differences, distance and compatibility, without taking broader questions of identity and power seriously (Vaara, 1999).

Nevertheless, the ramifications of major mergers transcend the boundaries of the focal organizations involved (Vaara and Tienari, 2002). This is because issues such as location of headquarters, choice of top management teams, division of roles and responsibilities, allocation of resources and decisions concerning layoffs and shutdowns have direct or indirect effects on a variety of stakeholders. The *symbolic* power implications of transnational mergers in particular can, however, be far greater than any traditional organizational stakeholder analysis would imply. Organizational and national identity-building processes involved in making sense of the implications of such mergers are complex.

In this article, we examine the ways in which symbolic power relations between social actors are discursively produced in a transnational merger. Our starting point is to focus on the discursive construction and reconstruction of social identities (Davis, 1983; Brown 2001). We are in particular interested in the (re)construction of national identities and the social dispositions and structures of domination associated with these identities (Clegg, 1989). Subjectively construed identities are in this sense power effects, which are articulated in mundane everyday language use (Billig, 1995; De Cillia *et al.*, 1999).

The popular media which address relational issues, differences and comparisons, are a significant empirical context for the discursive construction of national identities around the event of a transnational merger. Due to their significance and often dramatic appearance, mergers and acquisitions typically attract considerable amounts of media coverage, becoming something of a spectacle. The growing influence of media in the contemporary "global" world has been subject, for example, to sociological (Bourdieu, 1998a, 1998b) and critical linguistic (Fairclough, 1995, 2000; Chomsky, 1999) attention. There has thus far, however, been less interest on media and media texts in the field of organization theory and management studies (see, however, Mazza and Alvarez, 2000; Vaara and Tienari, 2002; Hellgren *et al.*, 2002).

The empirical focus in this article is on the merger between *Nordbanken* (Sweden) and *Merita Bank* (Finland), which was announced in October 1997. At the time, it was the largest merger ever to take place between a Swedish and a Finnish company, as measured in terms of personnel and turnover. Especially at its outset, the making of *Merita-Nordbanken* attracted a great deal of media attention in both countries.[1] In this article, we analyze the Swedish and Finnish press coverage of the merger by using the methods of critical discourse analysis (Fairclough, 1997). Our study illustrates the importance of media discourse in constructing and reconstructing national identities with specific power implications for organizations.[2]

NATIONAL IDENTITIES, POWER RELATIONS AND MEDIA TEXTS

The notion of social identities rests on the understanding that people define themselves as members of social collectives and categories (Tajfel and Turner, 1979; Turner, 1985; Ashforth and Mael, 1989). Identity building is a core preoccupation in sensemaking (Weick, 1995) where actors develop representations of the self (and others) in relation to others (and

---

[1]The geographical expansion strategy of the owners and executives in Merita-Nordbanken materialized when they announced a merger with the Danish *Unidanmark* in March 2000. The strategy was further strengthened through the acquisition of the Norwegian *Christiania Bank og Kreditkassen* in Autumn 2000. The Nordic financial services group is now called *Nordea*.

[2]Sweden and Finland share a common history. Already in 1150, King Erik of Sweden led a crusade to what is today the southwestern part of Finland. From the peace treaty of 1323 until 1809, Finland was a Dukedom in the Kingdom of Sweden. In 1809, Finland was incorporated as a Grand Duchy within Imperial Russia. In 1917, Finland for the first time gained its independence. As a consequence of Swedish influence during the period of colonization, the Swedish legal and social system took root in Finland. Also, there is still today a Swedish-speaking minority in Finland, amounting to approximately six percent of the population. The Swedish-speaking minority has been extremely influential in, for example, the domains of culture and business in Finland, and the Finnish-speaking majority has generally regarded it as an elite. Alongside Finnish, Swedish remains an official language in the country. Consequently, it is obligatory for all Finnish-speaking school children to study a certain amount of Swedish at school. Obligatory Swedish remains a contested topic in Finland.

themselves). The "social" identities of individuals are embedded in social relations. Identity building is also situation-specific as images of self are constructed in relation to particular others, making sense of new situations where the other is involved. A sense of community within a collective becomes mediated through symbols and rituals in these situations, drawing upon discursive resources. Identities are thus not fixed, stable attributes. Individuals aiming at distinguishing themselves from others constantly redefine their identities (Czarniawska, 1997). Constructed identities can often be temporary, ambiguous and even conflicting.

In this study, we explore power relations and (national) identities in the context of popular media, concentrating especially on understanding the "wider" circuit of power (Clegg, 1989). We consider subjectively construed identities as power effects, complex outcomes of processes of subjugation and resistance that are contingent and perpetually shifting (Clegg, 1994, cited in Brown 2001). Identity is a power effect as it reflects and reconstitutes broader discourse defining and redefining social dispositions and structures of domination, here, in terms of "nations" and national collectives (cf. Clegg, 1989).

Some social categories and categorizations with which individuals aim to be identified are relatively stable. A particular national collective is arguably one (for us, "nation" is a cultural construct rather than a political one). Nationalism depends on a set of deeply held images of historical time and community. Narratives of origin and destiny are central for the discursive construction and reconstruction of nationalism. Anderson (1983) talks about imagined, "invented" histories of nationalism. Peoples' imaginations are constantly fed. Notions of nationalism and national identity have experienced a revival as a means for researchers to attempt to make sense of contemporary large-scale social changes (Lyons and Breakwell, 1996).

National identities are discursive constructs (cf. De Cillia *et al.*, 1999). Billig (1995) uses the concept of banal nationalism to refer to the ways in which the construct of nation is often accepted and reproduced mindlessly and uncritically in everyday talk, rendered possible by mundane habits of language, thought and symbolism. De Cillia *et al.* (1999: 153) provide an illustration of how "national identities are discursively, by means of language and other semiotic systems, produced, reproduced, transformed and destructed". Narratives and identities, however, do not emerge from nowhere, and they do not operate in a vacuum. The construction and reconstruction of national identities involves a multifaceted process of linking contemporary events with existing cultural conceptions (Fiske, 1989a). If we accept that these conceptions are historically formed and reflecting broader discourses (re)defining symbolic structures of domination, a post-colonial theoretical lens may prove useful in understanding identities and the "wider context" and (symbolic) power relations (Prasad, 1997) in, for example, contemporary transnational mergers. Relations between particular peoples or "nations" may in this way be conceptualized to resemble a post-colonial condition (Said, 1995).

National identification in media discourse is the empirical focus of this article. The media have assumed a central role in contemporary societies. Politics, economy and business are examples of arenas where media are extremely influential (Fairclough, 1995, 2000). This means among other things that journalists create images that in turn may shape public views on the phenomena reported and commented upon. The media make sense of "realities out there" – and give sense and meaning in reporting and commenting upon these realities for their audiences (Fiske, 1989b; Gioia and Chittipeddi, 1991; Weick, 1995). The media represent and reproduce particular versions of "reality"; promoting particular voices and marginalizing and excluding others (Vaara and Tienari, 2002). The media also contrast different voices in texts to create what they consider will appeal to their audiences as good stories. This is one of the classic tricks of the trade, of which identifying "winners" and "losers" or heroes and scapegoats is an example (on top managers' own stories and narratives of mergers, see Vaara, 2002).

Journalists place their topics into specific discursive frames. This takes place under continuous pressure for space and time, where choices have to be made. In such a position journalists often reproduce commonly held views, for example, building on stereotypes. Limited space means that individual texts have to be as compressed as possible. On time pressures of journalists, Bourdieu (1998a) writes that journalists "think in clichés, in the 'received ideas' that Flaubert talks about – banal, conventional, common ideas that are received generally" (1998a: 29). In other words, journalists write what everybody already knows, and what they expect journalists to write. Bourdieu (1998a) calls these common-places, which work because everyone can ingest them immediately and their very banality makes them something the speaker (journalist) and the listener (reader) have in common.

Commonplaces are a part of the framing in media work. If the journalist chooses to frame the story with what everybody already knows, s/he reduces the uncertainty of how the story will be received and interpreted by the reader. In our view, there is an obvious link between commonplaces and banal, mundane ways of (re)constructing national collectives (cf. Billig, 1995; De Cillia et al., 1999). Working on national sentiments and stereotypes may be tempting for journalists in covering dramatic events such as a cross-border merger. The media can be effective in reinforcing national representations and stereotypes in a context in which its unconstraint may otherwise be challenged. Brookes (1999) provides an excellent example of this in his analysis of the British press coverage of BSE – "mad cow disease".

Further, it should be noted that media texts have power implications in the sense that they determine what view of the world – or versions of reality – will be presented to the public. According to Fiske (1989b) news as knowledge creation is power. He specifically refers to two aspects: "The power of knowledge has to struggle to exert itself in two dimensions. The first is to control the 'real', to reduce reality to the knowable, which entails producing it as a discursive construct whose arbitrariness and inadequacy are disguised as far as possible. The second struggle is to have this discursively (and therefore socio-politically) constructed reality accepted as truth by those whose interests may not necessarily be served by accepting it" (Fiske, 1989b:149–50).

The power of media over national identifications amongst its audiences is worth considering. The media may be an important source of support when people seek to justify their picture of self and the other (Weick, 1995; Garfinkel, 1967). For example, members of a merging organization may have a particular view of the other organization and then start to look for evidence in the media coverage in order to justify this view in the merger setting, which is marked by uncertainty (Frommer, 2001; Risberg, 2001).

Taking into account the apparent influence and power of the media in contemporary societies, and the popularity of mergers and acquisitions in business life, it is surprising how relatively little academic work has been published on the role of the media in the construction of these dramas. There are, however, some notable exceptions. Hirsch (1986) examined corporate takeovers as instances of cultural framing and institutional integration. He specified ideologies, genres and metaphors found in media texts concerning hostile takeovers, and illustrated how particular ideas on these events become legitimized and institutionalized. Schneider and Dunbar (1992) analysed the meanings ascribed to hostile takeovers using a psychoanalytical perspective, proposing a classification according to which most of these dramas can be interpreted as takeovers for growth, control, dominance or synergy. Hellgren et al. (2002) studied how specific issues are constructed in media texts on a transnational merger through interpretations of "winning" and "losing". They distinguished specific discursive practices in how this is accomplished in the texts; factualizing, rationalizing and emotionalizing.

In a discourse analysis of media texts on mergers, Vaara and Tienari (2002) identified four specific discourses, which they labelled as rationalistic, cultural, societal and individualistic. The rationalistic discourse constructs organizational change based on managerial concerns about competitiveness and rationalization (building its legitimacy on economic and financial rationale). This discourse, resembling the mainstream business rhetoric, dominates in the media in two ways; first, it is the only discourse in a large part of the texts, and second, it more often than not occupies a central role in individual texts where other discourses can be identified. Most relevant for the framework in the present paper, the "cultural" discourse specified by Vaara and Tienari (2002) is characterized by confrontation at organizational and national levels. Within this discursive framework, mergers are discursively constructed as confrontations between "us" and "them" (for the readers to identify with). In brief, the media texts both construct (national) identities and reflect commonly held stereotypes of self and the other.

In the following, we present our interpretation of the discursive (re)construction of symbolic power relations in the merger between Nordbanken (Sweden) and Merita Bank (Finland). The discussion with textual examples taken from Swedish and Finnish press material is based on a comparative study of national identification using critical discourse analysis methods (Fairclough, 1997).[3] The identities (re)constructed are embedded in the history of domination between the two nations. This shared history becomes activated in making sense of, and giving sense to, the contemporary business event.

MAKING SENSE OF A TRANSNATIONAL MERGER

A holding company was established when Nordbanken (Sweden) and Merita Bank (Finland) merged. In this holding company Nordbanken's shareholders held 60 percent and Merita's 40 percent of the stock. The voting rights, however, were divided equally between the owners

---

[3]*Methodological note*. The present research comprises a detailed analysis of media texts. Our point of departure is that all texts are "incomplete" and should be studied intertextually (Fairclough, 1997; Grant, Keenoy and Oswick, 1998). This implies that meaning is constructed when the reader-interpreter connects the text to another domain of meaning, text or context. Moreover, we assume that interpretations of media texts are constructed at the very moment the text is read. In this process of sensemaking, the reader is using what is already "known" to him or her. This process is firmly linked with identity building, which implies that the sensemaking process temporarily produces or reproduces the reader's identities.

Our focus is on the first six months of the merger between Nordbanken (Sweden) and Merita Bank (Finland), with a special emphasis on the two-week period following the initial merger announcement. In some instances in the following sections of this article we refer to texts outside our primary material in order to illustrate our points. Our basic Swedish material comprises a total of 79 texts in (1) *Dagens Nyheter*, a leading daily newspaper, (2) *Aftonbladet*, the leading tabloid, (3) *Dagens Industri*, the leading daily business newspaper, (4) *Veckans Affärer*, the leading weekly business magazine, and (5) *Affärsvärlden*, the leading monthly business magazine. Our Finnish material comprises a total of 84 texts in (1) *Helsingin Sanomat*, the leading daily newspaper, (2) *Ilta-Sanomat*, the leading tabloid, (3) *Kauppalehti*, the leading daily business newspaper, and (4) *Talouselämä*, the leading weekly business magazine. In sum, our material includes all relevant nation-wide printed media in the two countries (apart from the second largest tabloids and, in the Swedish case, the newspaper *Svenska Dagbladet*).

What we offer in this article is our construction of the constructions present in media texts (cf. Thomas and Linstead, 2002). In our analysis, we first identified characteristic themes in the Swedish and Finnish sets of texts respectively. We then focused specifically on texts that seemed to be built upon organizational and national contrast and confrontation. We then moved on to locate ways in which these texts framed and constructed the cross-border merger. Next, we read closely those individual texts and excerpts that seemed to adequately illustrate commonplaces (cf. Bourdieu, 1998a) that journalists use when linking the Merita-Nordbanken merger to the historical legacies of the two nations involved. Some of these illustrative texts are presented and discussed in this paper. Finally, an important part of our intertextual reading of the media material was also reflection on what was left "unsaid", that is, what could already be taken-for-granted by the Swedish or Finnish readers or what was not acceptable to express explicitly in the present context (cf. Fairclough, 1997). In all, the interpretations put forth have been reached through intensive debates between the authors, including careful re-readings of the original texts.

of Nordbanken and Merita. The making of Merita-Nordbanken was thus launched as a "merger of equals". Both banks were products of earlier domestic mergers and acquisitions (see *e.g.*, Tienari, 2000). At the time of the merger in October 1997, Nordbanken's market value was approximately 5.80 billion euros and Merita's 3.36 billion.

Managerialist discourse reporting and commenting upon financial and economic rationale through themes such as efficiency and competitiveness has been identified as the typically dominant discursive framework in the context of mergers and acquisitions (Vaara and Tienari, 2002). A large number of the Swedish and Finnish media texts on the Merita-Nordbanken (MNB) merger drew on such rationalistic, managerialist discourse. In the following, however, we concentrate on illustrating and specifying how power relations between the two "national parties" were produced in the media, and how particular national identities are constructed. In general, what we discovered was that in the Swedish texts, cultural discourse (*i.e.*, discourse building on notions of "us" and "them") was usually firmly embedded within a rationalistic frame. In the Finnish texts, cultural discourse framing the merger as national and organizational confrontation with, for example, frequent direct references to the historical relationship between the two "nations" emerged as a distinctive alternative for the rationalistic discursive framework.

Constructing a Superior Swedish Position

In the Swedish press coverage of the merger, a context-specific superior Swedish symbolic power position and collective identity vis-à-vis Finns was (re)constructed. Our first example is from a text in *Aftonbladet*, a major tabloid. Mr. Jacob Palmstierna, the former chairman of the board of Nordbanken and the newly appointed vice chairman of Merita-Nordbanken, was interviewed immediately after the merger had been announced (Palmstierna's comments are in italics):

No, We Never Sat in the Sauna

Merita does not really sound like the name of a large glorious bank. It sounds more like a hairdressers in Bandhagen. [. . .] But can you trust it?

– Yes, I can without a trembling voice say that Merita is a bank to trust.

And the new president is Vesa Vainio. That sounds like a snake. [. . .]

– Us Swedes, we've always had warm feelings for the Finns. More so, perhaps, than the other way around.

Why is that?

– The Finns have always had a big brother complex.

When it is time to gather the board of the new giant bank and sit down for a conference, which language will you use?

– The company language is Swedish. That has been decided on.

You and Vesa Vainio will alternate as chairman every second year. Why? [. . .]

– This construction is just a way to handle this national issue, as you understand.

No.

– I am speaking about psychology. This merger is an enormous thing to Finland. Merita is their largest, leading bank. For the merger to become accepted in Finland, one must have some balancing factors. One of those is the 50–50 voting rights, another is 5–5 on the board and another is that the chair of the president is alternated.

When did the [merger] negotiations end?

– At two o'clock last night, when we wrote the last comma. There were four of us. Hans Dalborg, Vesa Vainio, Timo Peltola and myself.

Where were you?

– At Palace Hotel in Helsinki, in an ordinary conference room. We celebrated with a glass of beer.

Beer! Shouldn't it be Kosken on a night like this?

– Well, I guess it should. But now it was beer.

But you blessed the deal with a sauna, didn't you?

– No, absolutely not.

[*Aftonbladet*, October 14, 1997 (Italics ours)]

We can only speculate whether the journalist in *Aftonbladet* is consciously provoking Mr. Palmstierna as an individual, merely playing a game in bringing up national stereotypes to write up a good story for a Swedish audience or whether he is being "serious". In any case, the title "*No, We Never Sat in the Sauna*" already frames the text in a particular way, equating Finnishness with a tendency to bathe in the sauna. It thus complies with a well-known stereotype. Further, it is interesting that many of the Swedish stereotypes of Finns activated in the text above are explicitly prejudiced. For example, Finns are associated with working class suburbs of Stockholm, such as Bandhagen (the name Merita sounds "*like a hairdressers in Bandhagen*"). This association is, in fact, not insignificant as there is a large Finnish working class minority in Sweden as a result of migration in the 1960s and 1970s, and a lot of ethnic Finns do live in Bandhagen.

The journalist also brings up the issue of Swedes not being able (or bothered) to pronounce and spell Finnish names correctly, and their tendency to joke about Finnish names in a condescending way. For example, Vesa Vainio (former CEO of Merita) "*sounds like a snake*". Further, Finns are also represented in the text as heavy drinkers. "*Kosken*" is an emblem of this. Koskenkorva is a typical Finnish brand of vodka-type strong alcohol. In Swedish everyday language the difficult name is often shortened to Kosken (which is incomprehensible in the Finnish language). For many Swedes, the text may bring into mind previous media coverage of violent crimes committed by (working class immigrant) Finns under the influence of alcohol in Sweden. In all, a relatively barbarian picture is painted of Finns in the text. Conversely, Swedes clearly occupy a superior position vis-à-vis Finns.

In the text, the interviewee Mr. Palmstierna is represented as the fair chairman who is well aware of potential conflicts in dealing with Finns. Yet, he too produces an image of Swedish superiority in his comments. On the basis of this particular text, Swedish readers are inevitably left with the understanding that the merger is crucial for Little Finland, while in Big Sweden this is a more minor issue. The equal distribution of votes, the building of the board of directors on the basis of national equality, and the alternating chairmanship are just some solutions to calm down the nationalistic emotions of the Finns. It is interesting that Mr. Palmstierna explicitly refers to the Big Brother – Little Brother setting in the present context (note that "Big Brother" does not refer here to the Orwellian idea of a control society). "*The Finns have always had a big brother complex*". This can be seen as a sign of cultural sensitivity but it can also be interpreted as an act of institutionalization of the superiority-inferiority relationship. It may be interpreted as patronizing. And "*us Swedes*" is in the text, too, measured against the Finns (cf. Billig, 1995).

It is important to bear in mind that the text deals with top managers' negotiations leading to a major transnational bank merger. Talking about "*snakes*" and making degrading references to "*sauna*" and alcohol consumption are thus particular choices made by the journalist. These choices are available to the journalist (and his audience) only due to the specific nature of the Swedish-Finnish relationship in general. The symbolic structure of domination overarching the relationship enables the discursive construction of a particular Swedish identity in this situation.

Construction of superiority and inferiority through the use of cultural stereotypes was by no means restricted to the genre of tabloids. An interview with Mr. Hans Dalborg, the former CEO of Nordbanken and the newly appointed CEO in Merita-Nordbanken, published in *Veckans Affärer*, the leading business weekly in Sweden, exemplifies this. The text is titled *"It is I who Decides"*. In the first part of the interview Mr. Dalborg makes it clear, arguing for the rationale of the merger, that *"his sole task is to money for the shareholders"*. The text then seems to change gear (Dalborg's comments in italics):

> Hans Dalborg is of the opinion that in Sweden we have not really understood how important this deal is in Finland, where Merita is the national bank before others. Sweden has four large banks of rather equal size, but Finland only one that now gets 60 percent Swedish ownership. It is a dramatic step.
>
> Moreover, Merita, with its parts from Kansallis and the Union Bank of Finland, is more than a bank. It is by tradition a great power player in Finnish economic life with a number of shares and personal connections to leading Finnish companies. It is said about the previous CEO of Kansallis that he was on the board of so many companies, some thirty, that it was well understood why he didn't have time to manage the bank. But the new CEO will not be inspired by his example.
>
> *– I am not interested in the Finnish power game – Vesa Vainio will have to take care of that. My only goal is to make money for our owners by increasing the profit per share.*
>
> But, will your role as a despotic CEO not become extremely limited? The representation on the board is half each from the Swedish and the Finnish side.
>
> *– This is not a conglomerate, this is a bank, with one management. The new management knows of no national borders and will be in charge for both the Swedish and the Finnish business. It is accepted that the top management of the company group that makes the decisions is large. If we agree, there is no problem, if we disagree, I make the decisions.*
>
> So you will perform some Finnish authoritative leadership style?
>
> *– In Nordbanken there are no limitations to what you are allowed to say, as long as the door to the outside is closed. But when the CEO has made the decision one will go out and implement it even though one disagrees. This model will work here too, I'm convinced about that.*
>
> [*Veckans Affärer*, October 27, 1997 (Italics ours)]

This text is not only interesting because of its provocative title. It illustrates how nationalistic sentiments intertwine with the dominant rationalistic discourse in the Swedish press coverage of the merger. Underlying the reported dialogue between Mr. Dalborg and the journalist is the association of rationalism with Swedishness. Construction of Swedish superiority is most clearly shown in the rendering of Mr. Dalborg's seemingly patronizing attitude towards the *"Finnish power game"*. He (as the Swede in control) stands above that game, but will let the (emotional) Finns continue with it if they wish to do so. It is evident in the way the text is constructed that there are no unnecessary power games in Sweden.

There is also a hint that if the problems created by the *"Finnish power game"* would require tough actions, Hans Dalborg (*i.e.*, as the CEO and a Swede) will have the final word. Rest assured, Swedish audience. Finally, the journalist's immediate association of *"I make the decisions"* (in Dalborg's remark) with *"Finnish authoritative leadership style"* is notable. This calls for more justification in the text from Mr. Dalborg who makes it clear that the archetypal Nordbanken (Swedish) management model – *"there are no limitations to what you are allowed to say, as long as the door to the outside is closed"* – will prevail; *"this model will work here too"*. In all, the structure of domination overarching the Swedish-Finnish relationship enables the journalist (and the interviewee) to discursively construct a particular Swedish identity; the rational self as opposed to the emotional other.[4]

---

[4]Similar discursive constructions seem to have emerged in relation to other transnational mergers. The aborted merger between the state-owned telecommunications companies Telia (Sweden) and Telenor (Norway) provides an example. The merger agreement was already negotiated, but widely publicized power struggles between the "national sides" in the early implementation phase led to the cancellation of the deal.

Finally, a less subtle example of Swedish superiority constructed in the Merita-Nordbanken merger. This is found in an article in *Dagens Industri*, the major Swedish daily business newspaper. The *"Finnish authoritative leadership style"* is expressed through another kind of vocabulary:

The End of Management by Perkele

Finnish managers are listening to their employees.

A wind of change has blown over the industrial life and its outstanding figures in Finland. Whisky and cigars in dim lighted cabinet rooms are out and management by *perkele* belongs to the past. [. . .] The new generation of Finnish managers are taking care of their health, playing ball with their children and demanding an open dialogue with their subordinates. And little by little they are beginning to learn about openness; press conferences are no longer arranged for the top management to show off and glitter; now it is about answering questions as far as possible. Jorma Ollila, the CEO of Nokia, is leading the development. He has managed to implement a totally new corporate culture among his employees (*Dagens Industri*, November 20, 1997).

Many readers of *Dagens Industri* are likely to recognize the Swedish stereotype of Finnish management style, coined in the Finnish swearword *perkele* ("devil"). *"Management by perkele"* is a term that became famous in Sweden in the mid–1980s when Finnish companies started to acquire companies in Sweden. The Swedish employees, apparently used to dialogue between managers and employees, were said to be shocked by what they considered as ruthless and authoritarian management style by Finnish managers (Laine-Sveiby, 1987, 1991; Ekwall and Karlsson, 1999). The tone in the text above indicates, then, that the Finnish managers are now making progress as they are working for *"open dialogue"* and *"little by little they are beginning to learn about openness"*. What is interesting here is that this progress is described as moving from the stereotypical Finnish management style as perceived by Swedes towards the archetypal Swedish style characterized by egalitarianism, co-operation and consensus seeking; *i.e.*, the *"open dialogue"* (Ekwall and Karlsson, 1999; Zander, 1999; Berglund and Löwstedt, 1996). For a Swedish audience, the obvious underlying message in the text is that the Finns are now *"little by little"* reaching a more advanced stage in management and managing which Swedes have mastered for quite some time.[5]

Why the particular discourse in the Swedish media? In commenting upon the merger between Nordbanken and Merita, the general tone in the Swedish press coverage seems to have moved from critical to neutral. Arguably, (re)constructing symbolic power relations between nations became necessary, because when the terms of the "merger of equals" were first made public, it seemed that the Finns had lured the Swedes in the merger negotiations (as pointed out above, Nordbanken's market value was approximately 5.80 billion euros and Merita's 3.36 billion at the time of the merger). The first reaction in the Swedish media was that the merger was not a good idea; the Swedish taxpayers (the Swedish state was a major shareholder in Nordbanken) and shareholders were portrayed as the losers in the arrangement. With regard to the line-up in top management, the apparent 50–50 balance of power appeared distorted. *Dagens Nyheter*, a major daily broadsheet, described this as *"fairness for the sake of fairness"* (October 14, 1997). At the outset, from a "Swedish position" there seemed to be no logical reasoning for the merger. A title in *Veckans Affärer* (October 20, 1997) read *"Nordbanken-Merita:*

---

[5] Swedish stereotyping of Finnish managers as ruthless and authoritarian brings an important difference to the fore. For Finns, these attributes are not necessarily negative. Nokia, the global company with strong Finnish roots, has been used as a positive example of *management by perkele*, which is depicted as flexible "guerrilla warfare" style management with quick decision making well suited to the increasingly fast-moving global world of business; *"there is readiness to confront change"* (Bruun and Wallén, 1999).

Expensive experiment", and the text made it clear that *"doubtful motives and weak arguments"* characterize the merger. *Dagens Industri* claimed already on October 14, 1997, that *"the merger does not create any value added for Nordbanken's shareholders"*.

After the merger announcement, CEO Hans Dalborg in particular held the role of justifying the rationale of the merger to the Swedish public through the popular press. After the initial criticism in the media, Mr. Dalborg seems to have carried out the justification work well. The representations of the financial rationale of the merger between Nordbanken and Merita shifted over time in the Swedish press. *Veckans Affärer* (April 27, 1998), for example, writes that merging with Merita may be viewed as positive for the Swedish shareholders in the long run. To put it provocatively, Swedish journalists were now able to conclude that Swedish rationality eventually prevailed in the merger.

Constructing an Inferior Finnish Position

In the Finnish press coverage of the merger, a context-specific inferior Finnish symbolic power position and collective identity vis-à-vis Swedes was (re)constructed. Finnish texts swarm with direct references to the historical relationship between the two "nations". This is illustrated by the following excerpt from a column by a well-known Finnish business journalist commenting on the reactions of the Swedish media immediately after the merger announcement:

> [. . .] The joy of the former eastern provinces of the Swedish Empire is made complete by the initial comments from Stockholm. *Dagens Industri*, always so convinced of the excellence of the Swedes, turned up its nose at Nordbanken, and the rest of the press wasn't exactly applauding the first Swedish-Finnish union in the financial world.

(*Helsingin Sanomat*, October 20, 1997)

From 1323 to 1809, Finland was colonized by the Kingdom of Sweden. It is apparent in the above text that the journalist is building on the notion that the Little Brother has come back to the Big Brother; *"the joy . . . is made complete"*. Interestingly, in the original Swedish text (in *Dagens Industri*, the business daily) the case was framed between Nordbanken and Merita, not Sweden and Finland. In the Finnish text, the same case is explicitly presented as one between the former colonizer (the self-promoted *"excellent"* Swedes) and its colony (Finland as *"the former eastern provinces"* of the colonial state). The historically determined, asymmetric Swedish-Finnish relationship enables the discursive construction of a particular Finnish identity – inferior but resistant – in this situation. This text also brings another aspect of the Swedish-Finnish relationship to the fore; while the Finnish press often commented and reflected on the writings of the Swedish media, the opposite was the case only very rarely.

Inferiority can be read in Finnish media texts through the theme of Swedes abusing or doing injustice to the Finns – and the Finns resisting. This is evident in the curious rhetorical leap made in the following texts. These texts make up an article that was published in *Ilta-Sanomat*, a Finnish tabloid. Again, the article reflects on the writings of the Swedish *Dagens Industri*, where a Swedish board member in MNB had been interviewed some time earlier:

A Wild Swedish Estimate: Merita to Cut Down its Personnel by as Much as 4000

Suspicion about the bank merger taking the bread out of the mouths of thousands of Merita's employees gets reinforcement from Sweden. Rune Brandinger, a board member in Merita-Nordbanken, promises that a lot of cost savings are due on the Finnish side. According to Dagens Industri, the paper that interviewed Brandinger, the reduction in Merita will be 3000–4000 people within a period of 3–5 years.

Merita's Pertti Voutilainen: Brandinger is Not Acquainted with the Matter

[. . .] Is it bitterness related to ice hockey that is behind all this? The story in Dagens Industri was published the same day as the Swedish tabloids, bitter from their defeat in ice hockey, were abusing Finland. Could Brandinger's comment be related to bitterness in hockey? – *I suppose not*, Voutilainen remarks. – *Coincidentally, I was in Stockholm on Wednesday when the result* [of the ice hockey match] *came out, and we thought that although there are no international matches in MeritaNordbanken, we'd allow this external one. – Let's enjoy this* [victory] *now, and they* [i.e., Swedes] *can be ashamed of being worse than we* [i.e., Finns] *are in ice hockey.*

[*Ilta-Sanomat*, February 20, 1998 (Italics ours)]

With ice hockey, the journalist refers to the quarterfinal match between Sweden and Finland in the 1998 Olympics in Nagano. Finland beat Sweden 2–1 and made it to the semifinals. Pertti Voutilainen is the former CEO of Kansallis. At the time of the interview, he was a member of the board of Merita-Nordbanken. The explicit reference to sport as a domain of confrontation between Sweden and Finland is here especially intriguing. It has recently been argued that sport continues to be a marker of distinctive cultural and national identities in a "global" world (Boyle and Haynes, 1996). Sports journalism produces a turn inwards toward national concerns, and a buttressing of a sense of difference (Blain *et al.*, 1993). What is interesting in our press material is that Finnish journalists seem to draw on sport precisely in this way when commenting on a business manouver, bringing an emotional flavour to it.

Sport in general has played a major role in the construction and reconstruction of national identity in Finland, especially since the declaration of independence in 1917. Competing against Sweden has been particularly important for the buttressing of Finnish national identity in, and through, sports. The rhetoric in the coverage of the Merita-Nordbanken merger brings the sensitivity involved in this to the fore. More specifically, as in the text above, it illustrates how the construction of Finnish national identity is typically defensive in nature, that is, competing from an inferior position vis-à-vis the other (Sweden). This is illustrated in a number of texts in the context of the Merita-Nordbanken merger. Merita is directly equated with Finland: "*Finland Loses 6–5 in the Organization Game*" (headline in *Kauppalehti*, October 14, 1997). Other typical examples include: "*Nordbanken – Merita 1–0*" (headline in *Ilta-Sanomat*, November 5, 1997), "*Business Units: Sweden 3, Finland 2*" (sub-heading in *Ilta-Sanomat* addressing the new organization structure of the bank, December 19, 1997), and "*The Score in the International Seems to be 0–1 for the Swedes*" (headline in *Helsingin Sanomat*, October 28, 1998).

Apart from sport, another recurring metaphor in the Finnish press coverage of the MNB merger is war. It is not unnatural for Finns to depict the Finnish-Swedish relationship as an ongoing battle. Although Finns and Swedes have never actually been at war as "nations" – due to the long colonial relationship and the immediate passing of Finland into the hands of Imperial Russia in 1809 – this kind of imagery is frequent in the public discussions in Finland. Associations with war and batt, again, enhance an emotional involvement in the Swedish-Finnish relations.

In an article titled "*A Finnish Counterattack Is Possible*", the major Finnish business weekly speculates on possible attempts by Finnish owners "*to regain power in Merita-Nordbanken to Finland*" (*Talouselämä* 35/1997). Further, when Merita-Nordbanken sold its stock in the major Finnish insurance company *Pohjola* in Janury 1999, commentary on Swedish recolonization of Finland mounted. The buyer was *Skandia*, the largest insurance company in Sweden. As Pohjola had been a part of the traditional "*Fortress of Blue-and-White Capital*" (*Helsingin Sanomat*, January 17, 1999), a power bloc of Finnish-nationalistically minded industrialists and businessmen, the deal evoked comments in a special tone:

The Gate was Opened

It is hard to describe a big event or feeling. You either hear excess or mundane words, Thursday 4 o'clock p.m. Merita-Nordbanken sold its shares in Pohjola to the Swedish insurance company Skandia. The fortress of the Finnish-nationalistic capital, over a hundred years old, was opened to the Swedes. "Skandia asked for the shares just before Christmas and we answered Skandia's question," Vesa Vainio, the chairman of the board in MeritaNordbanken described the atmosphere after the deal. On May 5, 1808, vice admiral Carl Olof Cronstedt surrendered Viapori, without notable opposition, to the Russians. [. . .] I admit that the analogy is limping and excessive.

(*Helsingin Sanomat*, January 10, 1999)

Vesa Vainio is Annoyed of Being Accused of Treason

(*Helsingin Sanomat*, January 17, 1999)

Viapori is a fortress on an island off Helsinki. Vesa Vainio (at the time, the vice chairman of the board of MNB) is put into the role of collaborating with the (Swedish) enemy; he is "*accused of treason*". The journalist above is aware of his particular choice of words – "*I admit that the analogy is limping and excessive*" – but he has yet found it relevant to activate the war metaphor, drawing upon a collective Finnish memory on the "loss" of the Viapori fortress. "*The Gate*" which is now "*opened*" symbolizes in our view Swedish recolonization of Finnish territory.

Further, in the Finnish media coverage of the Merita-Nordbanken merger, language became a particularly clear example of interpreted Swedish victory and (re)colonizing attitude. The laconic comment "*The company language is Swedish. That has been decided on*" by Jacob Palmstierna in the interview in *Aftonbladet* (Swedish tabloid) quoted above conceals a complex, sensitive and much-debated question in Finland. The Swedish CEO of Merita-Nordbanken, Hans Dalborg, was interviewed in *Kauppalehti*, the major Finnish daily business newspaper, immediately after the merger was announced. One of the sub-headings in the text was "*Does the Spirit of the International Match Live on?*". Among other themes, the journalist brought up the issue of language. Dalborg commented, referring to the merger negotiations:

Creating a joint corporate culture is extremely important, Dalborg emphasizes. He says that creating mutual understanding is made easier by the fact that Merita is a completely bilingual bank. According to him, language used in the negotiations has been Swedish all along. [*Kauppalehti*, October 15, 1997 (Italics ours)]

We do not know whether these were his "original" words, but Mr. Dalborg is presented in the text as if he believes it to be natural that all Swedes and Finns should communicate in Swedish, just like he had apparently done with Finnish top managers in the merger negotiations. The language question is, however, a highly contested terrain for Finns in general. Over 94% of the Finnish population do not speak Swedish as their mother tongue, and a large part of the Finnish speakers resent the compulsory Swedish – a remnant of the colonization era – that they are forced to study at school. Depicting Merita as "*a completely bilingual bank*" then illustrates Mr. Dalborg's ignorance of contemporary Finnish society at the time of the interview.

Some two weeks after Hans Dalborg's interview the decision to root Swedish as the "official corporate language" in Merita-Nordbanken was made public. This language choice was constructed in the Finnish media coverage as an unfair decision creating a great deal of practical problems for the Finnish employees in MNB who were now being forced to use a foreign language in their work. Language was also portrayed to mark a power imbalance in the organization. Vesa Vainio defended the language choice in an interview with *Ilta-Sanomat*, the leading Finnish tabloid:

Merita Chose Swedish Vesa Vainio: No Way to Management without Language Skills

When the Finnish Merita and the Swedish Nordbanken merge, the official language in the new bank will be Swedish, the chairman of the board in the new big bank, Vesa Vainio assured yesterday.

According to Vainio, the decisive thing is that the skills of the Swedes in the Finnish language are considerably weaker than the Finns' are in Swedish.

Among the top management in Merita, there have been dreams about English, the one and only international banking language, becoming the final official language in the bank. You can now say goodbye to these dreams.

Vainio said that, in routine work, you could use the local language in both countries. It is no use dreaming to get to the top management in the bank, however, if your Swedish isn't fluent. Skills in the Finnish language have, however, not been set as a requirement for reaching the board. . . . (*Ilta-Sanomat*, October 23, 1997).

The journalist's choice of words is intriguing. English and Finnish as corporate languages are presented as unattainable "*dreams*". The sarcasm is noteworthy; for example, it is well known among Finns that extremely few Swedes have made the effort of learning the Finnish language. The following text was published in *Talouselämä* almost a year after the interviews in *Kauppalehti* and *Ilta-Sanomat* quoted above. Note, again, the explicit link to sports:

The chairman of the board in Merita-Nordbanken, Vesa Vainio, is surprised over the extent of emotional turmoil that Sweden and the Swedish language still provokes among Finns. Nordic mergers and acquisitions are persistently commented upon in the spirit of sports internationals between Finland and Sweden. [. . .] – *The issue of language has been more significant than we initially imagined* [*Talouselämä*, 27/1998 (Italics ours)].

This is an illustration of how historical legacies live on in everyday life as they are activated in public discussion. Here, the legacy is related to the fact that the Swedish and Finnish languages have continued to structure the Finnish society and economy since the colonization period. In the MNB merger, the Swedish language emerged for the Finnish national collective (as constructed in the media) as a symbol of their asymmetric power relationship with Sweden and Swedes. It emerged as a symbol of recolonization. Further, if we assume that media coverage on the merger between Nordbanken and Merita is part of its public as well as the intraorganisational sensemaking, it can be speculated that when reproduced in the media, underlying images of superiority and inferiority may influence the internal sociopolitical struggles in the merging organizations[6] and become a self-fulfilling prophecy. Table 1 summarizes key features in the construction of superiority/inferiority in Swedish and Finnish media texts on the studied merger.

CONCLUSION

In this article, we have examined the (re)construction of national identities in the context of a transnational merger. Our critical discourse analysis of media texts has shown how the issues at hand reflect and reconstitute broader discourse defining and redefining social dispositions and structures of domination between particular peoples and "nations". Such analysis of power relations is in our view relevant and timely for mapping out and understanding the complex cultural and political implications of major contemporary industrial restructurings such as transnational mergers.

---

[6]Based on recent research on the organizing of the Merita-Nordbanken merger, for example, it is evident that the question of Swedish dominance was heatedly debated in the Finnish part of the organization, and the language question in particular triggered non-commitment and resistance among Finnish employees (Vaara *et al.*, 2000; Säntti, 2001). Apparently, when the Danish Unidanmark joined the Merita-Nordbanken group in March 2000, the top management immediately announced that the official corporate language is English.

TABLE 1   Key Features in the Construction of Superiority/Inferiority in Media Discourse

	Superior position	Inferior position
Role of nationalistic discourse	• Nationalistic discourse as firmly embedded within rationalistic discourse.	• Nationalistic discourse as a distinctive alternative for rationalistic discourse.
Role of legends and myths	• Lack of references to (nationally important) legends and myths.	• Frequent references to (nationally important) legends and myths, e.g. sports and war metaphors.
Typical stereotypes	• Normalized auto-stereotypes. • Patronizing and belittling stereotypes of the (emotional) other.	• National ideals as auto-stereotypes. • Envious stereotypes of the other.
Constructed subjectivity	• Modern and progressive subjectivity.	• (Re)colonized subjectivity.
Constructed dispositions	• Inherent dominance.	• Power/need of resistance.

In our study of the Swedish and Finnish press coverage of the merger between Nordbanken (Sweden) and Merita Bank (Finland), the media are understood as sensemakers and sensegivers in their practices of promoting particular versions of "reality" and marginalizing and excluding others (Fiske, 1989b; Gioia and Chittipeddi, 1991; Weick, 1995). National identification provides a discursive platform for the media to make sense of these complex phenomena for the benefit of their audiences (cf. De Cillia *et al.*, 1999). Cultural sensemaking in the form of (re)constructing national identities is an interpretive act which draws from historical legacies; stereotypes, myths and stories in different social domains. It is about constructing and reconstructing "us" and "them" in mundane everyday language use (Billig, 1995), based on these legacies. In the Swedish-Finnish merger, we have specified a particular feature of the discursive (re)construction of asymmetric power relations; superior (Swedish) and inferior (Finnish) national identities, which are embedded in the history of domination between the two nations. This shared history becomes activated in making sense of, and giving sense to, the contemporary business event.

The contextual and situation-specific nature of (re)constructing social identities does not mean that the theoretical apparatus put forth in this article cannot be used elsewhere. On the contrary: we talk about Swedes and Finns, but the setting could just as well be Swedes and Norwegians, the English and the Irish, the English and the Scottish or any other relationship between peoples with a shared past of domination and colonization. While national identities (re)constructed in relation to a specific other are experiential and temporary, legacies of national representations and stereotypes – the "building blocks" of identity in particular situations – are more stable and less subject to change. In all, a wider framework of symbolic power relations and national identification allows to interpret how socio-historical legacies, myths and stereotypes inform the discursive formation of contemporary business manouvers.

The findings of the present study show that a post-colonial lens is particularly useful in understanding the "wider context" of (symbolic) power relations (cf. Prasad, 1997). As in the Swedish-Finnish setting, on the one hand, the colonizer continues to dominate the former colony, reproducing a sense of superiority through discursive acts of patronization, drawing upon discourse where the colonized is constructed as exotic and primitive, but familiar enough to be defined and governed (Prasad, 1997; Peltonen, 1999). On the other hand, the colony continues to reconstruct its identity as inferior through discursive acts of subjugation and by constantly positioning and comparing itself against the former colonizer. An asymmetric symbolic power structure is reproduced.

It would be intriguing to explore contemporary British-French, German-French or British-German mergers or acquisitions in terms of national identity and power relations. These settings would probably reflect even more complex (re)constructions of identities and power as there is no self-evidently dominant symbolic national collective in the relationship. These relationships are yet loaded with proud nationalist sentiments due, in part, to the history of confrontation between the nations in question. The exchange of "compliments" between German and English tabloids in 1996, after Germany won the European Championship in football on England's home turf, is a banal example of this (Brookes, 1999). With similar rhetoric but less aggressively, a sense of German invasion was constructed in the UK media when the German BMW acquired the classic Rover brand.

Finally, it seems to us that nationalism and national identities have remained a neglected topic for most organization and management scholars, be they mainstream or critical. Perhaps the subject is too obvious and self-evident to be taken seriously. Or, conversely, perhaps it is too sensitive a topic for members of dominant nations as it entails a particular form of self-reflection: that is, from the perspective of national identification, its basis and consequences. This would, however, in our view vitalize discussions on power. It would also deepen understandings of the role and influence of the media in the contemporary, apparently "global" world. We hope that ideas presented in this article – written from a geographical periphery in Europe – will encourage a revived interest.

References

Anderson, Benedict (1983) *Imagined communities: Reflections on the origin and spread of nationalism*. London: Verso Editions and NLB.

Ashforth, Blake E. and Mael, Fred (1989) Social identity theory and the organization, *Academy of Management Review*, **14**(4), 20–39.

Berglund, Johan and Löwstedt, Jan (1996) Sweden: The fate of human resource management in a "folkish" society, In: Timothy Clark (Ed.) *European human resource management*, Oxford: Blackwell.

Billig, Michael (1995) *Banal nationalism*, London: Sage.

Blain, Neil, Boyle, Raymond and O'Donnell, Hugh (1993) *Sport and national identity in the European media*, Leicester: Leicester University Press.

Bourdieu, Pierre (1998a) *On television*, New York: The New Press.

Bourdieu, Pierre (1998b) *Acts of resistance – Against the new myths of our time*, UK: Polity Press.

Boyle, Raymond and Haynes, Richard (1996) "The grand old game": Football, Media and identity in Scotland, *Media, Culture and Society*, **18**, 549–64.

Brookes, Rod (1999) Newspapers and national identity: The BSE/CJD crisis and the British press, *Media, Culture and Society*, **21**(2), 247–63.

Brown, Andrew D. (2001) Organization studies and identity: Towards a research agenda, *Human Relations*, **54**(1), 113–21.

Bruun, Staffan and Mosse Wallén (1999) *Nokian valtatie*, Helsinki: Tammi [*Nokia's highway*].

Buono, Anthony and Bowditch, J. L. (1989) *The human side of mergers and acquisitions. Managing collisions between people, cultures, and organizations*, San Francisco: Jossey-Bass.

Calori, Roland, Lubatkin, Mikael and Very, Phillipe (1994) Control mechanisms in cross-border acquisitions: An international comparison, *Organization Studies*, **15**(3), 361–79.

Chomsky, Noam (1999) *Profit over people – Neoliberalism and global order*, New York: Seven Stories Press.

Clegg, Stewart (1989) *Frameworks of power*, London: Sage Publications.

Clegg, Stewart (1994) Power relations and the constitution of the resistant subject, In: J. M. Fernier, D. Knights and W. R. Nord (Eds.) *Resistance and power in organizations*, London: Routledge.

Czarniawska, Barbara (1997) *Narrating the organization*, Chicago: University of Chicago Press.

Davis, R. C. (1983) *Lacan and narrative*, Baltimore, MD: Johns Hopkins University Press.

De Cillia, Rudolf, Reisigl, Martin and Wodak, Ruth (1999) The discursive construction of national identities, *Discourse and Society*, **10**(2), 149–73.

Ekwall, Anita and Karlsson, Svenolof (1999) *Kohtaaminen Suomi-Ruotsi – kirja kulttuurieroista ja johtajuudesta*, Vaasa, Finland: Storkamp Media [*Meeting: Finland Sweden – A Book on cultural differences and management*].

Fairclough, Norman (1995) *Media discourse*, London: Edward Arnold.
Fairclough, Norman (1997) *Critical discourse analysis: The critical study of language* (2nd ed.), London: Longman.
Fairclough, Norman (2000) Guest editorial: Language and neo-liberalism, *Discourse and Society*, 11(2), 147–8.
Fiske, John (1989a) *Understanding popular culture*, London: Unwin Hyman.
Fiske, John (1989b) *Reading the popular*, London: Unwin Hyman.
Frommer, Ranja (2001) *Between expectation and experience – An analysis of post-merger integration in two mergers*, doctoral dissertation, The Royal Institute of Technology, Stockholm, Sweden.
Garfinkel, Harold (1967) *Studies in ethnomethodology*, Englewood Cliffs, NJ: Prentice Hall.
Gioia, Dennis and Chittipeddi, Kumar (1991) Sensemaking and sensegiving in a strategic initiation, *Strategic Management Journal*, 12(6), 433–48.
Grant, David, Keenoy, Tom and Oswick, Cliff (1998) Introduction. Organizational discourse: Of diversity, dichotomy and multi-disciplinarity, In: David Grant, Tom Keenoy and Cliff Oswick (Eds.) *Discourse + organization*, London: Sage.
Haspeslagh, Phillip and Jemison, David B. (1991) *Managing acquisitions: Creating value through corporate renewal*, Free Press, New York.
Hellgren, Bo, Löwstedt, Jan, Puttonen, Liisa, Tienari, Janne, Vaara, Eero and Werr, Andreas (2002) How issues become (re)constructed in the media: Discursive practices in the AstraZeneca merger, *British Journal of Management*, 13, 123.
Hirsch, Paul M. (1986) From ambushes to golden parachutes: Corporate takeovers as an instance of cultural framing and institutional integration, *American Journal of Sociology*, 91, 800–37.
Laine-Sveiby, Kati (1987) *Svenshet som strategi*, Stockholm: Timbro [*Swedishness as Strategy*].
Laine-Sveiby, Kati (1991) *Suomalaisuus strategiana*, Porvoo, Finland: WSOY [*Finnishness as Strategy*].
Lubatkin, Michael, Calori, Roland, Very, Philippe and Veiga, John F. (1998) Managing mergers across borders: a two nation test of nationally bound administrative heritage, *Organization Science*, 9(6), 670–84.
Lyons, Evanthia and Breakwell, Glynis M. (1996) Changing European identities and social change in Europe: A challenge for social psychology, In: Glynis M. Breakwell and Evanthia Lyons (Eds.) *Changing European identities: Social psychological analyses of social change*, Oxford: Butterworth/Heinemann.
Mazza, Carmelo and Alvarez, Jose Luis (2000) Haute couture and prêt-à-porter: The popular press and the diffusion of management practices, *Organization Studies*, 21(3), 567–88.
Nahavandi, A. and Malekzadeh, A. R. (1988) Acculturation in mergers and acquisitions, *Academy of Management Review*, 13, 79–90.
Olie, René (1994) Shades of culture and institutions in international mergers, *Organization Studies*, 15(3), 381–405.
Peltonen, Tuomo (1999) *Colonial forces in "global" HRD: Finnish expatriates, developmental subjectivity and resistance*, paper presented to the Critical Management Conference, UMIST, Manchester, UK, July.
Prasad, Anshuman (1997) The colonizing consciousness and representations of the other: A postcolonial critique of the discourse of oil, In: Pushkala Prasad, Albert J. Mills, M. Elmes and Anshu Prasad (Eds.) *Managing the organizational melting pot: Dilemmas of workplace diversity*, London: Sage.
Risberg, Anette (2001) Employee experiences of acquistion processes, *Journal of World Business*, 36(1), 58–84.
Said, Edward W. (1995) *Orientalism*, London: Penguin Books (first published 1978 by Routledge & Kegan Paul).
Schneider, Susan C. and Dunbar, Roger L. M. (1992) A psychoanalytic reading of hostile takeover events, *Academy of Management Review*, 17(3), 337–567.
Säntti, Risto (2001) How cultures interact in an international merger: Case Merita Nordbanken. University of Tampere, doctoral dissertation, Acta Universitasis Tamperensis 819.
Søderberg, Anne-Marie and Holden, Nigel (2002) Rethinking cross-cultural management in a globalising business world, *International Journal of Cross-Cultural Management*, 2(1), 103–21.
Tajfel, Henri and Turner, J. C. (1979) An integrative theory of intergroup conflict, In: William G. Austin and Stephen Worchel (Eds.) *The Social Psychology of Intergroup Relations*, Monterey: Brooks/Cole.
Thomas, Robyn and Linstead, Alison (2002) Losing the plot? Middle managers and identity, *Organization*, 8(1), 71–93.
Tienari, Janne (2000) Gender segregation in the making of a merger, *Scandinavian Journal of Management*, 16(2), 111–44.
Turner, J. C. (1985) Social categorization and the self-concept: A social cognitive theory of group behaviour, In: E. J. Lawler (Ed.) *Advances in group processes: Theory and research* (Vol. 2), Greenwich, CT: JAI Press.
Vaara, Eero (1999) Cultural differences and postmerger problems: misconceptions and cognitive simplifications, *Nordiske Organisasjonsstudier (Nordic Organization Studies)*, 1, 59–88.
Vaara, Eero (2002) On the discursive construction of success/failure in narratives of post-merger integration, *Organization Studies*, 23(2), 211–48.
Vaara, Eero and Tienari, Janne (2002) Justification, legitimization and naturalization of mergers and acquisitions: A critical discourse analysis of media texts, *Organization*, 9, 275–304.
Vaara, Eero, Tienari, Janne, Säntti, Risto and Marschan-Piekkari, Rebecca (2000) *Language as power in post-merger integration: The case of Merita-Nordbanken*, competitive paper presented to the 26th Annual Conference of the European International Business Academy (EIBA), Maastricht, The Netherlands, December.
Weick, Karl E. (1995) *Sensemaking in organizations*, Thousand Oaks: Sage.

Very, Philippe, Lubatkin, Michael and Calori, Roland (1998) A cross-national assessment of acculturative stress in recent European mergers, In: Martina C. Gertsen, Anne-Marie Søderberg and J. E. Torp (Eds.) *Cultural dimensions of international mergers and acquisitions*, Berlin: Walter de Gruyter.

Zander, Lena (1999) Management in Sweden, In: Malcolm Warner and Pat Joynt (Eds.) *Management in Europe*, UK: Thomson Learning Business Press.

Coffee and the Business of Pleasure: The Case of Harbucks *vs.* Mr. Tweek

CARL RHODES

In this paper, I examine the representation of organizations in the television cartoon series *South Park*. In particular the *South Park* episode 'Gnomes' is reviewed – this episode contains a direct parody of the role and conduct of organizations in society as its story revolves around a 'fictitious' coffee chain, Harbucks', attempt at a hostile takeover of a small town coffee shop. Drawing on the episode's *roman a clef* (or perhaps *cartoon a clef*) depiction of the global coffee retailing organization Starbucks, it is argued that this popular culture representation offers opportunities to critique and debate organizational behaviour in a way not available to modes of representation common to Organization Studies. Following Bakhtin's model of the carnival, *South Park* is read as exemplary of a subversive culture of folk humour that mocks, satirises and undermines official institutions – a culture rich in understandings of contemporary organizations and their relationship with society.

> These boys should learn how the corporate machine is ruining America. You see, I own a coffee shop and now some great, big multi-million dollar company is going to move in and try to take all my business, which means I may have to shut down and sell my son Tweek into slavery
> – Mr. Tweek, owner of South Park's coffee shop

> My argument is simple, this country is founded on free enterprise. Harbucks is an organization that prides itself on great coffee!
> – John Poston, Harbucks Coffee Corporation

INTRODUCTION

I love to drink coffee. Whether it is a frothy cappuccino over a mid-morning conversation, a bitter espresso following a satisfying meal or even a thermos of instant in the park on a cold day, coffee always seems to have a place. This is a global pleasure – over the past 500 years imperialists, missionaries, travellers and big business have ensured that the pleasures of the bean (and its cultivation) have spread to virtually all corners of the world. As a global pleasure and global business, how then might coffee inform an understanding of the relationship between business and culture? In this paper, I will discuss the popular critique of the business of coffee retailing as represented in the TV cartoon *South Park*. In particular the *South Park* episode 'Gnomes' (Parker and Stone, 1997) will be reviewed – this episode contains a direct parody of organizations in society as its story revolves around the attempt of a 'fictitious' coffee chain, Harbucks, attempt at a hostile takeover of a small town coffee shop. Drawing on the episode's *roman a clef* (or perhaps *cartoon a clef*) depiction of the global coffee retailing organization Starbucks, the paper will explore how this example of popular culture representation offers opportunities to critique and debate organizational behaviour in a way not readily available to modes of representation common to Organization Studies. Following Mikhail Bakhtin's (1984a/1965) model of the carnival, *South Park* will be read as exemplary of a subversive culture of folk humour that mocks, satirises and undermines official institutions. Such carnival is a site of open critique of official values and is a privileged location for anti-hegemonic discourse (Scott, 1990). In the case of *South Park*, this offers a culture rich in understandings of contemporary organizations and their relationship with society.

In reviewing the themes of the carnivalesque representation of organizations in popular culture, the paper advances in five parts. First, the potential relationship between popular culture (especially television) and knowledge about organizations is explored. Second, the logic of the carnival and the carnivalesque in popular culture and television is discussed as an example of this potential. Third, the *South Park* episode 'Gnomes' is reviewed in terms of how it represents organizations and their relationship with society. Next, the carnival logic of *South Park's* representation of organizations is explored in order to elicit the value of its ambivalent critique to the understanding of organizations. The paper concludes with a discussion of how popular culture, and carnival forms in particular, can be used as an important form of knowledge that should be taken seriously by the formal study of organizations.

ORGANIZATIONS AND TELEVISION HUMOUR

Butler (1997) has suggested that social inquiry might not only be informed by the practice of the physical scientist, mathematician and logician, but 'can learn from the art and craft of the novelist, dramatist, journalist, film-maker, soap opera creator' (p. 945) and so forth. In a similar vein, Phillips (1995) supports the use of literary forms of representation such as novels, short stories, plays, songs, poems and films as legitimate approaches to studying management and organizations because they can open up new possibilities for how we understand organizations. Such representations, Phillips suggests, can be used to provide 'a new intertextual arena within which theories of organization can come to life' (p. 635). Despite these possibilities, reference to and application of such creative forms in organization studies is limited.[1] At issue here is that researchers can easily become convinced of the supremacy of their own conventional genres of writing such that we do not account for knowledge that is represented outside of these genres. The situation is one where 'readers interpret texts as being factual in so far as they encounter appropriate textual conventions [genres] which can be read in appropriate ways' (Atkinson, 1990: 36). Genre, however, is not neutral – it exerts control over what it purports to represent such that genre influences what is definable as knowledge and what is not (Rhodes, 2001). To date the animated cartoon has not been commonly seen as a genre that might contain organizational knowledge. Part of my approach here is to say that this need not be the case and that in fact, looking to nonconventional genres offers possibilities for understanding organizations not available more commonplace forms.

Representational forms such as those associated with popular television are not commonly taken seriously in terms of their knowledge potential. While it is now perhaps conventional

---

[1] Although limited, there are some examples of how cultural texts have been employed in organization studies. Most commonly this is in the form of literary, as opposed to popular, novels (*e.g.* Czarniawsksa-Joerges and Monthoux, 1994; Knights and Willmot, 1999; de Cock, 2000). The representation of organizations in cinematic films has also been explored (*e.g.* Hassard and Holliday, 1998; Smith *et al.*, 2001; Grice and Humphries, 1997)

to suggest that the distinction between high and low culture is less meaningful that it once was (Storey, 2001), it still remains current for television to be viewed as a medium that panders to and exploits the 'low' tastes of the general public which results in 'populist spontaneism and demagogic capitulation to popular tastes' (Bourdieu, 1998: 48). In such a view, television has led culture to become 'shrivelled and absurd' and serious discourse has been replaced by 'mere' amusement and entertainment (Postman, 1987). This proposes that television merely titillates its audience by appealing to their 'lower' instincts and accounting for their laziness (Krönig, 2000). Such a pejorative view of the cultural value of television is then taken further by suggesting that people (like myself) who see television as being an important medium to 'read' have 'surrendered to one of the most perverse forms of academic pedantry' (Bourdieu, 1998: 9). As I hope to show, however, the humour of television itself intends to address the pompous seriousness of such criticism. Indeed, it is the carnivalesque humour that this paper will explore that provides an ambivalent critique of the pretensions of official culture.

In looking to animated television to understand the popular critique of organization, it must be noted that television is a medium that, in contemporary times, has become a platform for the development of cultural representations of organizations. Organizations are everywhere in television, whether it be in hospitals, law firms, coffee shops, factories or offices. It is therefore relevant to study these representations in order to understand the cultural meanings of work and organization. At the same time, television programs are produced and broadcast by organizations in pursuit of commercial interests. The result is that through television, commercial organizations are, in part, in the business of representing commercial organizations. As Rowe (1995) points out, the result is a close yet uneasy relationship between cultural and economic activity. It would be simplistic, however, to suggest that the relationship between culture and commerce was one where commercial institutions seek solely to create cultural representations that support or advocate commercial or capitalist discourses. Instead, in many instances popular culture exists in a paradoxical relationship with capitalist organizations; this paradox is such that popular culture produces representations of organizations that offer a critique of the modes of production and consumption that create and sustain them (Rhodes, 2002). Following Bataille (1991/1947) this relationship is one where popular culture can be 'excessive' of economic activity in that it is 'nonproductive' in a conventional economic sense yet it is created by the excess of energy that the capitalist system produces. Culture, in this sense, is both related to and more than that which is produced by organizations and the economy.

Whilst being excessive to the economy, culture has the opportunity to produce representations which are also excessive of the formal representations of capitalist interests. Such representations can be made important to understanding organizations in contemporary society, where as Hassard and Holliday (1998) have pointed out, 'popular culture offers more dramatic, more intense and more dynamic representations of organizations that management texts' (p. 1). Moreover, understanding the potential of culture is important as culture is a 'pedagogical force par excellence . . . through which people define themselves and their relationship with the social world' (Giroux, 2000: 10). Television in particular is an influential medium in that it achieves a mass audience and is 'like a Trojan horse introduced into the heart of the domestic fortress that we call "home"' (Weber, 1996: 122). As a result, certain forms of television provide the potential for significantly compelling and accessible critical understandings of organizations that operate beyond more formal representations.

An example of such critique can be seen in the television cartoon series *South Park*. The show tells the story of four children's experience of growing up in the fictitious Colorado town of South Park. This is not the story, however, of idyllic childhood in the American

Midwest. Indeed, it is a direct parody of such lifestyles as idealised in much American situation comedy. In the show's theme song this already becomes evident,

I'm goin' out to *South Park*, gonna have myself a time.
Friendly faces everywhere. Humble folks without temptation.
Goin' out to *South Park*, gonna leave my woes behind.
Ample parking day or night. People spouting 'Howdy neighbor!'

This rural utopia of simple, neighbourly folk is far from what actually happens in the show's stories. These stories focus on the lives of four children – Stan, Cartman, Kyle and Kenny; these are not, however, child-innocents growing up to be the model citizens of American sit-com dreams. Instead, they are foul-mouthed and at times nasty kids who constantly work to negotiate their identities amongst their dysfunctional relatives, bizarre school teachers and the general problems of growing up.

LIFE IS A CARNIVAL, BELIEVE IT OR NOT

In the book *Rabelais and His World* the Russian literary theorist Mikhail Bakhtin (1984a/1965) studied the popular sources used in the literary work of the sixteenth century author Rabelais. Bakhtin traces Rabelais' inspiration to the folk humour of the Middle Ages as manifested in the social practice of the carnival. Bakhtin identifies that the carnival had an important role in the life of medieval people and that in large medieval cities an average of three months of each year were devoted to carnival. He discusses that the rituals of the carnival, which existed in all countries in medieval Europe, offered a form of life that was non-official, and outside of the feudal, ecclesiastical and political forms that dominated medieval life. This 'carnival life' freed people from ecclesiastical dogma and operated outside of the religious sphere – carnival was subject only to its own freedom and was organised on the basis of laughter. As Bakhtin (1984a/1965) puts it himself, 'carnival celebrated temporary liberation from the prevailing truth and from the established order; it marked the suspension of all hierarchical rank, privileges, norms and prohibitions' (p. 10). A characteristic logic of the carnival is that of the 'inside-out' through which a second world of folk culture is constructed – this is an excessive parody of non-carnival life through travesties, humiliations, profanity and the comic crowning and uncrowning of kings. The result is a carnival laughter, which is not so much a reaction to a comic event, but rather a laughter of all of the people, including the participants in the carnival themselves. Such laughter is ambivalent in that it is both triumphant and mocking but does not place itself above the object of its mockery. As Bakhtin (1984b/1963) describes:

It could be said (with certain reservations of course) that a person of the middle ages lived, as it were, two lives: one was that of official life, monolithically serious and gloomy, subjugated to a strict hierarchical order, full of terror, dogmatism, reverence and piety; the other was the life of the carnival square, free and unrestricted, full of ambivalent laughter, blasphemy, the profanation of everything sacred, full of debasing and obscenities, familiar contact with everything and everyone. (p. 129).

Bakhtin suggests that the style of the carnival, the 'carnivalesque', is also employed in the novels of Rabelais (1494–1553). This style comes in the form of 'grotesque realism' in which the material human body, including eating, defecation and sex, are represented in grandiose and exaggerated imagery. This is neither the biological individual nor the 'economic man', but rather a festive and abundant body. It is the body at a material level – a degradation of the 'higher' principles of human existence; down to earth rather than up to heaven. This style has the attributes of exaggeration, hyperbolism and excessiveness where opposites are inverted and norms are transgressed. Such a carnival works to:

> liberate from the prevailing point of view of the world, from conventions and established truths, from cliches, from all that is humdrum and universally accepted. The carnival spirit offers the chance to have a new outlook on the world, to realise the relative nature of all that exists, and to enter a completely new order of things (Bakhtin, 1984a/1965: 34).

The carnival is thus a practice that both opposes and destabilises official views of reality. It creates itself in opposition to official culture on a series of planes; for example from seriousness to laughter, from the dogmatic to the open, from the immutable to the contingent and from control to identity (Storey, 1998). These oppositions question hierarchy by creating an ambivalent space between the high and the low where hierarchical distinctions are not respected – 'carnival breaks up and "reverses" the colourless and prosaic monopoly of the established order of power' (Jung, 1998: 104). Carnival does this in a way that is 'jesterly' – it distrusts and aims to deconstruct attempts at stabilising social systems by being playfully and non-violently subversive.

In examining Bakhtin's carnival, Stallybrass and White (1986) have noted that by the late nineteenth century the middle classes had rejected the carnival tradition both culturally and through acts of legislation that attempted to eliminate carnival as a feature of European life. What had happened was that modernisation, the movement towards urban industrialised society and the growth of the middle classes had removed carnival as a festive form. Despite this removal of popular rituals in the form of the carnival, Stallybrass and White also point out that without the carnival, the carnivalesque spirit had been sublimated. Although the carnival proper had largely been removed, carnival as a social practice re-emerged in an altered and broken down fashion through new formations of popular culture. Through its sublimation, the gratification of the desire for carnival was achieved through socially accepted behaviours instead of through the prohibited original. The carnivalesque became a repressed desire that in conscious terms was regarded merely as entertainment and sensationalism rather than as knowledge; despite this, the carnivalesque sphere of popular culture still refuses to lie down or to be regulated and remains 'outrageously omnipresent' in popular culture (Docker, 1987).

It is worth noting here that the analysis of the carnival presented by Bakhtin and by Stallybrass an White are in many ways attempts to historicise carnival in order to project 'the story of the European avant-garde back into the continent's past' (Pechey, 1998: 180). Historical 'accuracy' aside, however, what the carnival does provide is a framework and set of resources for understanding popular culture in the present. Where, then is carnival to be found today? Docker (1994) has argued that carnival, as a 'cultural mode' remains a strong influence on contemporary popular culture, such as television. He suggests that this is a culture that is creative, vigorous, exuberant and, importantly, excessive. Such a culture supplements, challenges, destabilises, relativises and pluralises official versions. Here television has significant continuities with descriptions of pre-modern carnivalesque forms. Carnival exists as an authorised transgression that is limited and set aside from the official – in this way: 'modern mass-carnival is limited in space: it is reserved for certain places, certain streets, or framed by the television screen' (Eco, 1984: 6).

As well as being a potential site for the carnivalesque, television is also an important medium in terms of its relationship with organisations. Like many other forms of popular culture, television did not emerge until the post Second World War period when new consumer products were designed and manufactured for new consumer markets (Davies, 1995). Television, as a mode of cultural (re)production is itself the product of big business.

Interestingly this does not seem to have stopped television programs from biting the hand that feeds them and offering critical views on organizations. This irony can be explained by suggesting that:

> Television's economics, which demand that it can be made popular by a wide variety of social groups, works against its apparent ability to exert ideological control over the passive viewer ... it is the audiences which make a program popular, not the producers. (Fiske, 1987: 93)

The implication is that capitalist cultural industries do not necessarily make products that promote capitalist ideology; instead they make products that will sell. The result is that there is not just one ideological position that is forced upon industrially produced texts – the products of the cultural industry, therefore, might contain more than just the seeds of resistance (Benshoff, 1992). Further, television representations of organizations provide useful understandings of work – in particular they represent workplaces as embodied, personal and emotional and explore everyday work settings and interactions that can contain implicit critiques of capitalist frameworks (Hassard and Holliday, 1998).

This critique shares the dynamism of the carnival spirit and the carnival can thus provide a way to understand popular culture.

> Bakhtin's notion of the carnival provides an inspired model for analysis of comic genres like the animated film, genres often overshadowed by more 'significant' cinemas. Where the clown once ruled or misruled in medieval comedy, it is now the turn of the animator to show his motley. (Lindvall and Melton, 1997: 203)

This carnivalisation is made possible particularly in animation because cartoons 'do not need the consistency or internal logic of a realist film. New codes can emerge where a reader encounters the unpredictable articulations of the cartoon' (ibid p. 209).

Based on the discussion above, my position here is that popular culture has effects beyond that of 'mere' or trivial entertainment and can indeed offer important critical possibilities in its reflections and representations of contemporary life. Further, I suggest that these possibilities are most notable in 'carnivalesque' forms of popular culture that can be read as being oppositional to, and destabilising of, official views of reality (Rhodes, 2002). This is a form of 'clowning' that dethrones established hierarchies and transgresses and transforms official orders of reality. It is here that popular culture can be considered as an important form of critique – one where:

> in relation to entertainment, carnivalesque as social critique doesn't have to be considered inferior to 'public sphere' reason; where playfulness, juxtaposition, heterogeneity, parody, inversion, grotesque humour, self-parody, are not inferior to more formal modes of argument and analysis, reflection and contemplation ... Carnivalesque, then, offers an ongoing challenge, to the narrowly conceived forms of reason of the 'public sphere', as well as to modernism desiring to legislate, in an equal imperial way, single standards for all culture; what's good for the modernist avant-garde is good for the world. In relation to both, carnivalesque remains an always dangerous supplement, challenging, destabilising, relativising, pluralising single notions of true culture, true reason, true broadcasting, true art. (Docker, 1994: 283–284)

This is not to say that all popular culture has critical potential, nor to say that all popular culture is carnivalesque – rather, the point is that in popular culture we can find examples of carnivalesque critique. Although this critique does not appear in the public forms in which one might expect to find them (Newspapers, Journals, Universities etc.) as I hope to demonstrate, it does not mean that the critique is neither important nor thorough.

GOIN' OUT TO SOUTH PARK, GONNA HAVE MYSELF A TIME

The *South Park* episode 'Gnomes',[2] first aired on 16 December 1998, is a prime example of how the carnivalesque critique of organizations is manifested in television and popular culture. The episode is particularly relevant as it explicitly examines the various aspects of big business both in terms of the ethics of business and in terms of its relationship with society more generally. The show features the plans of a large coffee chain, Harbucks, to open a new store in *South Park*. Harbucks, a thin disguise for the American corporation Starbucks, intends to take over the local coffee shop owned by Mr. Tweek. As we shall see, in telling this story the show provides a compelling and critical representation of business. If the logic of the carnival involves overturning and parodying official culture, this episode adopts a carnivalesque stance in relation to its depiction of American big business as exemplified by Starbucks.

Starbucks is exemplary of many of the characteristics associated with the supposed virtues of large organizations. The Starbucks Corporation's primary business is buying, processing and selling coffee. Its main distribution channel, and what it is famous for, are its retail stores that operate around the world either directly managed by Starbucks or through joint ventures. From Asia, to Europe to the Middle East, Starbucks is making its presence felt. The company states its objective as being to establish Starbucks as the most recognised and respected brand in the world. To achieve this goal it plans to 'continue to rapidly expand its retail operations, grow its specialty sales and other operations, and selectively pursue opportunities to leverage the Starbucks brand through the introduction of new products and the development of new distribution channels' (Starbucks Web Site, 2001). Starbucks' history is relatively short – the first Starbucks store opened in 1971 in Seattle. It was not until the early 1980s, however, that the contemporary face of Starbucks emerged when the then marketing director Howard Schultz visited Italy and decided to bring the espresso bar culture of Milan to America. By 1987 Starbucks was open in seventeen locations, by 1995 this had expanded to 676, and then in 1996 Starbucks opened its international division starting in Japan and Singapore. With continued domestic and international expansion, by May 2001 Starbucks was open in more than 4300 locations serving 12 million customers in 17 countries. Starbucks epitomises business success with its incredible story of growth resulting in US$2.2 billion in revenue in 2000 – Starbucks themselves suggest that their 'outstanding growth' is on account of the worldwide strength of their brand name. Starbucks is the leading retailer of coffee in the world.

Against the apparent success story of Starbucks, *South Park* refuses to take such dominant corporate logic for granted. The episode 'Gnomes' starts in the boys' schoolroom. Their teacher, Mr. Garrison, is under threat of being fired by the school board because it is claimed that he does not teach his students anything about current events. In order to assess the truth of this claim, the children are asked to make a presentation to the school board on a topic of their choice related to local news. The class is split into groups of five – the normal group of Stan, Kyle, Eric and Kenny are joined by Tweek. Tweek is the son of the owner of South Park's coffee shop – a jittery kid, who is said to suffer from Attention Deficit Disorder, but whose behaviour is suspiciously like that of a child who has drunk far too much coffee. Tweek suggests to the other four that they do their report on the underpants gnomes, who he describes as 'the little guys that come into your room real late-late at night and steal your

---

[2]The title is referring to a group of characters known as the underpants gnomes. Notably, this reference to underpants itself is carnivalesque as it immediately positions the gnomes scatologically in reference to what Bakhtin (1984a) calls the 'lower body strata'. Although not featured in the episode being reviewed here, a more dramatic example of this is the *South Park* character Mr. Hanky the Christmas Poo – literally a turd in a red Santa's helper hat who befriends the boys.

underpants'. The highly caffeinated Tweek, who can never sleep, is the only one who has seen them at their 3:30 am visits. The boys do not believe him, but they all agree to sleep over at Tweek's house to write their report and so that he can prove to them that the underpants gnomes do in fact exist. Planning to stay up all night to write their report and to witness the gnomes, the boys commence to drink pots of strong coffee prepared by Mr. Tweek. High on coffee (including from chewing on the grounds) time passes to 3:30 am and they have made no progress on their paper.

Earlier that day Tweek's father is visited by John Poston from Harbucks coffee corporation who offers him $500,000 to buy out his store. When he refuses to sell, Poston tells him that he will open his Harbucks store immediately next door to Tweek's coffee shop. When Tweek suggests that this could put him out of business, Poston replies, 'This is a capitalist country pal. Get used to it'. Mr. Tweek is worried about the fate of his business and, unsure of what to do, he complains to his wife that 'they really have my balls in a vice grip'.[3] Worried about his fate and how 'the corporate machine is ruining America', Mr. Tweek hatches a plan to get the boys to write their report about corporate take overs. In fact he writes the report himself and delivers it the boys complete just after 3:30 am. The boys agree to use Mr. Tweek's paper. In their excitement about having the report written for them, the boys (excepting Tweek) do not notice the underpants gnomes enter the bedroom to steal Tweek's underpants from his dresser. As they go about their business, the gnomes sing:

Time to go to work, work all night. Gotta get underpants we.
We won't stop until we have underpants. Lots of yummy underpants we.

The following day the boys present the report to the school board.

As the voluminous corporate automaton bulldozes its way through bantam America, what will become of the endeavouring American family? Perhaps there is no stopping the corporate machine.

The school board love the report, Mr Garrison gets to keep his job and the townspeople decide to join the boys in 'the fight against corporate takeovers'. They take the case to the Mayor who decides that if more than half of the town's population vote in favour, she will not allow Harbucks to open in South Park. The boys, relatively unaware of what is going on, are brought in as puppets to the anti-Harbucks campaign that ensues. The result is a battle by two sides each void of the principles that they espouse. Mr. Tweek and the school board use the kids in television commercials to sell their political beliefs. Poston, whose political arguments about free-enterprise fail, develops an advertising campaign targeting children to drink coffee – 'It's yum diddly-icious. It makes you feel super', he says dressed in a Joe Camel costume, 'I have a surprise for you. The new kiddycinno from Harbucks. More sugar and the other goodies kids like with all the caffeine of a normal Double Latte'. This is a stand off between cartoon advertising aimed at children and the use of children as mouth-pieces for adult political interests.

As the vote for or against Harbucks gets closer, the boys are required to make another speech. Realising that they do not know anything about big corporations, they are unsure of what to do. As they try to work out how to proceed, the underpants gnomes reappear – this time all of the boys see them. Kyle asks them why they are stealing underpants, to which one of the gnomes replies – 'Stealing underpants. Big business'. Kyle asks the gnomes to teach them about business. The gnomes agree to tell the boys about their own plans. The rationale is that phase one of their plan is to steal and collect underpants. They

---

[3]This reference to Mr. Tweek's testicles is again an example of a carnivalesque reference to the lower body strata. Further its implication of castration anxiety positions Tweek as subordinate to Harbucks paternalistic power. This motif continues through the episode as Mr. Tweek goes on to suggest that they also have his balls in a 'salad shooter' and a 'juice maker'.

go on to explain that phase three is 'profit'. The gnomes, who profess to be 'geniuses about corporations', do not seem to have yet developed the details of phase two – in fact the details of phase two seem unimportant as long as it leads somehow to phase three. The following day, the boys, armed with their new knowledge from the gnomes, address the town again. In contrast to their speech written by Mr. Tweek, they now suggest that 'Big corporations are good', because 'without big corporations we wouldn't have things like cars and computers and canned soup'. Moving on to talk specifically about Harbucks, Stan suggests 'Even Harbucks coffee started off as a small, little business. But because it made such great coffee and because they ran their business so well, they managed to grow and grow until it became the corporate powerhouse it is today. And that's why we should let Harbucks stay'. Mrs. Tweek, who all along had protested about her husband's use of the boys for his own commercial ends, addresses the group and suggests that before they pass judgement they should at least try the coffee from Harbucks. They do, and they like it because 'it doesn't have that raw sewage taste that Tweeks Coffee has'. The show ends as Poston and Mr. Tweek start negotiating a deal for Mr. Tweek to be the manager of the new Harbucks.

THE SOUTH PARK CARNIVAL

Clearly, *South Park* offers an irreverent depiction of organizations in society. This depiction draws on the logic of the carnival in order to create a parody of organizations that disrupts how such organizations choose to represent themselves and their role in society. In comparing *South Park*'s Harbucks to the 'real' Starbucks, the two organizations have much in common. The name Harbucks itself is a thin disguise – both organizations are large coffee retailers with plans to dominate their chosen markets. The question that I now turn to is that of how does *South Park*'s representation of Harbucks create a carnivalesque critique of Starbucks and what does this mean for the understanding of organizations in society? If carnival humour relies on the overturing of 'normal' hierarchical relationships of power, and the opposition to 'official' culture, then in order for a representation of organizations to be considered carnivalesque, it must contain within it an understanding of what such 'official' culture is. The carnivalesque, therefore, is not dialectical as it contains within it a synthesis of both the normal and the inverted order. Thus the carnivalesque is supplementary and excessive of what might be considered normal, but it does not seek to replace it or be 'better' than it; rather the carnivalesque critique is established by constructs within it what might be considered 'official' by pointing to its inversion.

In *South Park*, this coexistence of the official and the carnivalesque organization appears through the relationship between the main plot of the co-option of the boys in Mr. Tweek's retaliation against the competition from Harbucks, and the related sub-plot of the underpants gnomes. On the surface, it could be argued that *South Park* starts by providing a simple critique of big business imperialism as represented by Harbucks – the large corporation pushing out the 'little guy' in its unquenchable thirst for expansion. This is indeed the narrative that Mr. Tweek draws on in order to defend his own business interests. As the potential critical voice in *South Park*, however, Mr. Tweek's position is only thinly veiled as a front for his own (more modest) commercial interests. Neither he nor Harbucks appears as making any genuine ethical considerations in pursuing their business goals – Harbucks ruthlessly competes for the *South Park* coffee trade and when the argument for free enterprise fails to secure their entry into the market, they instead adopt the plan of marketing high caffeine, high sugar beverages (the 'kiddycinno') to children. Through this plot, ethico-political arguments that favour free enterprise are seen as merely convenient forms of rhetoric that allow for business expansion and the legitimation of greed in an ever-growing desire for corporate growth; if such arguments fail, however, other tactics need to be employed. Through Poston, Harbucks attempts to mobilise the discourse of American free-enterprise to counter the claims by the school council that its intentions are merely examples of corporate neo-imperialism – the desire to grow by taking over and conquering ever new markets. This echoes the letter to shareholders in Starbucks 2001 annual report where it states:

> Even during a year punctuated by unexpected trials, as well as a slowing economy, we achieved the highest net earnings figure in the history of our company and opened a record number of stores ... By December 2001, we opened more than 3,900 locations in North America and more than 1,000 locations in 23 international markets ... We believe that people in these new markets and around the world will embrace our brand and will enjoy the *Starbucks Experience* as part of their daily lives. (italics in original)

Starbucks too conceives of its growth and expansion as its ultimate medal – the marker of its success. Further the self-narrative of Starbucks is that this success is based on the excellence of its product. As they say about their 'Special Reserve' coffee – 'One person, one moment, one cup at a time. Welcome to Starbucks'. In *South Park* Poston defends his corporation by saying 'My argument is simple, this country is founded on free enterprise. Harbucks is an organization that prides itself on great coffee!' Upon being hissed at by the audience he is addressing, Poston responds 'Aw to hell with you!' The suggestion here is that political arguments about the righteousness of capitalism are mere fronts for expansionist corporate agendas – pleasantries that are well suited to the press release and annual report but out of step with the necessities of business.

In opposition, Mr. Tweek positions himself as the innocent small business man whose honest livelihood is being put at risk by the evil forces of big business. Here he works to mobilise a different discourse, one of honest work and family tradition. When first offered $500,000 for his shop by Harbucks, Mr. Tweek replies:

> When my father opened this store thirty years ago, he cared only about one thing – making a great cup of coffee. Sure we may take a little longer to brew a cup, we may not give it fancy names. I guess we just care a little more. And that's why Tweek coffee is still home brewed with the finest beans we can muster. Yes Tweek coffee is a simpler coffee for a simpler America.

As he talks, he holds up a small American flag. Like that of Poston, this is also a discourse of nationalism, but instead of invoking rights to freedom, Tweek draws more on the Protestant tradition of hard work and the nostalgic reminiscing of a bygone era when life was less complicated and honest business men (such as him) could go about their business affairs unencumbered by unfair competition. He positions himself in direct opposition to big business – in justifying his co-option of the boys into his fight against Harbucks he says to Mrs. Tweek:

> I'm serious hon. These boys should learn how the corporate machine is ruining America. You see, I own a coffee shop and now some great, big multi-million dollar company is going to move in and try to take all my business, which means, I may have to shut down and sell my son Tweek into slavery.

Tweek's espoused high minded American left-liberal ideals and his anti-business sentiments, however, are soon placed in contrast to his own tactics of using the boys as mouthpieces for his political convictions.

What we have, then, is the conflict between two different discursive legitimations of competitive business behaviour. The big business free enterprise of Harbucks and the small business anti-monopolism of Mr. Tweek. As has been discussed, each of these discourses is quickly revealed to be a way of legitimating particular instrumental and self interested forms of business behaviour, rather than being a form of reasoning through which business is conducted. In the case of Harbucks and Tweek the businesses that they run are done so through an ethic of survival at all costs (Tweek) and growth at all costs (Harbucks).

Against this background appear the underpants gnomes. Unlike Poston and Mr. Tweek, the gnomes do not attempt to legitimate their behaviour with any high-minded politico-economic discourse. Instead they offer an explanation that is more direct – they have a three phase plan – phase one is to steal and collect underpants, phase three is to get profit and phase two is either undecided or undisclosed. Indeed, it seems that phase two is relatively unimportant as long as it leads to phase three. Stealing underpants is the only thing that the gnomes appear to be able to do – in the parlance of business, it is their 'core competence'. Their goal is to turn this competence into a profitable enterprise. For them this phase two need not allude to meta-narratives of free enterprise or anything else, it merely needs to help them achieve their goal. In Harbucks and Tweek's cases, phase two of their respective plans to monopolise the *South Park* coffee retailing business involves the allusion to politico-economic discourse – in contrast to the gnomes, however, this discourse is not seen as a true conviction or an allusion to natural human rights – instead it is merely a step towards the true justification of profit making. This is the ultimate phase three and business will seek to achieve it through whatever means possible.

In the face of this conflicting discourse, how then is the conduct of business resolved? In *South Park*, it is consumption that wins out in the end. Harbucks coffee tastes better; as Mr. Tweek himself has to admit, the coffee is 'subtle and mild. Mild like the flash of sun on an April morning. This is coffee the way it should be'. This is an appeal to consumption and pleasure as the ultimate decider of economic activity – political and ethical considerations are swept aside and the best tasting coffee wins. This allows Harbucks, like the underpants gnomes, to continue their expansionist quest for profits. It is this appeal to hedonism that proves to be the elusive phase two of the plan. Phase one make coffee – phase two make it so enjoyable that people cannot help but drink it – phase three make profit. In *South Park*, however, the coffee is both pleasurable and problematic because it operates a mind and body altering stimulant. The boys use coffee as a drug in order to stay awake to write their paper. After drinking Mr. Tweek's coffee, Kyle yelps 'woo hoo!' and 'Totally dude, I feel awesome', Stan asserts that 'this stuff rocks', and Cartman says 'Seriously! I feel great!' True to the form of carnival's grotesque realism this pleasure soon turns against the boys and after five hours of drinking coffee they are feeling sick and vomiting.

This drug-like quality of coffee is further examined as Poston, the Harbucks representative develops his advertising campaign based on the Joe Camel cartoon character used to advertise Camel cigarettes. Pleasure is seen here as an illicit bodily experience; one which, with its connotations of drug taking and mind-alternation makes it taboo yet which implies that the pleasure of coffee is one that changes our body-mind experience. Coffee is enjoyable because it is a sensory experience – it is warm, it is bitter, it wakes you up, it makes you feel sort of 'high'. Corporations who, like Starbucks, sell coffee achieve their goals by altering bodies – they provide an ambivalent stimulant that can make you feel good, that can ruin your business, that can fill you with romantic musings and that can even make you vomit.

CARNIVALISING ORGANIZATIONAL KNOWLEDGE

The legacy of modernism is such that mass culture has come to be regarded as an inferior form of culture – at the extreme it is demonised as a danger to civilisation that will 'lead to mass acceptance of and lack of resistance to, all that is bad and wrong in the world' (Docker, 1994: xvii). Exemplifying the very views that Docker critiques, Postman (1987) has suggested that the ascendancy of the 'age of television' (p. 8) has recast the meaning of contemporary public discourse. He argues that 'under the governance of television, [public discourse] has become shrivelled and absurd' (p. 16) and has descended into a 'vast triviality' (p. 6). His proposal is that the growth of television means that we are 'amusing ourselves to [cultural] death', as culture becomes a burlesque where populations are distracted by trivia and culture becomes redefined as 'mere' entertainment. It is here, according to Postman, that 'serious discourse dissolves into giggles' (p. 162).

My point in this paper is that this is not necessarily the case and that popular culture can provide an important and considered critical perspective on the world we live in and of organizations. Carnivalesque humour in particular becomes important as it provides oppor-tunities to critique organizations and their behaviour in an open and playful way. As Docker puts it,

> Bakhtin dislikes the way the enlightenment identified its own notion of reason as reason itself, failing to recog-nise that the fearlessness, frankness, freedom and laughter of carnival table talk was itself a mode of critical reason. (p. 184)

Burrell (1997) has argued that organization studies 'ignores or, worse still, consciously hides that which is thought to be unacceptable in polite company'. Thus, many aspects of organizational life seem not to be discussed in certain formal or public contexts. The result is a virtually dual culture – 'the official culture filled with bright euphemisms, silences and platitudes and an unofficial culture that has . . . its own knowledge of shortages, corruption, and inequality that may . . . be widely known but that may not be introduced in public [official] discourse' (Scott, 1990: 51). This points to the significance of including popular culture on the agenda of organization studies as popular culture provides important under-standings of organizations that, in the case of the carnival, are other to and supplementary of more formal discourse. It is here that an approach closer to cultural studies can add to our knowledge of organizations. The transgressive profanity of carnival can thus provide a broader understanding of organizations as it enables a discussion of issues that might be otherwise considered taboo. It is here that such transgression 'does not deny the taboo but transcends and completes it' (Bataille, 1986/1962: 63).

In such a predicament, the carnivalesque, with its profanity, grotesque realism and mockery of the serious and official is a problematic contender to be considered as 'valid' organizational knowledge. Carnivalesque representations are irreverent and at times obscene; they offer ambivalence in place of certainty and valorise laughter and parody over serious-ness. This is a form of knowledge that is other to 'science' and 'reason' – it relates to an unofficial truth that knows no inhibitions or limitations. The laughing knowledge is one that,

> liberates not only from external censorship, but first of all from the great interior censor; it liberates from the fear that developed in man during thousands of years: fear of the sacred, of prohibitions, of the past, of power. (Bakhtin, 1984a/1965: 94)

In suggesting that popular culture can provide a critique of organizations, in conclusion it must also be noted that such critique is in no way inevitable. Any text, cultural or otherwise, may be open to potentially different readings based on the interests and intertextual resources that one brings to it (Rhodes, 2000). In relation to Starbucks, for example, the 1999 comedy film *Austin Powers: The Spy Who Shagged Me* sees Starbucks' product placements throughout the arch-villain Dr. Evil's headquarters. We also find out that it is investment in Starbucks that has funded Dr. Evil's attempts to achieve world domination. Unlike with *South Park*, however, this use of Starbucks' name was fully endorsed (although not paid for) by the Starbucks corporation. They saw the film not as an analogous critique of their own expan-sionist agenda but rather as a good form of advertising. As George Murphy, Starbucks' Vice President of Publicity, said of the film 'we thought [it] treated our size and identity in a humorous way' (cited in Wheat, 1999). Starbucks' reaction to the film did not acknowledge that it might provide a meaningful critique that would have any negative impact on them; this was both their reading of the film and the reading that they expected from their potential customers. What this highlights is that popular culture has a potential critique rather than an inherent one. It is this very potential, however, that a critical approach to understanding organizations might be able to develop such that popular culture can be used as a point of departure for the study of organizations. In part, it is the development of this potential that this paper has tried to contribute to.

As Czarniawska (1997) has described 'if we want to understand a society, or some part of a society, we have to discover its repertoire of legitimate stories and find out how this has evolved' (p. 16). The evolution of carnival humour, stretching back beyond the middle ages, is a good example of how understandings of organizations not available in conventional theory are manifested in the narratives that are legitimate in popular culture. Indeed, as well as being represented in genres different to those of theory, carnival mocks formal conventions whilst at the same time make them more transparent. If the 'main fount of organizational knowledge is the narrative' (Czarniawska, 1997: 21), then it is important to be aware of the diversity of narratives in which such knowledge is put forward and the diversity of genres through which it is constructed. My argument here is in popular culture, the use of carnivalesque in cartoons has much to inform us about knowledge or organizations. Its importance particularly is that rather than offering the finalised truths associated with more scientific approaches to organization theory, carnival representations do not tell us about the single right way, but rather work to parody and relativise power – to always suggest alternatives and keep power in check. Such critique is ambivalent in that it does not send a 'message' that stands over the narrative, but rather it laughs at a world to which it belongs. Carnival is thus opposed to dogmatic seriousness – its 'laughter purifies from dogmatism, from the intolerant and the petrified; it liberates from fanaticism and pedantry, from fear and intimidation, from didacticism, naiveté and illusion, from the single meaning, the single level, from sentimentality' (Bakhtin, 1984a/1965: 123). Perhaps organization theory can learn from carnival's example.

References

Atkinson, Paul (1990) *The ethnographic imagination: Textual constructions of reality*, London: Routledge.

Bakhtin, Mikhail M. (1984a/1965) *Rabelais and his world* (Hélène Iswolsky, trans.), Bloomington, IN: Indiana University Press.

Bakhtin, Mikhail M. (1984b) In: Caryl Emerson (ed. and trans.), *Problems of Dostoyevsky's poetics*, Minneapolis, MN: University of Minnesota Press.

Bataille, Georges (1991/1947) *The accursed share: An essay on the general economy* (R. Hurley, trans.), New York: Zone Books.

Bataille, Georges (1986/1962) *Erotism: Death and sensuality* (M. Dalwood, trans.), San Francisco, CA: City Light Books.

Benshoff, Harry M. (1992) Heigh-ho, heigh-ho, is Disney high or low? From silly cartoons to postmodern politics, *Animation Journal*, Fall, 62–85.

Bourdieu, Pierre (1998) *On television and journalism*, London: Pluto Press.

Burrell, Gibson (1997) *Pandemonium: Towards a retro-organization theory*, London: Sage.

Butler, Richard (1997) Stories as experiments in social enquiry, *Organization Studies*, **18**(6), 927–948.

Czarniawska, Barbara (1997) *Narrating the organization: Dramas of institutional identity*, Chicago, IL: University of Chicago Press.

Czarniawska-Joerges, Barbara and Guillet de Monthoux, Pierre (1994) *Good novels, better management: Reading organizational realities into fiction*, Reading: Harwood.

Davies, Ioan (1995) *Cultural studies and beyond: Fragments of empire*, London: Routledge.

De Cock, Christian (2000) Reflections on fiction, representation, and organization studies: An essay with special reference to the work of Jorge Luis Borges, *Organization Studies*, **21**(3), 589–609.

Docker, John (1987) In defence of popular TV: Carnivalesque v. left pessimism, *Continuum*, **1**(2).

Docker, John (1994) *Postmodernism and popular culture: A cultural history*, Cambridge: Cambridge University Press.

Eco, Umberto (1984) The frames of comic "Freedom" In: T.A. Sebeok (ed.), *Carnival*, Berlin: de Gruyter, pp. 1–10.

Fiske, John (1987) *Television culture*, London: Routledge.

Giroux, Henry A. (2000) *Impure acts: The practical politics of cultural studies*, New York: Routledge.

Grice, Shane and Humphries, Maria (1997) Critical management studies in postmodernity: Oxymorons in outer space? *Journal of Organization Change Management*, **10**(5), 112–125.

Hassard, John and Holliday, Ruth (1998) Introduction. In: J. Hassard and R. Holliday (eds.), *Organization – representation: Work and organization in popular culture*, London: Sage, pp. 1–15.

Jung, Hwa Yol (1998) Bakhtin's dialogical body politics. In: M.M. Bell and M. Gardiner (eds.), *Bakhtin and the human sciences*, London: Sage, pp. 95–111.

Knights, David and Wilmott, Hugh (1999) *Management lives: Power and identity in work organizations*, London: Sage.

Krönig, Jurgen (2000) Elite versus mass: The impact of television in an age of globalization, *Historical Journal of Film, Radio and Television*, **20**(1), 43–49.

Lindvall, Terence R. and Melton, J. Matthew (1997) Towards a post-modern animated discourse. In: J. Pilling (ed.), *A reader in animation studies*, London: John Libbey, pp. 203–220.

Parker, Trey and Stone, Matt (1997) *Gnomes/prehistoric ice man*, episode #217, South Park Series 2, Volume 9 Video: Comedy Central/Warner Vision International 3984-27533-3. Full Transcript of script at http://www.mrhatshellhole.com /scripts/217.htm accessed July 31st 2002.

Pechey, Graham (1998) Modernity and chronotopicity in Bakhtin. In: D. Shepherd (ed.), *The contexts of Bakhtin: Philosophy, authorship. aesthetics*, Amsterdam: Harwood, pp. 173–183.

Phillips, Nelson (1995) Telling organizational tales: On the role of narrative fiction in the study of organizations, *Organization Studies*, **16**(4), 625–649.

Postman, Neil (1987) *Amusing ourselves to death*, London: Methuen.

Rhodes, Carl (2002) Politics and popular culture: Organizational carnival in the springfield nuclear power plant. In: S. Clegg (ed.), *Management and organization*, Amsterdam: John Benjamins, pp. 119–138.

Rhodes, Carl (2001) *Writing organization: (Re)presentation and control in narratives at work*, Amsterdam: John Benjamins.

Rhodes, Carl (2000) Reading and writing organizational life, *Organization*, **7**(1), 7–29.

Rowe, David (1995) *Popular cultures: Rock music, sport and the politics of pleasure*, London: Sage.

Scott, James C. (1990) *Domination and the arts of resistance: Hidden transcripts*, New Haven, CT: Yale University Press.

Smith, Warren, Higgins, Matthew, Parker, Martin and Lightfoot, Geoff (2001) *Science fiction and organizations*, London: Routledge.

Stallybrass, Peter and White, Allon (1986) *The politics and poetics of transgression*, London: Methuen.

Starbucks 2000 Annual Report.

Starbucks 2001 Annual Report.

Starbucks Web Site (http://www.starbucks.com) accessed 1 July 2001.

Storey, John (2001) Postmodernism and popular culture. In: S. Sim (ed.), *The Routledge companion to postmodernism*, London: Routledge, pp. 147–173.

Storey, John (1998) *An introduction to cultural theory and popular culture*, 2nd ed., Athens, GA: University of Georgia Press.

Weber, Samuel (1996) *Mass mediauras: Form, technics, media*, Stanford, CA: Stanford University Press.

Wheat, Alynda (1999) One man's insult is another man's publicity, *Fortune*, August.

Fiction and Humor in Transforming McDonald's Narrative Strategies

DAVID BOJE, MICHAELA DRIVER and YUE CAI

The article builds on and expands a narrative perspective on strategy. Specifically, we develop a more Bakhtinian model in which corporate fiction and humor serve the firm's strategic dialogic imagination. We develop this model through an analysis of the McDonald's corporation. Through the grotesque humor of its fictitious Ronald McDonald world, McDonald's develops its dialogic imagination and transforms its strategic narratives. That is, strategic transformation is enacted narratively in and through its corporate fiction regenerating and revitalizing existing strategic narratives. Implications for research on McDonald's in particular and strategy in general are discussed.

INTRODUCTION

The view that strategy is a type of narrative seems to have arrived in mainstream organization research (Barry and Elmes, 1997). Since then linguistic and discursive analyses of strategy have been undertaken. For example, Rindova, Becerra and Contardo (2004) analyzed the language games of competitive wars and Starkey and Crane (2003) examined environmental strategy relative to narrative constructions of firm identity. These studies seem to validate Barry and Elmes' (1997) view on strategy in which multiple voices, such as authors and readers, co-create narrative fiction, which then can be examined, like fiction, in terms of various genres and attributes of success, such as credibility and novelty.

Building on this narrative perspective and particularly the Bakhtinian view, that strategy is a dialogical rather than a monological narrative, that is, a co-construction of various voices rather than one singular voice of some strategist for example (Barry and Elmes, 1997), we examine one voice that seems to be missing from the strategy discourse to date and that is the voice of corporate fiction and humor. While Bakhtin's theory has been applied in management studies of humor before, for example in Rhodes' (2001) study of carnivalesque grotesque humor in Homer Simpsons' popular culture and Boje's (2001) study of activist carnivalesque street theatre of resistance to Nike Corporation, we do not focus on humor as mocking, degrading debasement of corporations (nuclear power plant in Simpsons; Nike by the activists), but rather focus on the positive force of self-renewal and self-regeneration in fiction and humor and the role this plays for strategy.

Specifically, we will focus on the case of the McDonald's corporation to use Bakhtin's (1968) method as an illustration of how corporations may use narrative fiction to develop dialogic imagination and novel voices in strategy narratives. Using the cartoon series produced for McDonald's, the McDonaldland videos, we explore how grotesque humor degrades fictitious actors as they descend into a world of lower bodily functions, degenerating into grotesque and ridiculous caricatures of themselves. But because of and through this degeneration, the fictitious actors also gain access to miraculous transformation and redeem and regenerate as they ascend from this lower bodily stratum. The lower bodily stratum symbolizes death as well as fertility as the McDonaldland characters are reduced to excrement but are also re-born from the womb.

As such we explore how McDonaldland transforms McDonald's corporation in the lower material bodily womb of the earth and underworld to immortalize the 'spectacle of the marketplace' (Bakhtin, 1968: 393). We hypothesize that this occurs more through thrusting the fast food banquet into the underworld (McDonaldland) where it becomes transformed into the grotesque banquet. And in this way, McDonald's Corporation achieves double-body: the dying of the old McDonald's that has gone out of fashion; the regeneration of the new body in the hellish 'flames of carnival' (Bakhtin, 1968: 394).

In short, we suggest that a Bakhtinian reading of McDonald's use of fiction and humor uncovers a dimension of strategy and strategic transformation that has been missed in prior research. Management research has not examined the strategic use of fiction and humor, and, from our analysis as strategy being read primarily as rational, would likely consider corporate fiction and humor through Ronald McDonald videos, public relations and advertising, just another rational action to promote growth and profit maximization.

The paper proceeds as follows. First, we examine how McDonald's strategy has been researched in organizational literature making the case for the missing dimension of strategy. Then we explore what this dimension might look like from a narrative, particularly a Bakhtinian, perspective illustrating it with examples from McDonald's and then discussing its wider implications for organization studies.

MCDONALD'S STRATEGY IN THE LITERATURE

A review of some of the flagship management journals reveals 48 articles published on McDonald's strategy between 1985 and 2003 alone in three Academy of Management Journals, 11 in AMR, four in AMJ and 33 in AME. In these articles McDonald's is cited and researched as an example for a highly successful competitive strategy and for its exemplary application of rational, Taylorist, systems of operation. Bachmann (2002), for example, includes the saga of McDonald's using the QVC (quality, value and cleanliness) formula to be successful in a market that better-financed firms fumbled or rejected, and thereby McDonald's not only laid claim to the fast food era but also created opportunities for nearly limitless growth; McDonald's out competed Burger Chef (General Foods) and Burger King (Pillsbury):

> The odds against small, undercapitalized McDonald's competing with food industry giants were great. But they stuck to their strategy of providing inexpensive, quickly served hamburgers and maintaining a slavish devotion to their QVC formula—Quality, Value, Cleanliness. In the end they won the race, not by diversifying but by specializing. (Bachmann, 2002: 1)

The recurrent theme in this as in several other articles seems to be that McDonald's is attaining, if not limitless, certainly enormous growth of the kind only firms like Wal-Mart may match (Safferstone, 2002) through the single-minded adherence to a system standardized to Tayloristic precision (Kelly, 1997) and carefully micromanaged in every detail (Quinn et al., 1996; Usher, 1999).

McDonald's is lauded for its exemplary rational systems of production and product development (Meyer and DeTore, 1999), strategic planning (Beam, 1996) and knowledge management (Quinn *et al.*, 1996). Along similar lines, McDonald's is applauded for its exemplary and consistent strategy across the organization, its systems and culture (Robinson and Dechant, 1997) and for having measurable targets and progress checks at every level (Robinson and Dechant, 1997) allowing it to collect and act on corrective feedback for continuously improving quality (Usher, 1999).

Additionally, McDonald's is praised for the relentless application of rational systems of standardization and control that make McDonald's highly consistent across locations (Hallowell, Bowen and Knoop, 2002; Robinson and Dechant, 1997) and allow it to offer exemplary service reliability across time and locations (Usher, 1999). Along those lines, McDonald's has been lauded for its exemplary and strategic use of information technology (Quinn *et al.*, 1996) and its thick manuals of detailed procedures (Usher, 1999) that allow managers to create a nearly scientific approach to everything from service delivery (Meyer and DeTore, 1999) to the management of people. Mc Donald's has not only adopted elaborate technologies for employee scheduling (Quinn *et al.*, 1996) it has also sought to control employee values (Organ, McFillen and Mitchell, 1985; Starkey and Crane, 2003) and the display of emotions by employees at work (Ashforth, 1993; Wharton and Erickson, 1993). It has also attempted to engineer the behavior of its customers by providing role models who act out appropriate scripts for behavior in McDonald's restaurants (Bateson, 2002).

McDonald's has also applied a rational and consistent approach to franchising and has turned its experience and decision-making skills relative to the management of franchises as well as locations and design into a strategic resource (Combs and Ketchen, 1999; Nutt, 1999); so much so that it has been called 'the king of franchising' (Beam, 1996: 1). McDonald's has also developed a rational and aggressive approach to branding and capturing market share (Meyer and DeTore, 1999) and strategically used size and brand awareness to build competitive fortifications with 'moats' to protect against competitors (Sexton, 2001). This has allowed McDonald's to gain enormous power and sheltered it in industry shakeouts making it one of the Big 3 in the fast food business, alongside Wendy's and Burger King (Safferstone, 2002: 161), gaining it the reputation of being one of the 'gladiators of the competitive environment' (Brock, 2000: 259).

McDonald's exemplary application of rational systems strategies to almost every aspect of its business has made it a metaphor for a powerful if not glamorous organization that seems to mass-produce success in the same fashion that it mass-produces hamburgers (Marks and Mirvis, 2001). It has also made McDonald's an example of monolithic and perhaps overly simplistic strategic and managerial practices (Calori and Dufour, 1995) that verges on a cookie-cutter approach (Hallowell *et al.* 2002).

Yet, this cookie-cutter approach has provided the foundation for McDonald's global strategy, which seems to be overwhelmingly successful (Beam, 2002; Gupta and Govindarajan, 2001) accounting for over 60 percent of revenues in 1999 alone (Ireland *et al.*, 2001) and making it a symbol of globalization (Evans, 2002) as well as a powerful force in the global economy (Ireland *et al.*, 2001) with 30,000 outlets in 121 nations. McDonald's has been praised for pursuing growth as aggressively and systematically overseas as in domestic markets (Brock, 2000) and for its exemplary global value-chain management (Gupta and Govindarajan, 2001) and global knowledge deployment (Beam, 2002). It has also been lauded for its systematic and successful strategies of internationalization through strategic alliances, joint ventures, foreign direct investment and wholly owned new ventures and licensing (Burton *et al.*, 2000; Ireland *et al.*, 2001; Wright *et al.*, 1998). Such successful internationalization in turn allows McDonald's to leverage its global power, by, for example, getting preferential legal treatment around patent rights in Vietnam (Van Glinow and Clarke, 1995), and to prevail successfully in riskier, developing economies like Russia (Shama, 1993).

While McDonald's has been praised for its global-but-local approach (Gupta and Govindarajan, 2001; Hall, 2001; Kanter and Dretler, 1998), and its ability to stick to its core strategy (Nayyar, 1993) while allowing variation on the periphery around things like facility design and capacity (Usher, 1999), it has also had problems adjusting to the norms of other cultures such as, for example, in the former Soviet Union (Ashforth, 1993) and in the UK (Bateson, 2002). Consequently, McDonald's also had to modify its strategy and adapt to local conditions by, for example, varying its menu (Hall, 2001) or adjusting its training and recruitment practices (Gupta and Govindarajan, 2001) to accommodate local preferences. For example, in Hong Kong, McDonald's tried to move in on the local cooking territory not with the usual burgers and fries but with the traditional Chinese rice dishes. McDonald's stated that the reason these new items were created was to provide their customers with a variety of choices in the local setting. Another great example is McDonald's creation of Green Curry Burger in the Hong Kong outlets.

In fact, green curry is a taste of Thai but incredibly popular in Hong Kong. Attacking the local market taste with a third nation specialty is another one of McDonald's global-but-local approaches.

Along similar lines, McDonald's has successfully adjusted its part-time employment practices to switch from the shrinking pool of teenage workers to disabled workers (Hall and Hall, 1994; Reno, 1994; McWilliams, 2001) and a growing pool of senior citizens who, at little or no training cost, provide a reliable source of labor (Feldman, 1990; Mirvis, 1997; Paul and Townsend, 1993; Robinson and Dechant, 1997). McDonald's has also used a rational systems approach to adjusting its training strategy for its corporate lawyers enabling them to more effectively work around labor laws and avoiding having to hire temporary workers full time with commensurate benefits (Thomas, 2002).

While some praise such strategic adaptation and McDonald's rational systems approach to everything including the systematic circumvention of labor law as contributing legitimately to competitive advantage (Thomas, 2002), others criticize McDonald's for exploiting unfair advantage under the guise of rational strategic goals. In one such critique, McDonald's labor practices are used to illustrate the plight of the working poor who, in the absence of corporate strategies that develop their careers, seem stuck in jobs that do not pay enough to make a living and have no benefits (Kossek and Huber-Yoder, 1997).

Along similar lines, Seiders and Berry (1998) mention McDonald's in the context of firms who are at risk of losing their customers' credibility and loyalty and cite:

> The 1995 action brought against McDonald's by a woman who allegedly suffered extensive third-degree burns when she spilled a cup of the restaurant's coffee that is served at 180 degrees. The outcome was extreme and, in the view of some, recurrent—because McDonald's had previously received 700 reports of coffee burns. (Seiders and Berry, 1998: 6)

In this case, McDonald's seemed at risk of being perceived not only as unresponsive but also as negligent by customers again because it thought it more important to stick to its strategy and detailed procedures for serving coffee rather than adapting and being responsive to changing expectations.

By the same token, McDonald's has also made strides to be responsive and to adapt its strategy to better align with stakeholder expectations. For its acts of corporate social responsibility, for example, hiring disabled workers and accommodating disabled customers (Hall and Hall, 1994; McWilliams, 2001; Reno, 1994) or sponsoring Ronald McDonald houses, McDonald's has been praised as a an exemplary global citizen (Kanter and Dretler, 1998; McWilliams, 2001). It has also been praised widely for having extensive environmental programs (Anderson and Bateman, 2000; Berry and Rondinelli, 1998; Harrison and Caron, 1996) and for striving to be an ecologically sustainable organization (Starik and Rands, 1995) with a strategic reputation for environmental stewardship (Jennings and Zandbergen, 1995) strong enough to pressure other firms in its value chain to become greener as well (Russo and Fouts, 1997).

Highly publicized strategic alliances and collaborations, such as McDonald's partnership with the Environmental Defense Fund and The Natural Step group and its work on biodegradable containers with Earthshell (Berry and Rondinelli, 1998; Bradbury and Clair, 1999; Starik and Rands, 1995) enhance McDonald's reputation for being environmentally responsible (Rondinelli and London, 2003). Of course, they are also part and parcel of a strategy enacted specifically to signal social responsibility to McDonald's stakeholders (McWilliams, 2001). McDonald's alliances with environmental groups such as the Environmental Defense Fund illustrate how McDonald's seeks to carefully engineer strategic adaptations that seem responsive enough to stakeholders but do not distract from its core competitive advantage (Bachmann, 2002). Moreover, they illustrate the fine balance that McDonald's has sought between rigidity and flexibility, adaptation and renewal. As Starkey and Crane (2003) observe McDonald's cannot adopt a truly environmentalist strategy without losing that which provides its competitive advantage. The transformation that turns the golden arches green would threaten McDonald's very existence:

> In the story of green alliances, for instance, the prince must stay in some ways a frog because a transformative kiss from business would be the kiss of death for the environmental group and, indeed, for the legitimating aspect of the green partnership for business itself. Similarly, McDonalds cannot turn its golden arches green. (Starkey and Crane, 2003:13, quoted in Livesey, 1999: 33)

While this latter research adopts a specifically narrative perspective on strategy examining McDonald's strategic identity as constructed through stories of green alliances for example, the tenor of most of the research on McDonald's strategy seems to be that strategy is an uncontested narrative. That is, strategy serves as the grand narrative through which the organization's epic journey—away from weaknesses and threats toward strengths and opportunities (Barry and Elmes, 1997) is told. Hence, the literature we have reviewed is replete with examples of how McDonald's brilliantly implements one or another strategic move and how, eventually, even its greatest shortcomings may be turned into competitive strength.

A BAKHTINIAN READING OF MCDONALD'S STRATEGY

In contrast to the monological, grand narrative approach we have examined above in organization research, we suggest building on a Bakhtinian, more plurivocal, conception of McDonald's strategy (Barry and Elmes, 1997). In this conception, strategy is not only narrative but is served by the dialogic imagination (Bakhtin, 1981) developed through grotesque humor and fiction. Specifically, through strategy as dialogic imagination McDonaldland allows McDonald's corporation to descend into the lower bodily stratum where the mud slinging and degradation of its critics (McDonaldization) contributes to the 'spectacle of the marketplace' (Bakhtin, 1968: 393) and provides new avenues for degeneration but also regeneration. As McDonald's plays with grotesque fiction and humor in McDonaldland, it develops its dialogic imagination, so that transformations experienced by the fictitious characters of McDonaldland feed into its strategic narrative (Barry and Elmes, 1997) regenerating its rational strategy and contributing to its enormous success in the marketplace.

Dialogic imagination allows corporations to transform strategy through multiple voices and competing definitions (heteroglossia): 'there is a constant interaction between meanings, all of which have the potential of conditioning others' (Bakhtin, 1981: 426). Specifically, through the use of grotesque fiction and humor actors and behaviors undergo a dialectic transformation and metamorphosis in which degradation is turned into transformation in their social context. So the degradation and regeneration in the fictitious sphere allows for transformation in reality, which Bakhtin (1968) captures by analyzing a series of words all beginning with 'R': renewal, rebirth, regeneration, reconstruction, and revitalization. Grotesque humor, then defines a path of transformation by decent into the underworld degradations, that accomplishes rebirth in the cycle of decent (death) and ascent (metamorphosis). As individuals transcend in terms of metamorphosis either ascending or descending, the characteristics of the original physics of the body are abandoned while new images become the center of the system (Boje and Cai, 2004).

This focus on strategic renewal and regeneration is not only in contrast to the monologic, epic narratives of much of organizational research on McDonald's but also to applications of the grotesque method used by critics of McDonaldization. McDonaldization, a term coined by Ritzer (1993), suggests that McDonald's is a form of cultural imperialism and points to the negative impacts of McDonald's expansion (Boas and Chain, 1976). McDonaldization writings describe grotesque humor but focus on its degenerative role as it is used in the mudslinging by McDonaldization foes (including counter-globalization, slow food, vegetarian, & animal rights movements). José Bové, of France, for example, did dismantle a McDonald's restaurant one night, and deposit it (and dung) on the front lawn of a government official (Kincheloe, 2002: 7); women wear nothing but a bikini of lettuce to burlesquely protest animal rights for PETA (People for the Ethical Treatment of Animals). There is grotesque humor, parody and satire on the Internet; a 2003 United Kingdom exhibit featured a bronze casting called Last McSupper showing Christ and company eating a McMeal and Unholy Trinity shows Ronald McDonald crucified, flanked by also-crucified Hamburglar and a Big Mac.[i] We assert that these studies do not address the grotesque method for self-renewal as dialogic imaginings of the corporation.

The grotesque method, as part of a strategic dialogic imagination, allows the firm to regenerate itself as it develops ascending and descending images along the vertical line from higher official strata to the lower underworld strata. The grotesque method, as part of a strategic dialogic imagination, allows the firm to regenerate itself as it develops ascending and descending images along the vertical line from higher official strata to the lower underworld strata. Simultaneously, McDonald's corporate bodies are renewed for the next generation of employees and customers. Ronald, being the clown-symbol of McDonald's Corporation, he is carefully and detailed controlled, every aspect of his behavior is micromanaged. Ronald's clownery shows that the fashion, speech, and gestures change with the fashion, as a way to renew McDonald's to each generation of customers and employees (to old dies; the new is born) (Boje and Cai, 2004). The images are grotesque because they are material bodily images that involve animal, human, earthly and cosmic bodily tropes where each convexity (cave, stomach, womb, mouth, gaping jaws) has symbolic meaning. Bodily fluids and substances (spit, urine, dung, semen, and blood) also have grotesque meanings that are highly ambivalent (conveying both degradation/descent and renewal/regeneration). Degradation images include being disrobed (literally or rhetorically), having dung and urine tossed at you, being an official mocked in public, having official rituals degraded such as uncrowning the king. Finally, the grotesque method calls us to pay special attention to religious symbolism (transubstantiation, ecclesiastic travesties, gospel story theme allusions, and dying and being born again). In its ancient meaning carnival meant the 'procession of the dead gods' (Bakhtin, 1968: 393). Our task is to trace the full cycle of descent and ascent along the vertical plane and trace as well how it is incorporated into strategic advantage along the horizontal plane of time (historic renewal) and space (global expansion).

One illustration of the dialogic imagination is an exploration of a video (Have Time Will Travel, produced by Klasky/Cuspo) in which Ronald (clown-like leader of the gang, wears red and white shirt and socks, and has a yellow jumper, with a M over his heart, and it says Ronald on his back; can transubstantiate one material into another) goes on an adventure with his friends. These friends are themselves transfigured in some way as they represent various foods who as characters have risen from being dead meat. For example, there is Birdie who used to be a Chicken McNugget but now is part bird and part girl. She is the most intelligent and enthusiastic of Ronald's friends and has a bird's beak, bird's wings, with fingers, and bird's feet which she recently keeps shoed, and wears a pink jumper. Grimace is the most dim-witted, but a loveable purple blob symbolizing a milk shake who used to have four arms but in recent times has only two. Hamburglar is a boy with a hamburger head (in 1971 his head literally was a hamburger, in recent time the head is more like a Rugrat character, the bandit's mask replaced by sunglasses, the flowing black cape by a blue denim jacket with a big 'M' on the back). Hamburglar has an insatiable appetite for burgers, and his addiction prompts him to steal them; he also is a little prankster and is forever trying to get out of work (which gives Ronald opportunity to give him corrective sermons).

In the particular video, we'd like to examine (Have Time Will Travel) Ronald and the gang enter McDonaldland, a make-believe underworld into which Ronald descends for his adventures and is transformed from the normal human-like clown into a cartoon look-alike. In this adventure, Ronald and his friends travel in a time machine to a prehistoric land where a huge dinosaur eats their time machine. To save the day Ronald blows up a small burger into a giant patty, the size of a mini-McDonald's restaurant, in which he and his friends hide. Then they are eaten by a T-Rex as the giant burger is swallowed whole into the belly of the beast and travels coffin-like down to the belly floor. There the gang finds their time machine and fly out of the T-Rex, presumably through the digestive track and out the back end to safety and back to their own time.

In this 30-minute cartoon there are many images of transformation from the burger's transformation into a giant, restaurant-like, patty, which also serves as coffin or ship in a biblical Jonah and the whale story to the transformation from dinosaur meal to excrement, a descent into the belly and the ascent into rebirth as if risen from the dead. These images may demonstrate how McDonald's dialogically imagines itself. While competitors and McDonaldization foes may seek to undermine its strength or even contest its identity, in McDonaldland McDonald's is always reborn, always rises from the ashes and takes on biblical, and miraculous characteristics.

So while the underworld adventure journeys of McDonald's into McDonaldland in the cartoons may not directly explain how McDonald's crafts its strategy (Mintzberg, 1987), they nonetheless represent a voice, or multiple voices, in the multiple narratives that constitute strategy (Barry and Elmes, 1997). From this perspective it becomes possible to hypothesize a link between the material womb of bodily regeneration and the RAP (Recognition, Attitude of Competitiveness, & Patriotism) that was McDonald's management philosophy, taught in the early 1970s, in Hamburger University to counter restaurant infiltration by unionists (Boas and Chain, 1976). Unionization is one of the cosmic fears that its McDonaldization project might be halted; the other fear is that communities, as they did in the early 1970s might stop McDonald's from building more franchises. The 'P' in RAP, is the gesture of wrapping McDonald's in the flag of patriotism, with All American Meals, and all-American boys and girls behind the counter. This strategy worked during Vietnam, to protect McDonald's from the assault against all Americana symbols in that era, however, in contemporary times, McDonald's has come to symbolize negative aspects of globalization (the 'P' in RAP has become a problem). The Klasky and Cuspo Production video series is careful not to invoke patriotic symbolism; the more religious symbols come to the forefront; this we believe is the strategic shift: from patriotic imagery to carnivalesque banquet image that is wrapped in religious symbolism.

McDonaldland plays a very strategic role in dealing with McDonald's 'cosmic fear' by revitalizing official corporate management philosophy in the cosmic equivalent of the lower material bodily stratum of a specially crafted underworld grotesque banquet, where Ronald performs many miracles. In McDonaldland, official conceptions of management philosophy undergo a process of 'carnivalization: in every Whacky Ronald episode (Bakhtin, 1968: 394). There is even a Whacky vision of hell, a parody of a Disneyland theme park in Birthday World (read Disney World), where characters descend into theme park rides from an intimidating, gloomish, mechanical hell; as McDonald's is working more closely than every with Disney to merchandise characters in Happy Meals, this is a form of self-reflective humor and self-degradation, which we argue serves some strategic purpose.

Specifically, we suggest that one of the transformative roles of humor and fiction is to allow for the passing away of the old McDonald's strategy as its former corporate body, linguistically speaking, becoming imagined with new emergent meaning. We suggest that in the McDonaldland Klasky and Cuspo videos McDonald's is dialogically imagining strategic changes, developing biography, enshrining ancient culture and giving McDonaldization museum status, and exploring the galactic expansion of McDonald's fast food empire. We believe (consciously or unconsciously) corporate McDonald's is running scenarios of its destiny, deciding how to extend its greatness, and exercising creatively its managerial force while, not just globally, but with super galactic aims: boldly going where no fast food giant has gone before, conquering fashion tastes, renewing vitality, creating something of enormous strategic consequence.

When McDonald's invests in the production of videos like Visitors from Outer Space where McDonald's takes on galactic proportions, the carnivalizing of space, with grotesque planetary and alien bodies, embeds the spatial radii in the McDonaldization of future time. The animation is quite Baroque, lots of visual grotesque detail and exaggeration, interlaced graphically with corporate images. It is McDonald's corporate terrestrial space embrace of the temporality of human and nature time, where the corporation seems almost to swallow space and time in its gaping mouth. It is hyperbole and fantastic 'chronotopic artistic imagination' (Bakhtin, 1986: 46). This is a space fairy tale, yet also a realistic niche for futuristic corporate expansion; after all people in space need their fast food, and as such McDonaldization is double-bodied (on the threshold between globalization and Star Wars Empire). In our analysis, we pause frequently to analyze the mixing of real corporate markers (restaurant in McDonaldland Square, M's emblazoned on buildings, characters, and space vehicles) and how charming it is embedded in a space fairy tale that morphs into a legend of Fast Food Star Wars, a hyperbole. In this romantic tale, the rebellion is already crushed, the Jedi Knight (Hamburglar) is rescued by his father Darth Vader, played by Ronald McDonald, revealed behind the grotesque mask to be mechanistic rationality, all made concrete and graphically visible in the territorialization of outer space. This is not just artistic fantasy, it is corporately strategic infusion of fantasy time with corporate logo, and it is 'naïve realism' the idea that the public would put up statues in its metropolitan parks to the McDonaldland characters.

Striving for a polyphonic narrative that is graphically visualized, allows us to extend strategic narrative analysis into its visual imagination. As Bakhtin (1986: 49) puts it, 'time and space merge here into an inseparable unity, both in the plot itself and in its individual images'. The concrete locality of solar system, is an echo to McDonaldization, both its celebration, its parodic degradation, and in the process its renewal and regeneration descent and ascension; uncrowning and crowning), in fact, its metamorphosis as corporate futuristic strategic scenario. As we transcribe and analyze the dual-one (visual and verbal) dialog, we see that the videos are imbued with the mood of their contemplators, the McDonald's executives, the Leo Burnett ad agency, and the Klasky-Cuspo visual talent. Together, in this video, they condense strategy and space, into historical future; McDonald's strategic is chronotopic, its plan graphically imagined, McDonaldization globally, transformed into a galactic adventure, but also a strategic biography, in the early stages of becoming, a metamorphosis that could not occur with out grotesque humor (the carnivalesque). Temporally extending the corporate life cycle back to the past, into the future.

As a final illustration of dialogic imagination, we will look at another Klasky/Cuspo video (The Legend of Grimace Island). Grimace was created in 1971, part of the original McDonaldland gang; then he had four arms, and was furry; he lost two arms by the end of the 1970s. He is Ronald's most loyal and naïve friend. Grimace symbolizes chaos, a bodily doublet of cosmic chaos and fear. The word Grimace means to 'quince' in 'fear', his wry expressions seeking to amuse with twisting, contorting fright, not with disgust, not grim, but just anxious, timid, uneasy, ever-vigilant for danger. His corporate graphic material bodily construction is that of a purple mike shake, but symbolizing also the cosmic shake that accidentally triggers and always unleashes the chaos effect. His bodily character is grotesque: overweight, all stomach.

Grimace is a perfect example of what Bakhtin (1968: 459–61) means by ambivalence, the praise-abuse duality role-played in the episodes. He is the dual-body, the becoming chaos and the degraded fool. His praise-blame duality is blame and ridicule for being dim-witted and awe of his chaos power. His character is ambivalence, the double-body of shaking cosmic terror and accidental cosmic chaos. The comic drama series work out conflicts inherent in the praise-abuse of the other characters: Birdie is praised for her intelligence, and ridiculed by Hamburglar for her goodness; Hamburglar is praised for his inventiveness, but scolded often by Ronald and Birdie for his lack of team play, his low concern for others, his passive-aggressiveness, and his constant torture of Grimace. Of the four main characters (Ronald, Hamburglar, Birdie and Grimace), only Grimace never wears an 'M'. He is the straight man; his humor is literal, predictable, and dependable; only his chaos unleashed unexpected humor results.

This episode centers on Grimace, and allows the creative genius of Klasky-Csupo to unfold new semantic horizons in his character. To give Grimace courage is a revolution in his characterization. This episode is also a parody of Treasure Island, even a satire on the 1989 Brough's video, McTreasure Island. Since both deal (with the same theme, this is an excellent place to compare the two depictions. We can also see how the series progresses, what changes occur between the first and second episode. The McTreasure Island vessel is a 18th-century pirate's ship; the Klasky-Csupo vessel is a magic ship, exaggerated out of a tiny model ship in a bottle, into a pleasure vessel, where the two main sails are emblazoned with huge golden 'Ms' and atop the main mast flies a flag with a huge 'R'. This new history is much deeper than 18th century Treasure Island; this is a much more primordial island. This is not the linear, gradual evolution of Grimace, the new series discloses his semantic possibilities; the real treasure of Grimace Island is discovering Grimace's unrecognized, underutilized, and hidden power. In the 1971 Disco era (1971–1998) Grimace is a joke, a quivering fear, a docile character, of only dumbness. In the new series, he is a cosmic life force; able with Ronald's help to confront his cosmic terror.

This episode expands the bodies of meaning of Grimace and the community of Grimaces, their tribal warfare, their history, their underworld. This is no longer Treasure Island; this is ancient history 'already heavily laden with meaning, filled with it' (Bakhtin, 1986a: 5). The new episode travels past Treasure Island, to the semantic depths of native culture, returning with a boon more valuable than pirate's treasure. The milkshake character gets a primordial past, courage to overcome cosmic fear, and McDonald's corporation is resituated with new meaning, perhaps able to confront its own global terror. Grimace is squeezed into the McTreasure Island episode of 1989, but in 1999, Grimace is a double body: made primitive and able to contemporalize (another example of metamorphosis appropriated for corporate purpose). The exchange is dialogic, the contemporaneity of McDonald's characters, storylines, and images, but also the discourse of animation exploring the archetypal possibilities.

Grimace is not kin to 'materialist aesthetics' of corporate marketing; his aesthetics is more tribal, communal, and cosmic. Grimace's material body is a dual body: a dialog between corporate milkshake sales and cosmic forces. Grimace is part of peasant native culture, part of the struggle between premodernity and modernity; there are no golden arches on this island. The characters jump from the deck of their McYacht into a whirlpool, where they descend into the primeval underworld, beneath McDonaldland (also an underworld). They descend into the deep currents of primeval culture, to bring back the treasure to McDonaldland, and then to McDonald's world. McDonaldland and McDonald's world becomes more multifaceted.

Grimace's phraseology, his grammatical style, the 'D'Ah' utterance is rooted in the forces of cosmic fear. Grimace never wears an 'M'. He is an outsider, a foreigner, a communalist. We can picture the dialogue between the authors, the corporate executives speaking managerialism, the ad agency wanting 'Ms' emblazoned on every surface, the animation artists discourse of archetypal aesthetics, able to take corporate where it has never been before. This is a strategic dialogue, where behind every McDonaldland character, is the voice of an executive, ad agent, or artistic talent. In this dialogism, every utterance in The Adventure of Grimace Island has many authors and they have their respective addressees.

Grimace's utterances are part of the 'dialogism', the system of utterances (Bakhtin's most misunderstood concept). We know from the 1998 McDonald's press release (McDonald's, 1998), related releases (Hume, 1998; Kramer, 1999) and the credits at the end of each video, that a committee of McDonald's, Klasky-Cuspo, and Leo Burnett executives and creative talent, worked out the characters' utterances. The 1999 press release (Kramer, 1999) tells us that the executives were worried about the characters' utterances, not wanting, for example, to make Ronald too much a salesman, but wanting the characters to be edgy, timely, more in step with popular culture; the disco epoch of McDonaldland (1971–1998) was over; the new Rugrat epoch of the new video series was meant to rejuvenate, Ronald, Grimace (the whole gang) and McDonaldland; in the words of a Leo Burnett executive, 'to reignite the power of this icon', Ronald (Kramer, 1999: 14–18). Participants indicated that McDonald's corporate executives believed Ronald could do more that just being a figurehead spokes clown at 'high-profile public relations stunts such as delivering Happy Meals to the United Nations' (Kramer, 1999: 14–18).

Grimace cannot see his own cosmic power without Ronald's reflected gaze; Ronald can see Grimace's powers, and through the Ronald-mask we imagine the strategists can see it, and the animation talent in this episodes, reveals its semantic depths. Grimace's outsiderness, his foreignness, and nativeness, plays a powerful role in McDonald's. Ronald (and executives behind his mask) see possibilities for Grimace, see the courage of Grimace, see his great cosmic force, his power over chaos, and in this episode Grimace gets a transmutation magic (the ability to change his material body, at Ronald's request, into surfboard. Grimace sees the corporate world through a native's purple eyes. Grimace does not renounce his Grimace Island culture and worship the god of consumption; he does seek the protection of his savior, the one who addresses his cosmic fear, Ronald.

As such, Grimace's (like Ronald's) utterances have authors, corporate and animator ones, and addressees, superaddressees, beyond Ronald, Hamburglar, and Birdie. Holquist (1986: xviii) in his introduction to Bakhtin (1986) gives some introduction to superaddressee. The relevance of superaddressee is that it makes the utterance strategic, authored here by a corporate committee, to address audiences beyond the McDonaldland gang, possibly beyond kids. The corporate discourse and the native discourse of Grimace is a dialogic encounter between two cultures, which as Bakhtin (1986: 7) tells us, 'does not result in merging or mixing' since 'each retains its own unity and open totality, but they are mutually enriched'. McDonaldization too is a dialog between two cultures: McDonald's and 121 foreign nations. Grimace is a mask, where the corporate, ad agency executives, and animator's dialogue with the native, explore the semantic depths of the underworld. Grimace engages the McDonald's corporation in dialogue, to surmount their closedness, their rational managerialist philosophy, and see the depth of meaning in a non-materialistic culture. Grimace is part of the history of popular culture; each strategic change is rooted in a particular popular culture epoch: pre-McDonaldland (1948–1970); McDonaldland without women (1971–1980); Disco McDonaldland (1971–1998); the Klasky-Cuspo McDonaldland (1998–2002). Each utterance, each change in character material bodily form, is linked to 'socioeconomic factors', (Bakhtin, 1968: 2) to the dialogue of the strategic actors behind the masks of the McDonaldland characters.

In sum, this video, like the other videos, are not just corporate fiction and humor but part of the dialogic imagination. Grimace is the peasant native, the Island native, the carnival peasant confronting modern materialism, but appropriated by corporate handlers, to entice a new generation of consumers. Here, we show how corporate strategy can be reconceived in light of Bakhtin's concepts of dialogism, double-body, and carnival. Whether McDonald's stretches itself into mythical, prehistoric or galactic dimensions, the videos and clownery are not only part of a strategic narrative but in their polyphonic, carnivalesque and grotesque forms represent the dialogic imagination of the corporation. Through this imagination McDonald's can engage in transformation as it descends into the grotesque underworld and ascends reborn, revitalized and regenerated. To ignore this dynamic is to miss the dialogic imagination that not only forms part of the strategic narrative of the organization but also serves to transform it. As such, to examine the strategy of McDonald's merely as a purist narrative (Barry and Elmes, 1997) in which the corporation engages only in rational monologues, planning and implementing strategic moves with machine-like precision is to examine only the tip of the iceberg. To engage with strategic narrative at the level of dialogic imagination is to explore complexity that cannot be reduced to one, rational narrative.

CONCLUSION

The purpose of this paper has been to build on and expand a narrative perspective on strategy by exploring how fiction and humor may allow organizations to revitalize their strategic narratives. As we have seen in the case of McDonald's corporate narratives of fiction and humor, such as the Ronald McDonald cartoons, serve as dialogic imagination through which existing strategic narratives are revitalized and transformed. In turn, this transformation may be exactly what allows McDonald's not only to remain such a strong player in the marketplace but also to thrive in the face of new threats and criticisms. As such it may be McDonald's dialogic imagination that keeps it from being annihilated by a green identity (Starkey and Crane, 2003), and instead to emerge against all McDonaldization criticism with a revitalized image as an environmentally responsible corporation (Rondinelli and London, 2003).

From this Bakhtinian perspective then research on McDonald's strategy to date is missing one of the most important strategic dynamics. While much of it traces corporate actions as the outcomes of a rationalist monologue and purist narratives of some strategic model or another (Barry and Elmes, 1997), it sheds little light on underlying dynamics and the complexities of multi-voiced strategic narratives. We think that Bakhtin (1986: 63) got it exactly right, when he said to ignore the speech utterance, including its secondary subcategories, leads to 'perfunctoriness and excessive abstractness, distorts the historicity of the research, and weakens the link between language and life'. In this sense, the research we have reviewed earlier on McDonald's strategy shows only a weak link between language and life and ignores important speech utterances and subcategories such as narratives of fiction and humor. Most importantly it ignores how such utterances may revitalize strategic narratives and how strategy is narratively transformed. We suggest that beyond perfunctory abstractions of strategic models, see for example Porter (1980), much of the research on McDonald's strategy seems to miss what happens as strategy is narrated by many voices and through various primary and secondary utterances (Bakhtin, 1986).

The implication of missing these utterances is that not only McDonald's dialogic imagination has been overlooked but also that research on strategy in general seems to miss an important narrative dimension. If McDonald's uses fiction and humor to engage its dialogic imagination, then other organizations are likely doing this also. Consequently, future research needs to explore if and how other firms develop dialogic imagination. Prime candidates are firms, who like McDonald's, invest millions of dollars into official corporate humor, for example, Southwest Airlines. From there it could be explored whether other firms who do not officially invest in corporate humor or fiction also develop dialogic imagination, in for example, corporate myths and humorous stories, or maybe even in the official corporate visions developed as part of corporate PR and image making. In any event, expanding the narrative perspective of strategy to include dialogic imagining and strategic transformation through grotesque humor and fiction opens up many new avenues for research.

Particularly, it opens up a new field of inquiry into the primary and secondary utterances that may form the grammar, structure, styles and genres not just of Ronald McDonald (Boje and Rhodes, forthcoming) but of an entire linguistic theory of strategy. Some of the elements of this theory like double-bodied and double-voiced humor and fiction have been explored here, but many other remain open such as a more systematic treatment of the grotesque method and carnivalization. Finally, a linguistic theory of strategy might enable the systematic treatment of primary and secondary utterances through an entire dialogic speech chain in which strategic narratives are traced through multiple addressees and superaddressees as well as various chronotopes, or conceptions of time and space (Bakhtin, 1981). As such, the development of the corporation's dialogic imagination may serve as a point of departure for a broader perspective on strategy as narrative, one that can accommodate the complexities of language and life.

References

Anderson, L. M. and Bateman, T. S. (2000) Individual environmental initiative: championing natural environmental issues in the US business organizations, *Academy of Management Journal,* **43**(4), 548–71.

Ashforth, B. E. (1993) Emotional labor in service roles: the influence of identity, *Academy of Management Review,* **18**(1), 88–106.

Bachmann, J. W. (2002) Competitive strategy: it's ok to be different, *Academy of Management Executive,* **16**(2), 61–5.

Bakhtin, M. (1968) *Rabelais and his world* (Trans. Hélène Iswolsky), Cambridge and London: The MIT Press.

Bakhtin, M. (1981) *The dialogic imagination: four essays,* Austin, TX: University of Texas Press.

Bakhtin, M. (1986) *Holquist Speech genres and other essays,* edited by Caryl Emerson and Michael Austin, TX. University of Texas Press.

Barry, D. and Elmes, M. (1997) Strategy retold: toward a narrative view of strategic discourse, *Academy of Management Review,* **22**(2), 429–53.

Bateson, J. (2002) Are your customers good enough for your service business?, *Academy of Management Executive,* **16**(4), 110–22.

Beam, H. H. (1996) Value migration. how to think several moves ahead of the competition, *The Academy of Management Executive,* **10**(2), 72–4.

Beam, H. H. (2002) From global to metanational, *Academy of Management Executive,* **16**(2), 173–4.

Berry, M. A. and Rondinelli, Dennis A. (1998) Proactive corporate environment management: a new industrial revolution, *The Academy of Management Executive,* **12**(2), 38–51.

Boas, A.M. and Chain, S. (1976) *Big Mac: the unauthorized story of McDonald's,* New York: E.P. Dutton.

Boje, D. M. (2001) *Narrative methods for organizational and communication research,* Thousand Oaks, CA: Sage.

Boje, D. M. and Cai, Y. (2004) McDonald's: grotesque method and the metamorphosis of the three spheres: McDonald's, McDonaldland, and McDonaldization, *Metamorphosis Journal,* **3**(1), 15–33.

Boje, D. M. and Rhodes, C. (forthcoming) The leadership of Ronald McDonald: double narration and stylistic lines of transformation, *Leadership Quarterly Journal.*

Bradbury, H. and Clair, J. A. (1999) Promoting sustainable organizations with Sweden's natural step, *The Academy of Management Executive,* **13**(4), 63–75.

Brock, D. M. (2000) Multinational corporate evolution and subsidiary development, *Academy of Management Review,* **25**(1), 259–61.

Bruton, G. D., Lan, H. and Lu, Y. (2000) China's township and village enterprises: Kelon's competitive edge/executive commentary, *The Academy of Management Executive,* **14**(1), 19–30.

Calori, R. and Dufour, B. (1995) Management European style, *Academy of Management Executive,* **9**(3), 61–72.

Combs, J. G. and Ketchen, D. J., Jr. (1999) Can capital scarcity help agency theory explain franchising? Revisiting the capital scarcity hypothesis, *Academy of Management Journal,* **42**(2), 196–208.

Evans, P. A. (2002) Review of Gordon, P.H. and Meunier, S'.s 'The French Challenge', *Academy of Management Executive,* **16**(4), 161–72.

Feldman, D. C. (1990) Reconceptualizing the nature and consequences of part-time work, *Academy of Management Review,* **15**(1), 103–12.

Glinow, V. M. and Clarke, L. (1995) Vietnam: tiger or kitten?, *The Academy of Management Executive,* **9**(4), 35–48.

Gupta, A. K. and Govindarajan, V. (2001) Converting global presence into global competitive advantage, *Academy of Management Executive,* **15**(2), 45–59.

Hall, F. S. and Hall, E. L. (1994) The ADA: going beyond the law: executive commentary, *The Academy of Management Executive,* **8**(1), 1733.

Hall, F. S., Hall, E. L. and Reno, J. (1994) The ADA: going beyond the law: executive commentary, *The Academy of Management Executive,* **8**(1), 17–33.

Hall, J. (2001) Why global strategy is a myth and how to profit from the realities of regional markets: review of 'The End of Globalization', *Academy of Management Executive,* **15**(4), 140–2.

Hallowell, R., Bowen, D. and Knoop, C.-I. (2002) Four Seasons goes to Paris, *Academy of Management Executive,* **16**(4), 7–25.

Harrison, J. S. and Caron, H. (1996) Managing and partnering with external stakeholders, *Academy of Management Executive,* **10**(2), 46–61.

Holquist, M. (1986) Introduction, in: C. Emerson and M. Holquist (Eds) *Speech genres and other late essay* by M. M. Bakhtin, translated by V. W. McGee, Austin, TX: University of Texas Press.

Hume, S. (1998) He's wacky: he's the new Ronald, *Ad Week,* **39**(41), 5.

Ireland, D. R., Hitt, M. A., Camp, M. S. and Sexton, D. L. (2001) Integrating entrepreneurship and strategic management actions to create firm wealth, *Academy of Management Executive,* **15**(1), 49–64.

Jennings, P. D. and Zandbergen, P. A. (1995) Ecologically sustainable organizations: an institutional approach, *Academy of Management Review,* **20**(4), 1015–53.

Kanter, R. Moss and Dretler, T. D. (1998) 'Global strategy' and its impact on local operations: lessons from Gillette Singapore, *Academy of Management Executive,* **12**(4), 60–9.

Kelly, E. P. (1997) The one best way: Frederick Winslow Taylor and the enigma of efficiency, *Academy of Management Executive,* **11**(3), 101–5.

Kincheloe, J. L. (2002) *The sign of the burger: McDonald's and the culture of power,* Philadelphia, PA: Temple University Press.

Kossek, E. E. and Huber-Yoder, M. (1997) The working poor: Locked out of careers and the organizational mainstream?, *Academy of Management Executive,* **11**(1), 76–93.

Kramer, L. (1999) McDonald's execs explore makeover for Ronald icon, *Advertising Age,* **70**(34), 14–18.

Livesey, S. M. (1999) McDonald's and the environmental defense fund: a case study of a green alliance, *Journal of Business Communication,* **36**(1), 5–40.

Marks, M. L. and Mirvis, P. H. (2001) Making mergers and acquisitions work: Strategic and psychological preparation, *Academy of Management Executive,* **15**(2), 80–95.

McWilliams, A. (2001) Corporate social responsibility: a theory of the firm perspective, *Academy of Management Review,* **26**(1), 117–28.

Meyer, M. H. and DeTore, A. (1999) Product development for services, *Academy of Management Executive,* **13**(3), 64–77.

Mintzberg, H. (1987) Crafting strategy, *Harvard Business Review,* **65**(4), 66–75.

Mirvis, P. H. (1997) Human resource management: leaders, laggards, and followers, *Academy of Management Executive,* **11**(2), 43–57.

Nayyar, P. R. (1993) Performance effects of information asymmetry and scope in diversified service firms, *Academy of Management Journal,* **36**(1), 28–58.

Nutt, P. C. (1999) Surprising but true: half the decisions in organizations fail, *Academy of Management Executive,* **13**(4), 75–91.

Organ, D. W., McFillen, J. M. and Mitchell, T. R. (1985) In search of excellence versus the 100 best companies to work for in America: a question of perspective and values, *Academy of Management Review,* **10**(2), 350–5.

Paul, R. J. and Townsend, J. B. (1993) Managing the older worker—don't just rinse away the gray, *The Academy of Management Executive,* **7**(3), 67–75.

Porter, M. E. (1980) *Competitive strategy: techniques for analysing industries and competitors,* New York: The Free Press.

Quinn, J. B. Anderson, P. and Finkelstein, S. (1996) Leveraging intellect, *Academy of Management Executive,* **10**(3), 7–28.

Reno, J. (1994) Executive commentary, *The Academy of Management Executive,* **8**(1), 27–30.

Rhodes, C. (2001) The Simpsons, popular culture, and the organizational carnival, *Journal of Management Inquiry,* **10**(4), 374–83.

Rindova, V. P., Becerra, M. and Contardo, M. (2004) Enacting competitive wars: competitive activity, language games, and market consequences, *Academy of Management Review,* **29**(4), 670–86.

Ritzer, G. (1993) The McDonalization of society, *Journal of American Culture,* **6**, 100–7.

Robinson, G. and Dechant, K. (1997) Building a business case for diversity, *Academy of Management Executive,* **11**(3), 21–32.

Rondinelli, D. A. and London, T. (2003) How corporations and environmental groups cooperate: assessing cross-sector alliances and collaborations, *Academy of Management Executive,* **17**(1), 61–78.

Russo, M. V. and Fouts, P. A. (1997) A resource-based perspective on corporate environmental performance and profitability, *Academy of Management Journal,* **40**(3), 534–60.

Safferstone, M. J. (2002) The rule of three, *Academy of Management Executive,* **16**(3), 161–2.

Seiders, K. and Berry, L. L. (1998) Service fairness: what it is and why it matters, *Academy of Management Executive,* **12**(2), 8–21.

Sexton, D. L. (2001) Wayne Huizenga: Entrepreneur and wealth creator, *Academy of Management Executive,* **15**(1), 409.

Shama, A. (1993) Management under fire: the transformation of managers in the Soviet Union and Eastern Europe, *Academy of Management Executive,* **7**(1), 22–36.

Starik, M. and Rands, G. P. (1995) Weaving an integrated Web: multilevel and multisystem perspectives of ecologically sustainable organizations, *Academy of Management Review,* **20**(4), 908–35.

Starkey, K. and Crane, A. (2003) Toward green narrative: management and the evolutionary epic, *Academy of Management Review,* **28**(2), 220–43.

Thomas, R. E. (2002) Using the law for competitive advantage (book review), *Academy of Management Executive,* **16**(3), 159–62.

Usher, J. M. (1999) Specialists, generalists, and polymorphs: spatial advantages of multiunit organization in a single industry, *Academy of Management Review,* **24**(1), 143–51.

Watson, J. (1997) *Golden arches east: McDonald's in East Asia,* Stanford, CA: Stanford University Press.

Wharton, A. S. and Erickson, R. J. (1993) Managing emotions on the job and at home: understanding the consequences of multiple emotional roles, *Academy of Management Review,* **18**(3), 457–87.

Wright, M., Hoskisson, R. E., Filatotchev, I. and Buck, T. (1998) Revitalizing privatized Russian enterprises, *Academy of Management Executive,* **12**(2), 74–86.

'The performative surprise': parody, documentary and critique

Kate Kenny

Can parody help us to 're-imagine' the organizations and institutions we live with (Du Gay 2007, 13)? Or, like many forms of critique, does parody risk being incorporated: becoming part of the power it aims to make fun of? In this paper, drawing on Judith Butler's work, I argue that certain circumstances enable parody to destabilize hegemonic, taken-for-granted institutions (Butler 1990). I explore these ideas through a reading of the *Yes Men* documentary (Tartan Video 2005). This film features a series of humorous representations of the World Trade Organization (WTO). I show how these act to denaturalize and effectively critique this dominant force in global trade. This paper discusses the value of parody for helping us to re-think and re-make particular institutions and organizations. In doing so, I point to the importance of creating a spectacle in which parody can travel beyond its immediate location, so that it can reach ever newer audiences with its 'performative surprise' (Butler 1990, xxvi). I suggest that the rise of the Internet and inexpensive documentary techniques offer interesting new ways for achieving this.

Introduction

Representations of organizations in popular culture have been the focus of a significant body of work in the field of management studies (Butler 1997; Hassard and Holliday 1998; Rhodes and Westwood 2008). Such representations, it is argued, can provide a means to critique some of the institutions we take for granted (Hassard 1998). The recent proliferation of low-budget documentaries that highlight problematic aspects of business and management, such as *Supersize Me* (Sony Pictures 2004) and *The Corporation* (Metrodome Distribution 2005), are a significant part of this. While debates continue about whether these 'documentaries' represent fact or fiction, such films raise awareness about particular problems, and in doing so spark debate (Thompson and Bordwell 2002). This paper examines one such film, the *Yes Men* (Tartan Video 2005), and its use of parody to critique institutions. I focus on parody because both the film's protagonists and the journalists who write about them repeatedly refer to their performances as parodic spectacles (Myerson and Jain 2002; Yes Men 2002). Parody is generally understood as an imitation that aims to make fun of, critically comment upon or ridicule the original (Hutcheon 1985). In the process of imitation, the space between original and its parodic reproduction can flag up important features of the original, even as it reverses and pokes fun at them (Hariman 2008; Hopfl 2007; Rhodes 2002; Rhodes and Pullen 2007). Parody can, therefore, have a critical function: it helps us to laugh at power and imagine alternatives (Critchley 2007; Butler 1990). In particular, parody plays an important role in the ways in which we make and remake our understandings of particular institutions (Hariman 2008; Hodgson 2005). For example, in the *Yes Men* DVD, the 'original' WTO is parodied in order to draw attention to, and criticize, this institution's activities.

In considering how parodic representations help us to imagine alternatives to taken-for-granted institutions and critique power, an important question arises. Can parody *really* yield effective critique, or does it merely reinforce and legitimize that which it aims to change (Butler 1990)? If the former, what are the conditions under which parody is effective? I address these questions in this paper. I begin by examining the concept of parody, focussing on its role in questioning what is taken for granted and prompting political change (Butler 1990; Hariman 2008). I describe how parody is used to critique contemporary institutions and organizations, and highlight the importance of humour and spectacle in this. Next, I outline current debates on whether parody can be seen to be potentially subversive or is merely a 'safety valve' for the expression of criticisms that, in the end, have little effect. Having set the scene, I discuss these ideas with reference to the recent *Yes Men* DVD, which documents the parodic performances of this subversive activist group. I discuss the use of parody, spectacle and humour in this production, and argue that the relatively new media of DVD and Internet provide a unique fora for such critical humour to proliferate. Finally, I use this case to assess the role that parody plays in the critique of dominant institutions.

Parody

Parody is an act of duplication where the original is placed 'beside itself' and the copy is used as a joke (Hariman 2008, 249). In this process, the limits of the original become exposed. What appeared to be serious is shown as ridiculous, 'the powerful is shown to be vulnerable, the unchangeable contingent, the enchanting dangerous' (Hariman 2008, 251). In a useful history of the concept, Hariman shows how the 'turning upside-down' allowed by parody is essential for healthy political and cultural debate. Plato used parody to make fun of self-important Athenians who took themselves and their role as guardians of civilization too seriously (Hariman 2008). The tradition continues today; Hariman points to examples from contemporary popular culture, including *The Onion* and *The Colbert Report,* and examines their significance. Once a dominant discourse is 'set beside itself', the excessive, laughing imitations can destabilize the 'original' and highlight its tenuous nature (Hariman 2008, 254). For Hariman, parody is what keeps contemporary civilization going; it enables people to continuously look at the taken-for-granted in different ways. Parody is an essential part of political life.

Butler's *Gender trouble* (1990) is well-known for exploring parody's role in political change (Parker 2002). In the context of gender and sexuality, she explores how categories that are taken for granted in society can be troubled by parody. Butler begins by pointing out that terms such as 'masculine' or 'feminine' should not be thought of as pre-given, essential aspects of people. The concept of *woman,* despite how it operates in society, is not a 'foundational category', nor an essential aspect of some static self. It is, in fact, an 'effect of a specific formation of power' (Butler 1990, xxviii). Her project centres upon unpacking that power. When a baby is born, we rush to ask, 'is it a boy or a girl?' Why, she wonders, should this be our first question? Why is the male/female distinction one of the only *compulsory* boxes that require ticking on the newborn baby's birth certificate? Butler argues that society has long been invested in maintaining maleness and femaleness as primary and distinct categories. This distinctness reinforces discourses of both phallogocentrism and 'compulsory heterosexuality' (1990, xxviii), which in turn support the economic and cultural survival of a given nation state (Foucault 1990). Butler links the accepted primacy of the male/female binary with the idea that heterosexual alliances are foundational to social life and must be privileged above all other types of union. This has cruel implications for people who are left out. Homosexuals, transgender and childless persons find themselves outside of categories that determine what counts as a 'valid life' (Butler 2004). It is vital, therefore, that we try to 'open up' the ways we think about traditional, taken-for-granted categories like 'male' and 'female'; sex and gender are not 'givens' but are observable aspects of the exercise of particular forms of power (Butler 1990).

For Butler, then, *parody* plays a key role in opening up these traditional categories; aping and critiquing them, and highlighting their contingency. She uses the example of drag artists. While gender theory traditionally treats drag as degrading to women, reinforcing negative stereotypes of excessive femininity, Butler sees the practice somewhat differently. When a drag artist dresses up and parodies the notion of male or female, the effect is to challenge pre-held notions of gender binaries; drag can prompt us to question aspects of life we tend to take as foundational and unchangeable (Butler 1990). The *moment* itself, where we initially think that we see a woman but quickly realize that it is a man, throws up questions about the 'reality' of either gender. She notes, 'if you examine what knowledges we are drawing upon when we make this observation, regarding anatomy of the person, or the way the clothes are worn', then it becomes apparent that this is all knowledge that has been 'naturalized' through a process of normalization (1990, xxii). The question thus must be asked, 'What are the categories through which one sees?' (1990, xxii). For Butler, it is the vacillation that occurs between these taken-for-granted terms, when we are trying to work out whether it's a woman or a man that stands before us, which puts 'the reality of gender... into crisis: it becomes unclear how to distinguish the real from the unreal' (1990, xxiii). The *parody* here is important; it is in the 'pleasure, the giddiness of the performance' that we recognize the 'radical contingency' of categories of sex and gender (1990, 175).

If we are left questioning the 'reality' of the original, we are led to suspect that perhaps there is no actual 'original which such parodic identities imitate... the parody is of the very notion of an original; ... gender parody reveals that the original identity after which gender fashions itself is an *imitation without an origin*' (1990, 175, emphasis added). Again, the spontaneous, momentary laughter is key; it bursts out when we realize that 'all along, the original was derived' (1990, 176). In the years following the publication of *Gender trouble,* these ideas were welcomed and widely adopted by those concerned with sex and gender oppression and discrimination, even beyond the academic audience for whom Butler was writing. This highlights the political impact of Butler's parody (Blumenfeld and Breen 2001). Through parody, we laugh and we see things otherwise. In organization studies, Rhodes and Pullen (2007) discuss how depictions of men in *The Simpsons* cartoon show up the fragility of masculine stereotypes (2007, 171). By imitating and parodying dominant conceptions of masculinity, the *Simpsons* episode they discuss 'defamiliariz[es] the mundane', makes it ridiculous and leaves it open to question (Westwood and Rhodes 2007, 5).

Parodying institutions

While Butler focuses on parodying *norms,* the parody of institutions has long been an effective form of critique. An early example is Johnathan Swift's *A modest proposal* (1729), a critical imitation of a commentary on the British imperial system. The essay was published in the form of a 'normal' political pamphlet. It was a tongue-in-cheek argument for dealing with the 'Ireland problem' and suggested that, for example, poor Irish be encouraged to sell their surplus children to their British landlords so that they might eat them for dinner: 'No gentleman would repine to give ten shillings for the carcass of a good fat child, which, as I have said, will make four dishes of excellent nutritive meat.' Parodying the earnest political commentator, Swift stresses that the scheme offers benefit to all, 'the squire will learn to be a good landlord, and grow popular among his tenants; the mother will have eight shillings net profit, and be fit for work till she produces another child.' In presenting such arguments in a logical, rational tone, Swift critiques aspects of British imperialism: the prevalent anti-Catholic sentiment, the greed of landlords, the institutionalization of poverty in Ireland and the disengaged, cold nature of the political pamphlet as a means of representation. He achieves this by parodying the pamphlet form itself (Anderson 1991).

Parody can also perform such a 'critical function' in the treatment of *contemporary* institutions and organizations (Rhodes 2002; Rhodes and Pullen 2007). Westwood (2004) describes a corporate comedian who visits organizations and puts on a show that involves imitating and parodying the senior managers, corporate slogans and logos particular to that organization. Rhodes (2002) discusses how the TV show *South Park* frequently 'mocks, satirises and undermines official institutions' (2002, 294). In an analysis of one episode, he explores its portrayal of a global corporation, *Starbucks*. Presenting *Harbucks*, a copy of the original, the episode uses parody to make important points about the way Starbucks does business. For example, the episode implies that manipulative techniques are used by this organization in order to enter new markets when Harbucks is portrayed as ruthlessly taking over a local coffee shop and aggressively marketing a 'kiddycinno' cappuccino, high in sugar and caffeine, to the children of South Park (Rhodes 2002, 301). In this way, the cartoon imitates and critiques aspects of the original. In summary, there is a long history of the use of parody for critiquing particular institutions. This paper's focus on its use in criticizing the WTO adds to this.

Making parody work: humour and spectacle

If parody is to work, it needs to make us laugh (Butler 1990; Westwood 2004). For Hariman (2008), laughter enables us to 'relax' around power. Laughter takes away the 'fear and piety' we may have held in relation to a particular discourse; it makes an object familiar and, therefore, available for investigation (Hariman 2008, 255). The 'doubling' function of parody is vital here: we would not be able to directly laugh at the serious and taken-for-granted 'original', but we can laugh fearlessly at its more benign imitation. Rhodes and Pullen (2007) and Hariman (2008) show how Bakhtin's concept of carnival is useful for deepening our understanding of the role of laughter in parody. The carnival is a privileged place where the normal hierarchy is suspended and reversed. Here the 'comic crowning and uncrowning of kings' can be enjoyed by all (Rhodes 2002, 296). This idea, that humour allows people to say things they are normally not allowed to say, has been influential within organization studies. The privilege of critique comes from the compelling nature of laughter, from what is allowable through the medium of a good joke (Grugulis 2002; O'Doherty 2007).

In addition to the laugh, the *spectacle* is vital. Butler's drag is a performance: overt and noticeable. Hariman argues that for parody to effectively form part of political debate, the parodic object must be '*held up to be seen*, exposed and ridiculed' (2008, 255, emphasis added). To work, parody must push that which is powerful, yet taken for granted, directly into the spotlight to be copied and displayed as a 'carnivalesque' spectacle (Hariman 2008, 255). For example, Swift's pamphlet is shocking; his recommendation for serving babies advises that 'the fore or hind quarter will make a reasonable dish, and seasoned with a little pepper or salt will be very good boiled on the fourth day, especially in winter.' We notice, we laugh and we see things differently.

Parody and critique: subversion or incorporation?

While the critical intent of parody is clear, can it really be considered an effective form of critique? What can parody actually *do?* As noted above, an important aspect lies in parody's highlighting of the tenuous nature of much of what we take for granted (Butler 1990). However, parody offers more than simply highlighting such contingency. Parody takes fundamental 'givens' in society and 'cuts [them] down to size' (Hariman 2008, 254). This cutting can leave a particular norm open to question, and it is difficult to predict where this parodic re-examining might end up. For Butler (1990), parody shows us how a somewhat concrete 'given' in society is tenuous, and in fact is dependent on repeated performances. If that is the case, each successive performance, or citation of the norm, contains the potential for alteration and, perhaps, for subversion (Anderson 1991; Hodgson 2005; Rhodes and Pullen 2007). Parody plays a key role in these 'awry citations' (Butler 1990, 176). The play of parody in ongoing iteration of an identity can see the 'apparent ideal', 'elide, slide, alter [and] shift' in a number of interesting ways (Borgerson 2005, 71).

In the realm of the political, Hariman (2008) shows how parody can yield a plurality of perspectives: a multitude of ways of looking at a particular idea. Parody always works to keep power 'in check' (Rhodes 2002), though this can happen in unexpected ways. For example, power can be reversed; having mocked the repressor, jokes can be turned around to laugh at the repressed. Swift, for example, levels jokes at the peasants of County Cavan, Ireland, drawing on a well-known stereotype that people from this area are mean: Swift cites their renowned proficiency in the art of stealing (Swift 1729). Similarly Rhodes (2002) shows how *South Park* mocks the local coffee shop owner whose premises is targeted by Harbucks for takeover, showing him to be just as greedy as the corporation itself. Rather than implying a particular political position, these critical imitations do not necessarily 'tell us about the single right way, but rather work to parody and relativise power – to *always suggest alternatives…*' (Rhodes 2002, 305, emphasis added). This is not 'the stuff of revolutionary liberation', but rather the continuous, conspicuous and ridiculous inversion of the taken-for-granted (Rhodes and Pullen 2007, 176). For Hariman, these multiple, imagined scenarios are what keeps political life healthy: 'the long-term effect of a public culture alive with parody is an irreverent democratization of the conventions of public discourse' (2008, 258).

Parody and incorporation

This optimism is not shared by all commentators on parody. One view holds that such critiques merely give the *appearance* of a 'lessening of prohibitions' associated with a particular, oppressive form of power, where in fact little has actually changed. Critique can, therefore, represent 'a more devious and discreet form of power', because it leads us to think that a challenge is in progress (Foucault 1990, 11). For example, while humour can form an important part of employee resistance in workplaces (Taylor and Bain 2003), it can also contribute to the maintenance of 'routine and order', acting as a 'safety valve' for the expression of dissent (O'Doherty 2007, 199; see also Collinson 2002; Kavanagh and O'Sullivan 2007). For these reasons, humorous critiques and parodies are often considered to be ambivalent in their relationship to power (Grugulis 2002; Hodgson 2005; Westwood 2004).

Related to this argument about the ambivalence of parody is the idea that parody is *dependent* upon the original that it imitates and makes fun of. Parody is always, in some way, subject to this original. This dependency is dangerous, and means that parodic critique runs the risk of being compromised (Butler 1990). A parodic act will always take place from *within* a particular power–knowledge matrix; if 'subversion is possible, it will be a subversion from within the terms of the law' (Butler 1990, 119). Drag performances, for example, draw on representations of gender from the dominant, 'hegemonic, misogynist culture' (1990, 176). Westwood's (2004) account of a corporate comedian highlights this problem. The comedian is paid to perform at company get-togethers by senior managers, many of whom are made fun of in his act. In mocking these managers, however, the comedian has to be careful not to be too harsh. After one particularly scathing performance, his cheque arrived but was 'slow in coming, and then it was for only half the amount' (2004, 782). The comedian could transgress boundaries and parody power, but was only allowed to go so far. The danger of parodic repetitions being subsumed by 'the power one opposes', and becoming 'an instrument of [it]', is always present (Butler 1990, xxvi).

This leads to the question of what happens to its critical force, when humour becomes commercialized. If parody, for example, is put up for sale, has it 'sold out?' If we purchase *The Onion,* and this newspaper depends on sales to make profit, can it still be seen as a valid form of critique? Picasso argues that it cannot, in his *Protestation* over surrealist painters' forays into the world of commerce. He criticizes artists who engage in 'subversion for sale', including Max Ernst's designing of theatre backdrops, Magritte's work for Shell Oil advertisements, and Dali's *Vogue* covers. The debate continues into recent discussions of the political potential of organizational humour, where this humour is sold as a commodity (Kavanagh and O'Sullivan 2007). Parker discusses increased sales of 'anti-work culture' artefacts, such as mugs and framed slogans, arguing that such critique can only ever be ambivalent with respect to power (2007, 88). According to Boltanksi and Chiapello (2007), cynicism is big business in contemporary Western societies, and where it is mass-marketed and sold for profit the sharp edge of cultural critique is deadened. Discussing the commoditization of *parody*, Butler likens it to the way in which metaphors 'lose their metaphoricity, as they congeal through time into concepts' (1990, xxi). Similarly, when subversive, parodic performances are repeated over and over in response to demands from contemporary consumers, they 'always run the risk of becoming deadening clichés through their repetition and, most importantly, through their repetition within commodity culture where "subversion"carries market value' (1990, xxi). It appears, therefore, that parody can reinforce that which it aims to critique, and can be rendered 'deadened' through economic incorporation.

Incorporation or subversion?

In summary, parody and critical imitation can problematize aspects of life that we take for granted. They can, for example, help us to 're-imagine' the organizations and institutions that form part of daily life, a necessary step in political change (Du Gay 2007, 13). As we laugh, we realize the contingency of what we have taken for granted: the serious becomes ridiculous (Hariman 2008). Following Butler and Hariman, parody holds the potential for subversion of a given 'law', or norm, through the 'possibilities that emerge when the law turns against itself and spawns unexpected permutations of itself' (Butler 1990, 119). Like all forms of critique, however, parodic representations risk becoming incorporated, reinforcing that which they might wish to destabilize. As Hariman argues, parody is 'neither radical nor conservative' in relation to power 'but both at once', because of the inherent ambivalence described above (2008, 254). By itself, therefore, parody is not subversive (Butler 1990, 176). It is only 'certain kinds of parodic repetitions [that are] effectively disruptive, truly troubling', while other such performances risk becoming 'domesticated and recirculated as instruments of cultural hegemony' (1990, 176). For example, in her chapter, *Subversive bodily acts* (Butler 1993), she describes the kinds of 'parodic practices based in a performative theory of gender acts', which *do* effectively 'disrupt the categories of the body, sex, gender, and sexuality', leading to these being re-thought beyond 'the binary frame' (Butler 1990: 100). The point to note is that we cannot consider such things in the abstract, but only by examining a particular situation. Parody requires a *specific context* in order for it to be 'truly troubling' and to enable the kinds of mobilizations and subversions described above.

In this paper, I build on these ideas and ask how we can understand the role of parody in destabilizing perceptions of one institution: the World Trade Organization (WTO). I examine recent efforts by a group known as 'The Yes Men' to challenge the WTO's policies and practices. Through staging a number of pranks, releasing a DVD and continuing the conversation on the Internet, the Yes Men impersonated and poked fun at this organization. In doing so, they open up a new way of imagining the WTO, through pranks that are all the more compelling and difficult to ignore because of the laughter they provoke. Following Butler, I argue that this critique was effective due to the particular context of the parodic spectacle. I conclude by drawing out some of the implications of this for organization studies.

The Yes Men

Background

In 1996, two men, Igor Vamos, an assistant professor at the California Institute for the Arts, and Jacques Servin, a computer programmer in San Francisco, got together to set up a subversive activist group. 'The Yes Men' was formed in order to poke fun at powerful interests who are harmful to society, and to do so in such a way as to draw attention to the serious issues at hand. The group carries out 'identity corrections' (Lawless 2005; Yes Men 2005). These involve temporarily 'borrowing' the identities of particular organizations in order to speak and act on their behalf. In interviews, Igor and Jacques cite well known historical parodies as inspiration for their stunts, including Daniel Defoe's public suggestion that non-Anglicans be executed (Yes Men 2009).

Prior to forming the Yes Men and contributing to the subsequent documentary, earlier identity corrections were carried out by both men. Jacques was working as a computer programmer on *Grand Theft Auto*, a testosterone-fuelled computer game in which the player speeds around various cities in stolen cars. He replaced the normal 'extras', who walk around in the background of the action, with men in red swimming trunks who constantly kissed each other and the player's character (Silberman 1996). He was immediately fired, and became something of a hero in the gay community. In 1993, Igor had already carried out a similar 'identity correction' stunt, while working for toymaker Mattel. Having founded the BLO (Barbie Liberation Organization), he swapped the voice boxes between Barbie and GI Joe dolls just in time for the Christmas market. Little girls were surprised when their Barbie barked out 'Dead men tell no lies', while GI Joe complained that 'math is hard' before happily quipping 'I love to shop with you!' (Barbie Liberation Organization 2009). These pranks highlighted aspects of the world that the Yes Men saw as being problematic and yet taken for granted, including the misogyny and homophobia passed on to children in the gaming and toy industries. Forming the Yes Men enabled Igor and Jacques to embark on longer projects, usually taking the form of mini-performances. The idea is that the group 'turns up the volume' on the ideas, agendas and goals of its target organizations in order to highlight the problems it sees (Yes Men 2009). Through costumes, props and simulation programmes, their pranks maintain a continuous spectacle of ridicule and parody.

The documentary

The *Yes Men* documentary was directed by the filmmaking team behind the acclaimed Sundance Grand Jury Prize-winner, *American Movie* (Columbia Tristar 2000). Shot in a video diary style, the film follows the Yes Men's rise to worldwide notoriety for impersonating the WTO on television and at business conferences around the world between 2000 and 2002. This story is the main focus of the documentary, presented alongside vignettes about the history of the group and some earlier pranks. The tale begins in 1999, when Igor and Jacques set up a parody of the WTO website, using the domain name *gatt.org*. The website had a similar look to the original and could easily be mistaken for *wto.org* at a distance. On examining the text however, it is clear that the content on gatt.org forms a sharp critique of the WTO and its practices of, for example, prioritising free trade over the right to drink water for free, eat, treat the sick, protect the environment, organize trade unions, govern and have a foreign policy. Igor and Jacques began to receive emails about all sorts of trade matters from people who had mistaken their parody website for the real thing. One such email was from the organizer of 'Textiles of the Future', a conference of global textile manufacturers, inviting the WTO to present at the upcoming event in Tampere.

The documentary tracks the Yes Men's decision to go along. They adopt the pseudonyms Andy Bichlbaum and Mike Bonanno, and we are invited to watch as the pair prepare Powerpoint slides, purchase sombre business suits and shave their longish hair into military-style buzz cuts. The day arrives, and we see Andy presenting to the assembled delegates from the textile industry in a lavish conference hall. He begins by outlining what the WTO perceives to be two key management problems of the day: how to manage a remote workforce, while simultaneously remaining comfortable. These problems are related, Andy argues, and 'the solution is based in textiles' (Yes Men 2005). Pausing for effect, Andy whips off his business attire to reveal an all-in-one gold jumpsuit. Turning to face the audience, a three-foot-long phallus springs from the crotch, with a little television monitor sitting on the end level with Andy's head. This, he tells the audience, is the EVA, or Employee Visualization Appendage. It enables the effective management of an offshore workforce by administering electric shocks to sweatshop employees. In addition, he assures us, the suit is extremely comfortable to wear. We watch the audience's silent bemusement and listen as Igor and Jacques, post-conference, wonder why there was a lack of reaction in the questions and answers session. Surely, they wonder, given the number of PhDs and advanced degree holders present, a critical questioning of such an absurd schema ought to have followed (Yes Men 2005).

The remainder of the film follows the Yes Men on similar missions, and features excerpts of supportive talking heads, including a shot of Michael Moore discussing the WTO's role in maintaining abhorrent working conditions in Mexican border town sweatshops. Barry Coates, leader of the World Development Movement, is shown talking about the WTO's agenda of reducing the legislating power of governments. Other pranks featured in the film include a presentation at a university in Plattsburgh, New York, where the Yes Men, on behalf of WTO, proposed to solve global hunger by recycling human waste from developed countries to manufacture hamburgers for consumption by the poorer people of Western nations. At an international trade law conference in Austria, Andy proposes, on behalf of the WTO, that the auction of people's votes to the highest bidder would be a useful solution to the staleness of democracy. Finally, at an accounting conference in Australia, Andy, aka the WTO, announces that in light of all its mistakes, the organization now plans to shut itself down. In its place, it will found an organization whose goals are not to help corporations, but rather to help the poor and the environment. After this announcement, a hoax press release was sent out by the Yes Men to over 25,000 journalists, politicians and news agencies worldwide, and we watch a clip of the issue being debated in the Canadian Parliament. At its close, the *Yes Men* documentary urges viewers to visit the website yesmen.org, and through this medium to get involved and to carry out their own identity correction pranks. Igor and Jacques call for people to get out there and 'impersonate whoever holds power that needs to be criticized' (Yes Men 2005, 2009a).

The Yes Men parodies: effective critique?

Examining this documentary in light of existing studies of parody prompts a number of questions. Are the Yes Men correct in terming their DVD performances as parodies? If so, can these exploits form the basis for a critique of institutions such as the WTO? Are they actually subversive, and if so in what ways?

First, it appears that the performances presented on this DVD are, in fact, parodies. For Hariman, parody works through 'doubling' and 'carnivalesque spectatorship' (2008, 253), where a copy is placed beside the original, in a public manner, leaving both open for ridicule. Just as Swift smuggles his critique by parodying and publicly distributing an 'original' political pamphlet, so the Yes Men smuggle theirs into conferences as a sombre-suited WTO official. Both forms of parody create a doubling, which is used to 'turn up the volume' on aspects of the original and hold them apart for critique. At the Tampere conference, for example, the serious WTO becomes a 'site of laughter' (Rhodes and Pullen 2007, 164). Part of the joke involves putting forward incredible scenarios on behalf of the WTO; burgers made out of human waste and economic slavery in developing nations are presented as possible and desirable results of current WTO policies. The sudden appearance of the organization as a huge, golden phallus prompts imagining an alternative view of it; it symbolizes the WTO as an aggressive and cruel bully. In this doubling, the Yes Men's parodies confront the WTO with 'an image of itself that it constantly tries to hide' (Hariman 2008, 258). In addition to critiquing the WTO, these parodies invite us to imagine things as they might otherwise be. By vacillating between WTO as parodic bully and the 'reality' of the organization, we begin to question this reality. We see the contingency of what we may have taken for granted: it is the 'occasional discontinuit[ies]' prompted by pranks like this, which 'reveal the temporal and contingent groundlessness of this "ground"' (Butler 1990, 179). The authority and permanence of the WTO now appears to be fragile, sustained by 'repeated acts that seek to approximate the ideal' of a substantial, permanent and powerful entity (1990, 179).

Furthermore, through the Yes Men's parody, we see how a relatively unitary, coherent image such as the WTO's can be transformed into a 'field of proliferating voices', which point to a *multiplicity* of interpretations and possibilities (Hardiman 2008, 253). For example, by the end of the documentary, when we watch the WTO announcing that it is shutting down, we have already begun to imagine this as one alternative. In their declaration of the WTO's disbanding, the Yes Men prompt us to think, 'what if?' and 'why not?' Parody forms a key role in re-thinking political institutions (Butler 1990), and this is important in maintaining public debate (Hariman 2008). Of course, parody is not the only means of achieving this: NGOs, trade organizations and journalists are continuously engaged in earnest discussions about the ethics of global trade. However, by allowing the temporary suspension of normality, parody can reinvigorate discussions that have been numbed through repetition, and by entrenched positions on either side of a stale debate (Hariman 2008, 260). As Butler notes, although parody does not 'in itself, constitute a political revolution', it plays a role by promoting a radical shift in perceptions of what is possible, shifts that are necessary for political imagining. It is thus an essential part in questioning hegemonic, and potentially injurious, relations in society (Rhodes and Pullen 2007).

'Providing an excuse': the Yes Men spectacle

The case of the Yes Men allows us to theorize about the particular contexts in which parody can be effective for enabling such radical shifts. First, the *spectacle* is essential here. The formula is simple: the Yes Men create a performance, involving over-the-top pranks, and this draws the attention of journalists. Press releases detailing the WTO's disbanding even made their way into Canadian parliamentary discussions. The Yes Men feel that they provide reporters with the excuse to write about things that they find important but that are difficult to justify writing about. 'We can provide the fodder, sometimes, that lets these subjects (such as globalization) get covered.' (Yes Men 2009a) The golden jumpsuit and its three-foot phallus makes an excellent photograph, and the Yes Men's brazen gate-crashing of high-profile events makes a good story. For the group, attention from the world's print and television media is key. To date, their stunts have featured in *Fortune* magazine, *The Guardian, The Financial Times, Newsweek, The New York Times* and *Harpers Bazaar*. This kind of exposure is what enables the Yes Men to 'turn up the volume' on their target institutions, and ensure that the kinds of destabilization and re-thinking that their parodies can yield, reaches the maximum number of people. Without the ludicrous spectacles described here, the Yes Men would not receive the level of coverage upon which they depend. Routledge's (1997) study of Earth First! protesters at the M77 motorway site in Glasgow describes a similar phenomenon. The activists provided a continual supply of media friendly events and spectacles, such as dwelling in trees. Routledge describes this as an 'imagineering' of resistance, in which the *image* of the protest was seen to be paramount (1997, 359). Creating a spectacle is key.

Relatedly, in the case of the Yes Men, this spectacle is *not* a local one designed for the people who are actually present during the performance. The crowds were small at both the conference hall in Tampere and the meeting room in Sydney; each comprised less than two hundred people. In both cases, audiences reacted mildly, mainly just nodding quietly at what was being presented (Yes Men 2009b). The Yes Men appear reluctant to engage with these people who have turned up in their various professional roles to hear the WTO speak. Where Jacques and Igor do talk about them, it tends to be in a dismissive, somewhat patronizing manner; 'a couple of people admit being mystified by the appendage, but *no one* is bothered by the content of the speech, including when they're reminded about the slavery issue' (Yes Men 2009b). Without asking them directly, the Yes Men deem their audiences to be weak-willed dupes for not reacting more strongly (Yes Men 2005). Reasons for this non-reaction, which could vary between confusion, politeness or simply a culturally-embedded aversion to making a scene, are not considered. Non-reaction is interpreted as mindless acquiescence, but it could be that the Igor and Jacques have simply failed to engage their audience with their critiques. The Yes Men don't appear to care very much about the ambivalence that their performances prompts. They are open about the fact that they are more concerned about the resulting coverage in news reports (Yes Men 2005). In this way, local settings are overlooked in favour of the wider media of television, newspaper and Internet: the reaction of people who are present during their stunts is somewhat irrelevant. Routledge finds a similar phenomenon at the motorway protests. Here, the interests, needs and wishes of the local residents, whose lives stood to be drastically affected by the new road, were often overlooked in the quest for the attention of the wider press (Routledge 1997). These observations remind us, firstly, of the limitations of the documentary form of representation; as with any medium, film offers one version of events, in this case, the version held by Igor and Jacques (Hassard 1998; Rothman 1997). In addition, by focussing on that which is distant at the expense of the local, we see the problems inherent to such 'spectacular', imagineered forms of resistance.

Sharing the spectacle: DVD and Internet

In the *Yes Men* documentary, we have a spectacle that offers a critical re-imagining of problematic institutions. In sharing this spectacle with the world, the Yes Men make use of two relatively recent technologies: DVD and the Internet. This highlights the role of these media for enabling future parodic critiques.

First, the link between the DVD and its associated website is important for the success of the *Yes Men*. Film commentators report that the relationship between Internet and film is growing ever more complex and interesting, citing the Internet-based hype which heralded *Blair Witch Project,* and the online discussions between fans and director which led to rewriting parts of the script for *Lord of the Rings* (Thompson and Bordwell 2002). Internet discussions about activist documentary films have become a necessary adjunct to the film itself, such as with Al Gore's *An Inconvenient Truth* (2006). Michael Moore, a veteran of the medium, is currently using his own website to launch continuous counter-attacks against those who accuse his films of being less than accurate, calling the makers of the recent documentary *Manufacturing Dissent* (Liberation Entertainment 2007) a bunch of 'wacko attackos'. In the realm of organization studies, Sikka's work on Internet blogs highlights the unique political potential of web-based discussion and organizing for effecting change (Sikka 2008). In the case of *Yes Men*, visitors to yesmen.org are urged to debate the documentary and to join in themselves. The website encourages would-be activists and impersonators to just 'go for it' and carry out similar stunts with reference to other powerful interests in society. The site offers a discussion forum, help and advice on such pranks, and descriptions of identity corrections by would-be Yes Men. Interestingly, if such pranks are to attract the attention of the world's press and be successful, they must be funny. Humour must always move forward, transgressing boundaries, and must always be new (O'Doherty 2007). In order to be funny and effective, these pranks must always contain an element of newness, of performative surprise, and this implies that this kind of format encourages the proliferation of new forms of critique, rather than 'deadening cliché' of repetition (Butler 1990; Kavanagh and O'Sullivan 2007; Parker 2007). It appears that the medium of the Internet allows the laughter, the discussion and the parody to continue in the online debates that surround the documentary and the exhortations to repeat indefinitely. Yesmen.org provides an ongoing 'live' forum for critique and counterargument. The spectacle does not close with the final credit sequence.

A second interesting point relates to DVD technology itself. In the time between pranks, when the attention of the world's print media is elsewhere, the *Yes Men* DVD allows the spectacle to go further and to reach a wider audience. In this way, it joins the recent swathe of documentary films which highlight problems in society that 'people aren't talking about' (Yes Men 2005). We are currently witnessing an inordinate growth in similar DVD documentaries, due to changes in technology that makes them cheaper and easier to create (Thompson and Bordwell 2002). In addition, the Internet provides a very cheap and effective marketing channel for such films (Thompson and Bordwell 2002). This new genre is spreading widely due to such changes (Epstein 2005). This relates to Hariman's (2008) point that parody must be 'levelling' in order to work effectively. By this, he means that parody brings the elevated, the austere and the untouchable down to the level of the ordinary. In addition, everyone must be able to participate in the parody. We can see from the *Yes Men* documentary that the particular mix of inexpensive DVD documentary, widely-available Internet and press-release 'activism' enables such a levelling. The overall 'spectacle' of the *Yes Men* shows how the Internet, documentary and parody can form a potent mix for re-imagining dominant institutions and organizations.

Subverting the WTO?

Returning to the earlier discussion, it must be asked whether the *Yes Men* documentary represents an effective critique, or is merely entertainment. Revisiting Butler's ideas, we note that the parodic spectacles depicted in this film are always/already located in a 'commodity culture where "subversion"carries market value' (Butler 1990, xxi; Parker 2007). Certainly, the *Yes Men* have sold large numbers of DVDs and books in recent years. Despite this, the activists themselves claim that all such revenues are being channelled into future parodic spectacles, which echoes De Certeau's observations on the possibility for critique within contemporary modes of consumption. He describes how, in everyday life, 'the products imposed by a dominant economic order' can be taken up and used by people in a myriad of ways, and often towards 'ends' that are 'foreign to the system' itself (1984, xii-xiii). In this way, we seen how film production and Internet technologies can be used by 'ordinary' people to voice their resistance, and how even where these are commercialized, the impetus for critique can remain.

In addition, in considering whether the *Yes Men* DVD equates to subversion, it is useful to return to Butler's caution, that parody runs the risk of providing the necessary alterity that ensures the continuation of the 'the power one opposes' (Butler 1990, xxvi; Foucault 1990). It must be noted that it is this power that provides the very material for resistance and, therefore, resistance is always on *its* terms. However, this insight that we are always already mired in a particular set of power–knowledge relations also means that we cannot opt out of the game of repetition; we cannot choose not to partake. 'The task is not *whether* to repeat, but *how* to repeat... and, through a radical proliferation [of gender], to displace the very [gender] norms that enable the repetition itself' (Butler 1990, 189, emphasis added). In this way, activist groups like the Yes Men, who find themselves mired in a particular commodity culture that normalizes the WTO, either resist and subvert the culture or do nothing and let the norms reproduce according to the operation of power and domination. We are all invited to laugh at the 'vital instability' that is 'produced by that performative surprise' (Butler 1990, xxvi) and decide whether or not we want to join in the fun.

Concluding remarks

Butler argues that if norms are performative, reiterated over time, then parodic acts form a critical role in disrupting, subverting and altering the performance. When Yes Man Hans Hardy Unruh, a parody of a WTO representative, whips off his sombre business suit to release a three-foot-long golden phallus, complete with 'foreign worker control unit' at the tip, he provides both the textile executives in the audience and his DVD viewers with something of a 'performative surprise' (Butler 1990, xxvi). What such acts of parody *do*, following Butler and Hariman, is to highlight the constructed nature of commonly accepted identities; in this case, public perceptions of the WTO. In so doing, the comedic upturning enables us to hold these perceptions at a distance, to examine and critique them, and perhaps to imagine how things might be otherwise. If such acts are to continue, they must always be fresh, and always funny. The pranks must move forward in originality, and cannot be predicted (Critchley 2007). This new mix of parody, Internet and DVD documentary can help us to imagine and re-imagine institutions that often appear to be beyond reproach.

References

American Movie. Directed by Chris Smith, Columbia Tristar, 2000.

An Inconvenient Truth. Directed by Davis Guggenheim, Paramount Pictures, 2006.

Anderson, Benedict. 1991. Imagined communities: Reflections on the origin and spread of nationalism. London: Verso Books.

Barbie Liberation Organization. 2009. Operation newspeak. Barbie Liberation Organization video news release, http://www.rtmark.com/bloscript.html (accessed 3 March 2009).

Blumenfeld, Warren and Margaret Soenser Breen. 2001. Introduction to the special issue: Butler matters: Judith Butler's impact on feminist and queer studies since gender trouble. *International Journal of Sexuality and Gender Studies* 6, no. 1–2: 1–5.

Boltanski, L. and E. Chiapello. 2007. *The new spirit of capitalism.* London: Verso Books.

Borgerson, Janet. 2005. Judith Butler: On organizing subjectivities. *Sociological Review* 53: 63–79.

Butler, Judith. 1990. *Gender trouble: Feminism and the subversion of identity.* London: Routledge.

Butler, Judith. 1993. *Bodies that matter: On the discoursive limits of sex.* London: Routledge.

Butler, Judith. 2004. *Undoing gender.* New York: Routledge.

Butler, Richard. 1997. Stories and experiments in social inquiry. *Organization Studies* 18, no. 6: 927–48.

Collinson, David. 2002. Managing humor. *Journal of Management Studies* 29, no. 3: 269–89.

Critchley, Simon. 2007. Humour as practically enacted theory, or, why critics should tell more jokes. In *Humour, work and organization,* ed. R. Westwood and C. Rhodes, 17–33. Abingdon, UK: Routledge.

De Certeau, Michel. 1984. *The practice of everyday life.* Berkeley, CA: University of California Press.

Du Gay, Paul. 2007. *Organizing identity: Persons and organizations after theory.* London: Sage.

Epstein, Edward Jay. 2005. Paranoia for fun and profit: How Disney and Michael Moore cleaned up on Fahrenheit 9/11. *The Slate,* 3 May 2005, http://www.slate.com/id/2117923/ (accessed 3 March 2009).

Foucault, Michel. 1990. *The history of sexuality: Volume 1, an introduction.* London: Penguin.

Grugulis, Irena. 2002. Nothing serious? Candidates' use of humour in management training. *Human Relations* 55, no. 4: 387–406.

Hariman, Robert. 2008. Political parody and public culture. *Quarterly Journal of Speech* 94, no. 3: 247–72.

Hassard, John. 1998. Representing reality. In *Organization–representation: Work organizations in popular culture,* ed. J. Hassard and R. Holliday,. London: Sage.

Hassard, John and Ruth Holliday. 1998. *Organization-representation: Work organizations in popular culture.* London: Sage.

Hodgson, Damien. 2005. Putting on a professional performance: Performativity, subversion and project management. *Organization* 12, no. 1: 51–68.

Hopfl, Heather. 2007. Humour and violation. In *Humour, work and organization,* ed. R. Westwood and C. Rhodes, 33–45. Abingdon, UK: Routledge.

Hutcheon, Linda. 1985. *A theory of parody: The teachings of twentieth-century art forms.* New York: Methuen.

Kavanagh, Donncha and Don O'Sullivan. 2007. Advertising: The organizational production of humour. In *Humour, work and organization,* ed. R. Westwood and C. Rhodes, 235–49. Abingdon, UK: Routledge.

Lawless, Andrew. Identity correction – Yes Men style: Interview with Andy Bichlbaum. Three Monkeys Online, February 2005, http://www.threemonkeysonline.com/als/_the_yes_men_andy_bichlbaum_interview.html (accessed 3 March 2009).

Manufacturing Dissent. 2007. Directed by Debbie Melnyk and Rick Caine, Liberation Entertainment, 2007.

Myerson, Sylvie and Vidyut Jain. 2002. The art of confusion: Interview with Frank Guerrero. Subsol, http://subsol.c3.hu/subsol_2/contributors2/rtmarktext2.html (accessed 3 March 2009).

O'Doherty, Damian P. 2007. Heidegger's unfunny and the academic text: Organization analysis on the blink. In *Humour, work and organization,* ed. R. Westwood and C. Rhodes, 180–204. Abingdon, UK: Routledge.

Parker, Martin. 2002. Queering management and organization. *Gender, Work and Organization* 9, no. 2: 146–66.

Parker, Martin. 2007. The little book of management bollocks and the culture of organization. In *Humour, work and organization,* ed. R. Westwood and C. Rhodes, 77–92. Abingdon, UK: Routledge.

Rhodes, Carl. 2002. Coffee and the business of pleasure: The case of Harbucks vs. Mr. Tweek. *Culture and Organization* 8, no. 4: 293–306.

Rhodes, Carl and Alison Pullen. 2007. Representing the d'other: The grotesque body and masculinity at work in The Simpsons. In *Humour, work and organization,* ed. R. Westwood and C. Rhodes, 161–80. Abingdon, UK: Routledge.

Rhodes, Carl and Robert Westwood. 2008. *Critical representations of work and organizations in popular culture.* Abingdon, UK: Routledge.

Rothman, William. 1997. *Documentary film classics.* Cambridge: Cambridge University Press.

Routledge P. 1997. The imagineering of resistance: Pollok Free State and the practices of postmodern politics. *Transactions of the Institute of British Geographers* 22: 359–376.

Sikka, Prem. 2008. The internet and potentialities of emancipatory change: The case of the institutions and politics of accounting. *Critical Perspectives on International Business* 4, no. 1: 75–83.

Silberman, Steve. 1996. Boy 'bimbos' too much for game-maker Maxis. *Wired News,* 3 December, http://wired.com/news/culture/0,1284,775,00.html (accessed 3 March 2009).

Swift, Jonathan. 1996. A modest proposal: For preventing the children of poor people in Ireland from being a burden to their parents or country, and for making them beneficial to the publick. In *A modest proposal and other satirical works,* ed. S. Appelbaum. Mineola, NY: Dover Publications.

Taylor, Phil and Peter Bain. 2003. Subterranean worksick blues: Humour as subversion in two call centres. *Organization Studies* 24, no. 9: 1487–509.

Supersize Me. Directed by Morgan Spurlock, Sony Pictures, 2004.

The Corporation. Directed by Mark Achbar, Jennifer Abbott and Joel Baker, Metrodome Distribution, 2005.

Thompson, Kristin and David Bordwell. 2002. *Film history: An introduction.* New York: McGraw-Hill.

Westwood, Robert. 2004. Comic relief: Subversion and catharsis in organisational comedic theatre. *Organisation Studies* 25, no. 5: 775–95.

Westwood, Robert and Carl Rhodes. 2007. Humour and the study of organizations. In *Humour, work and organization,* ed. R. Westwood and C. Rhodes, 1–15. Abingdon, UK: Routledge.

Yes Men. 2002. The Yes Men dissolve the WTO. RTMark, http://www.rtmark.com/yestro.html (accessed 3 March 2009).

Yes Men. Directed by Chris Smith, Dan Ollman and Sarah Price, Tartan Video, 2005.

Yes Men. 2009a. F.A.Q. http://theyesmen.org/node/49 (accessed 3 March 2009).

Yes Men. 2009b. Beyond the golden parachute. http://theyesmen.org/hijinks/tampere (accessed 3 March 2009).

Organisational Gothic

MARTIN PARKER

This paper illustrates and theorises a tradition of 'gothic' representations of organisation in the last two centuries. It links Marx's conjunction between capital and the vampire, Dickensian melodrama, and Weber and Kafka's labyrinthine bureaucracy, to contemporary films that show power-crazed lunatics at the top of corporate skyscrapers. I argue that this represents a powerful form of cultural critique through representation. Organisational gothic is, I believe, one cultural trope that has commonly been employed in order to reframe sanitised visions of a brave new world. More generally, the paper also exemplifies a certain approach to the cultural aspects of organization, in this case by making a claim for the importance of a cultural history of representations of industry and organisation.

THE MONSTER AWAKES

The Goths, like the Vandals and the Huns, were nomadic tribes who brought the classical era of European history to an end. Where the Greeks and Romans had established learning and order, these central European hordes swept in and celebrated a mobile form of anarchic violence. After them was a thousand year long age of darkness, where the lamps of civilisation flickered in only a few places. No wonder the Goths have a bad name.

This paper is a small attempt to rehabilitate the Goths and the descendants who now claim their title. Since the 18th century, gothic has come to mean another form of darkness, and in its mobile transmutations, has celebrated various forms of disorder and transgression. In a wide variety of ways, gothic representations claim the dark sides of Western culture as their own. The seething desires of the unconscious, the night, the serial killer or sexual deviant, blood, loneliness, becoming animal or alien, the monstrous mob, the graveyard and the ruin. As several commentators have suggested (Botting, 1996; Davenport-Hines, 1997; Grunenberg, 1997), for more than 200 years, gothic has taken contemporary fears and made them its own. In this paper, I will excavate the specific conjunction between gothic and representations of industry and organisation. It seems to me that we can trace a stream of imagery that presents the urban world of work in ways that are heavily indebted to the gothic. I am going to argue that this represents a powerful form of cultural critique through representation. Organisational gothic is, I believe, one way of resisting sanitised visions of a brave new world, and it has haunted the culture of organisation for many years.

The wider point of this paper is to solicit certain forms of representation and conjoin them with a critique of contemporary forms of market managerialism. It seems to me that accounting frauds, anti-corporate protests, movements for business ethics and social responsibility, and the growth of critical management studies all point to a sustained political and ethical suspicion of large scale forms of organising. What I want to add in this paper is a cultural dimension[1], one based on an appreciation of the ways in which 'gothic' representations have become common ways of imagining our lives at work. I have explored this elsewhere in terms of the ubiquity of visions of the grey bureaucrat, the heartless corporation and the corrupt executive (Parker, 2002b), but in this paper want to explore the genealogy of these ideas as an enduring and radical critique of the modern world. Towards the end of the paper I will also consider whether invoking the gothic is necessarily a critical move, and also the status of a cultural criticism of organisations more generally.

GOTHIC

In perhaps its most consistent meaning, the gothic is that which diverges from Rome. If Rome represents the centre, order, visibility and civilisation then it is the Goths who seek something other. In cultural terms, the label was first applied during the later renaissance as a derogatory one to buildings that departed from the golden age of symmetry and proportion. Giorgio Vasari (1511–1574), an Italian painter, architect and writer, noted that there 'arose new architects who after the manner of their barbarous nations erected buildings in that style which we call Gothic'. Slightly later, John Evelyn (1620–1706), an English diarist, wrote that 'ancient Greek and Roman architecture answered all the perfections required in a faultless and accomplished building' but the Goths 'introduced in their stead a certain fantastical and licentious manner of building: congestions of heavy, dark, melancholy, monkish piles, without any just proportion, use or beauty' (both cited in Cram, 1909).

But if the gothic was here employed as a negative term that served to elevate certain classical virtues, its reincarnation in the middle of the 18th century reversed the assessment. By the time of John Ruskin's 1853 essay, 'The Nature of Gothic', the 'fallen Roman, in the utmost impotence of his luxury, and insolence of his guilt' (Ruskin, 1985: 80) has become the antithesis of virtue and authenticity. The corruption and sterility of neo-classicism provides the justification for an increasing celebration of the mediaeval, whether it be a conservative lament for feudalism or a radical celebration of craft guilds. Importantly, this later version of the gothic seems to begin at about the same time that notions of the 'sublime' and 'picturesque' become central to reorganising a relationship between the urban and the rural, the past and the present. The idea that wild and unruly nature was a source of beauty and awe would not have made much sense to those who spent their lives struggling with the earth, and in that regard it is hardly surprising that the educated and elite members of a newly stratified society began to valorise that which they had achieved some distance from. Tiring of the ordering that characterised neo-classical aesthetics, the rigid patterns of hedges and proper orders of column, the idea grows that yawning chasms, ruins and volcanoes could provoke reactions which were more than simply pleasing.

One hundred years before Ruskin, Edmund Burke's (1757) *A Philosophical Enquiry into the Origin of our Ideas of the Sublime and Beautiful* had provided the aesthetic rationale for willingly exposing oneself to the awe-fulness of nature. If smallness, delicacy, smoothness, sweetness and gradual variation were characteristics of the beautiful, then the sublime was characterised by vastness, darkness, danger, power and suddenness. It is because, Burke suggests, the latter phenomena remind us of our mortality and insignificance that

---

[1]The nascent idea of a 'cultural studies' of organisation is one that can be found elsewhere too. See some parts of Burrell (1997), as well as Hassard and Holliday (1998), Smith *et al.* (2001), Rhodes (2002) and ten Bos (2003).

exposure to the sublime provokes such strong emotions. Salvator Rosa's (1615–1673) images of the bay of Naples lit by Vesuvius and craggy Neapolitan landscapes populated by witches and bandits had already been brought back to Northern Europe as grand tour postcards. Withered trees and storms began to establish a new grammar for extreme experiences that were supposed to broaden the mind. By the middle of the 18th century Alexander Pope, Horace Walpole, William Kent and others had began to establish irregularity and artifice as principles upon which nature could be represented in design (Davenport-Hines, 1998; Munro, 2002). An increasing number of landscapes employed shell grottoes, hermits, obelisks and ruins to stage an emotionally dramatic movement from one prospect to another. The melancholy of decay also inspired the castellations and towers of houses and follies. One of Pope's engravings for his 1745 *Essay on Man* depicts a sea of derelict monuments, including a broken pediment inscribed, '*Roma Aeterna*'—eternal Rome. Rather than timeless order, it was now melancholy, mortality and insignificance that organised a new aesthetic.

At the beginning of Walpole's novel *The Castle of Otranto* in 1764, a gigantic helmet falls into the castle courtyard and kills the only heir just prior to his marriage. The intricate events that follow provide much of the imagery of the haunted house that has been so central to gothic ever since—ghosts, prophecies, murder and lust. Whilst Walpole's rather camp playfulness began to be made more formulaic in the writings of novelists like Ann Radcliffe, William Beckford and Matthew Lewis, it also feeds on some much darker forms of social criticism that emerge from the late 18th century onwards. Piranesi's prints of imaginary prison interiors (the *Carceri*), Goya's illustrations of the horrors of war, and the Marquis de Sade's incarcerated explorations of sexual desire and freedom all shared a deep pessimism (or realism) about the human condition. In many of these books we also find evil lurking in the representatives of the Roman Catholic Church, perhaps the global institution of its time and 'widely regarded as [*a*] sinister machine of cruel controls' (Davenport-Hines, 1998: 224). The arrogance of order and the cruelties of power were all too clear to those Europeans who lived through religious wars and the age of revolutions. A darker gothic sensibility seems to part company from romanticism at around this time. Terms that had been synonyms, the picturesque and the grotesque, were increasingly distinguished (Hollington, 1984: 23).

Fred Botting (1996: 2) has suggested that the gothic is concerned with excess and transgression, the 'negative, irrational, immoral and fantastic'. He is also clear that the figures of the gothic have been mutable, reflecting the hopes and fears of the age that they grow from. So, the desolate mountain becomes the haunted house, which in turn becomes the labyrinthine city or factory. The evil aristocrat or monk becomes the mad scientist or Machiavellian capitalist. It seems to be a genre which is continually concerned to celebrate that which is secreted away and oppose that which is deemed natural.

> It negates. It denies. It buries in shadow that which had been brightly lit, and brings into the light that which had been repressed. (McGrath, 1997: 156)

Yet, unlike more rational and illuminating forms of critique, the gothic suggests no tidy solution. There is no way out of the haunted house, the vampire never really dies, and the skeletal hand will always reach out of the earth to grasp your ankle just as you think you have got away. But we shouldn't understand the monstrous merely in terms of golems, blood-suckers and doppelgangers as if modern gothic were merely about transgressive bodies. Rather, and I will expand on this below, the gothic is also a way to represent social relations and institutions. In the form that it has taken from the 19th century onwards, the gothic has been profoundly concerned to show the darkness hiding in the light, to pursue a form of social criticism through cultural re-presentation.

INDUSTRIAL GOTHIC

As I suggested above, the emergence of concepts like the 'sublime' and the 'picturesque' began to make nature into an object of a new form of aesthetic interest. However, in another sense it also began to secure a new aesthetic vocabulary within which urbanisation and industrialisation could be represented. The dramas of light and shade explored by Rosa had been applied to industrial subjects by Joseph Wright of Derby (Hetherington, 1997: 109), and it is easy enough to see how echoes of hell could be forged from the smoke and fire of William Blake's 'dark satanic mills'. In a sense then, one element of the emerging critique of industrialism was to connect the manufactory and the city to established ideas from mythology (for examples, see Chapple, 1970: 93). If Eden was the pastoral idyll, then the growing industrial towns were far from green and pleasant—*The Nether World* of George Gissing's 1889 novel. But, perhaps most importantly, they were founded on new social relationships which problematised an older order. Much of 19th century gothic takes key figures in this new landscape and plays with the ambivalences that they contain.

The three key texts that provide so much of this imagery can illustrate this well enough. Mary Shelley's (1818) *Frankenstein*, Robert Louis Stevenson's (1886) *Strange Case of Dr Jekyll and Mr Hyde*, and Bram Stoker's (1897) *Dracula* are all novels set in the contemporary—told through letters, reports, diary entries and so on—but yet contain abnormalities that lurch through the text. In *Frankenstein*, the arrogance of science is exposed in a sorcerer's apprentice fable that illustrates hubris creating an external nemesis. In *Dr Jekyll and Mr Hyde*, Stevenson reworks older stories of possession and were-wolves into a tale of scientifically induced nemesis from within. Finally, in *Dracula*, the forces of reason and civilisation are pitted against something entirely unworldly that merges anxieties about class, sexuality, religion, human and animal bodies and even death itself in one heady mix.

There are, of course, plenty of other ways to read these stories, but the key theme I want to bring out is the massive tension they produce between their 'realism', being credible stories about modern people, and the eruption of horrific fantasy into the everyday. Of particular relevance here is the scientist or professional as a modern type who produces (Frankenstein), embodies (Dr Jekyll) or counters (Van Helsing) threats to order. These books are populated by doctors, lawyers and scientists, the emergent Victorian middle classes whose orderings did so much to create the modern world. Whether attacked by the disdainful aristocratic count Dracula or the 'stunted proletarian monster' Mr Hyde (Davenport-Hines, 1998: 312), the position of the professional classes is far from secure. So, if 18th century gothic was mediaeval, 19th century gothic used similar aesthetic mechanisms in order to insist that the battle between science and superstition has not been settled, and perhaps never can be.

However, 'superstition' is too loose and pejorative a word in these contexts. What these novels establish is the possibility that a wide range of 'Others' could be deployed to interrogate the present. Merely taking these three novels as exemplars, we have oppositions between food/blood, scientist/aristocrat, Western Europe/Eastern Europe, science/alchemy, human/animal, life/death, day/night, Christianity/paganism, reproduction/consumption in which the former term (perhaps the 'settled' term) is exceeded or inverted by the latter term. I will say some more about this (rather structuralist and moralising) understanding of gothic towards the end of the paper. For now I just want to note the power of gothic imagery as a way of condensing a certain moral censure. In summoning the image of Dracula, Frankenstein's monster or Mr Hyde, we can redescribe a person, thing or relation. Indeed, terms like 'vampyre' and 'blood sucker' had been used as derogatory alternatives to 'sharper', 'userer' and 'stockjobber' since the early 18th century at least (Davenport-Hines, 1998: 239). So when Karl Marx, writing before Stoker, uses various rhetorical flourishes in the *Eighteenth Brumaire, Grundrisse*, the inaugural address to the First International, and *Capital* (Godfrey, Jack and Jones, 2004) to apply the metaphor of vampirism to capital and the bourgeois order he is relying on an already fairly well established convention.

> Capital is dead labour which, vampire-like, lives only by sucking living labour, and lives the more, the more labour it sucks. (Marx, 1876/1976: 342)

Though there are economic issues being dramatised in quotes like this[2], there is also an important rhetorical strategy at work. In suggesting that capital is like a vampire, Marx (and also Engels) perverts the ideology of capitalism by equating the vitality of capitalist production with the sickening consumption of the parasite. The moral economy of value that Marx despised is re-described in terms that force the reader into some kind of imaginative leap. Whether they accept the implicit proposition that he makes is another matter, but Marx's metaphorical strategy is clear enough:

> …some of the most gruesomely archaic echoes of fairy-tale, legend, myth and folklore crop up in the wholly unexpected environment of the modern factory system, stock exchange, and parliamentary chamber: ghosts, vampires, ghouls, werewolves, alchemists, and reanimated corpses continue to haunt the bourgeois world, for all its sober and sceptical virtues. (Baldick, 1987: 121)

Yet these ideas and characters do not exhaust the gothic. Indeed, I would argue that they are merely the tip of an imaginative iceberg that throws a cold light on the modern world. In 19th century gothic, it is all too often the city itself that plays this role—a grim city populated by institutions of various degrees of cruelty—prisons, workhouses, schools, factories and laboratories. Take Charles Dickens, for example, an author who might not be termed gothic in a strict sense, but certainly continues what Hollington (1984) has termed 'the grotesque tradition'. In many of his novels, he employs extreme characterisation and chiaroscuro description to present the city and its denizens as polluted by money, whilst the simplicity and authenticity of the country lies beyond. Country folk are corrupted (*Great Expectations*) or easily hoodwinked (*Oliver Twist*) by the baleful influence of London, whilst Dickens continually expresses mock naivety about the motives of those populating various self-congratulatory yet cruel institutions. In his *Bleak House* of 1853, travelling to the 'iron country' involves leaving 'fresh green woods' behind and entering somewhere with 'coalpits and ashes, high chimneys and red bricks, blighted verdure, scorching fires and a heavy never-lightening cloud of smoke' (Dickens, 1853/1993: 695). Rouncewells' factory is described in similar terms:

> …a great perplexity of iron lying about, in every stage, and in a vast variety of shapes; in bars, in wedges, in sheets; in tanks, in boilers, in axles, in wheels, in cogs, in cranks, in rails; twisted and wrenched into eccentric and perverse forms, as separate parts of machinery; mountains of it broken up, and rusty in its age; distant furnaces of it glowing and bubbling in its youth; bright fireworks of it showering about, under the blows of the steam hammer; red-hot iron, white-hot iron, cold-black iron; an iron taste, an iron smell, and a Babel of iron sounds. (Dickens, 1853/1993: 696)

In Dickens' most celebrated 'industrial novel', *Hard Times*, he portrays Coketown as 'a town of machinery and tall chimneys, out of which interminable serpents of smoke trailed themselves for ever and ever' and factories which were 'vast piles of building full of windows where there was a rattling and a trembling all day long, and where the piston of the steam-engine worked monotonously up and down like the head of an elephant in a state of melancholy madness' (1854/1994). In perhaps his clearest anti-bureaucratic satire, *Little Dorrit* of

---

[2]To which might be added the relation between economics and desire. For a vein of speculation which has employed an admixture of Marxism and psychoanalysis, see Moretti (1983), Baldick (1987), Gelder (1994), and Brown (1997). Godfrey *et al.* (2004) usefully open an Althusserian gap between 'ideological' and 'scientific' readings of the vampires in Marx. This paper is primarily concerned with the former, theirs with the latter.

1857, we are introduced to the 'Circumlocution Office', an arm of government with the motto 'How not to do it'. Its particular expertise was in ensuring that any matters that were referred to it 'never reappeared in the light of day. Boards sat on them, secretaries minuted upon them, commissioners gabbled about them, clerks registered, entered, checked, and ticked them off, and they melted away' (Dickens, 1857/1994c: 106). The novel's protagonist is passed from office to office, through endless corridors and piles of forms that ensure that nothing is ever done.

> 'May I enquire how I can obtain official information as to the real state of the case?'
>
> 'It is competent,' said Mr. Barnacle, 'to any member of the – Public,' mentioning that obscure body with reluctance, as his natural enemy, 'to memorialise the Circumlocution Department. Such formalities as are required to be observed in so doing, may be known on application to the proper branch of that Department.'
>
> 'Which is the proper branch?'
>
> 'I must refer you,' returned Mr Barnacle, ringing the bell, 'to the Department itself for a formal answer to that inquiry.' (Dickens, 1857/1994c: 112)

But the 'industrial novel' is not, of course, limited to Dickens. Elizabeth Gaskell's 1855 *North and South*, dramatises the ugly town of Milton in the northern county of Darkshire and its contrast with the rural idyll of Helstone in similar ways. The first intimation of Milton that Margaret Hale sees is a 'deep lead-coloured cloud hanging over the horizon' (Gaskell, 1855/1995: 60), and, in her new house, 'thick fog crept up to the very windows, and was driven into every open door in choking white wreaths of unwholesome mist' (*ibid.*: 66). She meets Thornton, a local industrialist whose 'mill loomed high…casting a shadow down from its many stories, which darkened the summer evening before its time' (*ibid.*:159), whilst all around 'the chimneys smoked, the ceaseless roar and mighty beat, and dizzying whirl of machinery, struggled and strove perpetually' (*ibid.*: 407). In Emile Zola's *Germinal* of 1885, we find similar metaphors at work, though this time they are being used to describe a mine rather than a townscape. Village Two Hundred and Forty is surrounded by decaying factories, and the Le Voreux mine is the last major employer for its desperate citizenry. It is continually described as a monstrosity that swallows men. The pump of the mine is 'like the breath of an insatiable ogre… this god, crouching and replete, to whom ten thousand starving men were offering up their flesh' (Zola, 1885/1954: 80). The mental and physical suffering and disease caused by mining are described in hideous detail, and the lengthy winter strike that occupies most of the novel results in starvation, mob violence and the eventual destruction of the mine, which collapses into itself just as so many gothic mansions do at the end of the tale. 'The evil beast, crouching in its hollow, sated with human flesh, had drawn its last long heavy breath…. Soon the crater filled up and the place that had been Le Voreux was a muddy lake, like those lakes beneath which lie evil cities destroyed by God' (ibid. 452–3).

In Dickens, Gaskell and Zola the organisation is rarely treated as a problem in itself but provides an occasional scene for broader complaints. Instead, the industrial and the urban are co-implicated as the causes of a degradation in both ethical sensibilities and aesthetic experience, and this is expressed through a developing imagery of the manufactory and the city as grotesque places populated by stunted characters. Clearly this emerging anti-aesthetic is shared by the iconic gothic novels that all express a suspicion of the modern and, perhaps most importantly, employ a more or less explicit representational form of criticism. Just as empire and industry marched onwards to the future to the sound of a chorus of self-congratulatory approval, so did 'gothic's antagonism to the possibility of human progress' (Davenport-Hines, 1998: 276) provide a counterpoint, reminding readers that much darkness was also being manufactured by the industrial revolution.

ORGANISATIONAL GOTHIC

So it is not really until the early 20th century that organisations themselves begin to become represented as sites of darkness. Echoing the older image of the haunted house, we begin to see images of organisations as labyrinths with endless corridors and locked doors hiding evil secrets. Or, as the places where monsters are fabricated, and people themselves become monstrous. This is, in part, a shift from exteriors to interiors, from the dirty city street to the cramped office or nightmare factory. As good place as any to begin is with Max Weber's (1930: 181) deeply ambivalent description of the 'conditions of machine production which today determine the lives of all individuals who are born into this mechanism'. This is the 'iron cage' (*op cit*)[3] of bureaucratic administration in which the 'professional bureaucrat is chained to his activity by his entire material and ideal existence. In the great majority of cases, he is only a single cog in an ever-moving mechanism which prescribes to him an essentially fixed route of march' (Gerth and Mills, 1948: 228). Such mechanistic descriptions have echoed through 20th century politics and culture, articulating an intimate combination of ruthless efficiency and moral impoverishment.

Perhaps with Piranesi's *Carceri* in mind, the vocabulary of German expression in film from the 1920s onwards gives stunning visual illustration to Weber's terrors. Given post-war inflation, unemployment and war reparations Davenport-Hines (1998: 327) suggests that: 'all human institutions were thus discredited in Weimar Germany.... It was a ripe period for goths, although gothic could not be medieval and knightly in a period of sordid squabbles over percentages'. In Fritz Lang's 1926 film *Metropolis* 'the gloomy city is divided between a class of industrially roboticised human slaves forced to live a subterranean existence maintaining the awesome machines powering the city, and the rich who enjoy the luxuriously decadent pleasures of the world above' (Botting, 1996: 166). A key element of the imagery is that of workers being literally reduced to the appendages of giant machines.

> Dressed from throat to ankle in dark blue, men walk to their shifts with hanging fists and hanging heads. Row upon row, they shuffle into elevators taking them into the city's machine rooms. These machine rooms are places of roaring furnaces, heat-spitting walls, the odour of oil, and dark machines like crouching animals far below the streets. (Tolliver and Coleman, 2001: 44)

These industrial troglodytes are contrasted with the glorious indifference of the city above in which the suited managerial classes enjoy wood panelled offices. The towering masses of the cityscape are the new gothic castles and the monsters are now machines.

The visual imagery of *Metropolis*, as well as films like *A Nous La Liberté* (1932) and *Modern Times* (1936), may well reflect a Weberian diagnosis but there is another important influence too. As McGrath (1997: 156) has argued, 'psychoanalysis has in this century fulfilled the traditional function of gothic literature'. After all, the expressionist film set is also a landscape of the mind in which the suspension of disbelief allows for fantasy to mutate everyday features of the modern so that they become threatening phantoms. In fantastic fiction, whether these are real terrors or imaginary ones is not particularly important. 'Freud's remarkable achievement is to have taken the props and passions of terror Gothic—hero-villain, heroine, terrible place, haunting—and to have relocated them inside the self' (Edmundson, cited in Davenport-Hines, 1998: 325). There is no better source for this than the fiction of Franz Kafka, particularly his posthumous novels *The Trial* (1925/1953) and *The Castle* (1926/1957).

In both novels, the narrator is K—a bank manager in *The Trial* and a land surveyor in *The Castle*. The former tells the story of K's arrest, trial and eventual execution for a crime which

---

[3]In German, 'stahlhartes Gehäuse', perhaps better translated as 'shell as hard as steel'. See Baehr (2001).

is never specified, the latter of K's attempts to discover why he has been brought to a village beneath a towering castle to perform a task which no-one seems to want him to do. In each case, the ordered certainties of a smug professional are gradually stripped away as the logic of the organisation—'a rigid obedience to and execution of their duty' (Kafka, 1926/1957: 245)—exposes him to a series of increasingly bizarre humiliations. K is often sweating in low corridors, waiting in passages and being interviewed in chambers at the top of narrow staircases, the victim of confusion or conspiracy which no-one understands completely.

> The ranks of officials in this judiciary system mounted endlessly, so that not even adepts could survey the hierarchy as a whole. And the proceedings of the courts were generally kept secret from subordinate officials, consequently they could hardly ever quite follow in their further progress the cases on which they had worked; any particular case thus appeared in their circle of jurisdiction often without knowing whence it came, and passed from it they knew not whither. (Kafka, 1925/1953: 133)

K's eventual assassins in *The Trial* are two 'pallid and plump' (*op cit*: 245) gentlemen in frock coats and top hats who bow politely but say nothing. They don't know why they have been sent to administer 'justice', any more than K does.

In Kafka's world, cruelty is a bureaucratic matter, and the affairs of little people like K are of no consequence to those who merely carry out orders. Even misunderstandings are orders, after all. From *The Castle*:

> In such a large governmental office as the Count's, it may occasionally happen that one department ordains this, another that; neither knows of the other, and though the supreme control is absolutely efficient, it comes by its nature too late, and so every now and then a trifling miscalculation arises. (Kafka, 1926/1957: 62)

The person who is telling K this, the Superintendent, has a cabinet full of unfiled papers, and more piles of papers in the shed. Yet, because 'it is a working principle of the Head Bureau that the very possibility of error must be ruled out of account' (Kafka, 1926/1957: 66) the 'Control Officials', and those who control them, rarely intervene in such trivial matters. Indeed, even communicating with the Castle is a random matter, since there is so much important business to be transacted that the telephone is randomly switched between extensions.

Kafka's visions have since become archetypes, and the *Catch 22* type of organisational logic that he parodies has now made his name into an adjective. In an important sense, 'Kafkaesque' captures 20th century organisational gothic very nicely indeed. Darkly fantastic representations of work and organisations can be found in ever greater numbers as the 20th century develops. Adding to what we have covered already we could add Karel Capek's 1922 play *R.U.R.*—'Rossum's Universal Robots', Yevgeny Zamayatin's (1924) explicitly Taylorist 'OneState' of *We*, Aldous Huxley's 1932 *Brave New World* and George Orwell's *1984*. These visions variously dramatised the contrasts between industrial robber barons and mechanised worker slaves, the growth of scientific management and the bureaucratised violence of everyday life.

In the fifties and sixties organisational gothic seems rather eclipsed. Perhaps the contradictions of capitalism were no longer as stark or the industrialised agony of the killing fields of world war two was just too painful to consider, but the dominant message seems to be one of the organisation as a present day site for romance and upward social mobility[4]. However, Mervyn Peake's Gormenghast trilogy [*Titus Groan* (1946), *Gormenghast* (1950) and *Titus Alone* (1959)] is an important exception. Peake's Dickensian characters inhabit a gigantic sprawling castle that is run according to ancient ritual instructions contained in dusty volumes containing:

> ...the activities to be performed hour by hour during the day by his lordship. The exact times; the garments to be worn for each occasion and the symbolic gestures to be used. Diagrams facing the left hand page gave particulars of the routes by which his lordship should approach the various scenes of operation.... Had he been

---

[4]See Parker (2002b) for more on this.

of a fair skin, or had he been heavier than he was, had his eyes been green, blue or brown instead of black,
then, automatically another set of archaic regulations would have appeared… (Peake, 1968: 66)

Madness and bureaucracy become closely intertwined in a rambling story of intrigue and rebellion that, by the third novel, sees Titus the 77th Earl of Gormenghast escape to a city of strange
and wonderful technological marvels, of shimmering metal and glass buildings. Yet this is also
a city with smoking factory buildings, flying surveillance drones, a Kafkaesque court and
prison system and, like *Metropolis*, an entire culture of outcasts and fugitives beneath the city
itself in the 'Under-River'. Whether the institutions are feudal or modern, it seems Titus can
find no road to freedom, no place outside the sets of rules that constitute organised lives.

THE MONSTER WAKES

Gormenghast apart, it isn't really until the 1970s that organisational gothic begins to re-
emerge in a more generalised sense. Grunenberg (1997: 197) claims that contemporary gothic
is driven by 'an increasing weariness about the alienating power of technology and its disastrous social consequences', and adds: 'The Draculas of today are the greedy corporations,
automation, corrupt parties and politicians who deliberately erode the foundations of the
welfare state'. It was precisely the contemporary ubiquity of this demonology of the corporation that interested me in tracing some of the antecedents of contemporary gothic. It seems to
me that some very common motifs in fantastic fiction over the last three decades have been
the figure of the corporate tycoon conspiring at the top of their skyscraper; the organisation as
a place where monsters are spawned; and the visualisation of work as incarceration.

So when Dracula is relocated to London in *The Satanic Rites of Dracula* (1974) he is
disguised as D.D. Denham, a reclusive property developer with a corporate tower who is
secretly plotting to unleash a fatal virus upon the world. And when Damien, the anti-Christ,
returns in *Omen 3: The Final Conflict* (1981) he is a thirty-something CEO of a huge multinational corporation, Thorn Industries, who lusts for control of the world. Pretty much the
same figure of the corporate megalomaniac re-appears in a whole host of other films—
perhaps most splendidly in *Batman Returns* (1992) as the magnate Max Shreck (named after
the actor who played the vampire Nosferatu). In all these examples, and many more, the
image of the well dressed and dastardly chief executive looking out over the city from their
tower is a powerful continuation of gothic and melodramatic imagery. Indeed, such ideas are
now pastiched in comedy films like *Austin Powers: International Man of Mystery* (1997), in
which Dr Evil's henchman, Number Two, is portrayed as a corporate man with an eye-patch
and a briefcase who has built Virtucon into a global business. After Dr Evil's rather old fash-
ioned attempt to blackmail world governments with a nuclear device has failed, Number Two
turns to him and says:

I spent thirty years of my life turning this two bit evil empire into a world class multinational. I was going to
have a cover story in Forbes. But you, like an idiot, wanted to take over the world. But you don't realise there
is no world anymore—it's only corporations. (1997)

It seems that the easiest stereotype for a scriptwriter who wants to construct a villain is to call
upon wealth, class and gender and then embody them within the figure of the corporate executive. The melodramatic villain[5] no longer ties the innocent victim to the railway tracks, but
throws her from his corner office.

---

[5]A villain with a pedigree in melodramatic theatre and literature throughout the 19th century. For example, Alec
D'Urberville, from Thomas Hardy's (1891) *Tess of the D'Urbervilles*. Alec is a typical moustached Victorian rake, a
rich and morally corrupt seducer whose claim to the D'Urberville name is completely false.

Central to fantastic fiction films and novels are hence references to some part of the state or the military-industrial complex that has, because of greed, ambition or paranoia, invested in a dark conspiracy of money and power. In *Rollerball* (1975) for example, the hero 'Jonathan' is lectured by a senior corporate executive when he refuses to be retired from an exceptionally violent gladiatorial game which provides a circus for happy consumers. And, in a series of examples, the corporation produces or protects a monster that either rampages or rebels against its creators. Hence the Tyrell Corporation in *Blade Runner* (1982); the Weyland-Yutani Corp in the four *Alien* (1979–1997) films; Cyberdyne Systems in the *Terminator* (1984–2003) films; and Omni Consumer Products in the *Robocop* (1987–1993) films.

Indeed, this pervasive fog of organisational paranoia is constitutive of the many 'trust no-one' conspiracy narratives of the *X-Files* or films like *Conspiracy Theory* (1997), *The Game* (1997) and *Enemy of the State* (1998). Organisations, these texts repeatedly claim, are dark places where secrecy lurks behind closed doors and men in black are listening to every conversation (Parish and Parker, 2001). In a reversal of much of the post second world war organisational consensus, but a return to the narratives of *1984* and *Brave New World*, 'the technocrats are now the bad guys and the good guys are the reactionaries' (Franklin, 1990: 25). Images of rows of desks, endless corridors and insane bosses abound in *Brazil* (1985) where torture and repression are bureaucratised through the 'Ministry of Information'; *Joe and the Volcano* (1990) in which Tom Hanks' character seeks salvation from a grey dehumanised job; and *Being John Malcovich* (1999), where our hero works on the 7 1/2th floor with a ceiling that makes him have to stoop continuously. In these films, expressionist gothic is used to visualise the distorted lifeworld of the corporation, and the haunted house has mutated into a Weberian steel shell. Though not all anti-organisational representations draw on gothic imagery, many of them do—a law firm run by Satan in *The Devil's Advocate* (1997) as well as the TV series *Angel*; the 'Denmark Corporation' in the a remake of *Hamlet* (2000); and the Green Goblin in *Spider-Man* (2002), who is actually the CEO of Osborne Industries. Perhaps archetypally, in the cartoon series *The Simpsons* we have the etiolated Mr Burns, the evil capitalist who lives in a looming mansion with his fawning acolyte and plots against his employees and the residents of Springfield (Rhodes, 2001).

In the most general of terms then, we seem to see a mutation of themes and images over the last two hundred years of gothic, grotesque and melodramatic imagery. The evil villain twirling his moustache and plotting; the labyrinthine haunted house hiding secrets; the monster produced by mad science. All of these are now stock characters and settings, familiar to children and easily written into almost any piece of fantastic fiction. The corporation is taken to be their most credible site. Questions of motive are then simply assumed, because 'everybody knows' that corporations are motivational structures of greed, power and envy. So, at the very moment when global capitalism seems to be at its most triumphalist, and the ideology of market managerialism reaches down from the corporate tower into the crevices of the management of everyday life, careers, and relationships there is a simultaneous, and largely unremarked, 'common sense' that claims exactly the opposite. In the final section, I will conclude by further exploring the idea that the gothic can be treated as a form of representational critique, and then relate this to some general ideas about the role of a cultural criticism of organisations.

GOTHIC, CULTURE, CRITICISM

It gobbles whole mountains and forests, drinks rivers dry, spews toxic waste, and enslaves whole populations. It has all the rights of a citizen, but few of the limitations. It can cross national borders as if they were cobwebs. It is immortal, and can therefore amass wealth and power beyond the capabilities of mere mortals.... We are talking about the CORPORATION. (Earth First!, reproduced in Starr, 2000: 87)

It is easy enough to claim that there is a powerful gothic sensibility that stalks our age. Many authors have suggested as much, cataloguing 'horror, madness, monstrosity, death, disease, terror, evil, and weird sexuality' (Grunenberg, 1997: 210) as these themes are played out in contemporary sub-cultures, fiction, film and art (Latham, 2002). Yet, as this essay has hopefully shown, gothic representations of industry and organisation have been a pervasive feature of Western societies[6] for at least 150 years. Of course my use of the word 'gothic' is not at all precise here, and in fact I am really referring to some family resemblances between horror, the grotesque and melodrama—all genres that employ distortion and myth in order to achieve dramatic effects. Others have been considerably more precise in distinguishing the formal, classical, romantic and so on (Munro, 2002), and less cavalier in their generalisations.[7] However, I'm not sure that this confusion matters that much because my wider point is that this monstrous collection of texts represents a lengthy form of cultural struggle against the hegemony of a modern organised world. Following a cultural Marxism in the most general of terms, we can see these sorts of expressions as instances of contestation. Not the only ones, because there are plenty of examples of cultural contestation that are clearly not primarily gothic (comedic portrayals of management as stupid,[8] or romantic accounts of the freedoms that lie outside the work organisation, for example), and plenty of struggles that are not primarily cultural (trade union recognition, or the anti-corporate protests, for example).

But what does it mean to suggest that 'organisational gothic' is an example of cultural struggle? On the one hand, it is obvious enough that explicit gothic metaphors have played an important role as an imaginative resource for re-description. In referring to 'Frankenstein foods' to condemn genetic manipulation or describing people as 'Jekyll and Hyde' characters we are employing common clichés that rely on a metaphorical exchange between two domains. So when Garrick and Clegg reframe knowledge management as the transfusion of vital fluids, they title their chapter 'Organisational Gothic'[9] precisely to contrast the bright eyed utilitarianism of the knowledge managers with the seduction and coercion of the foul breathed vampire. For Garrick and Clegg (2000: 154), in the learning organisation the 'individual souls in the corporation that learn are those replenished by being sucked dry and recruited as brides and grooms to the new organisational Draculas'. Or when Pelzer and Pelzer (1996: 19) assert that 'organisations create fear, dread, helplessness', that they are self-created prisons, a 'threatening fact taking away our personalities, sucking life out of our bodies and brains without touching the surface of our skin', they rely on the same melodramatic grammar. In structural terms, the collision between a signifier for some form of horror and another domain (in this case, the work organisation) causes the latter to be infected or, let us say, re-thought. A commonly accepted, perhaps hegemonic, image is articulated in a different form. Whether this is the city as hell, the vampire metaphors in Marx, Weber's organisation-machines, or the CEO being revealed as the devil, it is the same operation at work.

However, to claim that this is necessarily a heroic form of criticism, in which the modern is *always* exceeded or inverted by the gothic, is to de-historicise both words and the movements that might happen between them. When Kenneth Gergen wrote in 1992 about the differences between romantic, modernist and postmodernist versions of organisation, he doubtless would not have anticipated that the term 'postmodernism' (or 'post-modernism') would often become

---

[6]And perhaps not only 'Western', though the ethnocentricity of this paper is clear enough. See Parish (2000) and Smith (2001) on occult capitalism in Ghana and Nigeria respectively.

[7]Further, as one of my referees noted, the mutation of themes from book, to film, to cartoon and so on, is also important in understanding their reception. I agree, and it is a further problem with the specifics of my argument.

[8]Which certainly links to older notions of the grotesque, and the carnivalesque laughter that turns the world upside down (see Rhodes 2002).

[9]The only other publication, to my knowledge, that uses this phrase directly, and hence the innocent victim of my textual vampirism.

a conventional way of celebrating post-Fordist economics, and not the endless unsettling that he anticipated. In the same manner, gothic imagery can itself become 'settled' or 'unsettling' depending on the context. Disorganising, revalorising closeted terms, soliciting the other, exceeding and inverting are all operations given meaning by a particular context, not having some transcendental or immanent meaning in themselves (Parker, 2002a). In a parallel fashion, there is a clear danger in treating gothic as it were necessarily always a great refusal which can and should be solicited by those who are excited by the romance of resistance.[10] Gothic ideas are the stuff of common cliché, and just as corporations can be described as the new Draculas, so can elected governments, or universities, or social workers. So can gothic be sold as a form of authenticity for middle class teenagers seeking community, or filmmakers seeking box office receipts, or nostalgics who wish to condemn versions of progress through science or urbanisation, or progressives who see the rural past as a haunt of irrational fears, or domesticators who wish to subdue the monsters from the Id, or punk academics selling rebellion for money. The point is that, as Botting (1996) argues, the gothic is mutable and hence it can be (and has been) employed for all these purposes and more. So in suggesting that the gothic can function as a form of representational critique, I am noting its power to denaturalise at one moment, but must also remember that it can itself naturalise as it becomes cliché, a metaphor that first shocks[11] and then becomes an excuse for not thinking. A (post-)Fordism of the intellect. Any colour you like, as long as it is black.

Nonetheless, there is something curiously powerful about this particular set of metaphors, because even whilst they decay into cliché they remain marked by such extremity. The images of horror, grotesquerie and melodrama that have haunted this paper seem to have a certain power, since once you have re-imagined the corporate tower as the castle on the hill, it is difficult to shake off that sense of unease. As Franco Moretti (1983: 107) comments, an older literature of terror 'presents society—whether the feudal idyll of *Frankenstein* or the Victorian England of *Dracula*—as a great corporation: whoever breaks its bonds is done for'. Nowadays, escaping from the great corporation might be just exactly what you need to do in order to survive. The message might be that you should stick to the path and stay out of the woods in case the wolf gets you, or that the wolf is already waiting for you at work. Or worse, that you look in the mirror of the washroom at work through yellowing eyes to discover that your eyebrows are thickening. Moretti describes horror as a 'literature of dialectical relations, in which the opposites, instead of separating and entering into conflict, exist in function of one another, reinforce one other'. But this is not, he claims, the mere functioning of ideology—generating the mists that obscure monsters.

> The more a work frightens, the more it edifies. The more it humiliates, the more it uplifts. The more it hides, the more it gives the illusion of revealing. It is a fear one *needs*: the price one pays for coming contentedly to terms with a social body based on irrationality and menace. Who says it is escapist? (Moretti, 1983: 108)

And here is a curious twist. If we do not treat culture as escapism, as an epiphenomenon of structure, then it can become both a topic and a limited resource for critique. If we treat the gothic, and specifically gothic organisation, as being an element in this 'literature of dialectical relations' then we have a way of grasping historical embeddedness fully. Dialectics explores the relation between opposing propositions, and hence the inter-connectedness of

---

[10]It seems to me that Pelzer and Pelzer (1996) and Pelzer (2002) seem to fall into this trap. I do not think that gothic should be treated as another synonym for cultural postmodernism, or as only a vehicle for a politicised post-structural understanding of language. Which is not to say that it can't play this function, just that it doesn't necessarily do it all of the time. Godfrey *et al.* (2004) claim that this paper falls into a similarly 'undialectical' trap.

[11]Smith (2001: 50) makes a connection between this and Brecht's 'alienation effect'. The point being that such an effect cannot rely on the same strategy every time if it is to shock an audience out of its existing state of consciousness.

supposedly separate terms. In general terms it therefore presumes a relationality between things which suggests that individual and context, particularity and generality are necessarily made in conjunction. In philosophical and political terms, this adds up to a radical attack on any approach which assumes an escapist separation between the romantic subject and their object of enquiry, or between the knower and the known. These, Baldick (1987:198) suggests, are precisely the limitations of realism, and in fact the only way in which the 'monstrous dynamics of the modern' can be apprehended are through the historically embedded techniques of estrangement that gothic has employed with such regularity. The reason that 'realists' like Dickens, Marx, Zola and Weber turn to monstrous metaphors is precisely because the 'conjuring powers available in language' (Smith, 2001: 51) can reveal through redescription, can unveil by veiling. At any given historical moment, the products of culture can label injustice in dramatic forms that can in turn provide resources to think about change.

Gothic criticism of organisations will not save anyone from the corporate beast, but it is a symptom of the times. Those critical of market managerialism may well employ such metaphors in their own attempts to sponsor change, to be (for a time, for our time) new Goths who oppose the ordered cruelties of a new Rome. As Ricardo Blaug (1999) has illustrated in his paper on the defeat of the well-organised XXth Roman legion by a swift and invisible gothic tribe in A.D. 9, 'hierarchism' causes a form of blindness to other organisational forms. In a parallel way, we could suggest that too much reliance on structural struggles inspires a kind of blindness to cultural struggles, and the tactics that they might employ. Not that either can be separated, since they are dialectically related and co-produced, but it seems obvious enough that seeing things differently might be a precursor to doing things differently. Which is, in a conclusively anti-gothic spirit, to end with revolutionary romanticism and hope that the dead hand of capital doesn't reach from the grave I am digging for it.

ACKNOWLEDGEMENTS

Thanks to the many who have listened to me ramble on about these ideas for years, and for their endless helpful suggestions which I have incorporated in the paper. You all know who you are, as do the four very helpful reviewers for this journal.

References

Baehr, P. (2001) The 'iron cage' and the 'shell as hard as steel', *History and Theory,* **40**(2), 153–69.
Baldick, C. (1987) *In Frankenstein's shadow,* Oxford: Clarendon Press.
Blaug, R. (1999) The tyranny of the visible, *Organisation,* **6**(1), 33–56.
Botting, F. (1996) *Gothic,* London: Routledge.
Brown, C. (1997) Figuring the vampire: death, desire and the image, in: S. Golding (Ed.) *The eight technologies of otherness,* pp. 117–33, London: Routledge.
Burrell, G. (1997) *Pandemonium,* London: Sage.
Chapple, J. (1970) *Documentary and imaginative literature 1880–1920,* London: Blandford Press.
Cram, R. (1909) Gothic architecture, *The Catholic encyclopedia, volume VI.* Online edition 1999. Available at http://www.newadvent.org/cathen/06665b.htm (accessed 31 October 2003).
Davenport-Hines, R. (1998) *Gothic. Four hundred years of excess, horror, evil and ruin,* New York: North Point Press.
Dickens, C. (1853/1993) *Bleak house,* Ware: Wordsworth Editions.
Dickens, C. (1854/1994) *Hard times,* London: Penguin.
Dickens, C. (1857/1994c) *Little Dorrit,* London: Penguin.
Franklin, H.B. (1990) Visions of the future in science fiction films from 1970 to 1982, in: A. Kuhn (Ed.) *Alien zone: cultural theory and contemporary science fiction cinema,* pp. 19–31, London: Verso.
Garrick, J. and Clegg, S. (2000) Organizational gothic: Transfusing vitality and transforming the corporate body through work-based learning, in: C. Symes and J. McIntyre (Eds.) *Working knowledge,* Buckingham: SRHE/ Open University Press.
Gaskell, E. (1855/1995) *North and south,* London: Penguin.

Gelder, K. (1994) *Reading the vampire,* London: Routledge.
Gergen, K. (1992) Organisation theory in the postmodern era, in: M. Reed and M. Hughes (Eds.) *Rethinking organisation,* pp. 207–26, London: Sage.
Gerth, H. and Mills, C. (Eds.) *For Max Weber,* London: Routledge and Kegan Paul.
Gibson, W. (1986) *Neuromancer,* London: Grafton.
Godfrey, R., Jack, G. and Jones, C. (2004) Sucking, bleeding, breaking: on the dialectics of vampirism, capital and time, *Culture and Organisation,* **10**(1), 25–36.
Grunenberg, C. (Ed.) (1997) *Gothic. Transmutations of horror in late twentieth century art,* Cambridge, MA: MIT Press.
Hassard, J. and Holliday, R. (Eds) (1998) *Organisation-representation,* London: Sage.
Hetherington, K. (1997) *The badlands of modernity,* London: Routledge.
Hollington, M. (1984) *Dickens and the grotesque,* London: Croom Helm.
Jancovich, M. (1992) *Horror,* London: Batsford.
Kafka, F. (1953) *The trial,* Harmondsworth: Penguin.
Kafka, F. (1957) *The castle,* London: Penguin.
Kafka, F. (1988) *The collected short stories of Franz Kafka,* London: Penguin.
Lang, Fritz (1926) *Metropolis.*
Latham, R. (2002) *Consuming youth: vampires, cyborgs and the culture of consumption,* Chicago, IL: University of Chicago Press.
Marx, K. (1876/1976) *Capital: Volume 1,* Harmondsworth: Penguin.
McGrath, P. (1997) Transgression and decay, in: C. Grunenberg (Ed) *Gothic. Transmutations of horror in late twentieth century art,* pp. 158–153, Cambridge, MA: MIT Press.
Moretti, F. (1983) Dialectic of fear, in: F. Moretti *et al.* (Ed.) *Signs taken for wonders,* pp. 83–108, London: Verso.
Munro, R. (2002) The consumption of time and space, in: M. Parker (Ed.) *Utopia and organization,* pp. 128–54, Oxford: Blackwell.
Parish, J. (2000) From the body to the wallet: conceptualising Akan witchcraft at home and abroad, *Journal of the Royal Anthropological Institute,* **6**(3), 487–500.
Parish, J. and Parker, M. (Eds.) (2001) *The age of anxiety: conspiracy theory and the human sciences,* Oxford: Blackwell.
Parker, M. (2002a) Queering management and organisation, *Gender, Work and Organisation,* **9**(2), 146–66.
Parker, M. (2002b) *Against management,* Oxford: Polity.
Peake, M. (1968) *Titus Groan,* Harmondsworth: Penguin.
Pelzer, P. (2002) Disgust and organisation, *Human Relations,* **56**(7), 841–60.
Pelzer, P. and Pelzer, M. (1996) The gothic experience. Paper presented at 14th SCOS Conference, UCLA, Los Angeles, July.
Rhodes, C. (2001) D'Oh: The Simpsons, popular culture and the organizational carnival, *Journal of Management Inquiry,* **10**(4), 374–83.
Rhodes, C. (2002) Coffee and the business of pleasure, *Culture and Organisation,* **8**(4), 293–306.
Ruskin, J. (1985) The nature of gothic, in: C. Wilmer (Ed.) *Unto this last and other writings,* pp. 77–109, London: Penguin.
Smith, A. (2001) Reading wealth in Nigeria: occult capitalism and Marx's vampires, *Historical Materialism,* **9,** 39–59.
Smith, W., Higgins, M., Parker, M. and Lightfoot, G. (Eds) (2001) *Science fiction and organisation,* London: Routledge.
Starr, A. (2000) *Naming the enemy: anti-corporate movements confront globalisation,* London: Zed Books.
ten Bos, R. (2003) Business ethics, accounting and the fear of melancholy, *Organisation,* **10**(2).
Tolliver, J. and Coleman, D. (2001) Metropolis, Maslow and the Axis Mundi, in: W. Smith, M. Parker and G. Lightfoot (Eds) *Science fiction and organisation,* London: Routledge.
Weber, M. (1930) *The protestant ethic and the spirit of capitalism,* London: Allen and Unwin.
Zola, E. (1885/1954) *Germinal,* Harmondsworth: Penguin.

Commodification of utopia: The lotus eaters revisited

Anna-Maria Murtola

This article responds to recent lamentations about the waning of utopia. Through an explanation of different concepts of utopia and an analysis of a recent shopping mall development project, the article shows how utopia has been appropriated by commercial actors. Drawing on the work of Herbert Marcuse and Giorgio Agamben and with the help of the Homeric allegory of the lotus eaters and contemporary popular culture, the article analyzes this state of affairs. It argues that an important part of the perceived decline of utopia is due to its commodification and that utopia, with the potential of being a 'means without end', is in need of what Agamben calls 'profanation.'

I sent two of my company to see what manner of men the people of the place might be, and they had a third man under them. They started at once, and went about among the Lotus-eaters, who did them no hurt, but gave them to eat of the lotus, which was so delicious that those who ate of it left off caring about home, and did not even want to go back and say what had happened to them, but were for staying and munching lotus with the Lotus-eater without thinking further of their return. (Homer 2008, 97)

Fiction is today a popular source of counsel in the analysis of contemporary organization. There are, for example, issues of journals concerned with this relation, such as the special issue of *Organization* (Parker and Rhodes 2008) concerned with popular culture and the issue of *Journal of Organizational Change Management* (Land and Sliwa 2009) concerned with the relationship between the novel and organization. An analysis of contemporary social and organizational phenomena through engagements with literature, cultural symbols, and works of fiction can also be found in several articles in this journal, such as in Beverungen and Dunne's (2007) analysis of Bartleby, Bristow's (2007) analysis of Harry Potter and Godfrey, Jack and Jones' (2004) analysis of vampirism. Utopia, a central literary theme in history, is an equally important concept for organization studies, as has been argued in the contributions collected in Parker (2002a). Recently, Rhodes (2007), for example, drew upon the concept of utopia in his analysis of expressions of utopia and its relations to work in the lyrics of rock music.

At the same time, there is a widespread concern about the perceived disappearance of utopia. Parker asks where all 'the radical utopias' are today and laments the current 'lack of faith in alternatives' (2002b, 5). Jameson argues that 'the waning of the utopian idea is a fundamental historical and political symptom' (2004, 36). Mazlish, although claiming that utopia is currently abundant in academic research, also agrees with Parker and Jameson that our current social context is 'not favorable to utopias' (2003, 43).

In this article, I discuss the contemporary state of utopia through recourse to a passage from Homer's *Odyssey* and its later adaptations. This famous but brief passage, often referred to as the lotus eaters, has inspired a long poem by Alfred Lord Tennyson, which I will return to later in this article. Its imagery has, also very recently, been taken up in popular culture in different forms.

Neophilia is defined as the love of, or enthusiasm for, the 'new.' But what this 'new' consists of is less straightforward. It can refer to something that has not existed before. It can refer to something that replaces something else that we call the 'old.' It can carry the exact same form as something else and still be new (e.g. a new television to replace the old one) or can mark a difference from an old form within a given category (e.g. a new model of an old television). The 'new' is thus a term used very broadly to indicate a particular relationship with something already existing, as a marker of difference from it. This marking of difference is a crucial aspect of what constitutes the new. On its own, the 'new' does not signify much. It is in relation to something that already exists that the new becomes meaningful. Evocations of the 'new' thus point to a temporal shift, in which the 'new' supersedes something that exists prior to it. In this sense, neophilia involves an enthusiasm for change. This does not necessarily mean a change in which the new already has a given form, but can also concern an open end in which the process of renewal is in focus regardless of the product that ensues.

In terms of the theme of this special issue, then, I will argue that utopia has a clear connection with the love of the 'new.' This relationship is not straightforward, and I do not argue that all utopias are about neophilia or that all neophilia is utopian. Although utopia is an ambiguous term, which I will discuss in more detail later on, the 'new' certainly plays an important role in many utopian concepts, in particular, in terms of an expressed difference from the present and a potential location in the future. Utopia is, in this sense, the eternal not-yet-here but potentially to come, and simultaneously also the potentially not to come. As such, it is the ever-new, the desired future that always eludes the present. Utopia, both as the new desired community to come and as the promise of the new, has throughout history been of great interest to humanity.

I will also argue that utopia is a perfect ally for capitalism. Obsessed with the new (new trends, new fashions, new innovations, and therefore new products for sale) in the attempt to satisfy customers' needs (existing or 'new needs'), it is no wonder that capitalist firms evoke utopia in their efforts to maximize profits. As the ever-new, utopia is the perfect commodity, the commodity that is inexhaustible and can keep profits rolling in. It is the promise of paradise at your fingertips, yet it never quite satisfies. The satisfaction gained from a taste of 'utopia' is always ephemeral, yet continued consumption can keep on feeding the illusion of a utopia having been reached. This, I will argue, is implicated in what many have identified as a 'waning' of utopia.

I begin the article with a discussion of utopia and its uptake in social theory. I then give a number of contemporary examples of commercial appropriations of utopia. I continue by discussing the implications of the commodification of utopia and then turn to a discussion of the concept of utopia in light of the commercial appropriations, drawing, in particular, on Agamben's concept of profanation. I conclude the article with an assessment of the present state and future intimations of utopia.

Utopia

Utopia is an ambiguous term. To start with, it often denotes an ideal society. In literary history, utopias are often elaborately planned, grand designs for the imagined life in, or organization of, new desirable societies. They are often imagined as existing in a void, a *nowhere*. This is important in enabling the free play of imagination when it comes to the ideal design of utopia. Utopias are, therefore, no modest proposals, but on the contrary, often quite radical propositions.

Throughout history, people have been fascinated with ideas of utopia, of harmony and happiness, freedom and abundance, escape from drudgery, sickness, and war. Although happiness alone does not constitute utopia, it is an important element in it. Happiness is, as Kant puts it, 'a purpose that can be presupposed surely and a priori in the case of every human being, because it belongs to his essence' (1996, 68). This search for happiness is implicated in utopian thinking.

History documents many different types of utopia. Some are presented as blueprints for the functioning of ideal societies, others as narrative portrayals of the life in an ideal society (Manuel 1966). Utopias often build on particular political ideals, with the abandonment of private property being a common feature. Some are utopias of abundance and excess (such as the medieval myth of the land of Cockaigne), others of moderation and restraint (Morris 1993). Some emphasize equality (Cabet 2003), others hierarchy (Plato 1997). There are utopias praising freedom (Fourier 1971), and also many hailing order and control (More 2004). Some utopias are primarily religious (Augustine 2003), others scientific (Bacon 1997) or technological (Wells 2005). Despite this wide variety, utopias, in general, have one thing in common: they are, in particular, characterized by harmony. Utopias are consensual unities that recognize no conflict, contradiction, or antagonism within their sphere. In utopia, these have been resolved in one way or another.

With the dawn of the Enlightenment and its focus on reason, as well as the scientific and technological developments that ensued, one might have thought that the time has finally come when humanity has acquired the means to reach the utopia it always wanted. To a certain extent, this is the case. The rise of affluence in the West, the freedom of choice that the capitalist production system has provided, and the development of medical, information, and other technologies have certainly brought us closer to some ideas of what utopia might look like.

At the same time, however, instead of a world free from toil, we face today a world where the greater part of the population still lives in poverty and hunger, where income inequalities are growing (Somavia 2008), where wars are fought over oil and water, and where excessive production has resulted in immense environmental degradation. As Adorno and Horkheimer (1997) argue, the dialectic of the Enlightenment consists precisely in this contradiction of contemporary reason. Despite the promises of the Enlightenment, this alleged Age of Reason still remains inexcusably unreasonable.

It would, therefore, seem plausible that the idea of utopia would still stay strong in the minds of both social theorists and others. But many have argued that utopia is not a prevalent concept today. Jacoby, for example, argues that the 'utopian spirit – a sense that the future could transcend the present – has vanished' (1999, xi). Utopia is not a term to celebrate, but rather to eschew, a term filled with ridicule or shame, a term that today either 'connotes irrelevancies or bloodletting' (Jacoby 1999, xi). It is this waning, end, or death, of utopia that Jacoby, Jameson, Parker, and others lament.

The ambiguity of the word 'utopia,' as devised by Sir Thomas More, is reflected in its meaning as both a good place (eutopia) and a no-place (outopia). This distinction lies at the very core of the concept. It is both within historical time and outside it. On the one hand, it is supposed to be an ideal place, the formation of which should not be restrained by the shortcomings and failings of the present. On the other hand, what is the point in having a dream image completely cut off from the possibilities of the present if there is no way of making it a reality? Although there is debate about how seriously More intended his work to be taken (see e.g. Carey 1999), there is no doubt about its subsequent impact in terms of the numerous literary utopias and practical experiments that ensued.

The tension between utopia as a good place and as a no-place, an ideal society and an impossible pipe dream, has long haunted the treatment of utopia in the social sciences. A common thread running through scholarly engagements with utopian thinking is the tension between the *desirable* and the *possible*, and much debate around the concept is based exactly on this tension. The tension comes to expression in various ways with different thinkers of utopia. Mumford, for example, describes the ambiguous character of utopia:

> The word utopia stands in common usage for the ultimate in human folly or human hope
> – vain dreams of perfection in a Never-Never Land or rational efforts to remake man's
> environment and his institutions and even his own erring nature, so as to enrich the possi-
> bilities of the common life. (2003, 1)

Here, Mumford expresses the core schism that utopia is endowed with. He points to the simultaneous strength and weakness of the concept.

The distinction between the desirable and the possible, the good society and the nonexistent (utopian) one, is also important for Bloch. He distinguishes between what he calls *abstract* and *concrete* utopias. Abstract utopias, as 'world-blind hope' (1995, 1039), are disconnected from the conditions of the present, whereas concrete utopias are clearly based on the material possibilities of a historical present, with 'path, compass, order' (1053). This argument echoes Mumford's distinction between conscious efforts to improve the common life and castles built in the air. It is also echoed in Jameson's distinction between 'wish-fulfilment' and 'construction,' although Jameson does emphasize that both of these 'perspectives' also have constraints (2004, 40–1).

Utopia is thus often criticized for its distance from reality or, as Cooke puts it, from 'the actual historical process, leading to a lack of connection with the potentials for emancipation implicit within existing social reality' (2004, 414). Or, as Levitas argues, one reason for being against utopian thinking is the 'suspicion that utopia is a distraction from political engagement' (2007, 295). Thus, focusing on hopelessly impractical utopian dreams might distract one from current issues that require urgent attention and engagement in the present.

Utopia is also endowed with further ambiguity. Critics of utopia such as ten Bos (2000) locate in utopia dangerous ideas of the perfect and the pure. Following Achterhuis (1998), ten Bos declares that he would not like to live in utopia because it, for example, 'subordinates the individual to the *collective*', 'is a world where nothing is left to chance', 'believes in the "unity of *totality and detail*",' is '*radical*,' has an 'obsession with *hygiene* and purity,' is based on a warped and utilitarian notion of happiness, and cannot avoid violence in order to ensure its harmonious order (2000, 12–13, emphases in original). Put in these terms, it is hardly surprising that ten Bos does not find utopia appealing. Although ten Bos, following Achterhuis, argues that utopia 'is not the land of Cockaigne' (2000, 12), others disagree, such as Jacoby who argues that ever since 'Greek and Roman ideas of a "golden age"… notions of peace, ease, and plenty characterise utopia' (2005, x).

But utopia is not only considered a distraction or, when it comes to its contents, too organized, too controlled, or simply boring, as ten Bos argues. Utopia can also be a dangerous concept. Attempts to implement utopia in different social and historical contexts have turned into the greatest tragedies in the history of humanity. Prevalent themes in the history of literary utopias have turned sour in attempts to realization, such as in the attempt to create a communist society in the Soviet Union, resulting in the persecution and death of millions, or the idea of a third Reich in Nazi Germany. As Jameson notes, in the second half of the twentieth century:

> Utopia had become a synonym for Stalinism and had come to designate a program which neglected human frailty and original sin, and betrayed a will to uniformity and the ideal purity of a perfect system that always had to be imposed by force on its imperfect and reluctant subjects. (2007, xi)

These atrocities are grounds enough for caution when it comes to utopian thought. There are, nevertheless, also those who argue that these kinds of monstrosities have nothing to do with utopia or classical utopian motifs of, for example, 'brotherhood and harmony' (Jacoby 2005, 15). Jacoby, for example, argues that 'it is, for the most part, nationalist, ethnic and sectarian passions – not utopian ideas – that drive global violence' (2005, xii).

Thus, utopia is a controversial concept, often dividing people into two camps: those who value the concept of utopia and those who consider it distracting or even dangerous. Some of the ambiguities of utopia can be understood through the differing concepts of utopia that are used by different writers. Jacoby (2005) makes a distinction between two different traditions of utopian thought: the 'blueprint' tradition and the 'iconoclastic' tradition. The blueprint tradition, Jacoby argues, was concerned with prescribing detailed instructions on how the everyday life in utopia would function. Thus, what they did was to 'map up the future in inches and minutes' (Jacoby 2005, xv). Jacoby argues that attention to utopia in history has mostly concerned this kind of utopia. The iconoclastic tradition, in contrast, comprised of thinkers who 'dreamt of a superior society but who declined to give its precise measurements' (2005, xv). Scholars of this tradition 'eschew the positive program; they specialize in negatives' (Jacoby 2005, 147). Although his division of utopian thought into two neat traditions might be too definitive, as Eagleton (2005) has pointed out, Jacoby insists that there is still much to be learnt from this latter kind of open utopian thinking.

For Marcuse, for example, utopia is neither clearly articulated nor hopelessly distant, but rather an opening achievable through persistent engagement in the form of negation of the present (see Marcuse 1970, 2009). Marcuse's approach to utopia is focused on the process toward it rather than on the explication of its attributes. As he puts it:

> Precisely because the so-called utopian possibilities are not at all utopian but rather the determinate socio-historical negation of what exists, a very real and very pragmatic

opposition is required of us if we are to make ourselves and others conscious of these possibilities and the forces that hinder and deny them. (1970, 69)

Here, utopia is not defined in structure and content, but acts through a negation of the ills of the present, acts on the particularities of the present, in response to the present, and at the same time includes aspirations to imagine possibilities beyond the restraints of current structures.

Many who value utopia often see its key power in this effort to summon alternatives to the present. These alternatives are not necessarily articulated to the minutest detail, but their engagement with the possibilities of a radically different and better future exposes their utopian character. Thus, Levitas, for example, argues that 'utopia embodies the refusal to accept that living beyond the present is delusional, the refusal to take at face value current judgements of the good, or claims that there is no alternative' (2007, 294). She also charges contemporary social policy with being too confined to the present constraints, that is, with not being 'utopian enough' (2007, 300). Cooke also refutes the argument of utopias being too detached from the conditions of the present, arguing instead that 'to give up utopian thinking on grounds of its metaphysical character would be disastrous for critical social theory, compromising its context-transcending, emancipatory perspective' (2004, 419). With respect to alternatives to 'organization as usual,' Parker, Fournier, and Reedy also emphasize utopia's 'critical, transgressive and transformative functions' (2007, x). Utopia, here as embodying a stark break with the present and a hope for the future, thus has a clear connection to the new, and specifically to the new as undefined. Similarly, Land and Jones ask 'Can we only imagine organised futures as an extension of the present? In what way might we be able to really think novelty – a transformation that is more than an extension of the present?' (2001, 104).

The concept of utopia that Cooke, Levitas, Marcuse and Parker, among others, work with is clearly more in line with Jacoby's iconoclastic tradition rather than his blueprint tradition. It is an open utopia, the particularities of which are not specified in detail but that operates as an affirmation of the potential for a radically better future through a negation of the ills of the present. It lies in stark contrast to the closed utopia of the blueprint type, whose content is defined in detail.

Thus, there are very different concepts of utopia in use today and, depending on the definition, also very different opinions about its usefulness and importance. There is, however, one space in particular where we find an abundance of utopia today. With this, I am referring to the sphere of commerce. But how has utopia been taken up in this sphere?

Commercial utopias

Although not an entirely new trend, utopia today has clearly been appropriated by commercial actors. Utopian elements can be identified in numerous commercial contexts. Instead of the Shangri-La that Hilton (1933) imagined, we have the Shangri-La mall, the Shangri-La resorts, and even a number of Shangri-La Chinese restaurants.[1] Instead of paradise, we have the Paradise Wildlife Park and Disney's Paradise Pier hotel.[2] The land of milk and honey can be found at Copenhagen Airport, which proudly announces: 'Welcome to the land of dreams and desires', 'love and beauty', 'passion and luxury'. In other words, welcome to tax-free shopping.

Disneyland, proclaiming to be the 'happiest place on earth' (2008a), shamelessly asserts that 'happiness is more than just a state of mind, it's a destination. And what better way to make yourself or someone else happy than to give the gift of shopping' (2008b). Utopia is also for sale in the context of gated communities, in which the promise of a slice of a conflict-free, safe space is attainable against a fee. There are companies building ideal cities such as Celebration in Florida (see e.g. Bartling 2004), not to mention companies such as ResidenSea with its 'floating luxury community' (WebUrbanist 2008) called 'The World' and its plans to build 'Freedom Ship,' which is to become a 'city at sea':[3]

> Envision an ideal place to live or run a business, a friendly, safe and secure community with large areas of open space and extensive entertainment and recreational facilities. Finally, picture this community continually moving around the world. You are beginning to understand the Freedom Ship concept of a massive ocean-going vessel … Freedom Ship would not be a cruise ship, it is proposed to be a unique place to live, work, retire, vacation or visit. (Freedom Ship 2008)

There have been other attempts in history to create utopias on earth, such as Owen's experiment of 'New Harmony' in Indiana or the phalansteries of Fourier's followers around America. One significant attempt in this direction, and the one that I will focus on in this article, is the shopping mall. Many scholars explicitly link utopia with consumption and the shopping mall (Crawford 1992; Backes 1997; Goss 1999; Jewell 2001; Maclaran and Brown 2001, 2005). Shopping malls are places of abundance, designed to provide visitors with whatever they might want. They are, in a certain sense, places of peace and harmony. Sometimes, this is summoned by a choice of serene music and tranquilizing water elements. The peace and harmony is, however, also always guaranteed by security guards. These are places of comfort where it never rains, as often pointed out in marketing materials. Like in some of the utopias in history, here, every day is alike and time stands still. Originally intended by its creator Victor Gruen in the 1950s as the heart of a community, supporting community life (Mennel 2004), this representative of an imagined capitalist utopia has evolved through the decades from a place where you can get more or less whatever you want into a veritable 'machine for consumption' (Beyard and O'Mara 1999).

But shopping centers, once appearing as commercial utopias in terms of abundance and availability, have today suffered inflation. They have become too numerous, too homogeneous, and uninteresting (see e.g. Max 2003; Dokoupil 2008; MarketingCharts 2008; *The Week* 2009). According to the *Shopping Center Development Handbook*, the 'industry is at a crossroads,' with much of the older shopping centers having become 'outdated' (Beyard and O'Mara 1999, 32). The shopping center industry today is facing a challenge to reinvent the retail form:

> Today, shopping center owners and developers must be more creative, more nimble, and more customer savvy than ever before to provide and maintain the type of shopping environment that consumers want. The necessities reflect not only a heightened competitive environment but also an environment that constantly demands new forms of shopping centers, new types of tenants, new retail formats, new shopping environments, new experiences for customers, new locations, and new ways of linking shopping centers with the broader communities around them. (Beyard and O'Mara 1999, 343)

One attempt to completely rethink the shopping mall can be found in Finland, where a massive 100,000 square meter mall, with close to 200 retailers, opened at the end of 2006. I studied the development of this mall for nearly three years, from early 2005 until the end of its first year of operation in 2007, through nonparticipant observation of management, planning and construction meetings, interviews with the designers and owners, public presentations, visits to the site, and discussions in the media (Murtola 2006, 2010).

Harmonia, as I call this mall here, focuses on not only fashion and furniture but also events. It was explicitly designed not to become a traditional shopping mall. Instead, the project was guided by two ideals: the city and creativity. Harmonia was, on the one hand, built on the image of a city. This shows architecturally. The aisles are called streets and each has its own street sign. There is a 'Central Park' with artificial trees, surrounded by terraces of cafés and restaurants. In the middle is an area where various events are organized: concerts, exhibitions, dances, and even ice skating sessions, with some events running late into the night. Harmonia includes an area called the 'Old Town' where arts and crafts professionals such as goldsmiths and blacksmiths have their small workshops and galleries. Harmonia has a radio station and its own newspaper. It is called a 'Commercial City' to distinguish it from traditional shopping centers.

The city as an ideal also brought with it other elements into the project. One of the owners, whom I call the Advocate, was in charge of the development of the concept of Harmonia and its marketing. He repeatedly emphasized that Harmonia was to be developed for the 'human being', not merely for the consumer. He asserted that the underlying values of the project were 'exactly the same' as those on which cities are developed and once explained the aspirations of the project in terms of creating a 'community culture'. He clearly wanted the project to reach beyond the sphere of the commercial. One of the important goals of the project, from his point of view, was to bring culture and commerce together, as supportive of each other. He also emphasized the heterogeneity that a city embodies, against the 'sterile' and 'boring' appearance of the shopping mall. These kinds of elements were emphasized throughout the project, beyond mere marketing.

On the other hand, it was important that Harmonia should not become a copy of anything else. From the very beginning, another focus in the project was on the 'new'. The Advocate continuously emphasized the need for creativity in the project and saw himself as a leader of a creative process, the outcome of which could not completely be ascertained in advance. The designers were encouraged to question all premises and to think of new and better solutions to traditional, established ones. The main architect of the project explained that when they designed Harmonia they started from a clean slate, from the question, 'What do we want?', without being confined to existing solutions.

In one public relations brochure, Harmonia was described as 'a combination of a shopping centre, a covered city milieu and an experiential travelling destination' as well as a 'meeting place for entrepreneurs and new ideas' (Harmonia 2006). The brochure also boldly stated that Harmonia 'is breaking the old notion that everything has already been done in the world' (Harmonia 2005). It declared that in Harmonia 'development and change are inbuilt' (Harmonia 2005). The very start of the Harmonia project was celebrated with a symbolic ceremony built on the old Finnish tradition in which the trees on the land were burnt down in order to create a nutritious ground on which new things can grow. This event sparked the slogan that kicked off the project and was diligently used throughout: 'We decided to clear 30 hectares in Finland to make room for new ideas' (Harmonia 2005). One of the architects of the project also explained that they had to, at times, ask themselves whether an idea was new enough to be used or whether it had already been used before (Architect 2006). These are just a few examples from the project of the urge to create something completely new.

As Advocate explained, the concept of Harmonia builds on four principles: (1) creativity; (2) profit as the means, not the ends, of business; (3) the importance of supporting people's personal development at work; and (4) the firm belief that there is no contradiction between 'responsible social behaviour and efficient enterprise' (Advocate 2006b). He explained to me the underlying logic of Harmonia:

> When the United States in its days was populated, the people from Europe who went there to realize their dreams arranged themselves into caravans. And every family sitting on the bench of a wagon had its own dream. In order to be able to realize their dream they joined a caravan ... which multiplied their chances of succeeding as compared to if they crossed the continent on their own. It is a bit the same with Harmonia, which is a non-hierarchical community of different actors where everyone is involved in realizing their own dream ... but they clearly understand that by being part of the Harmonia caravan, their chances of reaching that goal are multiplied ... This is perhaps the strength of Harmonia. (Advocate 2006a)

This is one of the allegories that the Advocate liked to use to describe the aspirations of the Harmonia project. Against the actual historical reality of the colonization of America, however, the Advocate's vision here is one of collective harmony. There are no contradictions or conflicting goals. There is no exploitation, no violence, no resistance. Instead, working together in a 'no-place' increases everybody's chances of individual success.

Harmonia is caught between two forces pulling it in different directions. On the one hand, it reflects commercial neophilia, an attempt to create something new, something that has never been seen before that can attract crowds of consumers. As the material presented here shows, this focus on creativity and newness was to be ongoing. On the other hand, Harmonia goes beyond this, expressing aspirations toward something deeper and more meaningful: a consensual unity in which there are no antagonisms, tensions, or conflictual interests; in which human beings are treated as more than commercial functionaries; and in which people can come together to realize their dreams. It draws not only on classical utopian themes of happiness and harmony and a betterment of life but also on a more open notion of radical improvement without a given goal. But what is noticeable throughout this case is that the vision of a consensual community builds on individual choice, individual aspirations, and the realization of individual dreams. This is the expression of an attempt to create a contemporary, capitalist utopia.

Capitalist firms continuously need to provide new things for sale in order to keep up their profits and not be run over by competitors, as the contemporary buzz around creativity, innovation, and entrepreneurship, also noticeable in Harmonia, testifies. This is, of course, not a new observation, as Marx and Engels had already, in 1848, remarked how 'in place of old wants, satisfied by the productions of the country, we find new wants, requiring for their satisfaction the products of distant lands and climes' (1950, 36). But in the case of Harmonia, this also concerns something more than just neophilia. Harmonia exhibits elements both of a 'love of the new,' whatever form it may take, and of what could be understood as utopian aspirations of a peaceful and harmonious social existence, a sphere without contradiction or antagonism.

Commodification of utopia

There are many gigantic commercial projects resulting in places designed to make people happy, to cure the ills of drudgery and fear in contemporary everyday life, places where, at least ostensibly, all contradictions have been eliminated. So far, I have positioned utopia in contrast to the present, as always distanced from it. There are, however, those who claim that utopia is no longer in the future or elsewhere but actually right here, right now. Fukuyama's (1993) famous *End of history* thesis is one example of it, as is Thatcher's assertion that there 'is no alternative.' Capitalism is the answer, and contemporary Western consumerism often appears as if without contradiction. Apart from a few tasks of fine-tuning, by and large, here we have it: a capitalist utopia of material abundance and individual freedom. We live in a utopia of market managerialism, built on a 'transcendent belief in the happy marriage between technology, capital and humanism' (Sørensen 2009a, 208). Is this utopia on earth?

But reality remains contradictory in many ways. Our acts on one side of the globe dramatically affect the conditions of life of others on the other side. When commercial actors take on the task of providing humanity with utopia, utopia is molded within the confines of the commercially viable and the interests served are not the interests of humanity on the whole. The capitalist utopia is a utopia for the individual, a platform for the fulfilment of individual dreams, as if cut off from any consequences for the rest of the world.

In the commercial sphere, utopia is on a leash. Here, the promise of utopia has been domesticated and reduced to a choice between specific given alternatives. Today, utopia has, I argue, not so much waned as it has been tamed. Today, our choice is, as Underhill puts it, between 'eighty different styles of sneaker or sixteen varieties of chocolate chip cookie' (2004, 4). Utopia has been reduced to an instrument of capital accumulation and turned into a form fitting the confines of commercial consumption. It has been enclosed and packaged to be sold for a fair profit, a true tool for any King Midas wanting to turn the hopes of humanity into gold. How has such a state come to be?

Here, the land of the lotus eaters, first described in the *Odyssey*, serves as a powerful allegory. It is a utopia of bliss and oblivion. It is a place where Odysseus' mariners land and find a people engaged in the eating of lotus fruit and flower all day long, which, like a drug, makes them feel happy. Once the mariners taste the lotus, they too forget about the pain and toil of the world and do not want to return to it but rather stay and continue to eat the lotus. As Tennyson writes:

> Let us swear an oath, and keep it with an equal mind,
> In the hollow Lotos-land to live and lie reclined
> On the hills like Gods together, careless of mankind. (2004, 6)

Tennyson adds an important element to Homer's tale: melancholia. He describes the lotus eaters as 'mild-eyed melancholy' (2004, 2) and the wish of the mariners to 'lend our hearts and spirits wholly/to the influence of mild-minded melancholy' (2004, 5). Thus, there is an element of sadness lurking behind the apparent happiness of the lotus eaters. This kind of utopia of abundance and 'immediate gratification' (Clacys and Sargent 1999, 71), if it is to be defined as such, is peculiar in nature. On the one hand, it appears as a utopia of plenty and promises harmony, happiness, and freedom from toil. On the other hand, there is, as Tennyson notes, something disquieting about it.

Today, this land, where people are immersed in a melancholic slumber, is the land of the commodity, of the shopping mall. The shopping mall, like utopia, is a 'land where all things always seem'd the same!' (Tennyson 2004, 2). This is the utopia of abundance, of immediate satisfaction. It is the utopia of forgetfulness toward the rest of the world, where, as Tennyson puts it, people lie reclined on the hills together, 'like Gods', 'careless of mankind' (2004, 6). It is the place you never want to leave, which caters to all your needs in the form of the commodity.

The commodity, like the lotus, is addictive. As long as you stay within this world and keep on shopping, you can feel happy. But the happiness is ephemeral, and the land of the lotus is, as Tennyson puts it, 'hollow' (2004, 6). Crawford describes this condition, which the shopping mall is designed to prompt, following William Kowinski, as 'a perceptual paradox brought on by simultaneous stimulation and sedation, characterized by disorientation, anxiety, and apathy' (1992, 14). The lotus eaters are never satisfied for more than a short moment; hence, the melancholia, which Tennyson introduces to the allegory. The lotus eaters know this. Yet they cannot or, better, do not want to stop eating the lotus.

Are the people of our contemporary polis lost in the land of the lotus eaters, desperately holding on to the illusion of utopia, unable or unwilling to give up the lotus that makes the illusion possible? The apathy created by the eating of the lotus, the unwillingness to look beyond the immediate present, is something that very much concerned critics such as Marcuse. His critique of advanced industrial society attempted to make sense of the silence of utopian aspirations through the twentieth century. He criticized what he described as a one-dimensional society for the concealment of contradictions and antagonisms that lie both behind and within it. Instead, society appears as unified and consensual. In other words, we seem to have reached a harmonious state and, through that, a utopia.

A one-dimensional society is a legacy of capitalist industrial production. It is a society beset with commodities, a society in which people 'find their soul in their automobile, hi-fi set, split-level home, kitchen equipment' (Marcuse 1972, 22). This is not only what the wealth but also the social cohesion of this society is built on: an 'immense collection of commodities' (Marx 1976, 125). It is an illusion of a utopia of abundance and freedom. As long as there are commodities to choose from, there is no need to focus on what lies beyond the immediate present. Today, we can buy our illusions of utopia. If the system in which we live can provide the things that we want and think we need, why should we want to look for anything beyond? As Marcuse argues, why would we want to reflect on the grounds, the underlying conditions of human exploitation and pollution elsewhere on which our utopian illusion builds? Rather than getting engaged with these issues, it is easier to keep ourselves preoccupied with the numerous important decisions right in front of us: which fruit to munch on next in order to uphold the illusion.

However, as Adorno and Horkheimer put it:

> The sufferer who cannot bear to stay with the Lotus-eaters is justified. He opposes their illusion with that which is like yet unlike: the realization of utopia through historical labour; whereas mere lingering in the shade of the image of bliss removes all vigour from the dream. (1997, 63)

But this is not an easy task, as Tennyson reminds us of at the end of his account of the lotus eaters:

Surely, surely, slumber is more sweet than toil, the shore
Than labor in the deep mid-ocean, wind and wave and oar;
O, rest ye, brother mariners, we will not wander more. (2004, 7)

Am I turning our contemporary mariners munching the lotus into 'naïve cubical drones moved around unwittingly by structural constraint or ideological mystification' instead of granting them knowledge, autonomy, and a capacity to be reflexive (Parker and Rhodes 2008, 633–4)? No. On the contrary, the melancholy of the munchers speaks exactly the opposite. There is awareness and there might be a will, but sometimes, the hill is just too steep or the sap too sweet. When Lily Allen sings in her recent song, 'I am a weapon of massive consumption/and it's not my fault it's how I'm programmed to function' (2009), this does not mean that there is no hope or resistance whatsoever. Allen's lines indicate not only a widespread melancholic surrender to consumerism, but, moreover, at the same time on another level, also an awareness of the illusion involved and critique of and resistance to it. Allen and others call on us to profane this capitalist utopia.

Profanation

Underlying many concepts of utopia, in particular those in the iconoclastic tradition, is a belief in the promise of the new, in that which is potentially to come. Whether explicitly defined in content or not and whether located in the future or not, utopia generally implies an element of hope: a hope for the possibility of another world, a hope for an alternative future, a hope not confined to the constraints of the present. Utopias are thus concerned with potentiality. They are concerned not with what is but with *what if*. They embed a glint of hope for a fundamental improvement of the existing state of affairs. That is what makes utopia such a powerful concept: it promises a radical potential for change.

This potential lies in the dialectical nature of utopia. Although often presented as an imagined place of happiness and harmony, a monad located in a void, utopia is always intricately linked to a material reality, a particular point in time and a particular social context. Utopias do not come 'out of nowhere,' even if nowhere might be their final location. They emerge in particular spatial and temporal contexts, often as a response to the perceived ills of a particular age. The possibilities and constraints of the present feed utopian thought. Such dialectics are perhaps more visible in the utopianism of the iconoclastic tradition, which explicitly works with a negation of the present, without a meticulously defined image of utopia in mind.

Utopia therefore exists in an ambiguous location. It exists in a tension between what is and what is not, between the historical reality of what is and the imagined sphere of what could be. Its radical promise for change relies on this relationship between the restricted sphere of the existing and the open sphere of the potential. The open sphere of the potential also enables imagination of radical alternatives not restricted by the bounds of the present. These images inspire change in the present. They are the call of the new. At the same time, however, these images, despite their form, are always connected to a present time from which they spring.

It is this existence between the actual and the potential, the material and the imagined, the here and the nowhere, the present and the future, that constitutes the dialectical nature of utopia. It is in this moment of the 'what is' *and* 'what if' that the radical potential of utopia lies. Utopia is and can be a useful concept as long as we recognize its limits. Cooke reminds us that utopia is a fiction and, by definition, '*not* attainable by finite human beings' (2004, 422, emphasis in original). It can, however, act as an impulse toward a radically better world. As Levitas argues: 'The recognition of necessary failure leads to the insistence on the provisionality of utopia. It is a method of considering the future, not the stipulation of a goal' (2007, 303).

The crucial aspect of utopia here is potentiality. The relationship between the potential and the actual is a question that goes at least as far back as Aristotle's deliberations on the relationship between *dynamis* (potentiality) and *energeia* (actuality) in book IX of his *Metaphysics*. Building on Aristotle, Agamben (1999) stresses that potentiality involves a potential to simultaneously both *be* and *not be*. Without both these elements, there would be no potentiality, only actuality. It is this power of suspension of the actual that lies at the heart of Agamben's concept of potentiality. But what matters here is not merely a lack. Mills points out that what matters, for Agamben, in potentiality is 'the maintenance of a suspensive state between being and not-being' (2008, 32). Agamben argues that: 'What is essential is that potentiality is not simply "non-Being", simple privation, but rather *the existence of non-Being*, the presence of an absence; this is what we call "faculty" or "power"' (1999, 179, emphasis in original). In this sense, potentiality encompasses actuality, even in its suspension. Thus, for Agamben, we might say that potentiality lies in a dialectical position between what is and what is not, between the actual and the potential.

For Agamben, potentiality is the defining characteristic of a human being. The human being is 'whatever being' (Agamben 1993). The human being has no set task, no given destiny beyond potentiality itself, beyond having 'faculty' and 'power.' This, then, also involves the faculty to suspend the immediate. Aristotle remarks that:

> While thought bids us hold back because of what is future, desire is influenced by what is just at hand: a pleasant object which is just at hand presents itself as both pleasant and good, without condition in either case, because of want of foresight into what is farther away in time. (Aristotle, 433b7–11)

That said, with Agamben, it is clear that the human being, the lotus eater, has the capacity not only to accept the immediate gratification in front of it or to suspend this actuality 'because of what is future' but also to do both simultaneously. Hence, the melancholia of the lotus eater.

Jameson notes that 'in utopia, politics is supposed to be over' (2004, 42). He asserts that 'utopia emerges at the moment of the suspension of the political' (2004, 43) and it might seem that we now have indeed reached utopia, a post-political age. However, as Marcuse shows, as long as there is contradiction in this world, we need politics, a way of engaging with different interests and different points of view. We need what Agamben calls a 'means without end' (2000).

The roots of Agamben's concept of a 'means without end' go back to Kant's utopian idea of a 'kingdom of ends' (1996, 83) and his later deliberations on the beautiful and the sublime (2000). In the *Groundwork of the metaphysics of morals* (1996), in which he analyzes the grounds for the possible existence of a categorical imperative, Kant makes his important argument about the human being always being also an end, and not just a mere means to an end: 'I say that the human being and in general every rational being *exists* as an end in itself, *not merely as a means* to be used by this or that will at its discretion' (1996, 79, original emphases). Kant argues for the necessary autonomy of rational beings as a presupposition for the possibility for human beings to come together and agree upon common laws to which they subject themselves, which also constitutes the possibility for their freedom: 'Now in this way a world of rational beings (*mundus intelligibilis*) as a kingdom of ends is possible, through the giving of their own laws by all persons as members' (1996, 87, emphasis in original).

The sphere where these laws are articulated is politics. Agamben argues that politics is a 'means without end':

> A finality without means (the good and the beautiful as ends unto themselves), in fact, is just as alienating as a mediality that makes sense only with respect to an end ... Politics is the sphere neither of an end in itself nor of means subordinated to an end; rather, it is the sphere of a pure mediality without end intended as the field of human action and of human thought. (2000, 116–7)

Utopia plays a part in this. And there are still a myriad of social movements, inspired by utopia, slowly working their way toward a better society (see e.g. Fisher and Ponniah 2003; Parker, Fournier, and Reedy 2007; Spicer and Böhm 2007).

As long as utopia stays in dialectical tension, it retains its power. But what commercial actors, such as in Harmonia, have done to utopia is that they have stripped it of its potential through an act of enclosure, trying to tie it down at one end of a dialectical relationship. The implementation of utopia in a material reality, always a restricted sphere, necessitates a reduction of utopia. Utopia as a force of change in its dialectical location opens up, rather than closes down, the possibilities of the future. Commercial appropriations of utopia, however, due to their commercial confines, restrict the possible and only allow a free play of the imagination within a given framework. Although it is, of course, important to remember that the imagination is never completely free and detached from a particular, historical reality, as I have argued here, it is the specificity and concreteness of the constraints in Harmonia and other commercial ventures that are at issue. Commercial appropriations of utopia can never provide a sphere of 'pure mediality.' Within a capitalist context, utopia is put to particular ends.

What is needed here is what Agamben calls profanation. Agamben sets profanation against consecration, which in religion as well as in capitalism involves the removal of things 'from common use' and their transferral to a 'separate sphere' (2007, 74). One such 'sacred' sphere is the sphere of exchange values. Profanation, in contrast, involves efforts to 'return to common use that which has been removed to the sphere of the sacred' (2007, 82). As such, profanation is again a dialectical concept. It is, as Agamben emphasizes, different from secularization. Secularization only moves things between the sacred and the profane, and in doing so, keeps the divide intact. Profanation breaks the divide between the sacred and the profane. It does not only entail abolition of separations but also requires us 'to learn to put them to a new use' (2007, 87). Profanation thus involves detachment from 'immediate ends' (2007, 91).

Utopia has the capacity to be a 'pure means' (Agamben 2007, 87). It is a concept capable of opening up rather than closing down. Something, however, has happened to it. Agamben writes about how language, as a pure means, has been captured and separated into a special sphere in order to obstruct language 'from disclosing the possibility of a new use, a new experience of the word' (2007, 88). Here, its profanatory potential has become nullified. The same could be said of utopia, which, as a commodity, has been separated from the common sphere and moved into the sphere of the sacred. What has happened to utopia in the hands of commercial actors is that it has become an item of possession. It has become the eternal commodity, the ever-new. Through this act of enclosure, consecration, the profanatory potential of utopia has been nullified.

Agamben argues that in 'its extreme phase capitalism is nothing but a gigantic apparatus for capturing pure means, that is, profanatory behaviours' (2007, 87). One such 'pure means' is utopia. The ability to imagine radical alternatives has been caught up in a web of exchange and consumption in which the alternatives have already been provided and the freedom that remains is to choose between the products on display: Disneyland, the shopping mall, or an apartment on board The World.

Utopia is thus not only an instrument of profanation. It has also been consecrated and is in need of profanation. Utopia needs to be wrested out of its sacred position, as a commodity, and returned to its dialectical one, as a pure means, as potentiality. It is in this dialectical position that utopia, as a tension between the actual and the potential, must remain.

Conclusion

In response to Jameson's concern about the waning of utopia and Parker's question about the contemporary location of radical utopias, my argument is that a transformation, rather than a waning, of utopia has taken place. Today, utopia has moved from its dialectical location to one-sided commercial appropriations, in which utopia is offered to the highest bidder and to those who can afford it, regardless of the effects on the rest of the world's population. Utopia has, in short, been commodified.

Today, there is, however, also a growing sense of disbelief. As Sørensen (2009b) has recently argued, our latest 'utopian experiment' is now over. With the financial crisis, and the economic crisis that followed, as well as the increased attention to contemporary environmental degradation, the idea of a capitalist utopia is seriously threatened. Although Sørensen's assessment of the end of this utopian illusion might be somewhat premature, it is clear that the smooth surface of our current, apparent utopia has been severely bumped and bruised. It might mean the end for Jameson's concern over the 'waning' of utopia, something he has already indicated in his later work (2007), with the dominant idea now making space for alternative conceptualizations of utopia. Perhaps utopia is neither here nor dead, after all, and instead, we are now entering a historical moment in which the lotus flowers are acquiring a bitter flavour and the lotus eaters are being forced to realize that it is time to return to the ship and continue the journey.

It 'still takes courage to be utopian,' as Sørensen (2009a, 218) puts it, but maybe there is a rupture in the present enabling utopian thinking, responsible utopian thinking, in a way that, for a long time, had not seemed possible. Jameson asserts that the 'desire called Utopia must be concrete and ongoing, without being defeatist or incapacitating' (2007, 84). But we must also, learning from history, keep in mind the dangers of both a consecrated and an undialectical conception of utopia. Jameson (2004) also points out that even a revival of utopia will not guarantee a politics leading to a new and better society. Nevertheless, as he and others have argued, without utopia and/as resistance, we will never get there. As Nick Cave puts it in his song, 'Night of the lotus eaters' (Nick Cave and the Bad Seeds 2008):

sapped & stupid
I lie upon the stones and I swoons

the darling little dandelions have done their thing
& changed from suns into moons

the dragons roam the shopping malls
I hear theyre gonna eat our guts

if I had the strength I might pick up my sword
& make some attempt to resist

Notes

1. Shangri-La Plaza is a mall located in Mandaluyong City, in the Metro Manila area, in the Philippines (website: http://www.shangrila-plaza.com/). The Shangri-la hotels and resorts markets itself as 'the world's leading Asia-based luxury hotel group,' with 57 hotels and resorts (website: http://www.shangri-la.com/). The Shangri-la Chinese restaurants are located in, for example, York, Pennsylvania (PA); West Bloomfield, Michigan (MI); Phoenix, Arizona (AZ); and Sydney, NSW, Australia (website: http://www.shangrilachineserestaurant.com/).
2. Paradise Wildlife Park is located in Broxbourne, Hertfordshire, UK (website: http://www.pwpark.com/). Paradise Pier Hotel is one of the Disneyland resort's hotels, located on Disneyland Drive, Anaheim, CA.
3. The World is a cruise ship with 165 residences, marketed as a 'seagoing community' and a 'luxuriously secure environment.' The World offers both short-term and long-term accommodation, and there are apartments for sale (website: http://www.aboardtheworld.com/, check also the company managing it at http://www.residensea.com/index.html). Freedom Ship's proposed 'voyage would continuously circle the globe' is available at http://www.freedomship.com/freedomship/overview/overview.shtml. Note: all websites were last accessed on 3 February 2009.

References

Achterhuis, H. 1998. *De erfenis van de Utopie* [The legacy of utopia]. Amsterdam: Ambo.
Adorno, T., and M. Horkheimer. 1997. *Dialectic of Enlightenment.* Trans. J. Cumming. London: Verso.
Advocate. 2006a. Interview with co-owner of Harmonia. 21 November.
Advocate. 2006b. Quote by William Kieschmick in information folder presented to the employees of Harmonia. 16 November.
Agamben, G. 1993. *The coming community.* Trans. M. Hardt. Minneapolis, MN: University of Minnesota Press.
Agamben, G. 1999. *Potentialities.* Trans. D. Heller-Roazen. Stanford, CA: Stanford University Press.
Agamben, G. 2000. *Means without end: Notes on politics.* Trans. V. Binetti and C. Casarino. Minneapolis, MN: University of Minnesota Press.
Agamben, G. 2007. *Profanations.* Trans. J. Fort. New York: Zone Books.
Allen, L. 2009. 'The fear,' from *It's Not Me, It's You.* London: EMI Records.
Architect. 2006. Interview with architect of Harmonia. January 11.
Aristotle. 1995a. On the soul. In *The complete works of Aristotle*, ed. J. Barnes. Vol. 1, 641–92. Princeton, NJ: Princeton University Press.
Aristotle. 1995b. Metaphysics. In *The complete works of Aristotle*, ed. J. Barnes. Vol. 2, 1552–728. Princeton, NJ: Princeton University Press.
Augustine, S. 2003. *City of God.* Trans. H. Bettenson. London: Penguin.
Backes, N. 1997. Reading the shopping mall city. *Journal of Popular Culture* 31, no. 3: 1–17.
Bacon, F. 1997. *New Atlantis.* Whitefish, MT: Kessinger.
Bartling, H. 2004. The Magic Kingdom syndrome: Trials and tribulations of life in Disney's Celebration. *Contemporary Justice Review* 7, no. 4: 375–93.
Beverungen, A., and S. Dunne. 2007. I'd prefer not to. Bartleby and the excesses of interpretation. *Culture and Organization* 13, no. 2. 171–83.
Beyard, M., and P. O'Mara. 1999. Shopping center development handbook. 3rd ed. Washington, DC: Urban Land Institute.
Bloch, E. 1995. *The principle of hope.* Vol. 3. Trans. N. Plaice, S. Plaice, and P. Knight. Cambridge, MA: MIT Press.

Bristow, A. 2007. Fragments and links: Organizational actor-world of the Harry Potter phenomenon. *Culture and Organization* 13, no. 4: 313–25.

Cabet, E. 2003. *Travels in Icaria*. Syracuse, NY: Syracuse University Press.

Carey, J. 1999. *The Faber book of utopias*. London: Faber and Faber.

Claeys, G., and L.T. Sargent. 1999. *The utopia reader*. New York: New York University Press.

Cooke, M. 2004. Redeeming redemption: The utopian dimension of critical social theory. *Philosophy and Social Criticism* 30, no. 4: 413–29.

Crawford, M. 1992. The world in a shopping mall. In *Variations on a theme park*, ed. M. Sorkin, 3–30. New York: Hill and Wang.

Disneyland. 2008a. *Theme parks at the Disneyland® resort*. http://disneyland.disney.go.com/disneyland/en_US/parks/overview?name=DisneylandResortParksOverviewPage&bhcp=1 (accessed 9 November 2008).

Disneyland. 2008b. PR brochure. August.

Dokoupil, T. 2008. Is the mall dead? *Newsweek*, 12 November. http://www.newsweek.com/id/168753 (accessed 7 July 2009).

Eagleton, T. 2005. Just my imagination. *The Nation*, 13 June.

Fisher, W.F., and T. Ponniah, eds. 2003. *Another world is possible*. London: Zed Books.

Fourier, C. 1971. *The utopian vision of Charles Fourier: Selected texts on work, love, and passionate attraction*. Boston, MA: Beacon.

Freedom Ship. 2008. *Overview of the Freedom Ship*. http://www.freedomship.com/freedom-ship/overview/overview.shtml (accessed 19 January 2009).

Fukuyama, F. 1993. *The end of history and the last man*. London: Harper Perennial.

Godfrey, R., G. Jack, and C. Jones. 2004. Sucking, bleeding, breaking: On the dialectics of vampirism, capital, and time. *Culture and Organization* 10, no. 1: 25–36.

Goss, J. 1999. Once-upon-a-time in the commodity world: An unofficial guide to the mall of America. *Annals of the Association of American Geographers* 89, no. 1: 45–75.

Harmonia. 2005. First version of the Harmonia project's PR brochure. 2 June.

Harmonia. 2006. Second version of the Harmonia project's PR brochure. 4 January.

Hilton, J. 1933. *Lost horizon*. London: Pocket Books.

Homer. 2008. *The odyssey*. Trans. S. Butler. St. Petersburg, FL: Red and Black.

Jacoby, R. 1999. *The end of utopia: Politics and culture in an age of apathy*. New York: Perseus/Columbia University Press.

Jacoby, R. 2005. *Picture imperfect: Utopian thought for an anti-utopian age*. New York: Columbia University Press.

Jameson, F. 2004. The politics of utopia. *New Left Review* 25, January/February: 35–54.

Jameson, F. 2007. *Archaeologies of the future: The desire called utopia and other science fictions*. London: Verso.

Jewell, N. 2001. The fall and rise of the British mall. *Journal of Architecture* 6: 317–8.

Kant, I. 1996. *Groundwork of the metaphysics of morals*. Trans. M.J. Gregor. Cambridge: Cambridge University Press.

Kant, I. 2000. *Critique of the power of judgment*. Cambridge: Cambridge University Press.

Land, C., and C. Jones. 2001. O cursèd spite. *Ephemera* 1, no. 2: 103–7.

Land, C., and M. Sliwa, eds. 2009. The novel and organization. Special issue, *Journal of Organizational Change Management* 22, no. 4: 349–449.

Levitas, R. 2007. Looking for the blue: The necessity of utopia. *Journal of Political Ideologies* 12, no. 3: 289–306.

Maclaran, P., and S. Brown. 2001. The future perfect declined: Utopian studies and consumer research. *Journal of Marketing Management* 17: 367–90.

Maclaran, P., and S. Brown. 2005. The center cannot hold: Consuming the utopian market-place. *Journal of Consumer Research* 32: 311–23.

Manuel, F., ed. 1966. *Utopias and utopian thought*. Boston, MA: Houghton Mifflin.

Marcuse, H. 1970. The end of utopia. In *Five lectures: Psychoanalysis, politics, and utopia*. Trans. J.J. Shapiro and S.M. Weber. London: Allen Lane.

Marcuse, H. 1972. *One dimensional man*. London: Abacus.

Marcuse, H. 2008. *Negations: Essays in critical theory*. Trans. J.J. Shapiro. London: MayFly-Books.

MarketingCharts. 2008. *Malls cause frustration, boredom for 80% of shoppers.* http://www.marketingcharts.com/topics/behavioral-marketing/malls-cause-frustration-boredom-for-80-of-shoppers-7145/ (accessed 7 July 2009).

Marx, K. 1976. *Capital.* Vol. 1. Trans. B. Fowkes. London: Penguin.

Marx, K., and F. Engels. 1950. Manifesto of the Communist Party. In *Karl Marx and Frederick Engels: Selected works.* Vol. 1, 21–61. Moscow: Foreign Languages.

Max, S. 2003. Malls: Death of an American icon. *CNN,* 24 July. http://money.cnn.com/2003/07/02/pf/yourhome/deadmalls/index.htm (accessed 11 August 2006).

Mazlish, B. 2003. A tale of two enclosures: Self and society as a setting for utopias. *Theory, Culture and Society* 20, no. 1: 43–60.

Mennel, T. 2004. Victor Gruen and the construction of cold war utopias. *Journal of Planning History* 3, no. 2: 116–50.

Mills, C. 2008. *The philosophy of Agamben.* Stocksfield: Acumen.

More, T. 2004. *Utopia.* London: Penguin.

Morris, W. 1993. *News from nowhere and other writings.* London: Penguin.

Mumford, L. 2003. *The story of utopias.* Whitefish, MT: Kessinger.

Murtola, A.-M. 2006. Negotiating identity: An excursion into the world of a business city. *Intervention Research* 2, no. 1/2: 59–72.

Murtola, A.-M. 2010. Against commodification: Experience, authenticity, utopia. PhD diss., Åbo Akademi, Finland.

Nick, C., and the Bad Seeds. 2008. 'Night of the lotus eaters,' from *Dig Lazarus Dig!!!* London: Mute Records.

Parker, M., ed. 2002a. *Utopia and organization.* Oxford: Blackwell.

Parker, M. 2002b. Utopia and the organizational imagination: Outopia. In *Utopia and organization,* ed. M. Parker, 1–8. Oxford: Blackwell.

Parker, M., V. Fournier, and P. Reedy. 2007. *The dictionary of alternatives: Utopianism and organization.* London: Zed Books.

Parker, M., and C. Rhodes, eds. 2008. Images of organizing in popular culture. Special issue, *Organization* 15, no. 5: 627–783.

Plato. 1997. Republic. In *Plato complete works,* ed. J.M. Cooper, 971–1223. Indianapolis, IN: Hackett.

Rhodes, C. 2007. Outside the gates of Eden: Utopia and work in rock music. *Group and Organization Management* 32, no. 1: 22–49.

Somavia, J. 2008. Preface. In *The World of Work Report 2008.* Switzerland: International Labour Organization and the International Institute for Labour Studies.

Sørensen, B.M. 2009a. The entrepreneurial utopia: Miss Black Rose and the holy communion. In *The politics and aesthetics of entrepreneurship,* ed. D. Hjorth and C. Steyaert, 202–20. Cheltenham: Edward Elgar.

Sørensen, B.M. 2009b. Book keeping: Faces and individuality in the new spirit of capitalism. Paper presented at the Management Philosophy Group Day Conference at Copenhagen Business School, 28 January, in Copenhagen.

Spicer, A., and S. Böhm. 2007. Moving management: Theorizing struggles against the hegemony of management. *Organization Studies* 28, no. 11: 1667–98.

ten Bos, R. 2000. *Fashion and utopia in management thinking.* Amsterdam: John Benjamins.

Tennyson, A.L. 2004. The lotos-eaters. In *Tennyson: Including lotos eaters, Ulysses, ode on the death, Maud, the coming and the passing of Arthur,* ed. A.L. Tennyson, 1–6. Whitefish, MT: Kessinger.

The Week. 2009. The vanishing shopping mall. 3 April. http://www.theweek.com/article/index/94691/The_vanishing_shopping_mall (accessed 7 July 2009).

Underhill, P. 2004. *Call of the mall.* New York: Simon and Schuster.

WebUrbanist. 2008. 5 Floating utopia and ocean city projects: From seafaring condos to oceanic micronations. http://weburbanist.com/2008/03/09/5-floating-utopia-and-ocean-city-projects-from-seafaring-condos-to-to-oceanic-micronations/ (accessed 18 November 2008).

Wells, H.G. 2005. *A modern utopia.* London: Penguin.

The man in the black hat

Ruud Kaulingfreks, Geoff Lightfoot and Hugo Letiche

A century after the American Frontier was closed, the cowboy remains an iconic figure. A sturdy individualism, a steely disregard for convention and the bravery to do what's gotta be done: these are powerful tropes that seemingly define a particular type of heroism. One that seems ageless despite the disappearance of the border environment in which the fictive cowboy operated.

Our aim in this paper is to explore the mythology of the cowboy as depicted in western films and fiction, demonstrating how it draws upon and develops particular kinds of individualism, sociality and morality that were first explicitly explored in the late eighteenth century. And, as theoretically-laden icon, we examine how the cowboy continues to shape writing and thinking about individuals and organizations, specifically focussing on the works of Ayn Rand and notions of entrepreneurship.

The man in the black hat

There is no Sunday west of Junction City, no law west of Hays City, and no God west of Carson City.
(Wild Bill Hickok)

The west is a country of the mind, and so eternal.
(Archibald MacLeish, 'Sweet Land of Liberty')

The town laid scattered wide… dotted over a planet of treeless dust, like a soiled pack of cards. Houses, empty bottles and garbage in a forever shapeless pattern. More forlorn than stale bones. It seemed to have been strewn there by the wind and to be waiting till the wind should come again and blow it away. Yet serene above its foulness swam a pure and quite light, it might be bathing in the air of creation's first morning. There the houses stood, rearing their pitiful masquerade amid a fringe of old tin cans, while at their very doors began a world of crystal light, a land without end, a space across which Noah and Adam might come straight from Genesis. Into that space went wandering a road, over a hill and down out of sight, and up again smaller in the distance, and down once more, and up once more, straining the eyes, and so away.

It was on this road that a rider rode towards town. His black hat sits deep on his head, his eyes hidden in the shadow of the brim. He was covered in dust and didn't seem to be in any hurry. Slowly he approached... (see Wister 1998, 18)

Cowboys always ride into town because their home is the wilderness ...

But the cowboy is not of and from the wilderness, like the Indian. Rather, he is from civilization: a civilized man who travelled into the wilderness of his own free will. He chooses solitude to escape from the power-riven society. He flees from the domination of man over man and finds *freedom* through living beyond society. For the cowboy, freedom is possible on the expanding border of the West 'the meeting point between savagery and civilization' (Turner 1994, 32) for only there can men live without the tyranny of society. But freedom is only attainable through individuality, through solitude.

In this paper, we want to entangle the myth of the cowboy with that of social theory and, in particular, we want to look at how the cowboy embodies a myth of freedom that permeates capitalist society, most clearly rendered today in writing about entrepreneurship. Essentially, the cowboy is a hero of civil society, but his heroism is both dependent upon and reinforces a specific type of morality wherein goodness is only achievable in the individual as opposed to the collective. Running through cowboy yarns is the assumption that society inevitably goes awry and, helped by the invisible hand of market forces, power struggles, coercion and the breakdown of civil society inevitably follow. The cowboy stands against, and in contrast to, this collapse of society. He is the epitome of individuality: by his mere presence he shows the alternative to the social war of man against man, and reminds civilians of the existence of freedom and justice, of goodness itself. And unconstrained by civil mores, he is able to restore morality with his six-guns and by doing things no civilized man dare.

'There are some things a man just can't run away from' – John Wayne

Our focus here is predominantly the *myth* of the cowboy. Not just from the western movie genre but also the tradition of writing about the West that the filmic genre draws upon – thus, for example, the introduction to this paper is a paraphrase of Wister's 1907 novel. Our concern is not with actual cowboys: their historical context or the grit and grind of their everyday lives. For, although western novels and movies derive some of their iconography from actual historic figures, and the history of the expanding frontier forms a backdrop to many tales, our interest is in how the western mythologizes the West in such a way that it continues to appeal to our present society. How, too, our understanding of the history of the American West is driven through the mythology of the western. And, to be honest, although many of the 'true' histories of the American West may be less colourful than their celluloid counterparts, they betray a tradition of similar mythologizing. Take Turner's famous lament on the closing of the frontier:

> to the frontier the American intellect owes its striking characteristics. That coarseness and strength combined with acuteness and inquisitiveness; that practical, inventive turn of mind, quick to find expedients; that masterful grasp of material things, lacking in the artistic but powerful to effect great ends; that restless, nervous energy, that dominant individualism, working for good and for evil, and withal that buoyancy and exuberance which comes with freedom-these are traits of the frontier, or traits called out elsewhere because of the existence of the frontier. (Turner 1994, 59)

Also, of course, the western movie does not stand alone. Not only does it permeate the written 'histories' of the West itself but the iconography seems through to other genres, particularly in action films: the latter-day cowboy now appears as detective, bank-robber, urban adventurer, army commando: essentially any individual hero who is forced to fight for his values when they stand against the dastardly dealings of society. And, as we shall see, this is nowhere more clearly expounded than in those derring-do capitalists that fight the moochers and looters of the bureaucratic state in the novels of Ayn Rand.

Cowboys embody a specific, glorious, vision of the western liberal ideology. As Wright pointed out: 'In an entertaining way it suggests to people in a market society what values they should have, what attitudes bring success, what actions they should take' (Wright 2001, 1). Yet we should avoid being overly glib. Cowboys are not a mere illustration of either liberalism or of a theory of civil society in popular culture. They change theory by incorporating and adapting it, enhancing some parts and weakening others. And the transient nature of these changes becomes evident with the way in which the iconography of the cowboy of the western – of fierce individualism, of steely unconcern to the social – can itself be incorporated and adapted by writers drawing different theoretical lines. Here again, as we shall later see, the 'fiction' of Ayn Rand serves as an unholy example.

The myth of the cowboy appears then, from the onset on, as a lost cause, as a nostalgic representative of a value that has already vanished. The myth appears *after* the border has been closed in 1890, when the railroad and the attached industrial model have already begun to take over the Wild West. The robber baron has his say and there is no room anymore for the free spirit. When historically the wilderness ends, the myth of the cowboy is born.

Cowboys' behaviour can be seen as extolling individualism, particularly through a marked disregard of social conventions, although this is not expressed in overt aggression directed towards the social. Cowboys do not aim to, and rarely do, confront a civil group (such as the troubled township), although the group can be (should be) threatened by the disrespect of the cowboy. Cowboys don't play by the rules: rather they act as individuals and seek their own solutions. They do not wait until consensus is reached but immediately move to action.

The benefit to the group legitimizes the cowboy's behaviour: he is not an egoist seeking personal gain. Rather his goal is wider – the benefit of society, a group of people or even that of an organization, even though he never fits in, is a very difficult person to deal with and has a deep scepticism for all group arrangements. In this, then, we see both communality with and a marked shift from libertarian logics where pursuing individual goals for individual benefit will, once the equations are worked out, benefit all society. Our cowboy, by contrast, works *for* the greater good by taking an individual position.

But for cowboys there is but a thin line between altruism and the socially unacceptable. He intends to do good but his unconventionality (often coupled with an ability to see the world in black and white) can be very dangerous for everybody and especially for himself. His individualism does not, in itself, guarantee the right outcome, and his course of action can cause problems and he may even harm the group he seeks to aid. In dealing with villains, he may kill innocent bystanders. He may be misled or mistaken and target the wrong person. He can even take the completely wrong course of action. Ultimately, he is never certain of his righteousness.

But what is key here is that *cowboys take the risk*. And once they accept that risk and make a decision, they never look back but pursue their goal with a tenacity bordering on single-mindedness. Not playing it by the book, searching and finding his own way outside the group's regulations and ways of behaviour, creates a substantial risk: one which other group members are not willing to countenance. Yet his individualism also can create risk for others, too. In a sense he creates victims through his contempt for others, in particular, those others who abide by rules that stabilize groups. He destabilizes the social through his open disregard of the rules which confronts and affronts the law-abiding citizens of the Wild West (or the organization team). He makes it impossible for a group to be in agreement because the cowboy has no interest in agreement – what he does, he does, and the group are left with a *fait accompli*.

Such heroic individualism is powerful medicine, especially when tied in to notions of risk. Unsurprisingly, admiration for the cowboy has resulted in attempts to institutionalize his individualist behaviour in the entrepreneurial organization. Workers are expected to behave like entrepreneurs, to take the risk, and to develop their own individual initiatives (see, e.g., Du Gay 1991, but also, as a corrective, Fournier and Grey 2001). They are encouraged not to behave according to the book but to pursue their own, self-governed opportunities. Yet already we can see the inherent problems emerging. Such pursuits do not match with good management principles: acting the cowboy seems unlikely to make an organization efficient. They jeopardize the enterprise by putting it at risk, by destabilizing conventions and working practices. Indeed, some mavericks, such as Nick Leeson at Barings or Jeffrey Skilling at Enron, leave a trail of organizational carnage. Yet just placing the cowboy into organizational harness seems to disturb the myth – an essential part of the cowboy story is that they come in from the wilderness. They come to town, perform their heroics, then ride off towards the setting sun on their lonesome. They are only ever temporarily engaged. They shrug and spit at the rhetoric of the modern corporation that seeks to possess ever more of the workers within.

However, it is not a narrow individualism that we are talking about here, for the cowboy first and foremost seeks the good of the community. He is a deeply ethical figure driven by moral values. Over-stressing individuality, making it the core of his being, strips him of his *raison d'être* and thus ultimately disregards his iconic value. His individuality is grounded in his morality and can not be seen as an independent quality. To get to an understanding of how this comes about, however, we need to look more closely at the history of individualist thought.

'A man ought to do what he thinks is right' – John Wayne

Theories of civil society started to be formulated in the seventeenth century, notably in the work of Locke and Hobbes, and were enlarged with the economic ideas of Adam Smith. These writers articulate the transition from a feudal society to modern times and are the voice of the emergent bourgeoisie. Without delving too deeply, one can suggest that this area of civil society theory is effectively part of the foundation of a philosophical theory of individualism that still holds today. The individual is placed at the centre of social behaviour: social structure and all collective arrangements are thus secondary and only permissible when supportive of individuality (although a closer reading of Smith, in particular, reveals a less monist argument, as we shall see later on).

This is in sharp contrast to feudalism. In feudal society a person was fixed within a social structure that determined absolutely the possibility and scope of individual action. There was no social mobility and no social change, nor could there be, for existing structures were sacred, backed up by tradition and religion. This transcendental order of fixed rules brooked no questioning, and the very idea of individual rights that could exist in opposition to this structure was unthinkable. And individuals themselves were of no importance: they only occupied subject positions within the given structure. In this society, dreams of changing one's fate or social position dictated by birth were pointless – the feudal system required and depended upon stability.

With the Enlightenment, this stability became seen as a problem in that it impeded the possibility of justice. The resolution, and itself one of the key levers of change, was the turn from structure to individuals as the foundation of society. Kant proclaimed that man can and should think by himself, by making use of his intellectual rationality. Each person must consider all claims of reality individually. Any claim on truth can and must be demonstrated intellectually – through convincing the other by intellectual means. Argument thus becomes a question of intellectual resolution on their own grounds, and it cannot be decided by appeals to tradition or authority. Thus, we find the autonomous individual: someone who has to be convinced (by intellectual demonstration) of the truth of a statement. The individual must think for himself. Enlightenment forms the condition for individualism. That is, of course, not to say that individualism appears as a result of Enlightenment, but that the transition from feudal to modern society brings forth a philosophical thinking wherein an autonomous *intellectual* individual takes centre stage. Reason, the highest faculty, must be used by the individual, as an individual. Hence Kant's famous claim to dare to think.

This shift radicalizes society. The components of the feudal structure – social relations such as lords, village, family, guild, etc. – can no longer be the cornerstones of a fixed social reality. Instead, reality is found by and through individuals – consequently they have the power to shape society. Individuals have equal opportunities and can develop according to their abilities. By thinking, reasoning and by earning a social position, each individual exercises their potential to influence the world around them.

Hobbes and Locke based their models of society on individualism: almost a contradiction in terms. A society, if it is individualistic, will be a kind of anti-society for, ultimately, greatest freedom comes with least contact with others. Even the modest ideal of equal opportunities carries with it the idea of competition: opportunity can only be realized in a struggle against the other for position. Thus the individualist core of civil society is not cooperation and mutual help but a Hobbesian struggle. For freedom – as the possibility to decide one's own life – cannot be completely realized within society, but to live without society will only reawaken the war of every man against every man, and fear and coercion will reign. These two positions are resolved by the social contract 'where a common power is set over men with right and force sufficient to compel performance' (Hobbes 1968, 196) which enables men to live together without continual strife. With the social contract, each man relinquishes part of his freedom in his own interest, a move made possible as together all men share a common interest in avoiding the war of all against all. Reason prevails, repressing innate aggression but within civil society there is always the danger of a return to Hobbesian war.

The myth of the cowboy is rooted in this conflict between individualism and society. He has great freedom because of his disconnection to society, his limited dealing with others. But he is not a representative of the natural state (like Indians) and so avoids the Hobbesian fate. Instead, he is on the margins of society. He has chosen to step away from society, but always remains related to it. Typically, as the movie begins, he rides into town, but after an hour and a half, he leaves again. Town, or society, is not the place to be happy or to be free, but it cannot be completely left behind.

Intriguingly, an individualistic society demands a lot from its members. Because feudalism was a closed society it offered a certain type of security and safety. One's future is fixed and relatively known: there are no existential concerns or fear over the outcomes of decisions concerning the 'entrepreneurial self'. Insecurity and fear still existed, of course, but they originated outside the realm of men. Gods and devils, fates and forces constantly endangered life. But these are beyond the ability of man to withstand: such supernatural powers demand of men merely a collective attitude of modesty and thankfulness. In one sense, then, disasters are not so terrifying: one cannot obviate them, so there is no question of responsibility. In an individualistic society, by contrast, individuals manage their lives and the world. Therefore they are accountable for what happens in the world, for the world, as it is, is the result of men's deeds. Thus, even natural disasters are seen as the result of political actions and we deal with them in terms of political accountability.

Accountability requires knowledge, to be informed. In place of certainties, individuals have to make decisions based on reason. Information is essential for a good decision, so as a consequence the individual is embroiled in an endless pursuit of information and knowledge. Like Sisyphus, man is continually trying to satiate his thirst for knowledge but continually discovers that he does not know enough. Man is continually aware of falling short, continually being reminded he has not enough information. Only what appears as a result of our decisions contains the promise of surety, but it must always fall short. Insecurity and displacement result, and we are doomed to live in continual uncertainty.

Society produces displacement by continually asking for individual answers and by regarding safety, as a false refuge in certainties, as a weakness. But in order to deal with displacement, it is necessary that displacement is not experienced as a lack. The myth of an autonomous individual thus makes displacement bearable by presenting it as something worthwhile, as a token of strength. The image of the cowboy, then, comes to play as the apogee of an individual without attachments: one who is able to live in solitude without having to deal with others. The myth of the cowboy represents and solves the main existential problem of civil society by reversing traditional values. Security and safety become weaknesses. The town dwellers (the community) huddle together for safety but they are still threatened by villains. They cannot stand up to the threat and need the gunman. He comes into town and challenges the villains. The cowboy's heroism comes from his outsiderliness. His detachment from society enables him to survive the wilderness, his strength and fearlessness that come from living alone are the qualities that enable him to be the one that can participate in a shoot-out.

'If everything isn't black and white, I say, "Why the hell not?"' – John Wayne

We can look at how this plays out through different westerns. And here we lean on Will Wright's (2001) book which looks at the cowboy as a metaphor for social theory. In his earlier (1975) structural analysis of westerns, Wright distinguishes four types of plot: the classical, the vengeance variation, the transition period and finally the professional theme.

The classical plot essentially develops as follows:

The hero enters a social group. He is initially unknown but then revealed to have an exceptional ability. The society recognizes a difference between themselves and the hero; the hero is given a special status but society does not completely accept the hero. There is a conflict of interest between the villains and society. The villains are stronger than society. Initially, there is a strong friendship or respect between the hero and the villain. The villain threatens society. The hero avoids involvement in the conflict. The villain endangers a friend of the hero. The hero fights the villain. The hero defeats the villain. Society is safe. The society accepts the hero. The hero loses or gives up his special status (Wright 1975, 48). *Shane* (George Stevens 1953*)* and *Duel in the Sun* (King Vidor 1947) are perhaps the best examples of this plot.

The vengeance variation alters the classical plot in that the hero is originally part of society and is harmed by villains. In order to seek vengeance he steps out of society, and from then on it reverts to the classical plot. *Stagecoach* (John Ford 1939, the film that made John Wayne a star) and *The Man from Laramie* (Anthony Mann 1955) are fine examples of this kind of plot (Wright 1975, 69).

In the transition theme the classical plot is reversed. The hero starts within society and ends outside. The hero is forced to fight society that has become closely identified with the villains. The woman doesn't reconcile the hero with society but joins him in his rejection. *High Noon* (Fred Zinneman 1952) is the example here (Wright 1975, 75).

Finally, the professional theme changes the classical plot in that the hero is a gunslinger hired to fight villains because society is too weak. Typically, it involves a group of heroes who operate as a team. *Rio Bravo* (Howard Hawks 1959) and *The Professionals* (Richard Brooks 1966) exemplified this plot (Wright 1975, 113).

Effectively, the latter are only variations because the three oppositions that underlie the classical plot endure: Strong/Weak, Good/Bad and Inside/Outside society. In westerns, society is almost always weak; the community is unable to defend itself and needs somebody with special abilities. The hero has these abilities because he is used to living outside society. The villains have the same abilities as the hero (also arising from a detachment from society) and may be as strong or even stronger than the hero. What distinguishes the hero from the villains is their ethics: the hero is good, the villains are bad. Because the villains are bad, their morals are low and honour is not predominant. Usually villains are not individuals; they tend to operate in a gang where they can hide their individuality and merge into it. Still, they are not completely unethical.

There are several types of villains. First, there are savages. Not part of society, they live in Hobbes's natural state and therefore are violent by nature. The hero, even when he is in a collectivity like the army, fights them single-handedly. He often goes against the army book and achieves results by so doing (see *She Wore a Yellow Ribbon,* John Ford 1950). Indians may have some ethics, but it is the exception in the classic western. Significantly, this image has reversed lately; Indians now are shown with strong morals. In a sense they represent Rousseau's '*le bon sauvage*' in a remarkable update of the old discussion between Hobbes and Rousseau. With this twist, civil society and its institutions represent evil by alienating men from their own nature. The Indians in, for instance, *Dances with Wolves* (Kevin Costner 1990) are morally superior because they are still in an original state of grace.

Next is the cowboy gone bad. He is as strong as the cowboy hero, has the same outsiderly power and is, in many ways, the mirror of the hero. But he becomes a villain because he loses (or never had) the moral sentiments of the honourable cowboy. He may get addicted to power, misuse his special abilities or even just be in 'the wrong place at the wrong time' (*Pat Garret and Billy the Kid*, Sam Peckinpah 1973) and becomes an outlaw against his will. Some are deceived into villainy by the worst villain of all. And then there are those born bad and who have never been good. These operate in gangs or act as hands for the main villain.

The capitalist is invariably a bad guy. Sometimes this will be a rancher obsessed with expansion to the detriment of other farmers, but the quintessential villain is the railroad baron (the robber baron). Ruthlessly he appropriates land for 'his choo-choo' and represents the expanding industrialization of the big cities in the East. He is a coward of low morals, his only ability is that of seducing people with his wealth. He hires gunmen to obtain his goals and destroys society with his capitalist blindness – exemplified in *Once Upon a Time in the West* (Sergio Leone 1969).

What Wright's analysis makes clear is how weak society is. So weak that it never can be the subject of the plot but is always the object. The conflict is one between outsiders fighting for or against society. The cowboy defends the group although in itself it has no value for the hero (unless *She* belongs to the group. The heroine is always the one that ties the cowboy to the group). And here paradoxes of the cowboy becomes clear, if we are to see him in terms of individualism. Lacking a home but defending the dwelling. Being tough, independent and not needing anybody, but defending and secretly admiring a home. And the cowboy, despite all his hardness, indulges in self-pity as he rides away leaving her with tears on her cheeks …

The drive to market

Does this suggest that cowboys, or individualists, are essentially unable to maintain relations or to get emotionally involved? Hobbes argues that if this were the case for individuals, society would disintegrate and thus the conditions for individualism would fall apart. Thus for Locke, and later Adam Smith, an ethics of individualism was needed, although this is ever problematic in liberal theory because it presupposes a 'thou shall not' thereby forcing people to obey rules and hampering free enterprise.

The solution is again man's intrinsic reason – his ability to choose what is best for him. Man's choice should never impinge upon others because then society would disintegrate (see Smith 1997, II: 51). Man's reason calls for sociability because engagement with others works for mutual benefit. Thus, no matter how calculated and reasoned our relationships are, they always presuppose altruism – a sympathy that cannot be reduced to the calculable – pre-figuring the self-interest of any relationship. (see Smith 1997, II: 37). This leads in unexpected directions: for Smith (and Locke) self-interest never means that one profits through other's detriment. Capitalism is foremost a social movement of engagement with the other based on equal competition: individualism opens the way for each to achieve self-realization without damaging the other, and without restrictions beforehand.

But equal opportunities for self-realization are only possible when there are unlimited resources, when everyone has the same starting point and endless possibilities. Capitalism, as the acme of individualism, fails when resources are limited and one is dependent of others, when one has to fight for a position in society, when one has to take a position which is already taken, when one has to dispose of another to take his position over. In the eighteenth and nineteenth centuries, the unlimited resources were available in the form of free land in the New World. 'So long as free land exists, the opportunity for a competency exists, and economic power secures political power.' (Turner 1994, 55) The Wild West and the expanding frontier of the United States gave the material basis for the theory of the civil society. Each man can work his own land and is free to do so. There will be mutual cooperation and at the same time competition, but no man shall be the victim of competition. As Turner puts it, in the West, 'Population was sparse, there was no multitude of jostling interests, as in older settlements, demanding an elaborate system of personal restraints' (Turner 1994, 67).

Freedom is threatened in an industrial society. The entrepreneur is dependent upon others and cannot just start an enterprise from nothing. He needs capital, which must be lent, and thus becomes dependent on the moneylender. The entrepreneur needs workers and thus makes others dependent on him, or he denies the possibilities for others. In industrial societies, the majority of people become workers contracted and dependent on wages from another for their sustention. Free enterprise itself comes to be dependent on workers and inequality. Similarly, industrial individualism has no place for respect for the freedom of the other: it is about profits and not self-realization. The more people an industrialist employs, the farther away he gets from the liberal ideal of free enterprise. Ultimately, his only concern is capital, and there is no relation whatsoever with the world, people, land, products except through rendering them into what can be calculable and realized within the price system. Civil society, reduced to monetary value alone, disintegrates and workers become alienated.

In industrial society, the liberal economy is doomed and freedom and equality are not possible. As Heilbronner remarked: 'He [Smith] did not see a revolution – The Industrial Revolution. Smith did not see in the ugly factory system … the first appearance of new and disruptively powerful social forces. In a sense his system presupposes that eighteenth-century England will remain unchanged forever' (Heilbronner 1980, 70). The Liberal economy is an agrarian economy where freedom is guaranteed by the open border of availability of land. It is this agrarian world that makes the cowboy the icon of liberal, individualistic society. The Wild West allowed for individualistic communities, where the ties were never so strong that anyone could not leave in order to start somewhere else. Communities of equals who need not obtain profits at the expense of the other: everyone owns his own land. The cowboy thus defends an ideal, a free and equal market.

According to Wright, in turn drawing on Turner, civil society can continue to develop as long as there is unsettled land – while there is still a frontier. Its end is therefore inevitable from the beginning. The West was steadily colonized and eventually the colonists arrived to the shores of the Pacific, ending the expansion, so that, by 1890, the Superintendent of the US Census could declare that the frontier no longer existed (Turner 1994, 31). Liberal society reaches its end at the same time. The ideals of endless expansion, of free land no longer hold. Now civil society is confined to cities and to industry, and the potential realization of the dream vanishes.

It is probably as a result of the closing of the frontier and the end of the dream that the mythical figure of the cowboy appears in popular culture. Owen Wister's *The Virginian,* was published in 1907, and its popularity was enormous. It was not the first cowboy novel – dime novels, with non-stop action guaranteed, had been around since the 1840s – but it was one that largely established the genre. It certainly set out the myth of the wild gentleman, who still had a strong ethical position, who was both very violent and compassionate, who was loving and ruthless, tough and unapproachable at the same time. Similarly, once the cinema came into being, western films translated the popularity of melodrama into the setting of the Wild West: the good fighting the bad in order to build an ideal society based around equality and freedom.

The cowboy comes to the fore after the dream he represents has ended. He romanticizes a vanished past, a past that was central in the development of civil society, and in doing so he keeps the dream of the civil society alive. He reminds us in the concealed way of popular culture of the ideals of liberalism and especially of the ethics of it. The need to fight the bad guys. This he does by playing up his individuality and toughness, his intransigence while completing the task at hand. *A man's gotta do what a man's gotta do* before he can ride on. He defends freedom and community against ruthless appropriation. His villains are people who take too much, who don't show respect for the property of small farmers and attempt to dominate the whole community.

'If you've got them by the balls, their hearts and minds will follow' – John Wayne

One central motif in the western is that a community can and must be defended with violence. Violence is, of course, for our liberal theorists, the natural state of mankind. In society, free men must yield some of their freedom to the state so that security can be guaranteed. But the state has a tendency to control citizens and to limit their freedom – it has to be watched and controlled. Thus citizens have the right to attack it when it appropriates too much power – even with violence. Thus, in this sense violence follows the same trajectory as freedom: both originate with to the individual; both are lent to the state. And when freedom is threatened, to reclaim their freedom, citizens have the right to return to violence.

The cowboy represents the nexus between the natural state and the community of the social contract. The cowboy is able to do the heroic things he does because he is able to return to and cope with the natural state of wilderness, he is used to freedom and thus to violence. But it is because he has made the *decision* to return that he is suited to be a hero.

Gangs of villains, by contrast, have fled society because they were unable to live by reason. Unsurprisingly, they then lack the honour of the gentleman gunman. Honour, in this case, is about unimpeachable integrity and moral consistency. Morality is based on a genuine virtuosity; it is what makes men surpass the passions of the natural state. In liberal terms, therefore, honour is bound into what it means to live a life based on reason. Not just in the sense of calculability, but also in the sense of engaging with the moral values of a community, civil responsibility, mutual help and respect for property. Honour is never putting one's own interest first when it would be at the expense of others. The cowboy is a gentleman because he does this continuously, even at the cost of setting his own interest (often in the form of love) aside for the benefit of the community. The gentleman gunman is especially able to take this altruistic position because he does not own property.

This lack of material interest that enables him to live in the in-between between community and wilderness also brings the dual structure of civil society into focus and highlights some of the intrinsic contradictions. Thus, although civil society is based on property and the protection of it lies at the core of its values, possession is at the same time a limitation of freedom. But property is not all: at a deeper level civil society is built not on property but on altruism. So, the town dwellers in whose name the shoot-out takes place have property, but their freedom and altruism is limited. The gunmen have no property but altruistically risk their lives for it. That is ultimately the principal morality of westerns.

But in his heroism, the cowboy lays bare the quintessential problem of the community. His deeds show the limitations of the community, their fears, their falling short of their own values. That is why he is not accepted in the community and has to ride out. If he remained in town, life for villagers would be unbearable; they would constantly be reminded that they are not heroes. They cannot be heroic: they can never be outsiders, tied as they are to hearth and home. But the community is formed as a community of equals, there is no place for someone different. The community needs the hero to leave. Fortunately, because of his love of nature and hatred of compromised honour displayed by the community, the cowboy will saddle his horse and ride away. Thus, in the final scene of *High Noon*, Gary Cooper takes his sheriff's star off and demonstratively throws it to the ground before mounting. A hero is an exile, can only be heroic as an exile.

Another aspect of this is the insight of the cowboy. He knows he cannot expect anything from the community – that they will not help him – an insight shared by the other outsider: the villain. The community is unaware of their paralysing fear. Only as the cowboy acts do the group become aware of their failings, and his heroism is accompanied by a veiling and an unveiling of their shame. The cowboy gets a kiss, breaks a heart and departs. The community covers its shame and carries on as before. The only one who really learns something is the heroine, who now understands the nature of her community. Unfortunately for her, she cannot now be happy: she now hates the community for their cowardice. The western myth is thus an icon of morality and honour, a metaphor for living according to strong moral principles, of engagement with community, of defending freedom and equality from an individualistic position.

It is this drama that underlines the popularity of the cowboy. Westerns refer to a time where it was possible to live by one's moral values and where corruption could be fought literally. Yet the dream of a civil society existed in the very empiricism of the expanding frontier, of continual conquest of nature. But any theory based on conquest, or on surplus to be used, is doomed to find a conclusion. Losing the land but retaining the dream means a search for new frontiers, new wildernesses to be conquered. The Digital Frontier or Space: the Final Frontier, perhaps? But these are but metaphors, and all attempts to create new Wild Wests fail because there is no new land to be conquered; only new ways of deploying capital. And that was exactly what our cowboys were opposing. How can an individual fight for community against capital when it is capital that creates the frontier? The cowboy remains an archaic figure who cannot exist in this new metaphorical West. So he becomes a metaphor of himself. Even the film becomes a metaphor of itself. The western is transported to the city and symptomatically the hero becomes poisoned and diseased. The morality disappears or becomes unclear. *Dirty Harry* (Don Siegel 1971) fights for the community against a member of that community. Harry, although a loner and in possession of real cowboy guns, cannot possess a strong morality. Rambo (*First Blood*, Ted Kotcheff 1982) is mentally ill as a result of his Vietnam years. These westerns show, if anything, the decay of civil society and the consequent downfall of the hero with it.

Urbane cowboys

But the metaphor of the cowboy remains vital in other ways. Henry Kissinger, in an interview with Orianna Fallaci, suggested: 'The main point stems from the fact that I always acted alone. … Americans admire the cowboy leading the caravan alone astride his horse, the cowboy entering a village or a city alone on his horse … He acts, that's all: aiming at the right spot at the right time" (Wright 2001, 8). Kissinger inadvertently exposes the problem of the cowboy. For him, the cowboy is *only* about individualism and not playing it by the book. He is even a leader whom others follow because of his greater knowledge. There is no reference whatsoever to morality or goodness, let alone to freedom and equality.

Elsewhere, the myth becomes even more ambiguous when stripped from its roots. Take Suge Knight, CEO of Death Row records, jailed for racketeering: 'Suge Knight had helped make his company, Death Row Records, one of the most successful black-owned record labels of all time. In four years the label had sold over eighteen million albums and earned more than $325 million (a record for a rap label) … Here was a man who settled out of court, who admired frontier justice used during the days of the Wild West. "Everything was so much simpler," he once said. "In those days, what was right was right and what was wrong was handled."' (Ro 1998, 2–3). Knight was, in many ways a successful entrepreneur (at least up until his jailing) but one not averse to using violence to further his own ends. For him, the black and white world of the cowboy has been further sharpened around the issue of violence. The innate morality, so important for our thesis, is entirely absent, and thus there is no difficulty with assaulting the community's values that the cowboy worked so hard to protect.

And this relationship to the cowboy in entrepreneurship is interesting. Not just because, in British English at least, the cowboy entrepreneur operates by violating all rules in order to gain benefit for himself at the expense of the community. The cowboy builder is an incompetent, overcharging and under-delivering swindler. Yet, this masks something deeper and darker in current society that we need to return to our liberal theorists to uncover. For our theorists of the enlightenment, individualism rested upon a fundamental morality. Without that pre-given morality in Smith, for example, all the ensuing individual rights cannot apply.

But individualism, with the entrepreneur as its ultimate representation, now stands for something very different in the world today. We should perhaps here turn to Mises, Hayek,and their followers, such as Rand and Kirzner, whose baleful influence contin-ues to influence the Anglo-Saxon right. (Alan Greenspan, ex-chairman of the Federal Reserve, for example, was one of Rand's inner circle, while Rand's book *The fountainhead* was reportedly inflicted upon the ideologues seeking to create a new direction for British Conservatism under William Hague.) Rand shows how the myth of the cowboy is used to praise entrepreneurs, to depict them as heroes of a free society. But only the individualism is underlined to drive towards the ultimate extension of self interest. Altruism has disappeared from this cowboy image – indeed the very idea of altruism is portrayed as being as much a handicap to individual action as rapacious and villainous appropriation of the fruits of individual endeavour. The entrepreneur is then much more a picture of the cowboy gone bad than a simple reinvigoration of the classic myth of the cowboy.

Now Rand is rather an easy target. Her entrepreneurs look fantastical today, with the constant revelling in the messier and more exploitative aspects of production. And her novels are pretty much unreadable as fiction. But she is not afraid to nail her position to the church door: her heroic entrepreneur John Galt, drawing explicitly on Mises, is quite clear. 'Do you ask what moral obligation I owe to my fellow men? None – except the obligation I owe to myself, to material objects and to all of existence: rationality' (Rand 1992b, 936). And in the same book, mining and shipping entrepreneur Francisco d'Anconias tells Dagny Taggart, rail entrepreneur: 'Don't consider our interests or our desires. You have no duty to anyone but yourself' (Rand

1992b, 802). At first cut, this appears to be two of the cornerstones of Smith's liberalism, reason as the essence of man, and of self-interest, taken to the extreme. Now to be sure, the first does avoid the transcendental move in Smith, with his natural duties of justice, of truth, of chastity, and of fidelity.

And the second moves from Smith, too. Smith identifies two driving forces behind man's actions. In *The theory of moral sentiments*, Smith describes the importance of 'sympathy' or 'benevolence' towards others – in the *Wealth of nations*, 'self-interest'. Both are essential for 'universal opulence', and indeed Smith points up the dangers for community in the market economy as 'self-interest' becomes more important. Not only that, but even his famous quote: 'It is not from the benevolence of the butcher, the brewer, or the baker, that we expect our dinner, but from their regard to their own interest' (Smith 1991, 14) really requires its context. Such as the next line: 'We address ourselves not to their humanity but to their self-love, and never talk to them of our own necessities but of their advantages' (Smith 1991, 14).

So Rand is no classic liberal, then. Nor are her entrepreneurs classic entrepreneurs. Howard Roark, architect and main protagonist of *The fountainhead*, will not work if the customer will not accept his (argreeably stark and modernist) designs in their entirety. Not for him, Mises's maxim, that: 'Monetary calculation is the guiding star of action under the social system of division of labor. It is the compass of the man embarking upon production. He calculates in order to distinguish the remunerative lines of production from the unprofitable ones, those of which the sovereign consumers are likely to approve from those of which they are likely to disapprove. Every single step of entrepreneurial activities is subject to scrutiny by monetary calculation' (Mises 1947, 229). Now it would be easy to rest here, safe in the knowledge that our audience are unlikely to find any of our protagonists heroic so far, and especially not Rand with her *Virtue of selfishness*. But disturbingly, it seems, for our epic story, Rand's entrepreneurs *are* uncannily similar to our mythical cowboys.

John Galt steps in and out of the wilderness. His strength comes from his ability to accept wildness, to enter the world of man against man as a reasoned choice and to return. He finds new land, Galt's Gulch, where owner-managers can settle and come together as equals in freedom. Here a man is reckoned by what he does, what he wrests from the wilderness, not by tradition, not by social standing. Violence can be re-appropriated, 'When a man attempts to deal with me by force, I answer him – by force' (Rand 1992b, 937). He stands up against organization, against appropriation (the Looters). Even the main actors look like cowboys: granite jaws, lean strength and steely gazes abound. And despite Rand's protestations, her principal characters act towards each other with compassion, truth and (in a specific way) of chastity and fidelity.

So where does this leave us, now? Have we just seen the endurance of a specific mythology, or is it possible that our cowboys, old and new, say something about the relationship between entrepreneurship and organization?

In part, yes (we hope). The first is that the entrepreneur, as a cowboy, is inevitably a fake. He cannot conceal that his work can only exist in an industrialized setting and is imbued in and dependent upon the very evil the cowboy was fighting against. This is the schism between Rand's ideals and reality. Dagny Taggart is doomed while she works within the system, Howard Roark will not accept compromise, while entrepreneurs, as Mises and Kirzner make clear, will adapt to even imperfect systems. This has consequences: the cowboy entrepreneur is flawed from the start and can never embody freedom and justice with the same distinction. Rand's work, in seeking to make stick this motif of entrepreneur as hero, merely makes its dissonance more visible.

Also, the cowboy entrepreneur may retain his individualism but now this translates only into self-interest and lack of engagement. Stuck in an institutional setting, he has to deal with law and order and can never go his own way. Most owner-managers, despite their frequent claims that they started their businesses so that no-one could tell them what to do, find that they are as constrained by regulation and economic calculation as when in employment. Acting in self-interest then becomes doubled in on itself as constraint, not freedom. And the link between employment and entrepreneurship becomes more critical. Despite her best intentions, Rand's entrepreneurs are the only really free characters – it seems impossible to wring freedom from within employment, even at the mythological level. Encouraging entrepreneurship from employees then appears, at best, a cruel trick, at other levels, simply immoral. Dirty Harry, for example, is just too enthusiastic in catching villains and uses too much violence. He is in a continual struggle with his superiors and even gets punished by having to work *in personnel*. John Wayne would never accept *that*. But then John Wayne would never be *employed*, at best he is a free-lancer... Returning from the myth, we see that the individualism of entrepreneurial cowboys can only exist within dependent relations, inside institutions. He can only be a cowboy, make a deal, by constricting others. The cowboy gone bad.

But figuring the entrepreneur as a cowboy also shows up our *ersatz* civil society. A civil society in an industrial setting, translates moral values into their opposite. The spirit of free enterprise has become the right to start a new company without having to bother about laws and taxes, without having to bother about the social impact and the dangers it may entail for the land and for society, and certainly not for the costs to people.

Also, the entrepreneur as cowboy is a tame translation of the original. A simulacrum almost in the sense that it is a copy of a copy of a copy... Each copy takes us further away from the original idea of the civil society. It is symptomatic that once the original idea has been diluted in the copies, organizations come to the fore. Could it be because goodness and moral values were envisaged as inexistent in them by the thinkers of the civil society? Industrialization and urban inequality have taken the West over but retained the images. So the cowboy is indulged as a name, as an image but inside an institutional setting. As Moss Kanter said: 'The cowboy strains the limits, but the corporation manager has to establish limits' (1989, 360).

> The sun sets over the vast expanse of prairie. A lone figure on a horse rides towards the horizon. His black hat is set deep over his eyes. The town he has just left is busy, as usual. Only one person notices his departure: a woman standing on Main Street watching him ride out. Her skirts move in the wind, a tear runs down her cheek...

References

du Gay, Paul. 1991. Enterprise culture and the ideology of excellence. *New Formations* 13: 45–61.

Fournier, Valérie, and Chris Grey. 1999. Too much, too little and too often: A critique of du Gay's analysis of enterprise. *Organization* 6, no. 1: 107–28.

Heilbronner, Robert L. 1980. *The wordly philosophers: The lives, times, and ideas of the great economic thinkers*. New York: Touchstone.

Hobbes, Thomas. 1968. *Leviathan* (original 1651). London: Penguin.

Mises, L.V. 1949. *Human action: A treatise on economics*. 4th ed. Indianapolis: Liberty Fund, 2007.

Moss Kanter, Rosabeth. 1989. *When giants learn to dance.* New York: Touchstone.

Rand, Ayn. 1992a. *The fountainhead* (original 1943). London: Corgi.

Rand, Ayn. 1992b. *Atlas shrugged* (original 1957). London: Corgi.

Ro, R. 1998. *Have gun, will travel: The spectacular rise and violent fall of Death Row Records.* London: Quartet.

Smith, Adam. 1991. *Wealth of nations* (original 1776). New York: Prometheus.

Smith, Adam. 1997. *The theory of moral sentiments* (original 1759). Washington DC: Regnery Publishing.

Slotkin, Richard. 1998a. *Gunfighter nation: The myth of the frontier in twentieth-century America.* Norman, OK: University of Oklahoma Press.

Slotkin, Richard. 1998b. *The fatal environment: The myth of the frontier in the age of industrialization 1800–1890.* Norman, OK: University of Oklahoma Press.

Turner, Frederick Jackson. 1994. *Rereading Frederick Jackson Turner: The significance of the frontier in American history and other essays* (originals 1891–1925). New Haven, CT: Yale University Press.

Wister, Owen. 1998. *The virginian* (original 1907). Oxford: Oxford University Press.

Wright, Will. 1975. *Sixgun & society: A structural study of the western.* Berkeley, CA: University of California Press.

Wright, Will. 2001. *The Wild West: The mythical cowboy & social theory.* London: Sage.

Index

Page numbers in *Italics* represent tables.